THE NUREMBERG FALLACY

THE
NUREMBERG
FALLACY

Wars and War Crimes

Since World War II

EUGENE DAVIDSON

The Macmillan Company, New York, New York

Collier-Macmillan Publishers, London

The Macmillan Company
866 Third Avenue, New York, N.Y. 10022
Collier-Macmillan Canada Ltd., Toronto, Ontario

Library of Congress Catalog Card Number: 72–84740

FIRST PRINTING

Printed in the United States of America

To S.M.D.

Contents

Foreword

IN the last chapter of *The Trial of the Germans*, written some twenty years after the major war criminals were sentenced at Nuremberg, I tried to draw up a balance sheet of the consequences of that trial on which so many hopes for a more humane world were placed. Since twentieth-century man obviously continues to be better armed with new weapons and lethal strategems than he is with the means of defending himself against them—or, as the Nuremberg judgments foresaw, making their employment unnecessary—the present book continues that inquiry on a larger scale.

The Nuremberg Fallacy seeks to explore the causes and methods of fighting some of the chief conflicts that have erupted since World War II and through these accounts to make possible a judgment on the cogency of the Nuremberg principles as they were applied first to the enemy and then, theoretically, to the nations that defeated the enemy.

Although only six wars were chosen to be dealt with from among the scores of conflicts that have been fought since the Nuremberg court declared aggressive war illegal, they may nevertheless provide an instructive guide to the moral, political, and military side effects of the trial and its doctrines. And because it seems evident that more efficacious ways of mitigating the scourges and horrors of war must continue to be sought for, other than those advanced at Nuremberg, the book also offers some modest proposals to this end.

In writing *The Nuremberg Fallacy*, dealing as it must with widely separated countries and immemorial problems, I have been fortunate in having the help of a number of people. I am deeply indebted to two old friends, Stephen D. Kertesz and Robert H. Ferrell, who have read the entire text and made many suggestions for its improvement. In addition, other scholars whose knowledge of the individual countries is far wider than my own have read separate chapters: Richard Brace, the one on Algeria; Walter Laqueur, that on the Arab-Israeli conflict; and Douglas Pike, the one on Indochina. Each of them made criticisms that I have gratefully taken into account.

I should also like to express my appreciation of the help of Mrs. Maria Chudzinski-Chase of the Law Library of Northwestern University, of the staffs of that library and of the Regenstein Library of the University of Chicago, the Bibliothèque Nationale, and the British Museum.

My thanks also go to Maria Abbadi who typed what was often an indecipherable manuscript and to the copy editor, Miss Carole Freddo, who worked with tact and expertise on the final text.

Chicago, September 1972

THE NUREMBERG FALLACY

1

The International War Order:
War in Our Time

O N October 1, 1946, the great trial of the major war criminals before the International Military Tribunal at Nuremberg ended with the sentencing to death of eleven of the defendants, prison terms for seven others, and the release of the remaining three. One other defendant, Martin Bormann, had been tried in absentia and sentenced to death. The trial of the twenty-two chieftains of the National Socialist state, of Hermann Goering, the generals, the admirals, the bureaucrats, the party leaders, had lasted 216 days, tons of documents had been fed into its machinery, hundreds of witnesses had been heard, and out of all this had come new principles of international law.

War, aggressive war, had been solemnly declared illegal by an international tribunal with judges from Britain, France, the Soviet Union, and the United States. Those who had committed it had been held criminally responsible for their political malefactions, hitherto considered acts of state for which the individual bore no personal guilt.

The four points of the indictment of the Nuremberg Tribunal had centered on war: two of the counts declared the responsibility for war a crime (to conspire to wage an aggressive war, and to wage it); the other two counts, charging war crimes and crimes against humanity, dealt with crimes both old and new. (The charge of committing war crimes had its roots in centuries of warfare and of accusations of improper or atrocious conduct on the part of the enemy; but the charge of committing crimes against humanity, like the charges of planning and waging aggressive warfare, made its first appearance at Nuremberg.)

Despite these sweeping declarations of a new legal world order,* we have lived since the Nuremberg trial in a time of unremitting international tension in which more than eighty wars or revolutions have been fought:† armed conflicts of all kinds waged with the full range of modern weapons (aside from the nuclear ones). The postwar years have witnessed wars between sovereign states, coalition wars, wars of national liberation, civil wars, guerrilla wars—none of them declared, all of them bloody, and some of them with episodes as barbarous as any that gave rise to the Nuremberg accusations. No comparable period in modern history has produced more wars than the years following World War II, and this is all the more striking when it is remembered that war in 1945 was formally declared by statesmen and international tribunals as exorcised, leaving to the victors of World War II only the task of policing an international order. Mr. Roosevelt at Teheran had foreseen four world policemen—Britain, the Soviet Union, the China of Chiang Kai-shek, and the United States—keeping the peace, and this project was institution-

* The London Agreement of August 8, 1945, established the International Military Tribunal at Nuremberg. The Agreement was drawn up by the United States, Britain, the Soviet Union, and France acting on behalf of the twenty-six nations that had gone to war with Germany. The phrasing of the clause on aggressive warfare had caused the only serious differences among the four powers. Mr. Justice Jackson, the chief American prosecutor at Nuremberg, had argued for the indictment of the perpetrators of any war of aggression as war criminals. The French expert on international law at the London Conference, Professor Gros, who held that individuals could not be tried for committing war, said: "We do not consider as a criminal violation a war of aggression. If we declare war a criminal act of an individual we are going further than the actual law." The Russians, who had themselves been declared aggressors in the Finnish war of 1940–1941 by the League of Nations, also opposed Mr. Jackson's sweeping definition. General Nikitchenko said: "Although when people speak of it they know what they mean, they cannot define it," and added that if the discussions dragged on the criminals would die of old age. Eventually the Russians produced a draft narrower than Mr. Jackson had hoped for but one acceptable to the four powers. It declared the crime to be: "Aggression or domination over other nations carried out by the European Axis in violation of international law and treaties." It was the contention of Mr. Justice Jackson, as well as of former Secretary of State Henry Stimson and many others, that Nuremberg was merely carrying out what was already established law; that the Kellogg-Briand Pact and similar instruments had, in fact, outlawed war before the start of World War II and the Nuremberg charges merely codified and would carry out their provisions. (Eugene Davidson, The Trial of the Germans, pp. 13–15.)

† The London Institute for Strategic Studies counted eighty military conflicts between 1945 and 1967. The New York Times lists eighty-three between 1945 and 1969, Istvan Kende tabulates ninety-seven. (Cf. note †, p. 3.)

alized a few months later with the founding of the United Nations and the designation of the four policemen as permanent members of the UN Security Council* In November 1947, the Assembly of the United Nations unanimously adopted the Nuremberg principles to be used by its International Law Commission as the basis for formulating the new codes of international law.

Not much peace, however, has emerged from all this. The United States has engaged in large-scale military actions in two of these eighty-odd wars, in Korea and Vietnam; it has intervened with military measures in Greece, Lebanon, Santo Domingo, Cuba, Guatemala, Laos, and Columbia, and indirectly in other countries as well.† Most Americans have believed, at least until the Vietnamese war, that despite this wide-ranging use of armed force the will to peace has not been lacking in the United States, and there is little doubt anywhere except in part of the Communist bloc that Mr. Roosevelt and his successors wanted nothing more than to disarm, to cooperate with other peace-loving states (as they liked to call them) to contain the aggressors, and to further the beneficent purposes of a world community. In this view, shared by a good many more people in the United States than in the rest of the world, the United States despite or because of its high-minded intentions has been continually forced to resort to arms.

The same conflict between the desire for peace and the resort to war has been evident in many of the other nations that have been involved in military actions, from their particular points of view, undoubtedly by all of them. World War II had been too destructive, with the loss of 30 million or more lives during its appalling course; the devastation of settlements and ways of life built over the centuries was too overwhelming to leave any desire for war as a heroic style. Nations in the past had gloried in their martial prowess, literature and

---

* Neither Churchill nor Stalin shared Mr. Roosevelt's confidence in China as a great power. Harry Hopkins, however, Mr. Roosevelt's close advisor, wrote a memorandum before his death in which he said that China was becoming most important in American foreign policy and would be its most likely partner in carrying democracy throughout the world. (Adam B. Ulam, *Expansion and Coexistence*, p. 473.)

† A Hungarian writer, Istvan Kende, lists ninety-seven wars waged in twenty-five years. Kende's analysis, while somewhat biased, includes, however, contrary to the Soiet view, the Russian invasion of Hungary in 1956 as a bona fide war. He has defined wars as actions that have involved the use of the regular armed forces on at least one side, continuity between the armed conflicts, "a strategical-tactical and organizational coherence between the individual actions," a degree of organization and organized struggle on both sides, the presence of a planning and organizing central activity on both sides. (Istvan Kende, "Twenty-five Years of Local War," pp. 6–22.)

the arts in Europe, Asia, and the rest of the world had celebrated it, but after World War II almost everyone seemingly rejected war as a test of civic virtue. No one anywhere wanted to assume the risks and burdens for the at best Pyrrhic victories of modern war on a grand scale. Whatever warlike moves were made were called by another name, or the word itself was modified in expressions like "Wars of National Liberation." The Communist forces in Greece, Poland, Yugoslavia, and Hungary were first regarded by both West and East as fighters in or with the resistance, and those that, with the help of the Red Army, formed new governments against the "reactionary forces" of the former governments in exile took their place in a status quo of sorts, a quickly established balance of power. These revolutionary forces, in the view of Moscow and the Communist party, did not take part in wars in a traditional sense but were engaged in a struggle against feudal, or crypto-Fascist, regimes that would seek to continue World War II in another form. Even in China, the full-scale military campaigns waged by Mao and Chiang after 1945 were regarded in both East and West as conflicts occurring outside the Nuremberg concepts; by the West as an unfortunate civil war, by the East as a continuation of the battle against imperialism, which in World War II had been waged against Japan and now was being fought against the puppets of the West. None of these military actions by Communist forces could possibly, in Moscow's view, be regarded as aggressions; on the contrary, they were a defense against aggression, against the attempt of capitalism to reconstruct archaic political forms out of which new wars must come. War was an inevitable, terrible product of the imperialist establishment and these national liberation movements were struggles against imperialism as well as against the wars it must generate.

For the West, however deplorable the continuing hostilities or however ruthless the Communist drive to power in the Eastern countries may have seemed, the findings of the Trial of the Major War Criminals and of the subsequent Nuremberg tribunals that continued to try the German malefactors of World War II remained in force. Nothing, no matter how much fighting took place, had changed the fundamental concepts that underlay the trials. The doctrines of the Nuremberg trials continued to be upheld, in a ceremonial fashion at least, and were reaffirmed from time to time: war in its traditional form was indeed a crime, and with the rapidly developing arsenals of destruction, an increasingly barbaric crime—both East and West were in agreement on this.

Those who were critical of Nuremberg had no brief for war, no desire to deal with it except as a grotesque survival of man's organized inhumanity to man. The only apparent differences were procedural—how was man to rid himself of its scourge? The Nuremberg verdicts had seemed a giant step toward this goal. Walter Lippmann compared Nuremberg with the Magna Carta, habeas corpus, and the Bill of Rights, Henry Stimson called it "a landmark in law," and in these sentiments they were joined by editorial writers, historians, and lawyers rejoicing that henceforth American and indeed all foreign policy would be based on the principles made into law by the trial. Collective security, it was very nearly universally believed in the West, had won over the isolationist misconceptions of the period between the two world wars. Isolationism had fostered the rise of Adolf Hitler and of the German and Japanese warlords; now with the defeat of the two aggressor nations, who had been joined by a misguided Italy, Finland, and the other satellite states of the Axis, a true world community was in the process of becoming a reality.

The success of this global enterprise, Mr. Roosevelt and his advisors became convinced, depended on convincing the Soviet Union that it could now trust the West and the nations that in alliance with the Red Army had brought down the attempt at world domination of the two marauding powers. Soviet Russia must be brought into the community of nations as a full-fledged cooperating member, it must have friendly powers on its borders, it must be encouraged to foster the Four Freedoms that Roosevelt in 1941 had promised the world would come about with the defeat of the Axis powers. With the Soviet Union joined in the search for international security, and the armed forces of Germany and Japan forever banned, the world might have its minor troubles but the cataclysms of the two world wars need never be repeated. This aim of securing a long period of peace, of wiping out the hideous products of a nihilistic, demoniacal drive for the domination of as much territory as might be seized, was by no means limited to Western heads of state. The atrocities of the war, the killing of some six million Jews, the abominable treatment of the peoples of conquered countries considered by the National Socialists as inferior or dangerous, or by the Japanese militarists as standing in the way of imperial greatness and Japan's domination of all of Asia, had left a suffering humanity with the conviction that it needed to assure a future purged of such monstrous powers. The nations of the world desperately needed a respite, but the form this respite took for some of them was a nonpeace: border wars alternating with periods of détente. None of these developments, however, had much to do with the principles of Nuremberg; they came about as a new and unsteady balance of power was established between the Soviet Union and the United States, and almost every war that has occurred since the end of World War II has been either caused or fueled by the larger conflict.

In the real world of hard events the dissolution of the principles enunciated at Nuremberg began even before the start of the trial. In 1944 as the Germans withdrew from Greece the Communist forces of the Greek resistance turned their guns against the royalist Greek soldiers, the government troops that had first resisted the Italian and then the German invasion. This tactic was followed in Poland, too, where with the advancing Red Army the Polish Communist cadres moved quickly to take over the administration of the country and to prevent the non-Communist Polish government forces, who had the support of the Western Allies, from regaining the power they had held when the war started in their defense. The battle in Greece was hard fought; the Communists were aided by the new satellite states in the Balkans, and the Greek government forces supported by the British, whose dominant position in Greece had been recognized by Stalin in his 1944 meeting with Churchill that parceled out spheres of influence in the Balkans.*

The bitter fighting in Greece continued with considerable Communist successes and by 1947 it had become clear to the British government that Britain could no longer maintain its military and economic aid, the costs were too great a drain, and the only power that could prevent Greece from falling to the Communist forces was the United States. By 1947 the division into two worlds was becoming unmistakable and Congress, at the request of President Truman, approved the sum of $400 million for aid to both Greece and Turkey as well as the dispatch of American military and civilian advisors to shore up the resistance of those countries to the Communist threat. It was, however, at least as much as American help, the defection

---

* Indirect measures too were used by the Soviet Union and approved by the Western Allies that could facilitate a Communist takeover. The Moscow Declaration of 1943 stated with regard to Italy, "It is essential that the Italian Government should be made more democratic by the introduction of representatives of those sections of the Italian population that have always opposed fascism." This formula, used in other Western European countries as well, provided essentially for the inclusion of Communists in any future Italian government, and it was not until 1947, with the proclamation of the Truman Doctrine, that Communists could be excluded from participating in governments where, as in West Germany, they were not wanted.

of Tito from the Soviet orbit in 1948, which dried up the flow of supplies and aid of all kinds that had been coming through Yugoslavia, that enabled the Greek government troops finally to win a victory. But whatever the weight of the American intervention, it and the Greek civil war had little relation to the peaceful world community that had been announced even while the Communists were attempting their takeover in the course of World War II. Greece was an early page in the chronicle of hidden and open struggle that was to dominate the postwar years, a conflict that reappeared in Czechoslovakia where Soviet tactics would succeed, and in Berlin where they failed, and that spread to the Far East, Southeast Asia, Africa, Iran and other countries in the Middle East, and Latin America.

A quarter of a century has passed since the Nuremberg principles were proclaimed, and it has become possible to see what they have done and what they have failed to do. This book will present some of the case histories of this period and attempt to determine whether, when the principles failed, it was because they could not possibly work in a world divided into hostile camps, or whether other factors, less sweeping and compelling, were involved. Does collective security, which is an integral part of the Nuremberg formula, help limit wars, or does it, as the critics of the League of Nations held, lead to an impossible attempt to keep things as they are, to hold a smiling or solemn mask before the faces of those who are bent on changing or maintaining the world to match their own image? If it is true, as more than one international lawyer has written, that law was never in such a chaotic state as it is today, how has its degeneration come about? What is the meaning of rules of war when the distinction between civilian and soldier threatens to be lost in modern war; when atrocities are taken for granted; when protection of nationals on foreign soil or of government or private ships and planes is often impossible; when prisoners of war have only such rights as the capturing power may grant them and they no longer have the protection of international agreements supervised by neutrals; when in the battles following World War II the torture of prisoners of war has been not only condoned but approved by the high commands of civilized governments? Why have these reversions to barbarism come about? Is it in the nature of the weapons and the callousness toward suffering that accompanies protracted resorts to arms? How far are the pretenses of legality and morality that cover what nations actually do, responsible? What can be salvaged from our experience of war, since the war, for the prevention or mitigation of its horrors? In short, what is there left in Nuremberg for us, and by us I mean all the people who stand to be blown up if the devices to keep the peace or limit the wars fail?

2

Aggression

War, Just and Unjust in History

WAR like disease has accompanied man from the beginning of recorded history. A nineteenth-century German historian calculated that from 1496 B.C. until A.D. 1861, that is, in the course of 3357 years, only 227 had been years of peace while 3130 had been years of war; for every year of peace there had been 13 years of war.[1]

Since these figures were compiled, many famous, and for the most part increasingly devastating, wars have been fought: the American Civil War, the Franco-Prussian War, the Boer War, the Spanish-American War, the Russo-Japanese War, World War I, the Russian Civil War, the Japanese occupation of Manchuria and the invasion of China, and World War II, to name some of them, plus the scores that have occurred since 1945. And with the increasing intensity of the nations' mobilization of resources and the insatiable demands of modern machinery of war, the need has grown to justify a war to an entire people, to demonstrate that a government had no alternative, that it had to resist an aggressor who would otherwise devastate or destroy the nation. A government must convince its people that the other side is responsible for hostilities even before they start.

The need to identify the enemy as the aggressor is not new; the Greek historian Polybius wrote of Rome in the second century B.C.: "The Romans were wont to take great care not to be the aggressors or to attack their neighbors without provocation; but to be considered to be acting always in self-defense and always to enter upon war under compulsion." Rome held that the just war required a formal declaration and religious ceremonies as well. It was legally waged against a people who violated Roman dominions or treaties with Rome, who did harm to Roman ambassadors, or gave support to the enemies of Rome.[2]

In the Christian era the Augustinian doctrine of the just war developed from the concept of natural law, the *Lex Naturalis*. It was a war fought against a state that had committed a serious wrong, above all, that had damaged the interests of Christendom, and in the view of Hugo Grotius, writing in the seventeenth century, almost 1200 years after Augustine, the victorious state, if it and its allies derived no undue advantages, acted for the entire Christian community when it punished the wrongdoer.[*]

Christian writers could justify organized killing only to take back one's own, or to avenge an injury. Wars could properly be waged to repel the enemy for a moral or for a religious purpose. This was evident in the views of Augustine writing in the fourth and fifth centuries, through Thomas Aquinas in the thirteenth century, who held not only that a war must be fought in a just cause, but also that the ruler must have a just intention in waging it. It was a view shared by the Spanish jurists, Francisco de Vitoria and Francisco Suarez writing in the sixteenth and seventeenth centuries. Vitoria and Suarez held that wars were expeditions of punishment to be waged in the Augustinian sense against a state that had violated the law. Both Suarez and Vitoria condemned the unjust treatment of the Indians by the *conquistadores*. They defended the natives against the claims of the Spanish throne, declaring that the spread of Christianity was no excuse for depriving the Indians of their lands and freedom.

---

* The belief in a natural law existing above the particular or positive law of separate states long antedates Christianity. Even Hesiod, the eighth-century B.C. didactic poet, has been claimed for international law by one scholar as having believed in a *Lex Aeterna*.

It was Cicero who invented the term *jus gentium*, which was the application of natural law, the law of reason, of the cosmos, and of the gods, to all mankind. The *jus gentium* applied to foreigners in their relations to Romans, without the technicalities of the *jus civile*, which affected Roman citizens only. The *jus gentium*, in its beginnings, unlike later international law, affected individuals rather than states. (Ernst Reibstein, *Völkerrecht*; Gerhard von Glahn, *Law Among Nations*.)

And in China during the Han dynasty, a Confucian scholar, Tung ch'ung-shu, in the second century B.C. told his emperor Wu ti: "The Way (Tao) comes from Heaven, Heaven is unchangeable and the Tao too is unchangeable." (Quoted in Mao Tse-tung, *Ausgewählte Werke*, Vol. I, p. 406.)

With the erosion of a universal Christianity the concept of a just war has been laicized, linked with the secular purpose of a war on behalf of a European order, or of civilization, or of humanity.

The eighteenth-century Swiss jurist, Emmerich von Vattel, in his *Droit des Gens*, wrote: "If therefore there is anywhere an unquiet nation, always ready to damage others and to cross them, to bring them to domestic troubles, there is no doubt that everyone would have the right to join together to restrain it, to punish it, and even to put it forever out of the possibility of doing damage."[3]

In the opposing views of the realists other maxims were adduced going back to the fifth century B.C. and quoted disapprovingly by Grotius: "For the ruler or for a ruling state nothing is illegal that is useful to their purposes; in political matters what counts is success, and without injustice no state can govern."[4] *Salus populi suprema est lex*, the well-being of the people is the supreme law. Thomas Hobbes held that the sovereign was bound by no rules but his own. Machiavelli dealt only with the facts of power and counseled his prince on how to succeed in a vicious world where life itself was always at hazard by ruthlessly and intelligently using the stratagems essential to consolidating and increasing his authority. Hegel, too, considered sovereignty to be absolute; disputes between sovereigns could be settled only by violence. Kant, who contrary to Hegel did believe in the possibility of attaining permanent peace, sourly observed that all the fine words of writers like Grotius and Vattel had not the slightest legal force and could not have, since states are not subject to collective coercion and such statements are no more than ingenuous justifications for any armed attack.[5]

The Humanitarian Missions

But while nations have operated with the guidelines of the realists, they have not wanted to live by them alone. Although men of the cloth, jurists, and theologians like Vitorio and Suarez, as well as secular leaders, wished to impose limits on the colonizers, such restraints never deterred the states concerned from their conquests of the Indian tribes on the North and South American continents or of the tribes of Africa, or their incursions into Asia. In the modern era France during its conquests pointed to its *mission civilisatrice* in Africa, Indochina, and the Middle East, and Britain to its *Pax Britannica* in India, among the warring tribes of Africa, and in Asia. In practice savage or barbaric peoples had no rights *per se,* although the obligation was often expressed to treat them humanely and the Germans, for example, had elaborate regulations governing the conditions of work for the natives under their rule in Tanganyika and the Cameroons.

While wars were no longer fought on behalf of Christendom, as a spiritual force it was replaced by admixtures of an encompassing humanitarianism. In 1827 Britain, France, and Russia intervened to put an end to the atrocities of the Greco-Turkish War; in the middle of the nineteenth century the European Great Powers protested to the Czar against the atrocious treatment by Russia of the Polish insurrectionists, and similar protests were lodged against the treatment of the Jews in Russia and of the Christians in Turkey. One of the chief reasons put forth for the American intervention in Cuba in 1898 was the ethical imperative to free the Cuban population from the atrocities of the Spanish overlords.

Individual Responsibility

Justifications for going to war against a barbarous or wicked enemy had nothing to do with trying him after the war was over. Napoleon, although he found himself in the hands of his conquerors, Britain, Russia, Austria, and Prussia, was not punished by any judicial procedures; the Congress of Vienna declared him to have placed himself "outside the civil and social relations and as an enemy and disturber of world peace (*du repos du monde*) is delivered to public obloquy." He was accordingly confined in political protective imprisonment on the island of St. Helena by Great Britain, the custodial power.[6]

At the close of World War I a special Commission of fifteen members representing the Allied powers, including the United States, deplored the waging of aggressive war but declared it was not illegal. The Commission found that: "The premeditation of a war of aggression . . . is conduct which the public conscience reproves and which history will condemn, but a war of aggression may not be considered an act directly contrary to positive law."*[7]

---

* The origin of World War I for many years was the subject of lively controversy —who was responsible for starting it? During its course it was widely believed in the United States and almost unanimously in the Allied countries that the two Kaisers of the Central Powers, but mainly Wilhelm II, were responsible. Then came the revisionist historians, who wrote in peacetime and based their research on new material includ-

Nevertheless, a short-lived attempt was made to bring Wilhelm II to trial, in the words of the Treaty of Versailles, "for supreme offenses against morality and the sanctity of treaties," although, as Clemenceau told the Dutch government, the accusation did not have "a juridical character but [was] an act of high international politics inspired by a universal conscience."[8] All this came to nothing when the Dutch, to the relief of everyone concerned, refused to surrender the former Kaiser for trial, a stand for which they were praised by a number of Allied jurists including an American representative on the Commission, James Brown Scott, who wrote: "Holland has made the world its debtor by refusing to surrender the Kaiser for the commission of an offense admittedly political. . . . That little country had too much honor to think of it."[9]

The Aggressors and the League of Nations

The League of Nations, although it was an organization based on collective security and in theory bound all members to take action, including economic sanctions and even military force, against any member state that went to war in violation of the Covenant, never did much more than shake its finger when a major power acted against League principles and never made any attempt to charge individuals with violations of them. In 1935 the League declared Italy an aggressor for its attack on Ethiopia and imposed economic sanctions but deliberately omitted the one commodity that might have affected the Italian war effort—oil. The only effect the imposition of the sanctions had was to drive the Italy of Mussolini closer to the Reich of Adolf Hitler, and when Italy conquered Ethiopia the League ended the sanctions, although it continued to recognize Ethiopia as a sovereign state. In 1939 the League expelled Soviet Russia from its membership for attacking Finland, and there the matter rested: the Soviet Union was no longer a member of the League and Finland was defeated. In Japan's invasion of China, the annexations by Germany of Austria and Czechoslovakia, and by Italy

---

ing secret documents released by the new Soviet state that sought to show what manner of government its predecessor had been and the infamy in general of the capitalist world. The Russia of Nicholas II and the France of Poincaré and Clemenceau took the place of the Germany of Wilhelm II and the Austria-Hungary of Franz Joseph as the countries chiefly responsible for the outbreak of World War I, and even though subsequent doubt has been thrown on this thesis, the black-and-white propaganda pictures of the Allied powers during World War I have not been restored.

of Albania, the League played no intervening role whatever, nor in any of these cases could there be any serious question of punishment for the perpetrators of aggression.

Acts of State

Jurists could not agree on the justice or propriety of trying heads of states and members of governments for their political sins. Acts of state, *Staatsräson, raison d'état,* have been recognized as human actions of a distinct category by historians and international lawyers, who have distinguished their exigencies from those of private life.* When, for example, Winston Churchill after the fall of France in 1940 ordered British warships to attack the fleet of their ally of the week before at Oran, and as a result over one thousand French sailors were killed, he was not acting out of pique or revenge or blood lust. He felt that for England's security he could not take the risk of permitting the French ships to fall into Hitler's hands. It was a decision made in sorrow, but one he and most of the non-French and anti-Axis world regarded as indispensable.†

The Kellogg-Briand Pact and Nuremberg

The Nuremberg Court after World War II was, then, not the first international body to declare aggressive war indefensible but the first to try the chief people believed to be responsible for it for their criminal acts.‡ The juridical basis for this proceeding was mainly the Kellogg-Briand Pact which had been signed by sixty-three nations in

---

* "Reason of State" has, since Independence, been rejected by some Americans as a European doctrine on a par with feudalism, monarchy, and balance of power. Nevertheless, it has been used by the United States as it has by other nations, but it was called in America by a different name—"National Interest." It was, for example, the concept of national interest that enabled the Roosevelt administration and the Supreme Court to approve the internment in camps of thousands of American-born Japanese during World War II for no crime other than being racially Japanese. (Cf. Alfred Vagts, "Reason of State in America," in *Jahrbuch für Amerikastudien,* pp. 237–244.)

† Churchill's orders gave the French four alternative courses: they could either join the British forces, sail to a British port, or to the French West Indies, or to scuttle their ships within six hours. If these terms were rejected, Admiral Somerville was to destroy the French Squadron. (Captain S. W. Roskill, *White Ensign,* p. 84.)

‡ Rudolf Hess, the deputy to Adolf Hitler who flew to England with a fantastic, not to say almost insane, scheme to make peace, was sentenced to life imprisonment at Nuremberg for having planned to wage and to have participated in waging aggressive war. Hess was the only defendant to be sentenced on these charges alone.

1928 and which formally outlawed war as an instrument of national policy. No penalties were provided nor any means for enforcing the Pact's provisions—in fact, since it permitted defensive wars, critics of the Pact said it was merely a meaningless genuflection before the shrine of peace. In at least ten instances it was violated by various powers among those who had signed it (by Italy in Ethiopia, by the Soviet Union in Finland, by Japan in China, by the intervention in the Spanish Civil War of Germany, Italy, and the Soviet Union, for example), but no one was ever tried for such breaches of the Pact, nor had any of its signatories imagined they could be. Nevertheless, it was invoked in Nuremberg as the legal cornerstone of the charges of committing war in violation of treaties. Although other conventions or declarations of policies were also cited, none of these had had the same panache or nearly as many signatures as had the Kellogg-Briand Pact. Nevertheless, despite all the loopholes and violations, the Pact not only repeated old preachments on how a nation should conduct itself but also expressed a contemporary doctrine, an increasingly widely held belief that recourse to war could be morally justified only on two grounds: for defense, or on behalf of the general peace. The Stimson Doctrine, proclaimed in 1932 after the Japanese occupation of Manchuria, reaffirmed the principles of the Kellogg-Briand Pact. In the post-World War II years any acquisition of territory by force has been either outright rejected or reluctantly recognized and called by another name. When Portuguese Goa was forcibly annexed by India in 1961, its new sovereignty was quickly recognized by the Soviet bloc as having come about through a just war of national liberation, and then, with some delay, the change was assented to by the United States and other Western powers, since there was nothing they could do about it that they were willing to do. Portugal was not a most-favored nation in either the Soviet bloc or the West.

The Elusive Definitions

The Soviet Union has always been an inveterate denouncer of aggression in general. In 1933 the Kremlin signed a convention with Latvia, Estonia, Afghanistan, Poland, Iran, Rumania, and Turkey which defined five acts of aggression, including a declaration of war, invading, blockading, or bombarding another state. In 1939, however, as soon as Stalin by virtue of his pact with Hitler had freedom of action in the Baltic, the Soviet Union promptly annexed Latvia and Estonia and occupied part of Poland.

But aggression, as such, remains universally condemned even if the powers are seldom agreed on when it occurs; no one has come up with a definition acceptable to the Communist and non-Communist worlds, or to the great and small powers.* The International Law Commission given the task of defining aggression in 1947,† a special fifteen-member committee established by the General Assembly in 1953, a thirty-five-nation Special Committee on the Question of Defining Aggression appointed in 1967, as well as other committees of the United Nations have been unsuccessful in their efforts to arrive at an acceptable definition, as have repeated attempts by historians and publicists. No international body has ever been able to state what exactly goes on when a nation commits an aggression. As a French jurist, Eugène Aronéanu, has written: "How to define aggression? A person asked to define an elephant answered: 'I don't know how to define an elephant, but I know it is something big.' "[10]

Some authorities have held that aggression is an essential truth, a primary concept beyond definition, a word like "justice," perhaps, or "righteousness." In any event, it is clearly a crime that can only be defined in a political context. The enemy is the aggressor; this is true *ab initio* because the charge of aggression is made whenever a nation is prevented by another power from pursuing or preserving what it believes to be its vital interests. It is a protean concept which, in some of its shapes, cannot be distinguished from affluence and

* When the forces of North Korea, on June 24, 1950, invaded South Korea, President Truman asked the Security Council of the United Nations to meet. The next day the Council passed a resolution calling the invasion a "breach of the peace" and demanding a cease-fire and withdrawal of the North Korean troops to the 38th parallel. The North Koreans, however, continued their attack, and on June 27 President Truman ordered the United States navy and air force to provide cover for the South Koreans who were retreating rapidly and in danger of being overrun. Later, on the same day, the Security Council unanimously recommended that "the members of the United Nations furnish such assistance to the Republic of Korea as may be necessary to repel the armed attack and to restore international peace and security to the area." The unanimous vote was made possible by the temporary absence of the Soviet delegate who boycotted the meeting to protest the United Nations' refusal to seat Communist China. Russia was, therefore, fortuitously unable to cast a veto against the resolution which, in any event, was of minor aid to the considerable American military effort. The action of the Security Council did provide the United States with some small additional troops from among the other members of the United Nations, but it did not prevent Communist China from sending crucial help to the North Koreans. The foreign troops in South Korea are still American, although they continue to be called United Nations forces.

† The Commission reported that a satisfying definition was impossible to formulate. (Eugène Aronéanu, *La Définition de l'Agression*, p. 1940.)

know-how. One of the new African nations, Dahomey, holds that aggression must be defined very broadly because a most common form in its experience is economic.[11] An eminent free market economist, Ludwig von Mises, expressed a similar view when he said that a high tariff should be considered an act of aggression against a foreign power able and willing to compete with the high-priced products of native, protected industries. Lin Piao, then Mao Tsetung's Defense Minister, declared that the impoverished, underdeveloped continents of Asia, Africa, and Latin America are continually subjected to aggression and enslavement by the United States as the leader of the imperialist powers.[12] In a not entirely dissimilar vein, the General Assembly of the United Nations on December 21, 1965, declared that no state had the right to intervene or to coerce another through economic or other measures, or to use force against its national identity.[13] Haiti, a few years later, called a film, *The Comedians*, that took a critical view of its one-man government and total lack of civil liberties "cultural aggression."

The ideological notion of aggression as a criminal act can be stretched to cover almost any contingency. A Polish draft code of criminal law drawn up in 1956 included crimes against peace, against humanity, and *against peaceful cooperation between nations*. As the world would discover in the invasions of Hungary and Czechoslovakia, and as we shall see in the claims advanced by the Brezhnev Doctrine, the Communist bloc may interpret such formulations very broadly indeed.[14] Israel and the Arab states call one another aggressors freely, and according to the Pan-Arab movement, the founding of the state of Israel was itself an act of aggression.[15] When the United States increased its troop strength and began the bombing of North Vietnam following the disputed attack on its warships in the Bay of Tonkin, it charged that it was responding to an aggression. To some observers six thousand miles seemed a long way to go to respond to an aggression committed by forces operating only a few miles from their own shores. The character of wars since World War II and the conflicting ideologies that justify or condemn them make any consensus on the use of the word "aggression" impossible in practically all the actual situations of crisis.

Partisan War and the Struggle against Imperialism

Partisan warfare, the dominant form of hostilities since World War II, has been developed and modified for the postwar contingencies. It is a form of war highly developed in the revolutionary strategies of China and Russia, well adapted to the nuclear age and its military stalemate, and for centuries it has been fought with marked success by small nations against great powers. When St. Paul appeared before the Roman commander, he was immediately questioned as a suspicious character, and asked if he was not the Egyptian leader who had started a revolt of 4,000 terrorists and then fled to the wilds some time before. Guerrilla war was successfully used against Napoleon in Spain and in Russia. In World War II it was one of the major weapons of the Russians against the Germans on the eastern front and in the Balkans, and it was waged on a smaller scale in the west—in France, Holland, Italy, and Norway. It has been a vital weapon in the crusade preached by Communist China against the Western powers on behalf of the poor people of the countryside revolting against the rich and decadent Western cities; and in the rhetoric of American Negro militants, it is the war of the revolutionaries of the urban poor against their oppressors. Partisan warfare with its hit-and-run tactics has played an important part in most of the battles in the wars of national liberation. The Israelis used it to help speed the British out of Palestine, and local populations to drive the French out of North Africa and Indochina; it was the main weapon of Castro in his Cuban revolution, and Mao Tse-tung, one of its chief prophets, based his campaigns against both Chiang and the Japanese on guerrilla tactics and strategy.

Guerrilla war is the spearhead of the wars against the colonial powers. Lenin called colonialism an absolute evil, a view shared by most African and Asian countries, and Communist doctrine in both China and the Soviet Union holds that any state possessing colonies is already convicted of criminality and aggression. Subject peoples have a right to take armed action to redress old crimes committed against them, as well as to undertake reprisals, and to use any means at their disposal to recover their independence. Every war of national liberation is therefore a legitimate response to the built-in provocation of an existing colonial power, and any opposition to native freedom movements is in itself an offense against international law and the United Nations Charter.[16]

Thus guerrilla warfare is part of the worldwide struggle against capitalism and imperialism, that is, against the imperialism of the Western powers or, as one observer has remarked, against imperialism that crosses water. Imperialism by way of land routes, if conducted as in Hungary and Czechoslovakia on behalf of the socialist order of peace-loving nations, is, of course, in the Communist view, legitimate. Khrushchev wrote: "The Socialist countries and the Communist parties all over the world will continue to aid and support the peoples who are waging an armed struggle against capitalism. Far from contradicting the principle of peaceful coexistence this is an affirmation of that concept since the issue at stake . . . is the right of all people to order their life as they see fit, to be masters in their own house."[17]

From the Communist point of view, "the struggle of people against reactionary regimes cannot be destroyed by international agreement. For this struggle to cease the causes eliciting it must be eliminated, i.e., capitalism must be liquidated."[18] By definition, no war resorted to by a socialist state constitutes an aggression and no war fought by a capitalist state can be anything but imperialistic. A socialist war is always a just war, and since those who fight on the other side are criminals, the North Vietnamese, for example, can legitimately, in the Communist construal, deny captured American airmen treatment as prisoners of war.

Capitalism Is Aggression

Capitalism is aggression and exploitation and the struggle against it is justified wherever and whenever it occurs. The Havana Conference of January 1966 called on the peoples of all countries to support national liberation movements and to undertake subversive action to overturn the governments of a number of members of the Organization of American States.[19] With the United Nations now dominated numerically by the Afro-Asian bloc plus the representatives of the Communist bloc, this is also the view of the United Nations. In its Declaration of January 1960, "On granting Independence to Colonial Peoples," the United Nations Assembly declared that every nation has the right to self-determination and that "The subjugation of peoples is contrary to the Charter and World Peace . . . the inadequacy of political or social or educational preparation should never serve as a pretext to delay independence. All armed efforts against such attempts must cease."[20] This doctrine applies to all the emerging nations as well as to countries with native populations that are not in power. Thus we have economic sanctions imposed by the United Nations (including the votes of the Western powers) against Rhodesia and South Africa because of their domestic policies, and a continuing demand for stronger punitive measures by the new African states.

The United Nations took no action against the dry-land imperialism of the Soviet Union, however, when it invaded with its allied forces of the Communist bloc the sister republic of Czechoslovakia and promulgated a new and powerful justification for such a measure in the Brezhnev Doctrine, which holds that when the socialist world is threatened by the actions of any of its member nations the Soviet Union has the right to intervene in that nation. The Soviet Union, joined by Hungary, cast a veto (Russia's 105th) in the Security Council against placing the question of the invasion of Czechoslovakia on the agenda of the Security Council. In the United Nations Assembly the American Secretary of State, Dean Rusk, berated the Soviet Union for the invasion and the Soviet Ambassador defended it declaring that Russia "will neither tolerate nor allow" any attempts to weaken the Eastern bloc.[21]

War Crimes and Crimes against Humanity

In the course of the years since Nuremberg the other counts of the indictment have also appeared in new contexts. The United Nations in 1948 adopted a convention against genocide based on Nuremberg, declaring that its perpetrators were to be tried by the state where the crime was committed and that the contracting states must hand over any such criminals they may apprehend to the state where the genocide occurred. The nations of the world were thus prepared to restate their belief that the destruction of civilian populations is a crime, but genocide is alleged to have occurred at least four times since the convention was adopted, committed by the United States in its bombing of North Vietnam, by the Nigerian government against the insurgent Ibo tribesmen of Biafra, by France against the Algerians, and by Pakistan against the Bengalis. In all cases the charges have been vehemently made and denied and there the matter rests.

With regard to the traditional laws of war many of them are in suspension or ignored. The treatment of American prisoners of war held captive in North Vietnam is subject to no international supervision and to no international conventions. This was also true of the imprisonment of the American prisoners taken when the USS Pueblo was seized by North Korean forces. If any of the traditional rules for the treatment of prisoners of war are observed by the government of South Vietnam, this may be owing to the American presence in that country (although, as we shall see, the United States' handling of prisoners of war has also been severely criticized by Americans as well as by neutral observers), which seems otherwise no more disposed to accept or to carry out the Hague and Geneva conventions than do the North Vietnamese. Torture has been widely used by both sides in guerrilla wars and those that have taken place since World War II are certainly no exception. We shall see in the accounts that follow what remains of the former humane provisions for the protection and treatment of captured enemy soldiers and of civilian populations, for limitations on how war may be waged against noncombatants and their property, for the treatment of the sick and wounded, and for the belligerent occupation of enemy territory—in short, for situations giving rise to crimes committed against the rules of war and against humanity. All such acts were linked at the Nuremberg trial with aggression, for it was aggressive war itself that was declared illegal and atrocities were its byproducts. In a number of wars since World War II atrocities have become an accepted part of military operations and of the defense against them.

NOTES

1. Johann von Bloch, *Beschreibung des Kriegsmechanismus*, Vol. I, p. xi.
2. Viscount Maugham, *UNO and War Crimes Trials*, p. 130. Quoted from *The Histories of Polybius*, Vol. 2, p. 549.
   Stephen D. Kertesz, *The Quest for Peace through Diplomacy*.
   H. Lauterpacht, ed., *Oppenheim's International Law*.
3. Hans-Heinrich Jescheck, *Die Verantwortlichkeit der Staatsorgane nach Völkerrecht*, p. 27.
4. Ernst Reibstein, *Völkerrecht*, p. 337.
5. Jescheck, *op. cit.*, p. 28.
   Alfred Verdross, *Völkerrecht*, Vol. I.
   Cicero, *De Legibus*, Vol. III, p. iii 8.
6. Jescheck, *op. cit.*, p. 31.
7. *Ibid.*, p. 52.
8. *Ibid.*, pp. 59, 62.
9. *Ibid.*, p. 63.
10. Eugène Aronéanu, "La Définition de l'Agression, p. 348.
11. John N. Hazard, "Why Try Again to Define Aggression?", pp. 701–710.
12. Richard A. Falk, ed., *The Vietnam War and International Law*, p. 110.
13. *Ibid.*
14. Bridge, *op. cit.*, pp. 1255–1281.
15. Bruno Frei, " 'Progressive' Auschwitz?", pp. 7–12.
16. S. Prakash Sinha, *New Nations and the Law of Nations*.

17. Cited George Ginsburg, " 'Wars of National Liberation' and the Modern Law of Nations," p. 939.
18. H. Dona, quoted in Robert D. Crane, "Basic Principles in Soviet Space Law," p. 944.
19. Alwyn V. Freeman, "Some Aspects of Soviet Influence on International Law," pp. 710–722.
20. Ginsburg, *op. cit.*, pp. 940–941.
21. *The New York Times*, October 4, 1968.

3

The Arab Wars

Aggression in Suez

IN 1956 in Egypt took place what is likely to be the last scene in the faded diorama of gunboat diplomacy, the traditional way of the great powers of dealing with a recalcitrant and weak nation that seemed to them to threaten their prestige or security. When Nasser nationalized the Suez Canal Company on July 26, 1956, in the view of the British and French governments he not only stole (in Eden's memoirs the chapter on the subject is called "Theft") the property of the private international company that built, and since 1868 had run, the canal, but he also confronted the two powers with an act of brigandage that both were convinced jeopardized their economic life lines. Britain and France were dependent on the canal for a large proportion of their oil imports (65 percent of Britain's requirements came through it), and if Nasser could strike down its international control, it would be the President of Egypt henceforth who would determine whether they would get the oil on which their economies so largely depended.

For France the matter was urgent for other reasons too: Ferdinand de Lesseps, a Frenchman, had built the canal, and the Compagnie Universelle du Canal Maritime de Suez, although an Egyptian company and subject to Egyptian law, was largely French-owned.* More

* That is, owned by French private citizens. Britain was the largest single shareholder with 44 percent of the stock. In 1956 sixteen members of the board of thirty-two directors were French, five British, five Egyptian, one American, and one Dutch. (Dwight D. Eisenhower, Waging Peace, pp. 35, 77.)

important, by 1956 a large part of the Arab world was ideologically at war with France. Although Tunisia and Morocco had been granted independence, France was fighting a bloody guerrilla war in Algeria, where the last and most cherished of her North African possessions was at stake. To accept a new affront by Egypt, which was already aiding the insurgent Algerian forces, would further weaken the precarious French position in North Africa and in the world, for Indochina had been lost two years before.

In other centuries such matters had been peremptorily dealt with: a warship would be sent up a river in China or Africa, force would be threatened and used if a native chieftain was obdurate, then he would either relent or someone else more amenable would be put in his place. In 1882 Britain bombed Alexandria following a massacre in that city and proceeded to occupy all of Egypt. But as the prime ministers of Britain and France, Anthony Eden and Guy Mollet, both knew, the spirit of the mid-1950s was very different. Eden was himself a good example of the change. He had always been a devout believer in collective security and a firm advocate of countering any violent measures undertaken by an individual state with the peacekeeping efforts of the League of Nations and then the United Nations. Guy Mollet, too, carried on a circumspect French tradition of placing a cautious reliance on the measures of collective security. It is true that General de Gaulle had spoken of the United Nations with unconcealed contempt, refusing to attend a session of "that thing the U.N.,"[1] but it was France that had originated the idea of the Kellogg-Briand Pact, and that had often called on the methods of so-called legality to keep Europe on the straight and narrow path prescribed by the Versailles and other treaties following World War I, until the system collapsed in the late thirties. With the establishment of the United Nations France had been added to the four world policemen as a permanent member of the Security Council and a pillar of the new organization.

Anthony Eden had never had any serious second thoughts about the necessity for supporting the international bodies that had followed both world wars. As a wholehearted supporter of the League and of the United Nations he was far from an original member of the gunboat school of diplomacy. His first thoughts as he tells us in his memoirs, were that the economic life of Western Europe was threatened by the seizure of the Canal Company; an international agreement—the Convention of 1880—had been flouted; and the

United States, which had precipitated the seizure of the canal by refusing to finance the construction of the Aswan High Dam in Egypt, should together with France and England take stern measures against the malefactor. He had no confidence at all in the beneficent intentions of Gamal Nasser; a man of that kind, he wrote in a telegram dispatched on July 27, the day after Nasser had made his announcement of the seizure, could not be allowed "to have his thumb on our windpipe."[2]

Gamal Abdel Nasser, for his part, was full of high purpose on behalf of a revivified Egypt and of Arab nationalism on the broadest possible scale. He was a man of the new Egyptian urban and semi-urban middle class. His father had been a clerk in the postal service, and Nasser had been educated in the military college at Cairo attended in large numbers by boys brought up in similar circumstances, with no love for the Effendi living in great luxury in contrast to the grinding poverty around them. Nasser had suffered the daily humiliation of being brought up in a country run by such an upper class and by a foreign power. Then he had had to endure the even greater humiliation of being taken prisoner in 1948 by the Israelis after having been wounded in the chest, and of seeing the Arab forces fail to drive the Jews out of their newly established country, which Nasser and thousands of other Arabs had immediately set out to destroy. The Arabs lost that war, but Nasser, together with brother officers, formed a military junta bent on political and moral revolution in Egypt. They succeeded in 1952 in bringing down the monarchy of King Farouk and ousting the parasitical functionaries who had long lived off the country and in their opinion had been responsible for the defeat and backwardness of Egypt.

Starting from the springboard of a successful revolution and the rapid consolidation of his own power, Nasser, after he became Premier in April 1954, was determined to go further, to get rid of not only the British troops, who under an agreement he made with Britain in July 1954 were to leave Egyptian soil within twenty months, but also the other vestiges of Egypt's colonial status, to destroy the corrupt feudalism that had kept Egypt weak and helpless, and to carry the torch of Arab unity to the entire Arab world. And he was having some success with these purposes. The British troops left Egypt a month and a half before the twenty months were over, Cairo was one of the chief sources of propaganda and material aid to the forces in revolt against French rule in Algeria, and to every

Arab country Nasser brought tidings of a pan-Arab order in the making, of liberation from their old domestic servitude as well as from their inferior status to European states. He introduced land reform in Egypt (no one was to be allowed to own more than three hundred acres), to the Sudan he promised self-determination and later full independence, and above all, he called passionately for an Arab crusade against the state of Israel. His many eloquent messages stirred deep emotions in his fellow countrymen and throughout the Arab world, and not the least of these was his call for Arab solidarity, which would mean military power and the rebirth of Arab pride after centuries of domination by foreign masters.

Opinions differed widely on Nasser's capacities. The Egyptians on the whole were delighted with him, despite an attempt at assassination in October 1954 by a member of an ultranationalist movement, the Moslem Brotherhood. But although his call for Arab unity aroused enthusiasm outside Egypt, many Arab leaders, among them King Hussein of Jordan and King Faisal II of Iraq, feared and distrusted his ambitions. Europeans and Americans had mixed impressions of him. Dag Hammarskjöld liked him, Eisenhower called him "dynamic, personable," Anthony Eden said he was "quite a likeable fellow, but far from being charming he is rather *gauche* . . . a man of considerable but immature intelligence."[3] Eden thought Nasser had had little experience with matters of state and showed it. Soviet leaders seem to have regarded him, as they did Fidel Castro, as an emotional, not entirely reliable, leader, extremely useful as a kind of Agitprop man in a strategic area, a leader who could be enlisted in the drive against Western influence and kindle the revolutionary fervors of thousands of followers. Nasser's anticommunism in local matters could be overlooked for his potential merits in furthering Soviet penetration into the Mediterranean and the Arab world. The Kremlin would undoubtedly have preferred a politically more dependable man, but such are hard to come by in the volatile politics of countries like Cuba and Egypt.

Nasser set out on the obvious and often productive course adopted by a large number of countries since the end of World War II of playing the East against the West. He had a conspicuous strategic position as well as a dramatic role to mark him out among the chieftains of the Third World, who wanted to remain as uncommitted as possible and to derive as much benefit as possible from a position of "positive neutralism." In his balancing act Nasser had considerable success; the United States and Britain seemed ready to finance the three-mile-wide Aswan Dam, the cornerstone of Nasser's plans for Egyptian economic improvement and the only hope for providing sufficient additional arable land for a too rapidly growing population. Nasser would point out later during the height of the Suez crisis that Egypt's wretched economic state actually gave her certain advantages: most Egyptians lived on the verge of starvation, their situation was getting worse every year as their numbers increased, and nothing the Western or any other powers might undertake against them would greatly worsen their situation.

It has not been very difficult to play one side against the other in the postwar constellations of power. Tito's Yugoslavia has been able to do that and so have Iraq and African and Asian countries. But Nasser needed uncommon skills to obtain what he required—armaments from both East and West and the financing of the high dam by either East or West on terms compatible with Egypt's meager resources and fierce resolve against overdependence on any foreign powers. In addition, he was dealing with some bristling, no-nonsense personalities, among them John Foster Dulles.

The American Search for Collective Security and a Balance of Power

President Eisenhower had complete confidence in his Secretary of State and the confidence was justified. The President and his Secretary shared the same views of what American foreign policy must be. Dulles held tenaciously to the tenets of the Truman Doctrine and would have liked to go beyond them. Communism was the principal danger to the security of the United States and the Free World, and therefore communism had to be contained and if possible rolled back. Both Dulles and Eisenhower, however, were also devoted advocates of collective security. They were convinced, as the Roosevelt and Truman administrations had been, that American failure to join the League of Nations after World War I had been a fatal error, that it had made possible the rise of Adolf Hitler, and that the same mistake must not be made again. Consequently, no differences had arisen between the two major parties on the desirability of American support for the United Nations and its principles of collective security. Eisenhower had entitled his book on the military campaign he had led in 1944 *Crusade in Europe*, and he obviously meant just that.

Not only had Hitler been a cruel and wicked dictator who had set out to conquer Europe, but he had also committed willful, criminal aggression, and if peace was henceforth to be maintained against such international lawbreakers it would be through the United Nations, the voice and sword and conscience of mankind.

Eisenhower like Roosevelt also deeply believed in the necessity to cooperate with the Soviet Union and to build a United Nations on the foundation of that cooperation. He wrote at the end of World War II: "Overshadowing all goals for us Americans was the contribution we might locally make toward establishing a working partnership between the United States and Russia. My persistence in this effort and my faith also in the ultimate success of the United Nations were both rooted in my experience as supreme commander."[4]

Almost a decade later, in the face of Nasser's unruly behavior, Eisenhower was as deeply convinced as ever of the rectitude and efficacy of the principles that had established the UN. As the Suez crisis peaked, he wrote: "In the kind of world that we are trying to establish, we frequently find ourselves victims of the tyrannies of the weak. In the effort to promote the rights of all, and observe the equality of sovereignty as between the great and the small, we unavoidably give the little nations opportunities to embarrass us greatly. Faithfulness to the underlying concepts of freedom is frequently costly. Yet there can be no doubt that in the long run faithfulness will produce real rewards."[5]

Eisenhower, however, had slowly become disenchanted with the Soviet Union; his friend, Marshal Zhukov, had had to decline an invitation proffered by President Truman to visit the United States because he had fallen into disfavor with Stalin, a circumstance, Mr. Eisenhower feared, that might have had a connection with Zhukov's friendly relations with him. As Stalin (and later Khrushchev) showed few signs of abating his hostility to the West, and after the Communist attack on Korea, Eisenhower came more and more to place his hope for a better world in the United Nations.

The mission of collective security, of holding down any aggressor, was therefore a chief salient of the American effort to maintain the peace. The other was to keep the Soviet Union in particular and communism in general from gaining any more territory and influence than they had already won in Europe and China. It was Communist China that had tilted the balance in Korea against the American and Korean forces and their allies who had sent troops to fight under the banner of the United Nations. It was Soviet Russia that had blockaded Berlin, divided Germany into two parts, and made a Communist fortress out of Eastern Europe. In the Middle East Eisenhower and Dulles were cautious and skeptical of the Soviet Union, but there as elsewhere genuinely devoted to the lofty principles of the new international morality. So strongly did they feel about the need to meet aggression, where they could, head on, that the President ordered a ship to the Mediterranean loaded with arms that were to be given to either the Israelis or the Arabs depending on which had been attacked.[6]

The United States had therefore two policies that were often difficult to reconcile: one was to stop Russian and other Communist expansion, and the other was to maintain the principle of law against all who rose against the peace whether friend or foe. If the United States kept resolutely to a policy of upholding law and principle in all contingencies, then perhaps at long last even the Soviet Union might be converted to the old glittering dream of a true international order.

In pursuit of both policies, the United States had joined with England and France in 1950 in issuing a Tripartite Declaration with the purpose of deterring aggression and a Soviet-fueled arms race in the Middle East. The three powers promised to take collective action, either within or outside the United Nations, against any attempt to change Arab–Israeli boundaries by force, and to supply the Arab states and Israel with arms to be used only for internal security and legitimate self-defense. So although the American ship had been sent to the Mediterranean with the old-fashioned aim of preserving the regional balance of power, and preventing the dependence of the Arab states on arms shipments from the Soviet bloc, it also had an ideological mission—to help stop the aggressor whoever he was.

But carrying water on both shoulders could wet both of Uncle Sam's pants legs. Soviet Russia was operating under its own rules. In 1955 what was then called the Czechoslovakian arms deal was arranged between Moscow and Egypt, whereby Egypt was supplied with tanks and planes on a scale unprecedented for the Middle East while the United States refused to send counterbalancing arms to Israel on the ground that this would lead to a heightening of tension and an open arms race between East and West. In 1956 new negotiations were in progress between Egypt and the Soviet bloc for still more arms. Although President Eisenhower and Secretary Dulles remained unwilling to send more American armaments to Israel, they expressed no objection to the French delivering what they told the President was a dozen Mirage planes; in fact, Eisenhower said he was pleased that the French had consulted him in the matter.* The President and his Secretary of State were well aware of the grave dangers of competition in the volatile Middle East between East and West, and while the case for helping Israel was well advocated in the United States by an important segment of American opinion both Jewish and non-Jewish, the economic and strategic importance of the Arab states kept American policy on a fairly even keel.

Israel

Israel was the only country involved in the Suez crisis whose very existence was at stake. It had no sooner been founded amidst violent fighting in 1948 when it was attacked by all five Arab states on its borders. Although it had managed to beat off the assault, and after a cease-fire and renewed hostilities had occupied Lydda, Ramleh, Nazareth, and western Galilee, territory it had not been entitled to according to the UN Resolution of 1947 but which it considered essential to its survival, it was still living at the edge of a volcano. Radio Cairo daily promised its extinction and by the end of August 1956 Egypt openly acknowledged responsibility for the repeated commando raids on Israeli territory and vowed her determination to continue them. Nasser said to the Israelis: "Wait and see, soon will be proven to you the strength and will of our nation. Egypt will soon grind you to dust."[7]

By the autumn of 1956 the commando raids became incessant, the guerrillas (fedayeen†) infiltrating mainly from their headquarters at Khan Yunis in the Gaza Strip, but also from Syria and Jordan under the command of Egyptian officers. In the period between 1949 and 1956 it has been estimated that 3,367 armed incursions were made into Israel from Arab territory, attacks in which 443 Israelis were killed and 963 wounded (in April 1956, 64 raids had occurred within five days).[8] Successful raids by the fedayeen were paid for by Egypt with cash bonuses and success could be proven by the display

---

* The actual number of Mirages Israel received was sixty, as Eisenhower, unpleasantly surprised, learned later.

† Fedayeen designates Muslims ready to make any sacrifice for their cause.

of trophies brought back from the raid—a finger, an ear, in some cases larger parts cut from the victim's body.[9]

Israel's response was massive retaliatory raids, a conspicuous display of force for which she was reprimanded by the Security Council in January 1956, which considered them disproportionate to the provocations and told Israel that if they continued the UN would adopt sanctions against her.[10]

The closing of the Straits of Tiran at the mouth of the Gulf of Aqaba was a more serious matter to Israel than the blockade of the Canal, and in addition it seemed to many observors contrary to international law. The Straits open onto the Red Sea from a littoral in the Gulf of Aqaba bordered by four powers, Egypt, Saudi Arabia, Jordan, and Israel, and under conventional maritime law no single state has the right to close such a passageway by unilateral action.* Moreover Egypt not only closed the water route, but threatened to shoot down Israeli planes crossing over the Straits so that El Al had to stop its flights to South Africa. Use of the Suez Canal had been denied by Egypt to Israeli ships since 1951 despite protests on the part of Israel and the Security Council which, however, took no action against Egypt. Since the end of 1953 all goods bound to or from Israel were barred and an Israeli ship, the *Bat-Galim*, that tested the blockade on September 25, 1954, had been seized. Since the approaches and the canal itself were in Egyptian territory, Israel could do nothing about that blockade short of going to war, although the canal, under the provisions of its charter, was always to be kept open in peace and war to the ships of all nations.

Despite these provisions, however, the canal had been closed by the British during both world wars to enemy shipping and to all neutral shipping suspected of supplying the enemy powers. Egypt could and did refer to this precedent when she refused to allow Israeli ships to use the canal, and she claimed that she was also acting legally when she closed the Straits of Tiran to Israel. Egypt said she considered herself at war with Israel despite the various cease-fires and armistices arranged since 1949 and the use of the canal could therefore be denied Israel as it had been Germany and her allies dur-

---

* The channel through which ships must pass to enter the Gulf of Aqaba runs between two islands belonging to Egypt and the Egyptian mainland, although the opposite eastern shore belongs to Saudi Arabia. Nasser claimed the right to control navigation of Israeli ships or ships bound to or from Israel passing through what were clearly Egyptian territorial waters because, he said, Egypt continued to be at war with Israel despite the cease-fires and armistices.

ing two wars; and as for the Straits of Tiran, Egypt said both shores of the passageway were Egyptian territory, which was true, and that she could legally do as she liked about the use of the Straits, which was much more doubtful.

With both the Suez Canal and her southern access to the Red Sea blocked, Israel had lost a trade route to the East, to which she shipped phosphates and potash and from which she received about 90 percent of her oil supply. Eilat, the newly built port in the south, was useless because of the blockade of the Straits, and the only sea route open to Israel was in the opposite direction, west of Haifa through the length of the Mediterranean. Haifa is far more important to Israel than Eilat, but if the closing of the canal seemed a threat to the economies of France and England, for a country in the precarious military position of Israel, the closing of both the canal and the Straits of Tiran seemed a tightening of the noose around her neck.*

The Canal and the High Dam

It is likely that Nasser had had in mind taking over the Suez Canal for some time before he acted in July 1956. The canal, owned by foreign powers, was another symbol of Egypt's subservience to European interests, and to nationalize the Canal Company would not only be a big step toward reestablishing Egypt's self-esteem and equal stature among nations, but would also provide a badly needed additional source of revenue. The company had an income of $100 million a year, much of which was spent by a provident management on capital improvements. The profit ran to some $30 million a year and only such untapped sources of wealth could provide Egypt with the large sums needed to pay her share of the costs of the Aswan Dam if she was to mortgage her cotton crop to pay for arms from the Soviet bloc.

Although the United States had rewarded Nasser with a grant of $40 million for signing the Anglo-Egyptian agreement of 1954 in which England had agreed to evacuate the Canal Zone and Nasser had promised to respect the rights of free navigation on the canal

* Although denial of access to the Suez Canal and the Straits of Tiran could not cut off Israel from essential supplies, which could be shipped by way of the Mediterranean, it seemed to Israel another act of attempted economic strangulation and made her growing trade with the East much more difficult and costly.

provided for in the Convention of 1888, Nasser soon made it clear that he considered this sum only a down payment on his further co-operation. He went off, in fact, in the opposite direction. He attended the violently "anti-imperialist" Bandung Conference dominated by The People's Republic of China in April 1955, with twenty-two other African and Asian nations, recognized Red China in May, and made his arms deal with Moscow in September.*

The occasion for seizing the canal was provided by Dulles' brusk withdrawal from the plans to finance the Aswan Dam. The 1955 arms deal with the Soviet Union and Czechoslovakia had been on a huge scale (estimates ran from $90 to $200 million) and it provided for nearly 200 fighter planes, plus bombers and transport planes, 530 armored vehicles, 230 tanks, 50 artillery pieces, together with destroyers, torpedo boats, and submarines. All these military supplies were to be paid for by bartering Egyptian cotton. Since the United States had been negotiating with Egypt on supplying her with a relatively modest consignment of arms worth $27 million, Egypt's decision to buy or trade in these dimensions was deeply disquieting to Messrs. Eisenhower and Dulles. Then, as negotiations were nevertheless proceeding in June 1956 for the Western financing of the dam, the United States learned that Nasser was in the process of arranging still another large purchase of arms and planned to go to Moscow to complete the deal after the final contract for the dam had been signed with Britain and the United States. If these two countries made their promised grant of $70 million available to him, Nasser would have considerable elbow room and a lot more money for his trading with the Russians and Czechs for the new arms.

His playing off of East and West, however, did not stop there. While the negotiations with the British and the Americans were proceeding, the Russians told Nasser that they too were ready to build the dam. In the Western view the Egyptians could not possibly afford to contribute their share to the building of the dam if they rearmed on the grand scale they were adopting, which was out of all proportion to the arms level in the Middle East, where up to 1955, when Nasser had concluded his first arms deal with the Communists, Israel and Egypt each had some 200 tanks and 50 and 80

* China had become the chief commercial buyer of Egyptian cotton. Economic and cultural missions from that country and from East Germany, Rumania, and Hungary were now prominent in Egypt and her capital goods came mainly from the Eastern bloc. By mid-1956 35 percent of Egypt's commerce was with Communist countries.

planes. The cotton crop was mortgaged, the average income of the
Egyptian peasant was about $60 a year, and Nasser had no way of
providing guns, butter, and a dam that would cost from $1 to $2
billion before it was finished in some fifteen years.[11]

The offers Britain and the United States made were based on
both political and economic grounds; they were ready to devote large
sums of money and engineering skills to the dam if they had a reasonable expectation that a portion of their investment would be
repaid over a period of time and that Nasser would remain relatively
peaceful and in the neutralist camp. The transaction, from their
point of view, had to be economically as well as politically viable.
Soviet Russia, on the other hand, the state founded on Marxist
principles of the primary importance of economics in the affairs of
mankind, makes its calculations far more on political than on economic grounds. Nasser knew that and he also knew that Russia expects and exacts concrete political compensations for such collaboration. It was best from his point of view to get the dam built by
the West and his arms, with Egyptian resources thus released, from
the East. But he was dealing with John Foster Dulles, a man in the
strict American fiscal tradition, implacably principled, with the highest standards of probity and small patience for the wiles of the Le-
vant when conducting large affairs of state and trade. Dulles had not
liked the arms deal Egypt had made with the Soviet bloc in September 1955 and thought a good deal less of the pending negotiations
for even more arms. In the opinion of the Americans and British
the new purchase of arms would preclude any likelihood of Egypt's
meeting its obligations to the International Bank for Reconstruction
and Development, which would be financing the construction of the
dam with a loan of $200 million after initial grants of $56 million
from the United States and $14 million from Britain. West German
firms were also to take part in building the dam with financial aid
from the *Bundesrepublik*. Egypt's contribution was to be $900
million, to be provided in local materials over a period of fifteen years,
a difficult matter with its cotton in pawn for the Soviet arms bought
and in prospect.

Nasser at this point overreached himself. Ahmed Hussein, the
Egyptian ambassador to the United States, told Dulles that he had
in his pocket Russia's promise to build the dam. He now demanded,
before signing a contract with the Western powers, a commitment
from the United States to make available to Egypt hundreds of mil-

lions of dollars over a period of ten years, which in effect meant that it would be the United States that would be paying for the dam. Dulles not only said no to that proposal, he informed Hussein that the United States was withdrawing all offers of aid.[12]

Dulles had acted impulsively but reasonably. He had consulted with neither the British nor close advisors like Robert Murphy before making his decision, and he never did explain to anyone why he had acted so abruptly and without consultation. No one of them, however, could really disagree with the justification for the decision. They knew it was unlikely that Congress would have approved the American grants and investments that were being demanded; it was already dragging its feet with regard to foreign aid and, in the case of Nasser with his close relations to the Communist bloc, such a large one-sided commitment of American resources would have had little if any chance of approval. Dulles probably acted as he did because he was deeply offended by the way Nasser, he felt, had misused him. The United States had refused to sell Israel additional armaments even after the large Egyptian buildup from Soviet sources, and Nasser, far from showing gratitude for this temperateness and for the promised American help with the dam, kept upping his prices. In addition, he was obviously planning to go to Moscow with the bargaining leverage of his contract with the West to get still more arms. Dulles thought that canceling American aid for the dam project would, among its other effects, deflate Nasser's triumphal visit to Moscow.

Five days later, on July 26, 1956, Nasser made a three-hour speech before a huge crowd of wildly cheering Egyptians. He told them that the Western nations were arming Israel against the Arabs, that 120,000 Egyptians had died digging the canal, and that Egypt, promised 44 percent ownership in the canal in 1888, had been cheated of it.* Egypt would now take over what was rightfully hers—the whole Canal Company. The concession for the canal, which was to run for ninety-nine years, would in any event expire in 1968 (the canal had been opened in 1869) if new arrangements were not made. Nasser told his delirious listeners that they were masters in their own house and would take over right now. In the course of his speech he re-

---

* The last two statements were exaggerated. Building the canal had not been dangerous work and few if any Egyptians died as a direct result. As for the Egyptian shares, Disraeli in 1875 had obtained 44 percent of them from the Khedive Ismail as part payment of Egypt's debts to Britain.

peatedly mentioned the name of Ferdinand de Lesseps, sometimes incongruously, and this, as it turned out, was the code word pre-arranged with Egyptian army and police officers to signal them to go into the offices and buildings of the Canal Company to take charge. It was a great day for Egypt. The canal and its revenues would henceforth be theirs, which would solve the troublesome matter of financing both the dam and new weaponry. Nasser promised that the canal would remain open, that ships would go through on schedule, and that the investors in the International Company would be compensated by Egypt for the value of their holdings.[13]

Reactions to Nationalization

The outside world was startled by the news of the nationalization. At 10 Downing Street Eden was dining with the King of Iraq and other Iraqi leaders when he heard the news and he was very angry, far more angry than Dulles had been when he learned of the Egyptian arms deal. In his opinion, and in that of French Prime Minister Guy Mollet, with whom he promptly got in touch, this was an act that simply could not be tolerated. To let Nasser decide if and when England and France would receive the vital shipments that went through the canal (almost 30 percent of the tonnage that passed through was destined for Britain) was out of the question. England in two times of great crisis had determined who could use these trade routes. An international company could not be replaced by the head of any single power, certainly not by a man like Nasser. Guy Mollet and M. Pineau, his Foreign Minister, agreed with Eden. So did Labour and Conservative members of the House of Commons, as well as the British and French press and public and Mr. Dulles, who said a way must be found "to make Nasser disgorge" his booty. The governments of Britain and France were determined to act firmly and Eden immediately called on the British chiefs of staff to make plans for armed intervention. From the start both countries believed they would have to use force against Nasser and they were prepared to do it. The commander of the eventual French expeditionary force, General Beaufre, says he told the British that the French were joining forces with them because the British were engaged in the operation, but if they had not been, the French would have gone ahead alone.[14]

The illegality of the seizure, alleged by Eden, was open to question if the owners were compensated and ships kept moving through the canal. The first act of concession authorized de Lesseps, in November 1854, to form the company; a second act of concession, signed on January 5, 1856, declared that the canal was to be open at all times to merchant ships. These agreements, which had been signed by the Khedive of Egypt, the Viceroy of the Sultan, had been confirmed by a Firman of the Sultan in 1866. The canal's neutrality, however, could be made formally legal only by international agreement. The Convention signed in Constantinople in 1888 by the leading maritime powers of Europe, Britain, France, Germany, Austria-Hungary, Russia, Italy, Spain, and the Netherlands, conferred on it a status of neutrality and stated that it was always to be open to merchant and war ships in times of peace and war.

Eden based his case on the concessions and the Convention, which he was convinced made it illegal to breach the canal's international status and for any single power to assume control. The canal had to remain international and always open. Both Britain and Egypt, as we have seen, however, had violated the Convention, and at the start of World War I, when British forces had occupied the canal, twelve German and seven Austrian ships had been seized. Britain contended then that she was acting under an agreement made with Egypt which granted her the almost unlimited power of prize court jurisdiction and that the Convention of 1888 did not apply to enemy ships using the harbor of Port Said. Ships that failed to leave there, the British insisted, could be taken out by force and captured outside Egyptian territorial waters. The British had maintained the same liberal view of their legal rights in the Second World War when they seized an Italian ship outside the three-mile territorial limit. Citing these acts as precedents, Egypt had captured and kept the Israeli ship, *Bat-Galim*, and imprisoned its crew for three months. Since the canal operated under Egyptian law and, although owned by an international consortium, was an Egyptian company, it seemed to some neutral observers that it could legally be nationalized by Egypt if the standards recognized by international law for the compensation of its owners and the continuous use of the canal were assured.[15]

It had been Britain that had imposed the conditions of peace and war on the canal. She had first opposed its being built, fearing that the resulting French influence in Egypt would have an adverse effect on her long lines of communication with the Far and Middle East, but she had come to value the utility of the canal for precisely these lines of communication. By the terms of the Anglo-Egyptian Treaty of August 26, 1936, any time England considered the canal in danger or, in effect, any time she believed her interests required it, the canal became her domain to defend.* In turn, Britain had recognized that the canal was an integral part of Egypt. When the League of Nations denounced Italy as an aggressor in the war against Ethiopia, the canal had not been closed to Italian ships, nor to Russian ships during the Russo-Japanese War when Japan was an ally of Britain's; but it was the British government that made the decisions, not the Canal Company.

The Canal Company was international but the city of Ismailia at the entrance to the canal was a British enclave with clubs Egyptians could not join and a high standard of living that only a few Egyptian Effendi could aspire to. When Nasser made his speech in 1956 Ismailia was still a British base; the troops were gone but British technicians remained, along with stores of supplies worth some 40 or 50 million pounds sterling. Nasser wanted everything he could lay his hands on, including foreign bank balances, and a few days after he made his speech he confiscated five million Egyptian pounds belonging to the Suez Company, which was being held by the Ottoman Bank in Cairo. In addition, he threatened the arrest of any Suez pilots who refused to work on the now Egyptian canal.

From Nasser's point of view such actions were not only necessary for his fixed purpose of asserting Egypt's sovereignty and stature vis-à-vis the Western powers, for rebuilding the country, and for leading the Arab world against Israel, but they were also legal and moral. Like the heads of many of the developing states, he accepted only such treaties or other international obligations inherited from the past as comported with present Egyptian interests. He was not a Communist, but he wholly accepted the Moscow-Peking doctrine that capitalism was robbery and exploitation and that its predations had to be fought. Why should hundreds of thousands of Egyptians be starving when the Canal Company had a profit of $30 million a year? Why should the British live in luxurious houses and clubs in

---

* The British Foreign Secretary, Sir Austin Chamberlin, when he accepted the Kellogg-Briand Pact, carefully pointed out that: ". . . there are certain regions of the world, the welfare and integrity of which constitute the special and vital interest for our peace and safety. His Majesty's Government has been at pains to make it clear in the past that interference with these regions cannot be suffered. . . ." (Cited Robert H. Ferrell, *Peace in Their Time*, p. 180.)

Egyptian cities when Egyptian peasants and workers were barely able to stay alive and their average life expectancy was thirty-five years?* International, especially British, control of the canal was a survival of the past, a thorny enclave of Western imperialism; it was Nasser's duty to exalt human rights over so-called property rights.[16]

In addition, Nasser said, the West was aiding Israel, an outpost of its imperialism, and that state, as Radio Cairo kept broadcasting, had to be destroyed. No compromise with Israel could be tolerated. Its very founding had been an aggression, it had driven hundreds of thousands of Arabs from their former homes, it had committed hideous atrocities like that of Deir Yassin, where 250 Arab villagers, half of them women and children, had been killed in a raid by the Stern and Irgun bands,† and it had no right whatever to exist. The Israeli victory of 1948 was a humiliation that must be wiped out in blood. So Nasser needed guns and the canal, and 99 percent of the Egyptians agreed with him when he asked for their approval in a plebiscite held after the seizure.

The Soviet Union's principles for the conduct of relations with the Western powers had been borne out in the act of nationalization and in much else that Nasser did with its help in international affairs. The Russians and their allies had played an important role in the founding of Israel, their votes in the United Nations Assembly had been weighty ones in that body's recognition of the new state,‡ and Czech arms had been furnished Israel in 1948, when Britain was supplying only the Arabs and the United States was embargoing arms to both sides. But here as elsewhere the Soviet Union had larger issues in mind than fashioning an Israeli state: it wanted

---

* The canal was a capitalistic enterprise, and its owners were paid dividends on their investments. Between 1876 and 1937 Egypt had been paid nothing because it no longer had any shares; in 1937 she was paid a token sum of 300,000 Egyptian pounds a year and allowed two administrative posts; and in 1949, after an Egyptian threat to apply new coercive laws, she was given seven percent of the profits plus seven administrators. (Benoist-Méchin, *Le Roi Saud.*)

† These were guerrilla fighters who, like the Arab fedayeen and the partisans of other countries, would use any methods that led to success. Their terroristic tactics helped hasten the British out of Palestine and the massacre at Deir Yassin helped embitter Arab-Israeli relations for years to come.

‡ A United Nations special committee recommended that Palestine be partitioned to include a Jewish state on September 1, 1947, and on November 29, 1947, the vote in the UN Assembly had been thirty-three in favor of the plan, thirteen against, with ten abstentions (of which Britain made one). The British High Commissioner left Palestine on May 14, 1948, and the Jews then proclaimed a state which President Truman, on behalf of the United States, recognized *de facto* eleven minutes later and Russia *de jure* on May 17.

to drive Britain out of the Middle East and creating Israel in Palestine was a useful move in that direction. After the state of Israel had been established, however, the British (and French) presence was still evident in Iraq, Syria, Jordan, Iran, and Egypt, so the Russians shifted to an anti-Israeli and pro-Arab policy with enormous rewards in prospect.

For Israel, Nasser's seizure of the canal presented an opportunity she was not slow to seize upon. No one had lifted a finger when her ships were barred from the canal and from the Straits of Tiran and no one had helped deter the Arabs from their incessant guerrilla raids. Britain was cool when not hostile. Seeking to maintain her position in the Arab world, she could not afford to appear too friendly to Israel, and as the crisis sharpened, British policy became so contradictory that General Dayan said only God could create more difficulties. Britain had a number of bilateral and multilateral pacts with Middle Eastern and Eastern states. One was the Baghdad Pact of 1955 with Turkey, Iran, Iraq, and Pakistan, designed, like NATO, as an alliance against Soviet incursions. She also had a mutual defense treaty with Jordan, paid that country a subsidy of $20 million annually, and when at one point in the autumn of 1956 it appeared that Israel might attack Jordan because of the fedayeen raids, Britain warned Israel that if she did the British were bound to come to Jordan's support. This after King Hussein of Jordan had dismissed his British military advisor, Lieutenant General John Bagot Glubb, who had formed a good Jordanian fighting force, the Arab Legion, and at a time when Britain and France were preparing their military expedition against Nasser and France and Israel were concerting plans for Israel's attack on Egypt! It was a monumentally contradictory policy that a more adroit man than Eden might well have avoided.

Eden was determined to make Nasser retreat from the canal. But in view of the complex international situation, with the Soviet Union certain to support Egypt, he needed the backing, or at least the benevolent neutrality, of the United States. When the news of the nationalization reached Washington, Dulles was on a good-will tour of Latin America. Eisenhower, in his absence, sent Robert Murphy, an experienced negotiator, to London "to hold the fort," as Murphy described his assignment, until Dulles got there. The matter was not nearly as desperate from the American point of view as it was from that of its allies. The United States was not a shareholder of the Suez Company, the trip around the Cape was not disastrously longer for cargoes bound for its shores than through the canal, and while Nasser seemed to be an unreliable and unruly character who ought to be put in his place, his acts should not give rise to the use of armed force if it could possibly be avoided. Both Eisenhower and Dulles deplored Nasser's high-handedness, both wanted him to retreat from his position, but force must be an *ultima ratio*, a measure to be applied as Eisenhower would later write, only in *extreme* circumstances or "in self-defense." The American President had written Eden that he did not rule out the use of force, a phrase greatly comforting to the British Prime Minister, but he certainly did not want to use it at an early stage or at any other time if a peaceful settlement could be arranged. Dulles was indignant at Nasser's behavior but he too was hopeful that world opinion and its pressures, including the good offices of the United Nations, would cool his fevers. Above all, it seemed to the Americans, it was necessary to gain time, to prevent any rash act on the part of Israel or England and France.

A lively interchange of telegrams and the visits of Murphy and Dulles were designed to slow down any bellicose measures, but more important in achieving this aim was the fact that neither Britain nor France could mount a military action by land, sea, and air without at least six weeks' preparation. The landing barges were not at hand, nor were planes available in sufficient numbers, nor troops. It had taken many months to prepare the landing in France in World War II, the British pointed out to themselves and to the impatient French, and while Egypt was not much of a military power she did have planes and tanks and troops that had to be taken into account. And to the British government the idea of allying itself with Israel and letting them take on the Egyptians was abhorrent. It would just about end British influence in the Arab world in general and in Egypt in particular. Because of these considerations Britain remained pro-Egyptian if anti-Nasser; after all, the vital canal was in Egypt.

The French generals Ély and Beaufre, who were sent to London to confer with the British on the common strategy, were not encouraged by what they found. The British high command was cool and determined but declared they could not mount a military action before October. The American Admiral Radford would later say that if the British and French had gone into the Canal Zone right away, while tempers were high, they would have been militarily successful, and Eisenhower and Dulles along with other Western leaders would have accepted the spontaneous action; it was the delay that was most damaging to their cause. The French indeed chafed at the long drawn out negotiations and preparations, but they themselves were not in a position to invade at this point. Most of their troops and war material were in Algeria and their concentration in that theater did not leave much left over for a large-scale military expedition against Egypt, which both France and Britain estimated had some one hundred Migs available together with 30 Ilyushin bombers and 100 medium tanks.[17] But France, many of her civilian and military leaders thought, could not permit another affront to her prestige. She had known nothing but defeat, one French general would later write, since World War II; Syria, Lebanon, Indochina, Tunisia, and Morocco were all gone, and now to let Nasser have a triumph at her expense while he was openly aiding the Algerian revolt would be a disaster.

One way the French thought the situation could be quickly saved was through the Israelis. Guy Mollet, who had just become Premier, was a Socialist and friendly to the Israeli state, the French general staff had a high opinion of the Israeli army, and the French foreign office was also pro-Israel. Both France and Israel were bound together by a common need, as they saw it, to stem the Arab attack against the borders of Israel and the French position in Algeria. Consequently a *de facto* military alliance was made between the two countries on August 7. A French military mission of Generals Challe and Martin and Colonel Simon traveled to Israel and came back with a glowing report on the Israeli army. Israeli officers journeyed to France in civilian clothes and returned piloting new Mystères.[18] Tanks were bought in France and unloaded at night on Israel's beaches in the Mediterranean by LSTs, and the dozen Mirages that Eisenhower had been told about multiplied in a remarkable fashion. The Israelis would be ready to fight much sooner than Britain, it became clear to the French military staffs, and one possibility, if the British gave up the action at the demand of the United States, or took too long about it, was to proceed against Egypt with Israel and without the British.

Though the Israeli officers who went to France traveled in civilian clothes, a man like Dayan with the patch over one eye is easily recognizable out of uniform, and sizable movements of military equipment are hard to conceal. Therefore there could have been little doubt in the American government, as well as in the Arab and the Communist camp, that large preparations were going on on the Israeli border. However, the attack was expected to be against Jordan rather than Egypt. Israel made it elaborately plain, as one of the many *ruses de guerre* she would be employing in the course of the next years, that it was against Jordan she was arming, for Jordan was the source of many of the fedayeen raids, and reinforcements of Iraqi troops had been sent there to bolster the forces of Hussein. The Israeli buildup was, as we have seen, looked on with obvious distaste by Britain, which was at great pains to demonstrate to the Arabs that she was not collaborating with Israel and specifically warned Israel against the dire consequences of attacking Jordan. Britain pointed out that during one of the Israeli retaliatory raids against Jordan, British planes had been very nearly ordered into the air against the Israeli troops and that they would be called upon for action if Israel invaded Jordan in force.

The Conferences

Eisenhower and Dulles took the same dim view of the Israeli preparations as did the British. Their efforts to work out a peaceful settlement of the Suez dispute were directed through conferences, the first one an international meeting in London of twenty-four nations. This, Dulles thought, would help to mobilize world opinion and lead to a resolution of the crisis under international auspices.* The United Nations, of course, figured importantly in his and Eisenhower's thinking, but Eden and Mollet were doubtful of appealing to the good offices of that long-winded body where Russia's veto in the Security Council and the voices of Asian and African nations in the Assembly did not seem likely to lead to any solution of the kind they thought essential.

Egypt and Greece refused to join the deliberations of the London Conference† and Israel was not invited. Twenty-two nations representing the chief maritime powers using the canal attended: India, Pakistan, Ceylon, Spain, Italy, Holland, Ethiopia, West Germany, Japan, Norway, Iran, Indonesia, Sweden, Portugal, the Soviet Union,

---

* World opinion is called upon or mobilized whenever a statesman, convinced of the moral unassailability of his position, is unable or unwilling to take the practical steps necessary to secure his aims. It is successfully mobilized only when its adverse propaganda value is considered by the accused as outweighing the advantages of continuing the disreputable practices.

† Egypt sent an observer; Greece refused to attend because of the alleged anti-Greek attitude of Britain on Cyprus.

Canada, and the United States, along with Britain and France and the nations of the British Commonwealth—countries that Egypt might be expected to regard with mixed feelings of friendship, indifference, and revulsion. The conference that opened on August 16 voted 18 to 4 to adopt a proposal made by Mr. Dulles stating that an adequate solution of the Suez Canal problem must respect the sovereignty of Egypt and its right to fair compensation for the use of the canal, but asserting the principle of international control. Any disputes were to be arbitrated and sanctions were to be applied if the agreement was violated, with some form of association of the conference with the United Nations. The resolution voted for by the eighteen countries declared that the canal must be insulated from the politics of any one nation and proposed that a new convention be negotiated. Soviet Russia, along with Ceylon, India, and Indonesia, refused to sign the document but a committee of five under the chairmanship of the Prime Minister of Australia, Robert Menzies, was appointed to go to Cairo to negotiate directly with Nasser. The Russian delegate to the conference said the proposal was no more than a maneuver of colonialism to "reimpose Western rule upon Egypt."[19]

Obviously, neither Egypt nor the Soviet Union had any intention of accepting even as a basis for discussion any plan that would return the canal to international control, and Nasser, although he met with Menzies and the members of the commission for some hours, would not budge. Later, Menzies would write that Nasser's intransigence was the result not only of Soviet support but also of an ill-timed announcement of President Eisenhower, who had declared at a news conference that there must be no use of force "and that if the proposals of the London Conference were rejected, others must be considered."[20] In any event, Nasser did reject the proposals of the eighteen members of the London Conference, and Eden and Mollet said they had never expected him to accept them. Their preparations for the invasion continued.

Dulles then came up with another idea for an international conference, this one to be called the Suez Canal Users Association. It was to be a projection of the London Conference, an international body that could run the canal and negotiate with Nasser, thus providing a buffer to any direct confrontation between Egypt and the French and British. These latter two countries were deeply skeptical of the usefulness of the proposed organization, but Eden's pursuit of the goodwill of Eisenhower and Dulles was not to be checked by refusing to join another international body with such transparently good intentions and purposes. The Soviet Union, however, called the Suez Canal Users Association "imperialistic" and refused to attend its meetings.

Dag Hammarskjöld, Secretary-General of the United Nations, also took a hand, negotiating behind the scenes with the countries involved including Egypt. He proposed a program of Six Principles,* which had the approval of Eisenhower and Dulles and was accepted by Eden and Mollet. At Eden's suggestion they were called not "Principles" but "Requirements" and they declared: the canal must provide free and open transit; the sovereignty of Egypt must be respected; the canal must be insulated from the politics of any country; tolls and charges should be fixed by agreement between Egypt and the users; a fair proportion of the dues should be used for development; and any disputes between Egypt and the Suez Canal Company should be settled by arbitration. The Security Council voted to accept the Six Requirements, which were in line with the earlier proposals of the eighteen powers, but the operational portion of the formula, which provided that the canal must remain open to the free passage of all ships (which would have included Israeli ships) and invited the Egyptian government to put forward its proposals for meeting the terms of the Six Principles, was vetoed by the Soviet Union and Yugoslavia.[21]

Dulles informed Eisenhower that the prospects were that direct negotiations would proceed between Britain, France, and Egypt under the auspices of Hammarskjöld. The Americans were still convinced that the course they were urging had a good chance of keeping the peace, despite Nasser's refusal to negotiate, the unmistakable sound of sabre-rattling on the part of France and England, and the objectionable and inexplicable resistance to American proposals on the part of the Soviet Union which, as Eisenhower said, had again shown that it was not interested in "a just resolution of any kind of the issues and problems facing mankind."[22] Britain and France, he thought, were still showing lamentable persistence in conducting themselves as if they were in a situation of crisis, recalling their nationals from Egypt and other countries of the Middle East and mov-

---

* These Six Requirements had first been advanced by Selwyn Lloyd, the British Foreign Secretary, on October 5 at a meeting of the Security Council. (Anthony Nutting, *No End of a Lesson.*)

ing more tanks, ships, and planes to Cyprus and Malta, bases from where Egypt could be attacked. Nevertheless, Eisenhower felt that American diplomacy was succeeding. He declared in a television interview in late October that progress toward a peaceful solution was "most gratifying . . . a very great crisis is behind us."[23]

Dead Ends

Eden and Mollet believed they had no more options. Despite their misgivings, they had tried everything that Dulles had proposed and as a result Nasser had conceded nothing, he had denounced the Menzies mission as "colonialism," and had accused the eighteen powers of "thuggery and imperialism," while the Suez Canal Users Association he had called "an association for waging war."[24]

Nasser had had no thought of compromise or negotiation, nor much incentive for either. On August 24 Khrushchev had said that in a conflict the Arabs would not stand alone; early in October Marshal Bulganin informed Anthony Eden in a letter that Russia stood at Nasser's side; and Eisenhower and Dulles assured Nasser they opposed the use of force as much as did the Soviet Union. Nasser's only concession was an indication that he might attend a conference of users of the canal if it included nations like Afghanistan, Albania, and Red China (whose favorable sentiments were assured no matter what his demands).

Limited sanctions had been tried. Britain had ceased all aid to Egypt and had frozen her sterling balances. It had been intended that the Users Association would pay its dues not to Egypt but directly into its own coffers, but this device, Eden thought, was sabotaged by Dulles when the American Secretary of State explained that the Users Association was supposed to collaborate with Egypt and expressed his belief that a considerable proportion of the dues collected should go to Cairo.

Not only were Eden's troubles mounting on the international scene, but he was having increasing domestic difficulties as well. The first reactions in Britain in support of his stand against Nasser had been spontaneous and bipartisan. The only paper that did not support a firm policy was the *Manchester Guardian*. The opposition Labour leader in the House of Commons, Hugh Gaitskell, made as belligerent a speech as any of Eden's. Aneurin Bevan, another leader of the Labour party, said: "If the sending of one's police and soldiers into the darkness of the night to seize somebody else's property is nationalization Ali Baba used the wrong terminology."[25] The entire House of Commons cheered when Eden announced on July 30 that Britain was stopping all aid to Egypt. But with the delay in taking action and the fruitless conferences, political opposition had formed within both the Conservative party and the opposition Labour party. Labour was traditionally pro-Israeli and some fifteen of its members were Jews but, like Mr. Dulles, they were anticolonial, favored cooperation with the United Nations, and opposed the use of force as a matter of principle. As Eden tried to explain in the House of Commons just what his policy was and where and how the Americans were backing him, the voices of those who wanted other and milder courses grew louder. Gaitskell turned from an ally into an opponent, and when it seemed that Eden was going ahead with his invasion plans, Sir Walter Monckton, the Minister of Defense, resigned his post although he stayed on in Eden's Cabinet as Paymaster-General.

The public reaction at first was as in the days when Britain ruled the seas and an empire. The Suez Canal was vital to Britain, every Englishman knew that, and Nasser, a small-time Hitler or petty Middle East despot, should be put in his place, which was not astride the canal. But then as passions cooled and American support weakened, more typical postwar attitudes arising out of weariness and self-doubt and a sense of diminishment in comparison with the superpowers reasserted themselves—the spirit of manfully facing up to Britain's now secondary position, of voluntary withdrawal from the old imperial outposts when the burdens of staying there proved too heavy or risky or simply not worth it. On dune and headland the fire was sinking and Dulles told Eden that British public opinion did not support his course.*

The Soviet Union was threatening Eden, and the United States, which he had desperately tried to persuade to take at least a position of benevolent neutrality, refused to tell the Security Council, as Britain and France wanted it to, that America would make common cause with them if Egypt refused to negotiate on the basis of the Six Principles. It seemed to Eden that the American position had changed from a willingness to see force used, if all else failed, to what

---

* Polls never showed the British public in favor of military action. In Early November 37 percent thought it right, 44 percent thought it wrong, and 19 percent were undecided. (Leon D. Epstein, *British Policies in the Suez Crisis*.)

was, in effect, a demand that he do nothing and do it slowly. Meanwhile Britain's position, Eden felt, was deteriorating in Egypt as in the rest of the Arab world. One Dulles proposal was that more oil be shipped from other sources, which would have penalized Britain's allies among the Arab countries who had already pointed out that Nasser had obtained more from Britain in the promised help for the Aswan Dam than they, her true and loyal supporters, were able to command with their policy of friendship and collaboration. Furthermore, oil in the northern and southern hemispheres could only be had for dollars, which England did not have. On September 13, after Eden told the House of Commons that the British government might be forced to take other steps, Dulles, to reassure Nasser, declared with regard to the tactics of the Users Association that "we do not intend to shoot our way through."[26] Two days earlier Eisenhower, when asked whether he would join England and France to prevent the canal's being closed, had said: "I am not going to be a party to aggression." What kind of leverage had Eden and the French left to restore their position with respect to the canal?

Bulganin wrote a second letter to Eden at the end of September telling him the Soviet Union disapproved of all the steps that Britain and the maritime powers proposed or had taken in the crisis; Dulles again explained that the United States did not identify with the colonial powers and, cruelest blow of all to Eden, said further that while there was talk of teeth in the Users Association, there were no teeth.[27]

With Time Running Out

Meanwhile the canal was running and running well under Egyptian control. Sixty Western pilots had resigned but others from West Germany and other Western countries had remained for the high wages, and the replacements included fifteen pilots from the Soviet Union and four from Yugoslavia. No serious delays had occurred; in fact, more ships than normal had passed through the canal after the first brief stoppages. Eden had been certain that the Egyptians could not run the canal, so another possible source for mobilizing public opinion was lost to him, as well as a legal justification for intervention.

It was Israel that came to Eden's rescue. With French help she was now prepared to end the fedayeen raids from the Gaza Strip

and to free the Straits of Tiran. On October 10 the French and Israelis agreed to make war against Egypt.* The plans that General
Dayan had brought to Paris evoked great admiration from the French
general staff. They were simple, bold—"prudent and audacious"
General Ély called them—and the French general staff was highly
enthusiastic. But the French did not immediately tell the British of
their approval. Only on October 25 did the British, according to
Eden, learn that Israel was mobilizing and, Eden feared, was on the
point of invading Jordan. If she did, Eden sternly told Israeli Prime
Minister Ben-Gurion, Britain would have to invoke the treaty of
assistance and come to Jordan's aid. But Israel was getting ready to
attack Egypt, not Jordan, and in this lay an opportunity for a fruit-
ful common policy for Britain and France. They could get rid of
Nasser, and act on behalf of the general peace. When Israel attacked,
they would demand a cease-fire and occupy the canal to separate
the belligerents and get back their property. French warships and
planes would provide support against air and sea attacks on the Israeli coast and aid the Israeli strike into Sinai. Israeli liaison officers
were provided to operate with the French but not with the British
forces. British policy was so obscure that Mollet had to ask what
Britain's attitude would be if Israel attacked Egypt, and only when
Eden replied that Britain could scarcely fight on the side of Nasser
was the British-French ultimatum drawn up. So elaborate was Britain's design to distance itself from any sign of collusion with Israel
that a British general said that if an Israeli officer showed up on
Cyprus he would shoot him. And actually at one point, after hostilities had started, when a British pilot had to land with his plane on
fire, British planes fired at the space around where he had landed to
prevent Israeli troops from attempting to rescue him. British policy
had the shape of a pretzel, but according to Anthony Nutting, Britain's Minister of State, Eden did know of the French-Israeli plans
as early as October 14 when M. Albert Gazier, Acting Foreign Secretary of France and General Maurice Challe, Deputy Chief of Staff
of the French air force, went to Chequers and told the Prime Minister of the intended Israeli attack and the plan for an Anglo-French
intervention, both of which Eden approved a few days later. Whatever the date when Eden learned of and approved the plans for the

---

* Conversations regarding possible military collaboration between France and Israel
had been going on intermittently since 1954 and a military accord had been drawn up
on August 7.

attack, whether in mid or late October, Britain persisted in her studied coolness toward Israel, which she took pains to demonstrate to the Israelis and, above all, to the Arabs, despite the combined operations being planned for the British-French-Israeli forces.

Not much went according to plan for the British-French military preparations. The landings in Alexandria, Ismailia, and Port Said had been given the code name "Hamilcar," which is spelled with an initial H in English and with an A in French. Accordingly the French vehicles were marked for action with a large "A" painted on them while the British had an "H." After this mix-up was discovered, the code name for the operation became "Musketeer," which has the same initial in English and French and is reasonably comprehensible in both languages. Ships taken out of mothballs were in poor shape with buckled plates and rotted wooden parts. Like the invasion plans, the ships were altered and realtered as their uses became more clearly defined. British tanks, which were to be shipped to central points in the Mediterranean, could not move along English roads because of the damage their treads cause, so they and other heavy war equipment were freighted by commercial trucks operating under union standards of an eight-hour day. Therefore it took almost twice as long as it would have if they had traveled under their own power to get to their debarkation points. The airlift to Cyprus was mainly accomplished with chartered planes. Seaborne war supplies have to be loaded so that those that will be used first when the ship lands are put aboard last, but some of the British officers in charge of logistics managed to do this in reverse order, so the unloading became a considerable tangle. Tanks and other supplies continued to arrive long after the fighting was over, still loaded in the wrong order. French troops too had their troubles. The 2,500 troops of the Foreign Legion sent to Cyprus had run out of food on the voyage from France and the famished men had to be fed by local restaurants and from British stores when they landed. The British were also unprepared for linguistic problems posed by the Foreign Legion contingents, who spoke mainly German, not French. (After World War II a number of Germans had joined the Legion in order to subsist, and others from the French zone of Germany had been forced by the French to join up on threats of a harsher fate if they refused.)

Worse still, the plans for the attack changed with costly and temper-frazzling delays. The British, because they held the island of Cyprus from which the parachute attack would be made and Malta where the seaborne operation was being assembled, and also because they knew the canal terrain well, were to be in charge of Musketeer. General Sir Charles Keightley, chief of the British Middle East land forces, was in command, with French Admiral Barjot as deputy commander. One early plan was to capture Alexandria and Ismailia, and after bombardment by French naval units, for the French to take Port Said with assaults by parachute troops (there is no port at Port Said). The plans were shifted because it seemed that undue difficulties would arise in landing, providing artillery support, and maintaining the flow of supplies. But when the final plan was eventually settled on, it worked like a landing exercise, in part because the preparations had been carefully made, but mainly because the Israelis had already defeated the bulk of the Egyptian army and sent it streaming back across the desert. Nor was very much left of the Egyptian air force.

Kadesh

The Israeli code name for their attack was "Kadesh"; it began on October 30. With deadly precision Israeli troops, provided with excellent intelligence that pinpointed Egyptian gun emplacements and troop concentrations, overran their objectives. They moved in to the west along the Gaza Strip and the Mediterranean and toward Ismailia and Suez, and south toward Sharm el Sheikh on the Straits of Tiran, the paratroops flying in low to escape detection by the Egyptian radar, the air force, when it was released for combat, shooting down the Egyptian Migs in the air or destroying them on the ground.* Some of the fighting was bitter, at Abu Agheila, for example, where Egyptian units held well-fortified positions that had been designed by German technicians. But they were no match for the Israeli soldiers. Sometimes they fled without firing a shot, sometimes after making a token defense, and the Israeli troops did not bother to round them up to take them prisoner. The Gaza Strip was quickly occupied. The Egyptians fled in columns and in small groups across the desert, and many of them lost their lives not to guns but to thirst and roving bands of bedouin who killed them and then stripped them of everything of value. Although they did not want them, the Israeli troops had to take thousands of Egyp-

---

* The Israeli air force was forbidden to fire the first shot against Egyptian planes to avoid being stigmatized as aggressors. Only after the ground fighting had been in progress for some hours were they given orders to attack Egyptian planes and support their own troops.

tian prisoners. They could not do much for such numbers—they were short of water and supplies themselves and had to move very fast before a cease-fire blocked them from reaching their objectives. The Israelis did make excellent use of the enormous quantities of supplies they captured at the Mediterranean ports of Rafah and El Arish. The Russians had been lavish in stocking the Egyptian army and the Israeli troops found curious things for use in desert warfare among the booty—including clothing designed to be worn in the far north. Apparently, someone in the Russian supply service had pressed the wrong button and the cold weather gear was sent to the desert and stored by the Egyptians along with other, more essential, equipment.

The Israelis were operating on a shoestring. General Dayan reports they did not even have enough wrenches to enable them to deal with the front-wheel drives of their jeeps, so that if a vehicle blew a front tire, it had to stay where it was. Troops traveled on trucks loaded with barbed wire because they had no other means of transportation; they used civilian vehicles and mounted bazookas on jeeps because they did not have enough tanks. They improvised, they patched together, and they moved forward. Mistakes were made and Dayan shifted commanders around, but the troops got to where they were supposed to and on schedule.

The Egyptians were unpredictable. They would fight well at some points and hold their ground with tenacity, but often they would leave their tanks and field guns without firing a shot. Their leadership was atrocious. Officers were often the first to leave a position and on one occasion they took a train and the only road to get themselves back to safety while their men trudged through the desert. Unfortunately for them, Israeli planes bombed the train and the road while they paid no attention to the columns plodding across the sands. The Egyptian high command on land and sea had little contact with the realities of the war.

An Egyptian destroyer, the *Ibrahim el-Awal*, that had belonged to England, set out to bomb Haifa and did lob some shells into the city before it put out to sea again. Its captain radioed Nasser that he had inflicted great damage on the city and that large sections were burning when he sailed away. Then Israeli ships and planes caught up with him, and after a ten-minute battle he surrendered, his ship was boarded by an Israeli crew and towed back to an unscathed Haifa. His resistance had been minimal, but he had sent messages to Cairo about the odds against him and the damage he had done the city, and Nasser had told him in one of the last messages the captain received before he surrendered his ship that his exploits would be written in letters of gold in Egyptian history.*[28]

It was to be called the Seven Days War but the Israelis had won almost all their main objectives by the fifth day. They had had to move with lightning speed. On October 30, according to plan, the British and French demanded an immediate cease-fire and the withdrawal of both the Israeli and Egyptian forces ten miles from both banks of the canal while British and French troops separated them and temporarily held Ismailia, Port Said, and Suez and guaranteed free passage of shipping through the canal. It was a plan conceived by the French General Beaufre, who was to lead the attack on Port Said, and it was gratefully adopted by Eden and Mollet, who saw it as a way to get rid of Nasser while the French and British assumed the role of the advance guard of the United Nations in keeping the peace—a solution that Eden thought particularly desirable since the League of Nations, he said, had suffered from the lack of an international force to back its decisions and the United Nations badly needed one. Now he was ready to supply it. Accordingly the ultimatum was sent to both Israel and Egypt giving them twelve hours to comply with its terms, in default of which Britain and France "would intervene with whatever strength may be necessary to secure compliance." Israeli forces had reached a point halfway between their border and Ismailia, and if they were to reach the canal, they would have to advance an additional eighty miles. Egyptian forces, on the other hand, were already stationed along the canal and if Nasser accepted the ultimatum it would be they who retreated. The Israelis, following the prearranged plan, accepted the British-French ultimatum; the Egyptians rejected it. The way was now clear for the long-planned Anglo-French attack which was to be concentrated on Port Said.

Advance and Retreat

But Eden's time of bad troubles was only beginning. On October 30, the same day the French and British sent their ultimatum, the Security Council met in an all-day session to consider a resolution offered by the United States demanding a cease-fire and Israeli with-

* The Egyptian crew had made no attempt to put out fires started in the vessel by direct hits, they had done nothing for their eighteen wounded, and they could not carry out an attempt to sink their ship because the water cocks were too rusty to turn. (Robert Henriques, *A Hundred Hours to Suez*.)

drawal from Egyptian territory and—this was directed against the British and French—calling on all members of the United Nations to abstain from the use or threat of force. Eisenhower and Dulles were furious with Israel. They suspected her attack had been timed with the American presidential election on November 6 in mind, in the belief that Eisenhower could not take a strong stand at such a political juncture. But the President was a man of firm resolve. He calls his book that recounts these events *Waging Peace,* and this he and Dulles were doing, with heavy hearts and valiant purposes, in a series of diplomatic moves that allied them not with their NATO partners but with Soviet Russia.

Britain and France vetoed the American resolution. Up to this point the veto in the Security Council had been a Russian specialty, and now Yugoslavia, her ally, moved to detour its effects when used by other powers. The Yugoslavian representative on the Security Council presented a resolution declaring that if seven of the eleven votes in the Council were obtained in favor, the Suez crisis would be debated by the entire Assembly.* The United States cast the seventh and deciding vote for the proposal, with Britain and France opposed and Austria and Belgium abstaining. There was talk in the Assembly of taking collective measures against the British and French. With the American representative to the UN, Henry Cabot Lodge, taking the lead, a resolution calling on all parties to join in a cease-fire and to send no military goods to Egypt or Israel was carried 64 to 5. Vice President Nixon, who like Eisenhower and Dulles was thoroughly convinced of the rectitude of the American position, said: "For the first time in history we have shown independence of Anglo-French policies which seemed to us to reflect the colonial tradition. This declaration of independence has had an electrifying effect throughout the world."[29] Britain and France nevertheless went resolutely ahead with their plans, though there still were maddening delays.

The Israelis had moved so fast that their representative in the UN promptly accepted the demand of the Assembly for a cease-fire provided Egypt also accepted. Israeli troops had reached their objectives in making the preemptive attack; they now occupied the Gaza

---

* Yugoslavia made use of the Uniting for Peace Resolution, adopted on November 2, 1950, under which deadlocked cases might be transferred to the UN Assembly from the Security Council by vote of seven members of the Council. (Cf. Stephen D. Kertesz, *The Quest for Peace through Diplomacy.*)

Strip and the Sinai Peninsula and had almost arrived at Sharm el Sheikh to open up the Straits of Tiran. By the time the Israeli and Egyptian governments approved the cease-fire, they would doubtless have captured that point too. But if the British and French accepted the cease-fire, they would be left without the cause cited for their invasion. Now it was the British who, by way of French intermediaries, had to plead with the Israelis not to accept the cease-fire. The paradoxes were remarkable. Britain, which had lately been warning Israel against the use of force against Jordan and threatening her with armed retaliation if she did, was now urging Israel to keep on with the fighting until England could join in.

Ben-Gurion reluctantly agreed. The Israeli representative to the UN explained to Dag Hammarskjöld that he had meant there already was a *de facto* cease-fire and that Israel's formal acceptance was conditional on Egypt's answering these questions: Did she agree to a cease-fire? Does she still maintain that she is at war with Israel? Is she prepared to negotiate to establish peace? Will she lift the blockade of Israeli shipping on the canal? Will she recall the fedayeen bands? This stall enabled Britain and France to join the war.

Anthony Eden, explaining the attack, told the House of Commons: "I have been a League of Nations man and a United Nations man. And I am still the same man with the same devotion to peace. . . . I believe with all my heart and my head that this is a time for action effective and swift."[30] In the British view, then, the invasion was a police action on behalf of international order. The bombardments and landings on Port Said began on November 5. With the majestic pace that had characterized Musketeer from the start, the invasion plan called for the occupation of Ismailia on the 8th and of Suez by the 12th. But this was to be a one-day war—it was all over by the 6th of November. Port Said was captured in a well-conducted military operation, but that was as far as the British and French could go for they had no political cover.

The skies fell on Eden.* The House of Commons was in an uproar. Even a sizable section of the Conservative party was revolting

---

* Eden was physically ill. He had a duodenal ulcer, which two bile-duct operations had not been successful in correcting, and would soon have a third one. He was in considerable pain and had a high fever. Ben-Gurion was down with influenza as the Israeli army was ready to strike and had a fever of 103° F. Dulles, too, was seriously ill. On November 3 he had to be operated on for the cancer that was to kill him two and a half years later.

against his leadership. He had lost support everywhere, abroad and in Britain. Marshal Bulganin proposed on November 5 joint action by the United States and Russia against the Anglo-French forces and threatened in notes to England, France, and Israel that the Soviet Union was prepared to use force to crush the aggressors and might even resort to the bomb. Eisenhower told the French President René Coty that France had "espoused the cause of evil."[31] Hugh Gaitskell called Eden's actions "disastrous folly." A run on the pound had been gaining momentum and threatened to dislocate the entire British economy—15 percent of her gold and dollar balances had been lost since September.

Eden and Mollet could only agree to withdraw from Port Said and to let their troops be replaced by United Nations contingents, but not before they added a final touch of irony to the proceedings. They had inserted in the Assembly resolution of November 4 this statement: "The two governments continue to believe that it is necessary to interpose an international force to prevent the continuance of hostilities between Egypt and Israel, *to secure the speedy withdrawal of Israeli forces* [italics supplied], to take the necessary measures to remove obstructions to traffic through the Suez Canal, and to promote a settlement of the problems in the area."[32] This a day or two after they had persuaded Israel to continue the fighting.

Israel was slower to retreat, but Ben-Gurion, too, who had gained, with UN contingents replacing the Egyptian forces, a ten-year respite against the fedayeen raids as well as Israeli access to the Straits of Tiran, ordered the Israeli troops to pull out of the conquered territory.

While this successful performance of an international morality play was taking place, the Hungarian revolt was being put down by Russian tanks. Soviet troops had moved into Hungary in force on November 1. Two Russian divisions had encircled Budapest, with five more in reserve, and on November 4 they attacked the city. Some 50,000 Hungarians died in Budapest alone (Anthony Eden calculated about 200,000) and 150,000 fled the country into exile during the few days the Iron Curtain was open.

The United Nations, which had been so deeply shaken by the use of force by Israel, France, and Britain, was much slower to act in this crisis. The American ambassador to the UN seemed to regard the concern of the British and French with Hungary as no more than a diversionary device to take the minds of the members of the

United Nations off their own misdeeds. The Security Council met and adjourned, and when on November 3 it called for a cease-fire in Hungary and for the withdrawal of the invading Russian forces, the Soviet member of the Council vetoed the resolution—the 79th veto for the Russians. The Assembly took up this crisis, too, and by a vote of 50 to 8 with 15 abstentions called for a cease-fire, for the withdrawal of the Russian troops, and for UN officials to enter Hungary as observers. But the Assembly's resolutions have no more force than a superpower may wish to grant them and the Soviet Union would permit no observers to come into the country, not even Dag Hammarskjöld. The Hungarian Prime Minister, Imre Nagy, was granted asylum by the Yugoslav government when he and his entourage took refuge in the Yugoslav embassy in Budapest on the last day of the revolution. Three weeks later the Hungarian and Yugoslav governments granted them safe conduct, but when they left the embassy they were immediately arrested by Soviet soldiers and their execution was announced nineteen months later.*

The British and French troops departed from Port Said and were replaced by United Nations contingents. Nasser had won a great victory. Britain and France were reduced to impotence in their claims against him. The Suez Canal was his without international control, or any Users Association. Dulles and Eisenhower had their victory of a kind too. They had demonstrated their adherence to high principles and their firm belief in the United Nations; they had treated their friends no differently from their foes; they had smitten the aggressor and shown all the world that the United States remained on the side of law.

Israel was a partial victor. She had refused the demand of the Secretary-General of the UN to withdraw her forces unconditionally from Sinai; she first obtained guarantees for the freedom of her shipping through the Gulf of Aqaba and for protection against the fedayeen raids. UN forces occupied Sharm el Sheikh and the Gaza Strip in the place of Egyptian troops and guerrilla bands.

Britain and France had been humiliated. Their position not only in the Middle East but in their own estimation as well was greatly diminished, and many Britons and Frenchmen were bitter although

---

* Kádár, as President of The Hungarian Council of Ministers, wrote to the Yugoslav government that no sanctions would be taken against Nagy or his group and they could proceed freely to their homes. (Kertesz, *East Central Europe and the World*, p. 132.)

others approved of the American, the United Nations, and even the Soviet course. When the French ambassador to the United Nations learned of the attack on Port Said he had been so shocked he had wanted to quit his post.[33] But the defeat would long rankle and in the case of France played some role in the country's subsequent decision to manufacture nuclear weapons and to leave the ranks of NATO. Dulles' policy of containment, not to mention rollback, had been sacrificed to his and Eisenhower's stubborn belief in the peacekeeping role of the United Nations and in the iniquity of aggression. But only in Suez, not in Hungary.*

It was Soviet Russia and Egypt that made the major gains. Russia was now firmly ensconced as the protecting power of the Arabs against Western imperialism, builder of the Aswan dam, and upholder of the sword of Islam. NATO was badly shaken. It seemed to many European observers in a continent used to making cynical judgments that America dealt with the Soviet Union in Hungary by one standard and used another with the French and British in Suez.† The operational portions of the preachments of Eisenhower and Dulles about the rights of small nations and the wickedness of the use of force applied only to the Suez Canal. Since they did not, could not, encompass Poland and Hungary, what kind of principles were they except principles of bumbling naïveté or hypocrisy?

And as for the UN, it had not made the slightest protest against Nasser's confiscation of international property, and while it had made similar demands on the Soviet Union as on Britain, France, and Israel, nothing whatever was done in response to its resolution on Hungary. Any enforcement of its decrees could only occur in the rare case when the Soviet Union and the United States were on the same side, as in the Egyptian crisis, or when Russia was absent from the Security Council, as in the Korean War.

---

* The mortality tables on the two military actions were heavily weighted on the Russian side. Egypt, according to a British report, lost 650 men killed, 1200 lightly wounded, and 900 hospitalized. In addition, there were 2700 civilian casualties. In the engagement against Israel 1000 Egyptian soldiers were killed in action, 1000 more died in flight, and 6000 were taken prisoner; while 172 Israelis were killed, and 817 wounded. The Hungarian dead were perhaps twenty times the numbers of Egyptians killed. (Eden, Memoirs; Connell, The Most Important Country; Paul Camille, Suez.)

† Mr. Dulles cabled Ambassador Bohlen in Moscow instructing him to tell Khrushchev and Zhukov: "The United States has no ulterior purpose in desiring the independence of the satellite countries. . . . We do not look upon these nations as potential military allies. We see them as friends. . . . We are confident that their independence if promptly accorded, will contribute immensely to stabilize peace throughout Europe, West and East." (Eisenhower, Waging Peace, p. 71.)

The international tides, however, ran deeper than the suspicions or passions of the critics. Had the United States supported the British and French, what then? Even with Nasser deposed and assuming that the Soviet threat to use the bomb was a bluff, how long could England and France have held the canal and maintained their supplies of oil against sabotage, and could they have reimposed on Egypt a government friendly to them? One Arab diplomat told a French historian before the Port Said attack that it could not possibly succeed—either Nasser would flee to another Arab country and conduct guerrilla war from there, like the one he had been waging against Israel, or if he were killed, someone else would take his place and the fight in any event would continue.[34] France had enough to do fighting the rebellion in Algeria; to move into Egypt would be to widen an already effective guerrilla front, making ever greater demands on the French army and economy. With Soviet Russia behind the Arab cause, Britain and France would have been more and more compelled to explain their military presence in Egypt, not only to the Arabs but to their own people. Nasser might be deposed but Egyptian and Arab nationalism could not be swept away by occupying Alexandria, Ismailia, and Port Said. A compromise with honor, by Western standards? How could that be arranged with Nasser and how enforced? One battle was over, but no peace was won. The Israelis held on precariously to their lives and their state, 2.5 million people in a sea of 100 million Arabs. What would keep them alive, aside from their own tenacity and fighting qualities, was pointed out much later by Ben-Gurion, who said the Soviet Union needed them, for without Israel, Russia would have little leverage with the Egyptians or the other Arab nations, which had nothing much in common with Russia or one another except their hatred of the Israelis and their need of outside support to drive them into the sea.

Postscript

The lawyer who had defended Rudolf Hess, Alfred Seidl, sent a telegram to Winston Churchill as the Suez crisis ebbed asking him whether any plans were afoot to try Anthony Eden for crimes against peace in accord with the new law established at Nuremberg.

NOTES

1. Adam B. Ulam, *Expansion and Coexistence*, p. 643.
2. Anthony Eden, *The Memoirs of Anthony Eden—Full Circle*, p. 474.
3. Eden, *op. cit.*, p. 526.
4. Dwight D. Eisenhower, *Crusade in Europe*, p. 458.
5. Dwight D. Eisenhower, *Waging Peace*, p. 42.
6. *Ibid.*
7. Eden, *op. cit.*, p. 575.
8. John Connell, *The Most Important Country.*
9. A. J. Barker, *Suez: The Seven Day War.*
10. Eisenhower, *Waging Peace*, p. 28.
11. *Ibid.* p. 25.
    Robert Murphy, *Diplomat among Warriors*, pp. 375–376.
    Moshe Dayan, *Diary of the Sinai Campaign.*
12. Herman Finer, *Dulles over Suez.*
13. Robert Murphy, *op. cit.*
14. Général Beaufre, *L'Expédition de Suez.*
15. Burgt Broms, *The Legal Status of the Suez Canal.*
16. Hugh Thomas, *The Suez Affair.*
17. *Ibid.*, rev. ed., p. 51.
18. Général Paul Ély, *Memoirs.*
19. Eisenhower, *Waging Peace*, p. 47.
20. Murphy, *op. cit.*, p. 387.
21. Eden, *op. cit.*, pp. 562–563.
22. Eisenhower, *Waging Peace*, p. 47.
23. Murphy, *op. cit.*, p. 388.
24. Eden, *op. cit.*, p. 542.
25. Thomas, *op. cit.*, rev. ed., p. 37.
26. Eden, *op. cit.*, p. 539.
27. *Ibid.*, p. 557.
28. Merry and Serge Bromberger, *Secrets of Suez*, pp. 23, 24.
29. Eden, *op. cit.*, p. 606.
30. Barker, *op. cit.*, p. 95.
31. Benoist-Méchin, *Le Roi Saud*, p. 498.
32. Cited Dayan, *op. cit.*, p. 183.
33. Ely, *op. cit.*
34. Benoist-Méchin, *op. cit.*

4

Algeria

WHEN on the night of October 31–November 1, 1954, Radio
Algiers and some seventy other widely scattered French installations
in Algeria were attacked in a well-coordinated uprising, a war flared
up that had been smoldering with recurrent massive outbreaks for
more than a century. It was a guerrilla war and a racial war where,
despite what anthropologists may say about race distinctions in that
part of the world, each side could identify the likely enemy by his
features and color as readily as by any uniform or flowing robes he
might be wearing. It was also one of the post-World War II wars
between the north and the south, the north and south of countries
like Korea, Vietnam, and the Congo, and between nations like China
and India, Russia and China, Pakistan and India, Egypt and the
Yemen. Algeria, with the exception of the Al Moravid, the Saharan
Berber Conquest, had been invaded in its history of more than two
thousand years from either the north or the east, and this war was
no exception.

Seen from Peking, it was an action in the universal war between
the whites and their victims, between "the wretched of the earth"
(as Frantz Fanon, one of the black men who espoused Algeria's
cause, called the colonialized off-white, brown, black, yellow, and red
peoples of the world, everywhere in his and Chairman Mao's view

colonized and exploited) and their white oppressors.* Seen from Moscow, it was another uprising against capitalist imperialism of any color. Like the 1946–1954 war in Indo-China this was waged against its French version led, as was often the case in Arab countries, by men who might be useful but were rarely disciplined enough material for the Communist Party. The party regarded Muslim movements as reactionary, the leaders obsessed with religion and narrow, sectarian nationalism not much better than the foreign imperialisms they fought against. In this battle against a common enemy they could be used, but they were to be supported in a general way and directly only under propitious circumstances.† The Algerian Communist party, a branch of the French Communist party, was mainly made up of Europeans, many of them intellectuals like Henri Alleg, who wrote a book, La Question, about his experiences in French torture chambers. La Question, like Uncle Tom's Cabin written a hundred years before, had a wide sale and an even wider influence on both sides of the Atlantic. A large number of members of the Algerian Communist party were of Spanish origin, and when the party attempted to take over the revolutionary movement with the same strong-arm tactics that had been used in the Spanish Civil War, the consequences were similarly disastrous, except that in Algeria it was the party not the revolution that lost. Party cadres were assigned foolhardy and costly missions by the Muslim leadership, and after suffering heavy losses played only a minor role in the organized rebellion.

To most Frenchmen and to the French government, Algeria was part of France, of the French community, one of the crown jewels of its overseas empire. On the mixed population of tribes of Berbers and Arabs, Moors, the descendants of Jews (many of whom had migrated in the fifteenth century from Spain), and Negroes (who had been brought in as slaves from the Sudan) the French *mission*

* The indigenous population of Algeria included the Caucasoid Berbers who, though darker now, still as in preceding centuries occasionally have light hair and blue eyes, blacks from the Sudan, Arabs (some, like Abd-el-Kader, blue-eyed), nomads, and *métis*, who by tradition took on the caste of the father. They were, however, in almost all cases, physically distinguishable from the European population, which made the perception of psychological and cultural differences easier than it was in purely European wars. "Arab" will often be used as a generic term in this chapter for the mixed native population of Algeria, although in fact a majority are Berbers.

† In the 1930s, after the rise of Hitler, the French Communist party, following Moscow's Popular Front line, kept aloof from the Algerian resistance. Only in the changed political climate of the mid-1950s, when Muslim organizations were already battling the French, did the party lend direct support.

civilisatrice had bestowed the boons of the modern world—electricity, scientific medicine, highways, airplanes, hospitals—in short, civilization. Many eminent Frenchmen had been born in Algeria—Albert Camus was one, Marshal Juin another—and a personage more exalted than either could be claimed by the region—St. Augustine, whose mother had been a Christian in a time before the Berbers were converted to Islam. For more than a century the country was governed by its French, or rather by its mixed European, population. Among the thousands who migrated to Algeria in the nineteenth and twentieth centuries were as many different peoples as among the indigenous population. Only half of them were of French origin; Spaniards had settled there in large numbers, as had Maltese, Balearic Islanders, Italians, Corsicans, Sardinians, even Germans and Swiss. Those who had stayed had invariably taken French nationality, which was readily granted them in contrast to the native population. The *colons* were convinced of their indispensable part in the *mission civilisatrice*. Like colonists everywhere they were able to point out and take pride in the beneficent effects on the Muslims of the physical and cultural improvements they had made in a country arid and barren in many sections, that had been badly ruled under a foreign power (Turkey) when the French armies had invaded. The French commander of the expeditionary force, General de Bourmont, had told the Algerians that his troops came as liberators to free them from the cruelty and repression of Turkish rule. And while it is true that the French had invaded Algeria with fire and sword, together with the scrolls of the Rights of Man, and conducted a scorched-earth policy with wholesale destruction of lives and property in a war of conquest that lasted seventeen years, the French unlike the Turks had brought the country and some of its people into the nineteenth and then the twentieth century.

In a sense, since the war of the invasion and then the occupation had been followed by only relatively short periods of tranquillity, the conflict begun in 1830 had never ended. Insurrections and uprisings had occurred again and again, and the new guerrilla hostilities in 1954 differed from those that preceded them mainly in the well-knit organization, with a central command, that undertook them. Muslim leaders declared that they had given orders against killing,[1] but with the attacks on the French oil tanks, gas works, and radio and telephone installations came shooting, and the first person killed was a French schoolteacher gunned down in the street along with a

Muslim who had tried to save him. Still, no heavy loss of life took place in the first actions: seven Europeans in all were killed and seven more wounded. But it is hard to see how the leaders of the revolt could have expected to accomplish their ends in this surprise operation without bloodshed since one of their objectives was to acquire arms, which meant that police stations had to be attacked. The French reacted vigorously but in such a way, they said, so that reprisals would be taken not against the Muslim population but only against the actual perpetrators. Here, too, however, despite humane intentions, it would not be possible to destroy the revolt at its source without increasingly repressive measures. The new phase of the war escalated quickly because of the hit-and-run tactics of poorly armed, hard to identify, and fanatically determined bands of revolutionaries who were outwardly indistinguishable from peaceful citizens and could only be quickly routed out of the cities and countryside by wholesale measures against entire communities. The rebel strength was estimated at only some three thousand fighters in the 1954 uprising, a number that rose within two years to more than eight thousand with almost three times as many auxiliaries, but the damage they could cause to life and property was considerably out of proportion with what they might have accomplished in conventional warfare.

Thus the hostilities that erupted on November 1, 1954, and that were to last almost eight years, had small beginnings; the rising might have burned out like so many of its predecessors had it not been for its timing—it came when the tide of anticolonial nationalism was running high and when the belief of most European countries in their civilizing mission had worn thin. This 8-year war, or these last 8 years of a 130-year war, was to cost more than 200,000 lives and 50 billion new francs ($10 billion). It was an endless drain on lives and money and national energy that increasing numbers of Frenchmen thought out of proportion to the value of Algeria as part of a dwindling overseas empire. If the French-Algerian War may be said to have begun as soon as the French landed in 1830, its final phase could only be mounted in the mid-twentieth century, when what might be called the anthropological view of races and peoples, of cultural relativism, where each has a theoretical equality and right to its kind of order and disorder, took the place in the credos of Western societies of the notion of the civilizing imperatives of a so-called higher culture.

In the Time of the Invasion

The Muslims had taken this view or something like it even in 1830, when despite the deep impoverishment of much of the country and its mixture of tribes, the inhabitants had a sense, if not of nationality, at least of identity as other than that of the invaders, and they had fought tenaciously against them. It was easy for the Arabs to identify the invaders, not only because of their race and language but because the French took the land for themselves; decrees of 1844 and 1845 declared that all land without buildings on it was the property of the government, as well as land on which hostile acts had been committed. From the French point of view, unused land belonged to no one but them.[2] The Berbers, converted to Islam by the Arabs in the seventh and eleventh centuries, had never completely assimilated with the Arab population, and they spoke Arabic, if at all, as a second language. The Turks had been able to maintain a precarious sovereignty over Algeria only with the aid of highly trained mercenaries—Janissaries—and when the French invaded they had to battle all the tribes as well as the Turkish forces.* Other invaders— the Phoenicians, Carthaginians, Romans, Vandals, Byzantines, Arabs, and Spaniards—had managed to hold the shoreline, but only the Arabs and the Turks had penetrated into and held the interior against the warrior Berbers, who may have come to Algeria from Egypt as much as 2500 years before and acknowledged conquest by no one.

The whole area of northern Africa—Tunisia, Morocco, Algeria (Arab historians often include Arabic Spain and Libya)—was called the Maghreb in Arabic, meaning the Arab West as against the Makresch, the East, and the Misr, the Middle Country. The center of the Maghreb was Algeria, and centuries before the French conquered the country it was known as the breadbasket of the Roman world despite the droughts and infertile stretches in much of the interior. But a broad belt fifty to 100 miles in depth along the Mediterranean was a growing region with a more productive agriculture than most of Europe had. And although piracy was anchored in the Barbary Coast (as the shoreline of the Berbers' country was called),

---

* A Muslim jurist, Mohammed Bedjaoui, has argued learnedly that Algeria was already an autonomous nation before the French invasion, that the Deys had concluded treaties in its name, and that the French hold on the country was no more than a belligerent occupation since Algeria had never ceased to exist. (Mohammed Bedjaoui, *La Révolution Algérienne et le Droit*.

Algeria was also, in the early Middle Ages, a beneficiary of Islamic culture and literacy with Koranic schools that compared favorably with the narrow learning taught in Europe. A French general, Valazé, reported in January 1843 that: "Almost all Arabs know how to read and write. In each village there are two schools."[3] Nevertheless the word "barbarous" probably comes from Berber. Originally, a "barbarian" was a man who spoke Latin or Greek, or for that matter Arabic, badly (*barbar* in Arabic means to stammer), but the word came to mean in the Christian world a Saracen, a nonbeliever, a pagan, and the Barbary pirates were regarded by Europeans as barbarians of both sea and land.

From their fortified base in Algiers and other cities along the coast, until the beginning of the nineteenth century, the pirates preyed impartially on the shipping of the Mediterranean, exacting tribute and capturing the vessels of those who refused payment and enslaving their crews, who had to pull an oar in the pirate galleys or ransom their way back to freedom. The only European powers exempt from the Barbary exactions were Austria and Russia, both of which were in a strategic position to threaten Constantinople. As for the others, whether they paid tribute or made presents which the Hansa city of Hamburg preferred to call its protection payments, all—the United States, Holland, Naples, Sardinia, Portugal, Denmark —put cash or goods on the line. Sometimes the Europeans retaliated: the French bombarded and sacked Algiers in the seventeenth century, and attacks were made on the pirate city by Holland and England in the early nineteenth century. The United States conducted two wars against the regent of neighboring Tripoli to stop the payment of tribute to the pirates and to release American prisoners. But when such assaults were made in force the pirates usually withdrew into the interior, where few cared to follow them. Later on, when the heat cooled, they would return to their ships and to their lucrative trade.

Two attempted invasions of Algeria were defeated. The one in the sixteenth century was led by the Holy Roman Emperor and King of Spain Charles V. He commanded a great armada of 65 large galleys with 12,330 sailors and a landing force of 23,900 soldiers, but before they reached Algiers a storm scattered the ships and the invasion came to nothing, although Spanish forces continued to occupy Oran and Mers-el-Kebir until the Turks drove them out.

In 1775 Spain again, under King Charles III, attempted to occupy Algiers, sending a fleet of 40 war vessels and 344 transports carrying 22,000 men. They too had no luck and were defeated by the Muslim forces.

The wars of Spain against Turkey, and France against Spain, had given the Barbary pirates the same kind of opportunities patriotic European and American privateersmen made good use of when they were given an official blessing, in the form of a letter of marque, to prey legally on the commerce of an enemy. For the Berbers, the Moors, all infidels were enemies; anyone with a ship they could plunder or who might pay something to avoid being plundered was fair game. But by the time the French were prepared to invade Algeria, the pirates were gone, shot out of the water by long-victimized naval powers whose patience had run thin and by the decline of Algiers, ravaged by an invader against which it had inadequate defenses— disease. Only the breadbasket remained and the French turned to it, as the Romans had before them, to supply their population and their army. It was, in fact, the grain from Algeria for which the French contracted that led to the French invasion.

The French consul at Algiers, M. Deval, had considered himself gravely insulted in April 1827 when the Dey of Algiers, a young man of twenty-five, had flicked him on the wrist (or on the face, accounts vary) with his fly whisk after the Dey had pressed the consul for the long overdue payment (the grain had been contracted for during the French Revolution) which had been haughtily refused in what the Dey considered provocative language.* The sum of money France had agreed to pay for the grain was 27 million gold francs. It had been owing for over thirty years, and while a settlement had been arranged providing that 4,500,000 francs be paid outright with 2,500,000 more to come, the latter sum was so bound up in red tape that it seemed more than likely it would never be paid unless sterner measures were adopted by the Dey.

As a result of the fly whisk incident Charles X, the Bourbon monarch restored to a shaky throne which his political ineptitude did nothing to strengthen, immediately ordered a naval blockade of Algiers allegedly as a reprisal for the insult to his envoy. The blockade lasted three years and its only visible results were the high costs

---

* M. Deval was fortunate. At the end of the seventeenth century two successive French consuls along with a number of Christian slaves had been fired from the mouths of cannon as a retaliation against French bombardments and demands for indemnities. In return the French Admiral d'Estrées decapitated seventeen influential Turks he had on board and floated their corpses on rafts into Algiers.

of maintaining it and the capture by the Algerians of the French commercial concession, the Bastion. Thus the French were forced to undertake something more if they were to avenge the insult to their envoy. This they did. They proceeded to capture Algiers in a planned operation that was to be more spectacular than anything offered by the *Théâtre Français*. A French entrepreneur advertised in a Paris paper that seats might be had on his vessel lying off the harbor of Algiers where for 15 francs a day, with board, the purchaser could watch the bombardment from a prudent distance.

More lay behind the bombardment, however, than the fly whisk. Charles X was having a troubled time ruling France. The great overseas empire that once had included Canada and Louisiana was gone, lost through military defeat or sold to pay the bills of other wars. Algeria was close at hand and in many material ways a tempting prize as well as another step toward recapturing a vanished *gloire*. A successor of Charles X, Napoleon III, would dream of becoming emperor of an Arab kingdom based on the French possession of Algeria (not only the King of England could be an emperor by virtue of overseas possessions, a good many of them formerly French).

The capture of Algiers went according to plan, but while the commanding general, de Bourmont, assured the inhabitants of the city they had nothing to fear from the French, that none of their rights would be diminished, and that the French came as liberators, it soon seemed to the inhabitants that he spoke *pro forma*. Algiers was thoroughly plundered by the French troops and General de Bourmont confiscated the entire Algerian treasury amounting to 50 million gold francs. In June 1830 a Catholic paper asked: "Has not one the right to exterminate Algerians as one exterminates ferocious beasts with all possible means?" And on November 30 General Clauzel, who declared that he, too, wanted to see the natives exterminated, said: "I have ordered battalions to destroy and burn all that they find in their way. When one makes war it is not to increase the human species." At the entrance to one French camp sixty-eight heads were exhibited impaled on bayonets, according to the French paper *Le Moniteur*, which called it perhaps ironically *une très belle affaire*. On at least one occasion prisoners of war were massacred, French sources said, and at Saad 2300 women and children were reported killed, at Muru 1500.[4]

The generals made no secret of their activities or of the difficulties of their job. One, General Wimpffen, declared: "After we had destroyed some thousands of fruit trees and killed the Arabs, hardly were our columns gone when we had to send new troops to the same place." Another, General Baraguey, said that in conducting his campaign he had had 5000 olive trees chopped down, and a later commander-in-chief and governor of Algeria, General Bugeaud, defending the ferocity of his troops in the Chamber of Deputies, told his listeners that a war in Africa could not be fought without measures foreign to Europe or it would last an eternity.[5] The greatest figure among the French generals in Africa, Marshal Lyautey, although an enlightened supporter of indirect rule, summed up the matter: "You do not colonize," he said, "with choir children."[6]

In 1833 a French commission of inquiry declared that the French had taken for their own uses the property of "pious foundations," "sequestered that of a class of inhabitants we have promised to respect," made a forced loan of 100,000 francs, taken over private property without payment, and made the owners pay the costs of the destruction of their own property "whether it belonged to private persons or to mosques." In addition, the commission said: "We have profaned the temples, tombs and the interiors of houses that are sacred to the Muslims."[7]

Such admissions and charges, like the war itself, were to continue during all the years the French remained in control of Algeria. As the French armies moved from the coast into the interior to protect the cities they had captured, they were confronted with increased resistance. Battle was given wherever local leaders were on hand to take the field against the invaders. The French were facing some 10,000 armed men and an army numbering 100,000 men would be needed to subdue them.* The leader of the Algerian forces was Abd-el-Kader, a young man of twenty-five with no previous military experience who developed, nonetheless, formidable abilities as a tactician and strategist. General Burgeaud, who succeeded General de Bourmont as commander-in-chief, was singlemindedly determined to make Algeria a place fit for French colonists. He said in 1841 that wherever the water supply was good and the land fertile "there we must place colonists without worrying about previous owners."[8]

Harsher measures were instituted as the resistance became more

---

* Arab sources tell of as many as 70,000 men "nominally" at the disposal of Abd-el-Kader and say that 30,000 cavalry and 6000 infantry were used against the troops of the French Marshal Valée. But such numbers, if they were ever available, were fleeting. As may be seen from Abd-el-Kader's reports, he never had more than 10,000 tribesmen under his command and often far fewer. (*The Life of Abd-el-Kader*, written from his own dictation and compiled from other authentic sources by Colonel Henry A. Churchill, Chapman and Hall.)

difficult to overcome, and the war was waged increasingly against the civilian population. Arab horsemen were simple tribesmen in their daily life before the French came, but they turned into fanatical warriors. The Berbers, who for centuries had resisted every foreign intrusion, maintained a stiff-necked opposition to French rule.

The Algerian War in its earliest phase lasted long enough to bring out the refinements of barbarism and cruelty, in complete disregard of any customary rules of war by European powers, that accompany all long wars against a tenacious enemy. Arab civilians who had taken refuge in caves were gassed by the primitive but effective measures then at hand. French reports admitted that thousands of civilians were killed and the slaughter was accompanied by a wholesale expropriation of both land and buildings of the hostile tribes, especially where the land was fertile.

The Pre-French Algerian Scene

But the French were not invading a country of Rousseauesque peace and tranquillity. Life before the French came was hard and cheap, and for most of the people of whatever tribe or race in Algeria, it was desperate even where the land was fertile. Peasants paid taxes at every turn—a direct tax of 10 percent on their fields and herds permitted by the Koran, and then supplementary taxes, some of them levied arbitrarily by local officials who also expected and received gifts for their dubious services. The Turks were top in the chain of command; they were the rulers (all of them were officials of one kind or another), the rest were the ruled, and the overlords had no confidence in a light rein. Some 4000 Turks lived in Algiers, which in 1830 had between 30,000 and 35,000 inhabitants, including 12,000 to 16,000 Moors, in addition to Arabs and *Koulouglis* (children of Turkish fathers and Arab mothers), and 5000 foreigners. Negro slaves, about 500 a year, were brought into the city mainly from the Sudan, where they had been sold for bolts of cloth, headdresses, or Turkish slippers, or had been captured in raids.* Thirty thousand slaves, many of them white Christians who were the property of the Dey, were said to have been held in Algeria in the seventeenth century and their numbers did not diminish until piracy was

---

* Arab sources place the number of inhabitants of Algiers at 75,000 in the eighteenth century and ascribe the reduction in the Muslim population in the nineteenth century to people fleeing the city to escape the French. (Mostefa Lacheraf, *L'Algérie: Nation et Société.*)

stopped. In 1815, when an American ship neared the harbor of Algiers, a large number of such slaves were put in irons to prevent a mass attempt to board her. A year later, when Lord Exmouth landed in the city, he liberated some 3000 slaves there and elsewhere along the Barbary Coast. But although slaves were bought and sold in the market, their lives, aside from those in the galleys, were not very different from those of the free population. In some cases, when slaves belonged to dignitaries, they might run small businesses; in more humble circles they were considered members of the family although they might often be beaten.

Law and order were chancy things. In the eighteenth century a massacre of Jews had taken place—the Jews were one group that could unite the disparate peoples in a common pogrom. And Algerian prisons were overcrowded with prisoners awaiting punishment after having been sentenced by the Turkish authorities. There were mainly two penalties: death and the bastinado—beating the victim on the soles of his feet while he was strapped down with his legs at right angles to his body, in some cases until he was crippled. Anywhere from 30 to 1200 blows might be administered and they were exactly counted. The death penalty for Turks was carried out by strangulation, but no Turk could be punished in public. Jews were burned alive, Christians hanged. Women charged with infidelity were drowned by being tied in a sack and thrown into the sea. For killing a Turk the penalty was death by impalement. Other crimes were punished by flinging the culprit from a high rampart, and highway robbers were torn to pieces as they fell by hooks driven into the walls. A Moor caught stealing any article of even the slightest value had his right hand cut off. For minor offenses lips and noses might be cut off, a punishment that has continued to the present day. When one of the resistance leaders in the 1954 war ordered his men not to smoke, those who disobeyed were punished in this fashion.* It was a cruel society accustomed to violence, to drugs, to the exactions of one's betters. Jews were not permitted to ride horses, which were too noble for them, or to carry arms or lamps at night (to carry a light on the street after dark was obligatory and the Jews had to use candles), and they had to move aside for Muslims. Algiers was filled with prostitutes and its sexual perversions were well known along the waterfronts of the seven seas; there were two words

---

* Women, too, might have their noses cut off although in their case the punishment was considered merely disfiguring while men, it was believed, lost their masculinity with their noses. For a man to lose his nose was the worst penalty short of death.

in the argot for pederasty, one for the passive form, the other for the active.[9]

The professional Turkish soldiers, the Janissaries, became so powerful in the eighteenth century that they virtually took over the government in Algeria as well as in Istanbul. More than half the Deys who nominally ruled Algiers after the mid-seventeenth century suffered a violent death, many of them at the hands of Janissaries recruited for their protection. The Janissaries were themselves subject to strict discipline and infractions were punished by their commanders with a violent hand. They were celibates but sodomy was an approved vice among them and they were known to rape and plunder and on occasion to use occidentals for target practice. They became powerful enough to choose the Dey, and he could not rule without their support, which he needed far more than the approval of the Sultan in faraway Constantinople. They had certain privileges, among which was the right to earn money in a side line, and many of them engaged in trade that was lucrative because they were members of the privileged caste. Between the Janissaries and the pirates, any central government was limited in its pretensions to power, and although four Deys administered Algeria (under them were the Beys of the districts and the Caïds of the subdistricts), the government held precarious power and was constantly threatened by its own forces.

It was also a corrupt society. Islamic law is in theory a majestic edifice with the Imam, who is its chief representative, a religious as well as secular authority passing legal-moral judgments which are the more solemn because they are related to a divine order. No distinction in Islamic theory is made between legislative, judicial, and priestly functions. In practice the Imam transfers his functions to the Caïds, the lesser functionaries, and the Caïd, riding on a mule more impressive than most as a symbol of his office, is the one the ordinary man does business with and before whom he appears as before a court. A court of appeals could amend the judgment of the Caïd as could the sovereign. In the complex dealings with authorities the payment of bribes was part of the system's functioning and the public had no reason to have great confidence in the justice handed out. The institutionalizing of justice through the Imam remained respected because of its divine origin, but everyone knew the system had to be dealt with in mundane fashion.[10]

Since in the Islamic view one of the highest values is to procreate and provide more believers for the True Faith, Algerian society tended to produce more people than its resources could support. A man could have four legal wives in addition to concubines, as many slaves as he could afford, and children by all of them. Child marriages were often contracted although they could not be consummated under Koranic law until the bride was twelve and the groom fifteen years old.* Since women, with too much child-bearing, close quarters, and endless hot baths, and fattened as adolescents according to Oriental prescriptions of feminine beauty, were considered old at thirty, they had in any event a short time to be admired and cherished for their attractiveness.† Much of their time was spent with one another, talking, combing their hair endlessly, dyeing it with henna, deepening the shadows of their eyes with kohl, putting on and taking off ornaments, and even at times, it was said, making advances to Christians whom they might chance to encounter while their husbands were away on male errands of work and recreation, the latter often in the cafés the Turks had introduced with much success to the life of the Algerian cities.[11]

But if such encounters took place they were rare. The Muslim girl said farewell to the outside world when she married. So abrupt was the change that her last days as an unmarried girl were often spent "seeing the world," that is, walking to the outskirts of her town or village, visiting the marketplace, seeing all she could before entering her husband's house. She would spend the rest of her days in its seclusion, or behind the curtains of the family tent where she would meet only her woman friends and relatives and her husband. Her husband's permission was needed to leave the house, and if she traveled she was supposed to avoid crowds and any kind of conspicuous behavior, to be always veiled, often, even today, with only one eye showing, and never by a look or gesture to call attention to herself.‡

The devout Muslim, Abd-el-Kader, like the Prophet, held that a

---

* Among the Berbers, a French general reported, a girl might be a mother at eleven years of age and a grandmother at twenty-two. (General E. Daumas, *La Vie Arabe*.)

† Childbirth was a precarious event not only in the past but in recent times too. Hygiene was unheard of, women were cared for by female neighbors or members of their family and midwives, and one doctor in a study made during World War II reports that as many as 30 percent died in childbirth. In difficult cases doctors might be called in but only after traditional methods had failed and little could be done to save the life of the patient. (Jacques Bouchet, *Contribution à l'étude des fléaux qui menacent la mère et l'enfant indigènes en Algérie*.)

‡ Women, however, under Islamic law and custom had their rights, too. A man could be bastinadoed for not supplying his wife with adequate clothes in winter. If she had a fortune she was not supposed to use it for her own maintenance but for good works and presents and finery. Among the Berbers, women in later years might work in a proper environment, a store, for example. (A. M. Goichon, *Le Vie Féminine au Mzab*.)

man should not marry for riches that make a woman proud, or for beauty that fades, but for piety that endures. He, the Emir, who became the Sultan when he was called to the leadership of the tribes united against the French, had married young (at fifteen), as the Koran adjures a man to do, and he held womankind, especially in the person of his mother, in high reverence. He continually praised her life of good works for the poor and her piety, which he prized above all female virtues. But men were the rulers of the Muslim world, and though a woman might go to a mosque to pray, she need not, in the view of the Muslim savants, for to love and respect her husband was religion enough for her in the eyes of both men and women.

Abd-el-Kader

Abd-el-Kader was the Muslim, and often the European, ideal of the *preux chevalier*, the "Desert Hawk," as more than one English writer called him, learned, courageous, generous, a man to capture the imagination of the drab world of nineteenth-century industrialism. (In 1848, after he went into captivity, W. M. Thackeray wrote a poem about him: "Abd-el-Kader at Toulon, or the Caged Hawk.") French generals who fought against him praised him. He was the romantic Arab of picture and story, wearing the simplest attire, scornful of riches. Born to the saddle, he could vault from one side of the horse to the other at a full gallop and stand in the saddle and fire with precision. A warrior taking up arms only for the freedom of his fierce desert people, he fought with gallantry, improvising, attacking and retreating with unexpected moves, winning battle after battle until only the superior numbers and resources of the French finally defeated him. But not before almost the entire military might of France had been brought to bear against him and he had time and again defeated the best it had to give.

Born in May 1807 in a family village on the banks of the river Hammam in the province of Oran, the fourth son of an eminent Marabout (one of the Arab aristocracy whose piety and religious knowledge were the chief sources of their hold over the people), he had been an unusually timid boy, a trait he soon outgrew. He was given to hunting but also to the seclusion of the study and he collected a wide-ranging library that the French destroyed when they captured, in his absence, his womenfolk and retinue—the traveling hearth of tents for 60,000 people, the *Smala*, as the Arabs called it.

When Abd-el-Kader learned of the loss of his people, his manuscripts, and all his wealth, he was deeply shocked and retired for some hours of meditation, refusing to see anyone. When he emerged from his solitude he was his old self; he characteristically and rhetorically asked his followers why he should mourn—the dead were in Paradise, now he was free to fight the infidels unencumbered by his goods, which he now knew he had valued too highly.[12]

About five-feet-six in height, with black hair and dark eyes some observers thought black and some blue, he was the kind of handsome, graceful, erudite warrior for whom later generations, under the spell of T. E. Lawrence in film and story, would have a special place in their pantheon of heroes. He learned to read at five, at twelve he was proficient in the Koran, and at fourteen he was a Hafiz who could recite it by heart. He was one of the learned by any standards. He read Aristotle, Plato, and Pythagoras as well as the Muslim philosophers. He was ascetic and deeply religious but with a tolerance that was often lacking in his allegedly more civilized opponents. Although he preached the holy war, the Jihad, against the French invaders, he treated his captives with the courtesy of a medieval prince, forbade any mistreatment of them, and took the same care for their well-being as he did for that of his own troops. The tributes to his gallantry and skill in war come not only from Arab and literary admirers among the Europeans but also from the men who fought against him, men who like General Daumas were suspicious of all Arabs, and who like Marshal MacMahon and General Changarnier had time and again felt the lash of his onslaught and endured his unswerving resistance to their own true faith and civilizing mission. It was Napoleon III who finally conquered him—not on the field of battle, for that had already been done by the time their paths crossed, but by a generosity similar to Abd-el-Kader's own. And it seems to have been as a response to the treatment accorded him by Napoleon III that the leader of the holy wars against the Christians that were waged for seventeen years saved the lives of some 12,000 of them during a Muslim uprising in Damascus after his return to the Muslim world.[13]

For all his chivalry Abd-el-Kader could not always impose his views on his men. In a battle at Macta where he had surprised and routed the French in a narrow defile, attacking them suddenly with cavalry and foot soldiers who had been brought to the battlefield by riding behind the saddle of each horseman, he was successful in defeating the enemy, but he would have done even better if his troops descending on the French rear guard had not stopped to massacre the wounded and to chop off the heads of the men they had killed, making pyramids of them. The delay gave the French troops in the forward part of the column an opportunity to establish a line of defense and eventually to escape a trap where they would all have been killed or captured. When the Emir, who had ridden to the forward part of the defile, learned of the conduct of his men he was furious. But he could not always bring them up to his own standards, and this was not the only time his troops got out of hand. The Koran taught that the worthiest death of a believer was to die in the Jihad fighting for his faith against the infidel; this was conduct holier than a journey to Mecca and to the Prophet's burial place. The man who died in battle against the unbeliever was instantly transported to Paradise. With such prospects the troops of Abd-el-Kader would fight well and tenaciously and with conspicuous willingness to sacrifice their lives. But they also had a tradition of collecting trophies of battle, and heads were among the best of these.

Nor were Abd-el-Kader's orders with regard to the treatment of prisoners always followed. At one point he discovered that French captives he had ordered to be sent to him for questioning had been clothed for the occasion, that they had been living in rags and on starvation rations. He could and did order punishment for such disobedience, but even more compelling than the fear of his wrath among his men was their hatred of the Christian who had come to despoil and to conquer their land, and the shortness of supplies which they had to share with their prisoners. Abd-el-Kader was able to organize a long-lived resistance to the French and some of his followers remained loyal during all the years of the battle against the invaders. Others, however, brought up above all to survive in this life, were on the side of the strong battalions of whatever religion or purpose, and they joined the French or kept out of the fight when the fortunes of the Emir failed to prosper.

Abd-el-Kader's vengeance on what he regarded as unworthy or traitorous conduct was swift and terrible. He himself tells the story of decimating the Borgia tribe that had collaborated with the French and driving out the survivors from their native villages to find subsistence where they could.[14] He lopped off the heads of traitors and enemies, but the latter only in the course of battle, and he punished any of his followers who decapitated French soldiers they had killed, ordering one man to be given 250 blows three times in succession on separate counts for his failure to obey orders against a practice the Emir abhorred. He was himself an ascetic, wearing no gold or silver on his robes and forbidding any such adornments, along with wine and tobacco, to his soldiers.

The Civilizing Mission

The French troops, on the other hand, were expected by their generals to do as well as they could for themselves; General Changarnier, one of the best commanders in Africa, like General Sherman in the American Civil War, believed the quickest way to victory lay through the destruction of enemy property as well as lives and he ordered his troops to seize all Arab goods and harvests. Another French officer, Colonel Forey, told his men in 1843 to ravage the country, take possession of the flocks, and especially the women and children, and thus force the Arabs to submission. Pierre de Castellane, son of the Marshal de Castellane, described in 1844 how the French had destroyed the fig harvest, adding: "When we left the country was completely ruined." These measures he thought necessary because the Arabs only understood brutal force. Another Frenchman reported in 1842 that poor and rich Arab villages alike had been destroyed and their harvests as well, "a sad and cruel method for which I have the greatest antipathy."[15] In the diary of Saint Arnaud de Lettres were a long series of entries telling of destruction and killing of civilians. One such entry for October 5, 1842, read: "Today I am making a halt to continue emptying silos and burning villages and huts. I shall leave them no peace until they submit." On January 14, 1843, he writes: "I shall not leave a single tree standing in their orchards, not a head on the shoulders of these wretched Arabs. . . . These are the orders I have received from General Changarnier, and they will be punctually executed. I shall burn everything, kill everyone. . . ." Sometimes he did even better than he intended, for example, when he drove the inhabitants of the Beni Naâseur tribe from their homes and the next day found their huddled frozen bodies on the road where they had died in a heavy snowfall during the night.[16]

Arab warfare could match the French in ruthlessness; the Arabs, too, killed civilians and prisoners of war and they, too, burned and pillaged. On one occasion they fell upon some drunken French sol-

diers, cut off their heads, and displayed their trophies to acclama-
tions of joy on the part of the native population. Another time a
group of seemingly harmless Muslim pilgrims dressed in wretched
rags who were permitted by the French to enter a tent where
wounded were lying, suddenly pulled out guns from under their
burnouses. A two-hour battle followed in which all but two of the
Arabs were killed. In another incident 300 French prisoners were
massacred by one of Abd-el-Kader's lieutenants when he had no food
for them and he learned that Moorish allies of the French were approaching and feared the prisoners might be released.[17]

French sources also tell of the methods, since then become more
familiar, of the recently established Foreign Legion. One of their
captives suspected of robbery was lowered down a well on a rope
and intermittently kept under water until he told them where he
had hidden the loot. Against the Oulad Riah tribe in 1844 the
French commandant had brushwood fires lighted in front of the
caves where, according to the French count, 500 tribesmen and
women and children had taken refuge and they were asphyxiated
(Arab sources say not hundreds but thousands were killed in the
caves). Two months later the same thing happened when French
troops under Saint Arnaud de Lettres lighted fires in front of caves
where tribesmen had taken refuge and 1500 died; not one escaped.[18]
At Constantine, Arabs said, the population had tried to flee from a
French attack down the cliffs on which the city was built by means
of ropes, many of which broke and thousands died. Oran, according
to Arab sources, had a quarter of a million people in 1830, but the
city was nearly empty a year later, and in 1838 only 1000 natives remained (2120 in 1845 and 12,721 in 1881).[19] There was a similar
wholesale exodus from other cities.

Thus the struggle for independence began at the start of the
French invasion, and although periods of calm followed outbreaks
of violence, it never ceased. One French author writing in the 1830s
said that the Arabs were certain of their eventual victory. Allah had
permitted the evil of the French occupation to befall them because
their sins had been great, but in the long run, the French, the infidels, the Roumis (as the Europeans had been called from the time
of the Roman empire), would be swept from the country. Allah and
his faithful would defeat them.

The French were, however, often able to buy support or to get it
voluntarily from dissident tribesmen; intertribal feuds were many

and the tribes could be played off against one another. Even a Turkish battalion was recruited to take part in the French investment of Constantine. Arabs had always hated the Turks and their harsh suzerainty; many of them preferred French to Turkish rule and the Turks returned their animosity. Achmed, the Turkish Bey of Constantine, told the French he had decapitated 12,000 Arabs.[20] But some of the Berber and Arab tribesmen were implacable enemies of the French. To one of Abd-el-Kader's lieutenants, Sidi Mohammad, the French offered 500,000 francs, the restitution of his vast properties, and an annual pension of 50,000 francs if he would submit to French sovereignty and continue to live in Algeria. But Sidi Mohammad refused in an eloquent letter:

From Djebel Darda to l'Oued Feddah, I command, I slay,* I pardon. In exchange for the power I exercise for the glory of God and the service of Monseigneur the Sultan Abd-el-Kader, what do you propose to me? My estates, which powder will be able to return to me as it has taken them; money and the name of a traitor.[21]

Others among his followers, as Abd-el-Kader sadly observed, including some of those who had sworn eternal loyalty to him if he would lead them as Sultan, did submit to the French and some of them made common cause with the invaders. Arab loyalties could be fickle, as the French too would discover disadvantageously when apparently peaceful tribes who had long accepted their authority suddenly rose against them and massacred all the Europeans they could find. In general it was the well-to-do urban classes, the religious leaders, the Marabouts, and the Caïds who went along with the French, accepting jobs and money and protection. A lower class of civil servants, the *beni oui oui,* as the French called them, were brought into the administration of local communities and these yes-men were most useful during the entire period of French rule in Algeria until the later years when collaborators were often murdered by the Algerian underground.

But the French were caught on the horns of a dilemma. If Algeria was to be made a part of France, it had to be heavily colonized, and no matter how much land was reclaimed from the desert and swamps, more would have to be taken away from tribes that owned it. This

* An Arab historian says that this accepted translation is probably wrong. The verbs "combat" and "slay" have the same root in Arabic and he believes the true sense to be "I fight." (Lacheraf, *L'Algérie,* p. 104.)

policy required protecting the *colons'* lives and, from the Arab point of view, their stolen property, and at the same time pacifying the natives with reclaimed land and new economic opportunities, and by allowing them to keep their own customs and religion (although in the early years of the occupation French generals had talked of their mission of continuing the Crusades and converting the entire population to Christianity) and promising equality and French citizenship to those who qualified for it—a mirage that always remained in the far distance. If, however, the *Métropole* (the government in Paris) conceded too much to the natives, the *colons*, who more often than not were having a hard time too living in an inhospitable climate where they were constantly threatened by endemic diseases (malaria, typhoid, typhus, and cholera), the depredations of wild beasts, and native uprisings, were certain to do their best to defeat the proposals. Any new measures that would enfranchise Arabs and bring them into the higher administration, threatened the whole structure of European privilege and dominance. The *colons* for the most part lived a circumscribed life on small farms or, in the cities, owned small businesses, and they earned on the average somewhat less than their counterparts in France. For many of them the struggle for existence proved too harsh to bear.[22] In some years almost as many returned to Europe as migrated to Algeria, and the European population never grew to more than a tenth of the Algerian. For those who stayed, who managed despite the rough conditions to make a life for themselves, there was a strong sense of pride and accomplishment. Had they not changed the face of a barbarous country writhing under Turkish misrule and brought it to a hitherto unknown degree of stability and order? And was it not true, as the *colons* could demonstrate until the end of French rule in Algeria, that France had spent far more on the country than she took out of it? When the French had come to Algeria not more than 1.4 million acres had been planted in grain, and in 1954 there were more than 7 million acres of grain, 6 million made fertile out of brush and swampland and desert.[23]

Even a man like Albert Camus, a humanitarian of the deepest convictions—it is above all Camus' perception of justice, and the constant struggle imposed on man to attain it in some measure, that have differentiated him from so many merely socially-minded writers —could not bring himself to do more than plead for an Algeria open and common to both Muslims and Europeans. He, too, regarded himself as an Algerian and like so many others among the *colons* had worked to build the country into a truly civilized society, one of the rarest constructions on the whole globe. Camus writes that his own family in Algeria exploited no one; they were poor and worked their land for a far from luxurious living. The Arab case, Camus thought, was a strong one but so was the French side. He denounces the use of terror by the French; for any innocent lives that may have been saved by its methods fifty new members had been recruited for the Algerian resistance. Terror, he said, had also led to the demoralization of the French, and conceding the past failures of administration, he thought the country should be federalized like the Swiss Republic, with the Arabs freed from the colonial system and the *colons* retaining their rights.[24]

Camus and others like him had no interest in a rule of force and racial airs ("We are condemned to live together," Camus wrote), and they thought it possible for the two cultures to complement each other, to intermingle and create a society that was both French and Muslim in an Algeria that would take to itself the virtues and strengths of both races.

But too much had gone wrong to make possible such a reasonable and civilized solution. The Arabs had lost their best lands, they had followed the precepts of the Koran and multiplied up to and beyond the limit of the nourishment that any crops or herds could provide on the land available, and antibiotics enabled more of them to survive every year, only to live miserably for the rest of their days in a state of unremitting hunger and deprivation. Algeria, in the conventional French view, was a part of France, to be governed by France and to provide a refuge and second homeland for Frenchmen. François Mitterand, Minister of the Interior, said in November 1954: "Algeria is France; from Flanders to the Congo one law, one nation, one Parliament. That is the Constitution and that is our will. . . . The only negotiation is war."[25] Jacques Soustelle in February 1955 said that France would no more leave Algeria than she would Provence or Brittany; she had made her choice and that was integration.

To gain colonists in the nineteenth century Frenchmen were offered two and three hectares of land free and more land at low cost. In addition they were given 1200 francs in government aid for stocking and running their farms, plus plants and free grains and free passage for a family. Arab lands had been confiscated wholesale; whenever a revolt occurred, the tribe responsible was punished by expropriating its land. In some cases the tribe could buy it back and the money thus obtained was used to compensate other native owners whose land had been expropriated. In addition land was bought from Arabs by gullible Frenchmen who did not know that under the tribal system tracts were often held in common and a part-owner would often be delighted to sell his share and shares that belonged to other co-owners to a *Roumi*. One French buyer spent twenty years looking for a property he had bought but which he could never find. Some of the new *colons* followed the army, and shouldered a gun on their way to properties the army would in any case have to defend for them. Big companies were set up in France, like the Société Algérienne Générale. They held huge tracts of land made available to them by the French government and which they either resold to colonists or rented, in some cases, to the Arabs who had once owned them.

The economy of Algeria was shifted from one based on grazing and cereal raising to one based largely on viniculture. The French discovered that good wine could be made from Algerian grapes, and when the blight of phylloxera hit France in the late nineteenth century, the demand for Algerian wines increased in France as well as in other European countries. Wine grapes became the chief cash crop of Algeria—an acre of vines was worth three times more than an acre of cereals—and since Muslims drink little or no alcoholic beverages, the natives witnessed much of their best land, previously used for food crops, being planted to wine grapes which brought in a much higher return than the cereals but fed no one except the owners and other Europeans. Two fifths of the best land of Algeria (one third of all the arable land) was owned by the French, much of it used for viniculture, and the proportion of food available for the rapidly increasing Arab population was very small.*

In 1911 there had been two sheep for every native; in 1954 the proportion was 1.8. Erosion of the land and planting of former pasture lands accounted for the difference. Native Algerians got along,

---

* Before independence about 16,600,000 hectares were cultivated, of which Europeans owned one third. Jean-Paul Sartre, whose point of view was strongly anticolonial, summarized the comparative figures as follows: in 1850 the *colons* owned 115,000 hectares; in 1900 1,600,000; in 1950 2,703,000, with 11 million owned by the French state. Seven million hectares were left for the Muslims. (Jean-Paul Sartre, *Situations*, Vol. V, p. 32.)

Cf. Thomas Oppermann, *Le Problème Algérien*, p. 54, who writes that in the 1950s 25,000 *colons* owned 2,700,000 hectares as against 7,700,000 hectares owned by the entire Arab population.

it was calculated by French experts, on 1500 calories a day, two thirds of what the Europeans lived on, and just enough to keep many of them alive to produce more children, who in time would have fewer calories to nourish them no matter how much the land produced. In 1954 forty-seven Muslim babies were born per 1000 of population; the death rate was 11 per 1000. As for education, Arab sources said that over 90 percent of the native population was illiterate in 1960. Schools were mainly for the European population, although a small proportion of Arabs did attend and a few went on to secondary schools and even to the university the French founded in Algiers or to the French universities in the *Métropole*. But 18 million native children were not in school in 1954 because no schools existed for them. For every 227 European inhabitants there was one European student, but for the Muslim children the ratio was one student for 15,432.[26] French generals in the very beginning of the occupation had opposed increasing the literacy of the native population (General Ducrot Furone had wanted no Arab schools) and the attitude never changed very much during the entire period of occupation.

Arabic was a secondary language in the schools and in the central administration and was taught badly, the Muslims said, by the French. The Arab was a second- or third-class citizen, or a nondescript with no citizenship the French cared to identify. By the forms of voting permitted under the statute of 1947, the *Loi Cadre*, the Muslim population could elect representatives to a Parliament equally divided between Europeans and the natives, with sixty in each college of the legislature.* But the Parliament was not permitted to discuss political issues; those were resolved by the Chamber of Deputies in Paris. In addition, to guarantee French control, the Governor-General could, after a delay of twenty-four hours, call for a second vote on any measure and in that case a two-thirds majority was required. An Algerian election was a model that not even Chicago or Latin America could compete with. In Algiers, because of the size of the native population and the relative political sophistication, the native parties could vote, and have their votes counted, but in the hinterlands the returns were very different. In the election of June 1951 the administration lists were returned unanimously

---

* The Algerian Assembly, which had administrative functions, was elected in its first college by 464,000 Europeans and 58,000 élite Muslims with French citizenship; the second college represented 1,400,000 Muslim electors. (Brace, *Ordeal in Algeria*, p. 70.)

or better outside Algiers. In Algiers the Nationalists actually recorded 7550 out of 8000 votes, but in the countryside, where the polls were unsupervised except for government personnel, the count was overwhelmingly for the official candidates. At Aumale, for example, the government candidate received 1240 votes from 1240 registered voters and in Beni-Rached 728 out of 728. At Boudjerba the returns were even more gratifying to the officials. There the government candidate received 800 votes from a list numbering 500 eligible voters.[27]

An Algerian election became a synonym for a wildly faked election, just as an Algerian war had come to mean one waged without pity or any heed to the conventions of war. Even in the continual fighting of the 1950s the French high command did not recognize what was going on in Algeria as war, and a combatant could not be awarded the *Croix de Guerre*, which was a decoration earned only under hostilities duly recognized as war. As in the case of the Americans in Vietnam, the French were engaged in a good deal of bombing, shooting, strafing with planes and helicopters, and all other activities of modern warfare but they were not officially at war; they were engaged in putting down an insurrection conducted by guerrilla bands.

Algeria was founded on juridical pretenses. That it was part of France was one, and when Napoleon III, wanting to be an emperor like his illustrious ancestor, had spoken of an Arab kingdom under his scepter the *colons* had objected. Algeria for them was French, as proclaimed by the law of 1848 that had annexed the country to France. Louis Napoleon had also declared that all Arabs who wished to be admitted to the benefits of French citizenship could become citizens, but in 1871 when the Muslim inhabitants of Bougie visited the French judge of the peace to be sworn in, they were arrested.[28]

Time after time the Algerians were promised that they could become citizens but this was never to be, never, at least, on a large scale; even in 1935, after seventy years of such promises, only 2500 Muslims actually were citizens. Algeria existed for France, not the other way around. Conscription for Algerians was introduced in 1912, and after a man had completed his military service he was entitled to vote only in communal elections. In the 1950s a million Muslims were either unemployed or underemployed, taking part-time jobs when they could get them, and some 350,000 went to France to seek work, eventually becoming one of the chief sources for financing the revolution. It was not that France was totally deaf and blind to the needs of the native population; as the uprising continued, for example, more schools were promised. In de Gaulle's Constantine speech on October 3, 1955, he predicted that by 1963 two thirds of Algerian children would be in school. Also salaries and wages, de Gaulle said, were to be raised to levels comparable to those in France, more land was to be made available to Muslim farmers, housing for a million people was to be provided. But even as the French pointed out that one third of the investments in Algeria were made on behalf of social purposes, the Algerians were convinced that not a school would have been built and not a law passed and enforced for their benefit if it were not for the threat posed by the rebellion and the need to keep the Arab population as tranquil as possible.

The word "independence" was not used in Algeria until after World War I, in which Algerian troops had fought and many of them had won high French decorations. But the hopes of the native population that fought in France's wars for increased participation in their government, for equality, and a better life were never realized then or later. Men like Georges Clemenceau, aware of waning French strength in Europe as well as of the contributions the Algerian contingents had made to the Pyrrhic victory of 1918, wanted to concede more rights and privileges to the Muslims. In 1922 Clemenceau, from his retirement, said he favored granting the natives progressively equality of rights, and the same demand was made by a Muslim who had won the Legion of Honor, Emir Khaled. But these were voices in a tumult; Emir Khaled was exiled and Clemenceau ignored or resisted by the *colons* who had political clout in Algeria. Measures continued to be proposed by successive French governments to accomplish such ends but they never came to fruition. Assimilation, integration, citizenship—these were all promised but never attained. Nor were they to be won after the Second World War.

The Muslims continued through indirect taxes to pay three times the amount paid by the Europeans, for as in the times of the Turkish rule taxes were many and special for them: a 10 percent tax on their harvests and animals, taxes for licenses, tolls, dogs, permits, for the upkeep of forests and rural roads, and visits of functionaries, and they had to be paid five or six times a year often at places some distance from where the taxpayer lived. Consumer taxes, bearing most heavily on the native population, went up steadily from 1938 to 1954, but capital imposts, which would hit the Europeans, were cut by more than half in the same period. In 1954 taxes on consumer goods accounted for 54 billion francs in revenue to the government, the income tax for 16 billion francs, and the capital imposts for only 5.5 billion francs.[29]

The revolution was made by men who deeply resented their inferior status. Some of them, without overtly preaching the *Jihad* of Abd-el-Kader, had a modern version of it; one of them, Ben Badis, who in 1931 created an association called "The Elect," proclaimed their platform: "Islam is my religion, Arabic my language, Algeria my country." And he added that "independence is the natural right of every people on earth."[30] Ben Badis was a reformer; he started schools where Arabic grammar and syntax as well as the Koran were taught. Another Arab leader, Ferhat Abbas, an early assimilationist who considered Algeria to be French territory that should evolve from a colony to a province and who wanted an Algeria integrated with France, had declared in 1936: "I don't want to die for the Algerian *patrie*, because this fatherland does not exist. I have not been able to discover it; I have interrogated history, the living and the dead, I have visited cemeteries and no one has answered me. One does not build on wind."[31] It would take almost twenty years for Abbas to come to the conclusion that independence was the only possible route to genuine freedom.

France and its *mission civilisatrice* for a long time had a powerful appeal to many Arab intellectuals who had studied in French universities, and knew how far removed from the modern world all the Arab countries were and how much they had to learn from Europe in general and France in particular. Always, however, their hopes for achieving some sort of equal coexistence with the French, the European population, were dashed. And then came World War II, when France was defeated on the battlefields of Europe and its possessions in North Africa were disputed by the French warring between themselves, one faction representing Vichy, the other de Gaulle and the French Resistance. The Vichy government pleased many Muslims when it rescinded the Crémieux decrees that had granted citizenship to Jews in Algeria at a time when only a handful of Muslims had attained citizenship.* But beyond such considerations what the Muslims heard from Allied statesmen was the promise

---

* In order to qualify for citizenship under M. Crémieux's law the Muslims would have had to relinquish the Koranic statute and law.

that every people should have the right to govern themselves and to decide their own destiny.

Still only a small number of their leaders spoke of independence. Ben Badis continued to exalt Muslim fraternity and an Algerian nation that might well be fitted into a formula of cooperation with France. Ferhat Abbas, continuing on his moderate course despite having been jailed and then liberated in 1943, had told the French government in a manifesto that Algerians wanted autonomy, and they would participate in a war of liberation on condition that the liberation would occur without regard to race or religion, and that after the war a conference would be held with the Muslim organizations to work out a political, economic, and social statute.[32] Abbas founded a party to further his program, Les Amis du Manifeste et de la Liberté (AML).

Only Messali Hadj, who had once been close to the Communist party, spoke openly of independence. He had founded the Party of the Algerian People (PPA) in 1938, had been condemned to sixteen years of forced labor in March 1941, but had been liberated by General Giraud in 1943 and placed under house arrest. In 1946 he replaced the PPA, which had been outlawed, by the *Mouvement pour le Triomphe des Libertés Démocratiques* (MTLD), a working-class and revolutionary party. Nevertheless all the native groups including the AML, whose autonomous Algerian republic was to be federated with France, soon moved toward a harder line. The Atlantic Charter, the repeated statements on behalf of self-determination and the rights of man that were parsimoniously borne out in a French ordinance of March 1944 promising citizenship to 60,000 Muslims, incited the Algerian native movements to expect far more than they would be likely to get by means of making demands and voting. Then an event occurred that changed the resistance movement in all its variations to a revolutionary program.

Beginning of the End

On the day of the German surrender, when all over the world celebrations were being held to mark the downfall of the Hitler tyranny, at Sétif in Algeria hundreds of natives were shot down in the streets. Again the leaders were arrested, Messali Hadj and Ferhat Abbas, the latter as he was congratulating the Governor-General, Chabaigneau, on the Allies' victory.

A series of minor incidents triggered the disaster. On May 1, 1945, an Algerian flag was ordered flown at a meeting held by the PPA, a provocative demonstration that resulted in the death of one Muslim in Algiers and wholesale arrests by the jittery French in the hinterlands. The Prefect of Constantine, a militant *colon* determined to maintain France's position, gave strict instructions to the police to maintain order. As a result, when the police inspector at Sétif, a man by the name of Laffont, left a café on May 8 and saw another group of demonstrators carrying an Algerian flag and a placard with the seemingly innocuous words: "Long live the victory of the Allies," he feared the worst. Laffont fired three shots, killing the man with the placard. Other demonstrators were shot in the melee that followed, including a young man named Bouzid who was carrying the green and white flag of Algerian independence.

French authorities proclaimed martial law, to which the Arabs replied by crying the *Jihad*. A number of Europeans were killed including the socialist mayor of Sétif, Deluca, who was considered pro-Arab. The government then called up overwhelming forces against the native population: the Foreign Legion, Senegalese troops, the militia, and even Italian prisoners of war. They struck with airplanes and tanks and the guns of the crúiser *Duguay-Trouin* that shelled the coastal region of Kerrata. The French say 1500 Muslims were killed but Algerian sources say from 5,000 to 10,000 Muslims died in these reprisals. That was the result of a day of freedom that began at Sétif with a demonstration celebrating the Allies' victory.

The *colons*, as always fearful of a mass native uprising, armed themselves and took the law into their own hands, a use of lynch justice that was never condemned by the government. The massacre turned moderate Muslims into staunch, sometimes fanatical, supporters of independence. Former commissioned and noncommissioned officers who had fought in the French army (Ben Bella, who had been a sergeant, among them) became revolutionists when they learned of the killings that began in Sétif and spread to Bougie, Bône, Souk-Ahras, Heliopolis, Millesimo, and Villars where Muslims were slain and then burned in the limestone ovens. May 8 was to be long remembered in Algeria for reasons different from those in the rest of the world.

The massacre of Sétif led directly to the rising of 1954. Algerian leaders, as well as the simple rank and file, believed that none of the promises made them would be kept if they would possibly lead to equality with the French. Between 1945 and 1954 sporadic bombings and shootings continued along with wholesale arrests as plots were discovered; the prisons were filled with alleged conspirators. Many of those arrested went on hunger strikes, some lasting for three and four weeks, and torture became part of the procedures of interrogation.

Groups and parties continued to be formed among the Muslims; elections were faked the same as before. On November 1 a new group, the *Comité Révolutionnaire d'Unité et d'Action* (CRUA), composed of Ben Bella and other activists, ordered the rising that would end only with Algerian independence. On November 5 the existence of a clandestine army, the *Armée de Libération Nationale* (ALN), was announced, a tiny force with nothing like the 25,000 men claimed for it. Toward the end of the year the political arm of the revolution, *Front de Libération Nationale* (FLN), was formed as a rival of the *Mouvement Nationale Algérien*. Both of these parties had their beginnings in Messali Hadj's *Mouvement pour le Triomphe des Libertés Démocratiques* (MTLD), but the factions were contentious and divided. It was the dissidents of the MTLD, working through the revolutionary committee, who started the military uprising in 1954. Their program was taken over by the FLN, to which, it was claimed, half the Muslim population of Algeria belonged by 1956, and which had become the dominant force of the resistance together with the ALN, at the expense of all the other scattered parties of revolt. The organization of the FLN was far superior to those of its rivals and one example of its efficiency may be seen from an event in 1956 when five of its leaders, including Ben Bella, were captured. The French had forced an airplane chartered for them by the King of Morocco, and flying from that country to Tunis, to land in Algeria where the five men were made prisoner, but the FLN continued its policies precisely as before. The durable Arab formula for revolt based on a charismatic leader was not nearly as evident in the FLN as in many of the other resistance organizations. The romantic tradition of Abd-el-Kader was replaced by the efficient functioning of a built-in steering committee within the party apparatus.

The Dirty War

The war begun in 1954 was a ruthless one on both sides. Arab guerrilla bands swept down on French farms and killed everyone on them. They placed bombs anywhere Frenchmen were likely to congregate—in cafés, restaurants, public buildings—and the French Algerian newspapers reported almost daily new outrages, many of them against women and children killed on their farmsteads. In their turn, the French began to use torture as a reliable means of obtaining information—the only means, the military command thought, of getting knowledge of where the next bomb would be planted and of breaking up the innumerable cells of the FLN and its army. Borrowing from the methods of the French resistance during the war, from the precepts on conspiratorial organization and guerrilla war of Mao Tse-tung and the Soviet Union, the FLN was divided into cells of three members, no one of whom knew more than what he had been ordered to carry out. The French used everything they had in their arsenal of defense. To augment the police and the Foreign Legion, they brought in paratroops who had fought in the guerrilla wars of Indochina and who became the units most dreaded and detested by the Muslims because they tortured prisoners and made no secret of it. They would use any methods provided they made their victims talk and could thus forestall the next attack.

It was a dirty war even by the declining standards of the Second World War. Prisoners were beaten up routinely, tortured with electrodes placed in their ears or genitals, attached to dynamos capable of increasing the intensity of the shock up to and beyond human endurance. They were given the water treatment, which meant drowning them until they were ready to signal their willingness to talk, pieces of flesh were cut from them, and candles were placed on their bodies until they burned out. All the familiar horrors of the Nazi concentration camps appeared again in Algeria and some new refinements were added. When Ben Bella, after independence was won, journeyed to Moscow and on his return through Czechoslovakia was taken to Lidice, he told his Czech audience that Algeria had had a thousand Lidices. Villages had been wiped out, he said, their male inhabitants shot and the women and children often killed, too, in the wholesale reprisals undertaken by French troops against the Muslim guerrillas. At one camp a group of prisoners, one of them blind, was forced to crawl some 800 meters on their knees (it took them an hour), carrying their luggage, and they were beaten all the way. Other prisoners were buried up to their necks in the desert sand, and only during the midday hours were they given a covering for their heads to keep them alive. Although the Geneva Convention of 1949 forbids collective punishment, the French took reprisal measures against entire communities. In November 1956, as a result of a road being damaged, the inhabitants of Ouadhia were fined 5.5 million francs, ordered to evacuate their two villages, and told that anyone found in them would be interned, and if they fled, shot. For the shooting of a French soldier another village was burned to the ground together with the year's harvest of grain, which meant no food was left for a population with no other reserves. One French general, Paris de la Boulardière, protesting against the terrorist orders given him, asked to be relieved of his command in the Atlas Mountains and was thereupon sentenced to sixty days' fortress arrest. Other French officers, appalled by what they saw, and sometimes by what they themselves had done, described the horrors to their compatriots and in newspapers. Official investigations were held and promises of reform made but they could not be kept. As General Massu, one of the commanders most feared and hated by the Algerians, said, there was no other way to fight the kind of war that was being fought in Algeria.[33]

Massu was a rigorous commander but no enemy of the Muslims per se (he and his wife had adopted two native children). The enemy's conspiratorial network had to be broken up or innocent people, guilty of no crime whatever, would be blown up or shot down; the captives had to be made to talk and to talk quickly or the bombs they knew were to be planted would explode, and the news of their arrest would become known to the underground and the leaders would escape. Massu's tactics were successful. The most densely populated quarter of any city in the world, it was said, the Kasbah, was "cleansed" in a series of raids, and the clandestine organization was penetrated and fragmented although it continued to function, often weakened but regaining its strength and striking anew. The guerrilla war spread to France where bombs went off. Hundreds of thousands of Algerians who were working there were divided into districts, *Willayas*, like the six the FLN had established in Algeria itself, and the workers were either forced, or volunteered, to contribute to the war effort just as did those who remained at home. A regular tax of 200 francs a month (at the then current rate, about 50 cents) was imposed by the FLN; it rose to 1000 francs for employed workers and to as much as 40,000 to 50,000 francs a year in the case of well-to-do businessmen.[34]

In 1957 the French banned from sale all medicaments that might be used on behalf of the wounded native soldiers, anaesthetics and antibiotics among them, and Frantz Fanon, who was a doctor, reported that many of them died of tetanus. Massu's severe measures and his corps of Arab informers were effective. He countered every Arab move. When a strike was called and shopkeepers lowered their shutters, Massu ordered them torn down. When the Arabs killed, he took prisoners and executed them. In September of 1957 no assassinations were reported as against 120 in December of 1956, and Massu's parachutists had confiscated more than 100 bombs. But the counterterror had its limits, and that included the patience of the homeland. The FLN returned with fire and sword and bomb and General Massu, a savage critic of anyone who impeded his plans for the defense of French Algeria up to and including de Gaulle, was dismissed from his command after telling a German reporter from the *Sueddeutsche Zeitung* that he and the army disagreed with General de Gaulle's Algerian policy.

Although the French did not recognize the FLN as a belligerent, claiming they were engaged in putting down an insurrection, the Geneva Convention of 1949 has rules for civil wars too. And while the FLN, although it was not a party to Geneva, declared its willingness to respect the Convention, the French would never accept either the FLN's offer or the validity of the Convention with regard to the Algerian War.[35] When on February 8, 1958, an FLN patrol operating out of the small Tunisian village of Sakist-Sidi-Youssef crossed the frontier into Algeria and killed fourteen French soldiers, French planes bombed the Tunisian village in reprisal, killing large numbers of its inhabitants. One German paper called it another Oradour.[36]

The rising was not a unified, mass reaction of the peoples of Algeria. The same tactics used by guerrillas in Indochina, Soviet Russia, Poland, the Ukraine, Yugoslavia, and France were as successful among the disparate tribes and peoples of Algeria as they often were elsewhere. The FLN demanded collaboration from the native population in the form of money, supplies, and manpower, and if it was not forthcoming there were harsh reprisals. The population of one village, Melouza, was wiped out because it was regarded as anti-FLN and francophile. No one knows how many Algerians were killed by the revolutionary cadres seeking to liberate them, but the numbers were certainly high.

The revolutionaries knew that the war had to be ruthless if they were ever possibly to win. Vastly outnumbered in the field, in technical resources, in equipment, they had to get along with a fraction of the armaments and men the French could throw into the battle. The only way they could balance or nearly balance such force was to use every legal and illegal method open to them. Their officers were for the most part former Algerian soldiers who had served in the French army, and no one held a rank higher than colonel. For the first time in the history of a Muslim country, women were brought directly into the fighting line. Girls, who by tradition were not permitted to leave their houses in the company of men outside their family, went out into the field with resistance groups, carried bombs under their burnouses, and planted them in the public places where they would do the most damage. When the French caught up with them they, too, were tortured, and in addition, the Algerians said, raped and shamefully mishandled. This was a revolution within the revolution, for women were suddenly freed of shackling conventions a thousand years old so they, too, could blow up the *Roumis*, including European women and children who happened to be near where they had left their bombs.

The Algerian newspapers reported almost daily incidents of terror perpetrated by the FLN or its army, the ALN: entire families were wiped out, rockets were fired into hotels, delayed-action bombs were left in churches. On March 9, 1956, guerrillas chatted for twenty minutes with their seven victims before killing them; on April 29–30 *Le Journal d'Alger* reported nine attempts at assassination within forty-eight hours; in Oranie the *Echo d'Alger* on May 8 reported fifty farms burned and sixty people massacred; on May 10 *Le Journal d'Alger* reported that forty-six villages had been attacked, in one seventeen people had been killed, six had their throats cut and were burned. In Biskra the *Journal d'Alger* reported on May 27–28 that twelve Europeans had been killed; on August 21–22 *La Dépêche Quotidienne d'Algérie* reported fifty Europeans killed in a revolt in Oued-Zin; a few days later the father of eight children was killed by a shot in his back; early in November three bombs exploded in Algiers killing six and wounding thirty-six, including eleven women and ten children (*Le Journal d'Alger*, November 13, 1956); on December 16 a grenade exploded in a cinema killing one child and wounding sixteen (*Le Journal d'Alger*).

Such events went on day after day for years. In 1962 104 explosions of plastic bombs were reported in one day in Algiers (*Le Journal d'Alger*, March 6, 1962). Nor were Europeans the only victims.

At Melouza and Wagram early in 1957 338 Muslims were killed in one night by the partisans and their homes burned.

One military maxim that has been borne out over and over again in the post-World War II wars is that you can do anything with bayonets but sit on them. The French had no chance of remaining in Algeria unless they could somehow bring the native population and the *colons* together into a society which both would feel was a worthy one, or at least a supportable one in which to live. In the years between 1919 and 1954 the *gros colons* successfully prevented the introduction of the measures of equality and reconciliation that might have brought the two peoples together. It was no good telling the native population to rejoice in the railroads, airfields, and penicillin the French had brought to the country. These amenities did not mean anything to a half-employed or unemployed worker and to a city and peasant population struggling to keep alive on a starvation diet. On the other hand, nothing the French could do would solve the problem of the Muslim birthrate—not the marshes they reclaimed to make arable land, or the methods of modern farming they introduced, and as for their medicine it could only contribute to the magnitude of the problem. The French, many of them, meant well. They passed laws and decrees conferring citizenship, made large outlays for public purposes, and offered higher education, although for a very few it is true, in Algerian and French universities. The fine phrases of French generals and politicians like de Gaulle in his manifesto of 1943 promising equality between Algerians and French, the references to France as the home and source of the Rights of Man, which of course applied to Algeria as they did to France itself, not to mention all humanity—these were not rhetoric for mere display or cover.

The French, in fact, exhausted their arsenals both of powder and persuasion. They resettled 1,250,000 villagers where they could be protected against reprisals of the resistance by the French army. They built an electrified fence along the Moroccan border to keep out infiltrators. Under General Challe groups of twenty men were sent into native villages to act as medics and teachers and to win over the people. But how could they win them? No matter what efforts these or any other Frenchmen made, the dreadful poverty remained. It could only be ameliorated with extra rations, or other well-intentioned temporary measures, and then the future closed in again.

The need for an improvement in French Algerian policy had been recognized for years by French authors like Anatole France, Albert Camus, and François Mauriac, by all shades of politicians from men like Clemenceau, who knew how much France needed Algerian manpower in its armed forces, to Léon Blum, who wanted to extend the suffrage gradually, and Guy Mollet, who declared that he recognized the existence of an Algerian personality.

It is no wonder then that de Gaulle, who had dreams of French grandeur far beyond the confines of North Africa, when he returned to power in 1958 began his faltering and zigzag steps to end the conflict. France was mortally tired of the war. It had cost billions of francs and thousands of lives. Five Frenchmen and sixteen Muslims continued to die every day in combat. The war took so many troops from continental France that her power to fulfill what de Gaulle took to be the destiny of the first state in Europe was seriously damaged. The French people were fed up with the war. They wanted their conscripted sons home again. The conflict had lasted too long, it had never been won, they pointed out, and never would be won.

De Gaulle was operating between the extréme Right and the Left: in Algeria between the *colons* and the generals on one side, with the exception of some who shared de Gaulle's views, and the FLN on the other; in France, between similar forces on the Right and the Communists on the Left. The Communists up to 1958 were usually the largest single party in France, and after that date the second largest party, and however shifting their policies with regard to the Algerian independence movement, Communist leaders lost no opportunity to attack France's colonial policy in general, from the alleged killing of 50,000 Madagascans in 1946–1947, to the atrocities at Sétif.[37]

On June 4, 1958, de Gaulle was in Algiers. He was introduced to a wildly cheering throng by Jacques Soustelle, himself a Gaulliste and integrationist who could, however, toy with the idea of using the bomb to win the war. Soustelle, presenting the President of the Republic, said: "De Gaulle is among us. He is here because faithful Algeria wants it, because she wants to remain forever French." To the introduction and the frenzied acclamation of the crowd, de Gaulle replied in his characteristically oracular style: "I have understood you. I know what has happened here. I know what you have wanted to do. I see that the road you have opened in Algeria is that of renewal and fraternity."[38] But de Gaulle had not entirely made up his mind, or if he had, did not wish to disclose his conclusions. He praised Algiers as a great French city and said what so many had said before him, that henceforth there would be only one category of inhabitants, all Frenchmen, all with the same rights and duties. But not even de Gaulle could talk the war away; it continued in the midst of promises and hortatory messages and despite de Gaulle's feeling that France's civilizing mission was not completed. On December 4, 1958, he shouted: "Long live Algeria, the Community, France!" But the war went on, and on September 16, 1959, de Gaulle said Algeria had three choices: secession, becoming French, or association. A few days later he promised Algeria, under certain rigorous conditions, the right to self-determination once the country was pacified. In January 1960 he dismissed Massu, on June 14 he offered to negotiate with the leaders of the insurgents,* although earlier he had said he would never negotiate with the FLN, and on May 9 he assured the *colons* that France would not abandon her children.

He was on a steep and narrow path and it was impossible to bring both warring sides along with him. Together with the Algerian resistance, the hard-nosed ones were the *colons* and some of the French military who were still thinking in terms of empire and promotions. The *colons*, like the Algerians themselves, had endured the climate and diseases, worked long and hard hours, and for the most part made the most modest of livings. They had come to an undeveloped country and despite all the attendant evils had made it the most flourishing of the Arab countries. They had abolished slavery—as late as 1934 a French general, Latour, had put an end to the traffic in Morocco.[39] Who was de Gaulle or anyone else to say they had to leave the country where many of them were born or had lived for decades and where only a few *gros colons* had gotten rich. Had they not found it a primitive, often desert land and made parts of it bloom that had never been anything but wasteland before they came?

---

* A provisional government in exile, the *Gouvernement Provisoire de la République Algérienne* (GPRA), with Ferhat Abbas as Prime Minister, had been set up in Tunis in 1958. Abbas resigned in August 1961 and was replaced by Ben Yusuf Ben Khedda with Belkacem Krim as Foreign Minister. It was Krim who conducted the secret negotiations with Louis Joxe, the French Minister of Algerian Affairs. Ben Bella was released from his imprisonment in March 1962 and elected Prime Minister by the National Assembly in September. He later became President and was deposed in 1965 in a coup by the army and the Minister of Defense, Houari Boumedienne.

Even Albert Camus admitted that if the program of the FLN were fulfilled, over a million Europeans would be forced to leave the country, and was that justice?

On April 11, 1961, de Gaulle said he foresaw a sovereign Algeria, and on April 22 the French generals in Algeria led a revolt against him and his policies. This revolt was the last gasp of French colonialism—Indochina had gone, so had Syria, Madagascar, Tunisia, and Morocco, and one black African state after another. During July and August of 1960 eight African states, former colonies of Belgium and Britain, renounced colonial status; Katanga proclaimed its independence, as did Dahomey, Niger, Upper Volta, the Ivory Coast, the Central African Republic, the Congo,* Gabon, and in addition, the Mediterranean island of Cyprus. For a short time it was feared the revolt of the generals might spread to France. An airborne landing of parachutists in Paris itself to take over the government seemed a possibility, for many of the dissident officers had the deep affection and abiding confidence of their troops and what de Gaulle was proposing seemed like treason to many of them. Other soldiers, however, especially the draftees, resisted the orders of the rebel generals, using transistor radios to keep in touch with Paris. De Gaulle proclaimed a state of emergency. But the revolt sputtered out. The bulk of the army and of the French people followed de Gaulle in his Algerian policy. Algeria did not mean that much except to the people who had dug themselves into its soil or who saw it as a last symbol of France as a world power. The generals who had revolted were either captured by the forces loyal to de Gaulle or escaped into exile. Those who were captured were tried and given either the death penalty or long terms of imprisonment, none of which, however, was carried out.

The French army had been deeply shaken by its succession of defeats. It was not difficult for many of its officers to blame France's lost battles on treason at home, a stab-in-the-back explanation of defeat very like the one used by high officers in the German army in 1918. Some of the most renowned names in the French military hierarchy took part in the revolt, which lasted four days—Generals Maurice Challe, Edmond Jouhaud, Raoul Salan, André Gardy, and André Zeller—and Jacques Massu might well have been among them had he not been recalled to France the year before. Five generals and

* King Baudouin of Belgium proclaimed the independence of the new state on June 30.

200 other officers were eventually arrested and tried. Jouhaud and Salan, who was captured later, were sentenced to death, as was Gardy, who escaped to the Argentine; Challe and Zeller were given fifteen years, but de Gaulle commuted the death and prison sentences, although two of the younger officers involved were executed.

Independence

So the die-hard generals and the *colons* lost and the *colons* had no recourse, when Algeria became independent, but to leave their farms and businesses and return to France. By the end of September 1962 only 250,000 of them remained in Algeria and most of these left in the years to come. The FLN had not fought a long and bloody war to share the country with the invaders and few *colons* had much desire to stay under the new rulers. The *colons*, Camus among them, had always foreseen this contingency. They had told de Gaulle and any other French officials who proposed granting autonomy or freedom to the Muslims that this meant abandoning everything that France had tried to accomplish in the 130 years of its occupation.*

France had had no allies in this battle. The United States continued on its anticolonial course, attempting to keep France in NATO by supplying planes, helicopters, and weapons to the French, while at the same time furnishing wheat to the Algerian refugees, but it was luke warm or cool in its political support of French Algerian policy. And in Algeria as in Suez it was in the political arena that France was weakest. During World War II Franklin Roosevelt had had grave doubts about returning any of France's colonies including Algeria; when the American landing in North Africa was carried out neither de Gaulle nor any other French general was consulted about the operation. John Kennedy spoke in 1956 in the United States Senate on behalf of recognizing the "independent personality" of Algeria. The AFL-CIO protested against any American military equipment going to France to be used against "the Algerian National Liberation forces."[40] It was the time of anticolonialism in the West as well as in the East. This was as true of Britain and other allies of France in the United Nations as it was of the United States. The Arab countries represented in the United Nations con-

---

* Camus, in 1936, had been booed off the stage by *colons* when he advocated reforms to benefit the Muslims. Undoubtedly torn between both sides of the conflict, he fully identified himself with neither.

ducted an adroit campaign to get the Algerian question on the agendas of the Assembly and the Security Council. France steadily refused to recognize the competence of the United Nations in what she said was an internal matter and subject to discussion by France alone, but the Arabs denied that this was true, pointing out that the independence movement and the war affected the maintenance of peace in the region if not of the world, and they had powerful supporters for their position among the countries of the African and Communist blocs. Only the two-thirds rule had prevented the adoption of a Pakistani resolution supporting the right of Algeria to self-determination in 1959, and in 1960 when the motion was again presented by the Afro-Asian bloc, now including the right to independence, it was adopted.

The extremist and terrorist organization of the *colons*, L'Organisation de l'Armée Secrète, (OAS), even after the French and the FLN concluded a cease-fire at Evian-les-Bains on March 12, 1962, would not accept its terms that, in effect, granted independence after reserving minor rights for France and the holding of a referendum. The OAS, under General Salan, who was still at large, continued its bombing and shooting directed against both Muslims and the French population. But the counterterror had no widespread support and collapsed. Its purpose had been to provoke a *Jihad* in the cities so the French army would have to be called in to save Christian lives and thus delay independence, but the strict discipline of the FLN-ALN kept the resistance firmly in line. Salan was captured on April 20, 1962, the referendum was held in France on July 1, and more than 90 percent voted in favor of an independent Algeria which would cooperate with France, 5,975,581 for and 16,534 against. Two days later de Gaulle recognized the new state.[41]

It was mainly in Algeria that the battle was won, in Algeria and then in France. In Algeria, by the determination of relatively few but enormously determined men, conducting their operations as Mao Tse-tung had instructed, within a population that would be like the all-encompassing water to fish, a population that felt itself aggrieved and despised but that never rose *en masse*; in France, by battle fatigue brought on by guerrilla war. The numbers of the FLN went up and down with the fortunes of war, and the thoroughness of the repression, and while a majority of Muslims certainly favored the forces of independence, or of native rule, nothing like a majority ever actually joined the battle. In 1956 the French calculated the

Algerian forces at some 8050 regulars with 21,000 auxiliaries, to which the French could oppose 400,000 troops in Algeria and 150,000 more in Tunisia. The French forces rose to a half million but they were never enough. Their units made use of all the manpower France could spare, even from the Algerian population (150,000 *Harkis*, Muslim auxiliaries, served with the French army), but such units, although useful, sometimes changed sides since they knew they would have to live in the country after the fighting was over.

The war was won by tactics that are particularly adaptable to the conditions of modern, political war, where a weak power confronts a strong one but where the stakes are unequal in the minds of the contestants, the one fighting for all the heady slogans of these times —freedom, self-determination, a better life for all, the end of imperialism, of exploitation—the other side no longer convinced either of its civilizing mission or even of its right to stay in a territory that was not its own to begin with. The courage and ruthlessness of an embattled few, and attrition, won the war for the Algerians; war-weariness and an uneasy conscience lost it for the French. The great moral question for contemporary societies—whether life is really better for the great majority of the Muslim population, to say nothing of the *colons*, with the victory of Algerian nationalism—has still not been answered.

There is no doubt, however, that the Arabs rejoice in their independence despite the continuing problems arising from their impoverishment. Primary education for children under the Arab government is compulsory and illiteracy will eventually disappear. Unemployment and underemployment remain very high and taxes have been trebled since the French left. Nevertheless people pay the higher imposts with far less reluctance than they did under French rule for they tell themselves that freedom cannot be measured by tax payments. Now, if they are misgoverned, it will at least be by their own people and not as second-class subjects of a foreign power. They live with enormous differences between the upper political and economic strata and the working and farming population; under a semi-police state and a one-party system where a former leader, Ben Bella, has simply disappeared into what has been said to be a form of house arrest, charged with promoting a personality cult similar to Stalin's, among other crimes.

Algeria is a quasi-socialist country permitting only a limited participation of capitalist enterprises and of foreign capital. Confiscated

French lands have been assigned to rural cooperatives, vineyards are being uprooted to provide land for grazing and cereal crops. The people with their high birthrate and meager resources work on as best they can, still hungry a good deal of the time but feeling themselves more nearly masters in their own house than they ever have been since 1830. The *colons* have returned to the *Métropole*, leaving behind them not only their fixed property, but the bombs and slaughter too.

NOTES

1. Johannes Maas, "Algeriens politische Geschichte bis zur Unabhängigkeit 1962," pp. 116–129.
2. Richard and Joan Brace, *Ordeal in Algeria*, pp. 17–18.
3. Mostefa Lacheraf, *L'Algérie: Nation et Societé*, p. 73.
4. Michel Habart, *Histoire d'un Parjure*.
5. Maas, *op. cit.*, pp. 116–129.
6. Pierre Lafont, *L'Expiation*.
7. Charles-Henri Favrod, *Le FLN et L'Algérie*, p. 2.
8. Brace, *op. cit.*, p. 17.
9. *L'Algérie, Un siècle avant l'occupation Française*. Témoignage de Shaw, Religieux Anglais (Paris: Carthage, 1968).
10. Jean-Paul Charnay, *La Vie Musulmane en Algérie*.
11. Pierre Boyer de Latour, *La Vie Quotidienne à Alger à la Veille de l'Intervention Française*.
12. Churchill, *The Life of Abdel Kader*, p. 223; see also Wilfred Blunt, *Desert Hawk*.
13. Churchill, *The Life of Abdel Kader*.
14. *Ibid.*
15. Général Changarnier, *Mémoires du Général Changarnier*, p. 81.
    Lacheraf, *op. cit.*, p. 93.
16. Quoted in Blunt, *op. cit.*, pp. 167–168.
17. *Mémoires du Maréchal de MacMahon, Souvenirs de l'Algérie*.
18. Blunt, *op. cit.*
19. Lacheraf, *op. cit.*
20. Changarnier, *op. cit.*, p. 26.
21. *Ibid.*, p. 219.
22. Yves Courrière, *L'Heure des Colonels*.
    Bruno Etienne, *Statistique du CNRS*.
23. Brace, *op. cit.*
24. Albert Camus, *Resistance, Rebellion and Death*.
25. Favrod, *op. cit.*, p. 313.
26. Favrod, *op. cit.*, p. 178.
27. *Ibid.*, p. 119.
28. *Ibid.*, p. 70.
29. *Ibid.*, p. 35.
30. *Ibid.*, p. 91.
31. Thomas Oppermann, *Le Problème Algérien*, p. 33.
32. Favrod, *op. cit.*, p. 97.
33. Saadi Yacet, *Souvenirs de la Bataille d'Alger*.
    Hafid Keramane, *La Pacification*.
    Bechir Boumaza et al., *La Gangrène*.
34. Jules Roy, *Autour du Drame*.

35. Oppermann, *op. cit.*
36. Lafont, *op. cit.*
37. Erich Kern, *Algerien in Flammen.*
38. Favrod, *op. cit.*, p. 325.
39. Pierre Boyer de Latour, *Le Martyre de l'Armée Française.*
40. Brace, *op. cit.*, p. 138.
41. Paul Henissart, OAS.

5

Aggression in the Holy Land

THE wars between the Jews and the Arabs, like the century of Algerian wars, never ended in a peace. The Israeli-Arab hostilities might quiet down, be stilled for a time, but they always erupted again in small or large actions with a continuing barrage, even in the periods of formal cease-fire, of charges and countercharges of aggressions. Each side held a position completely irreconcilable with that of the other. From the point of view of the Zionists, they had no alternative to survival; either their state remained free and intact with Israelis in control of it, or it went down in the sea of Arab rejection and hatred that surrounded them. Israel was the only state in history in the creation of which the nations of the world formally took part, in this case a two-thirds majority of their representatives in the Assembly of the United Nations, and its appearance had even brought together for a fleeting moment the foreign policies of the two superpowers, both of which had voted for the founding of a Jewish state. But Israel survived as the Jews themselves had survived for 2000 years—precariously, dependent on its wits and inner strength, and, far more than it liked, on the policies of powers with interests remote from its own.

The Arab enmity was implacable. For the Arabs Israel was an affront, a foreign body in their midst, a cancer, as some of them said, that had to be destroyed. Whatever chances may once have existed for some kind of condominium, of a shared living space, had long since been lost in a witches' cauldron of hatred and recrimination with nationalist, religious, economic, and political differences so deep, with each side so convinced of the justice of its cause, that any kind of reasonable compromise would have been rejected as the equivalent of unconditional surrender by either Jews or Arabs if any statesman had proposed it.

The United Nations' decision on November 29, 1947, to partition Palestine in order to establish an autonomous state of Israel grew out of the ashes of Auschwitz, which the Arabs were quick to point out was not an extermination camp of their making. The killing of some five to six million Jews in the gas chambers of what had been one of the most civilized nations of the world, where Jews had long thought of themselves as being Germans and good Germans, was a blow from which the self-esteem of the Western world, long convinced of the steady progress of its mores and institutions and the increasing benignity of its gods, would never entirely recover.

Earlier attempts to create a Jewish state had always run out of steam. The Balfour Declaration issued in 1917, which stated that the British government looked with favor on the establishing of a Jewish homeland in Palestine, was based on some hard political calculations as well as on the emotional appeals of the Zionists, but it ran counter to other British promises to other peoples. Lloyd George said, perhaps fancifully, that he had been converted to Zionism by the alchemy of Chaim Weizmann, without whose acetone, cordite* would have been a lot harder to come by for a Britain engaged in its first major war in a hundred years. The Allies, however, needed more than acetone; they were competing for Jewish support in the United States, in Russia, and in Poland against the Central Powers who had been fighting a czarist Russia where the word "pogrom" had been coined. The German conquest of Poland had been aided by Jewish hostility to Russia, where Jews were to play an important role in the revolution, and the ally on whom the British in 1917 placed their chief reliance was President Wilson, who was thought to be pro-Zionist. What the Allies were seeking was a propaganda weapon to win the Jews and at the same time not antagonize either the forces of the Russian monarchists or of the emerging revolution. No one representing either the Czar or his enemies would object to a

* The British had tried unsuccessfully to manufacture the powder with the aid of wood alcohol (David Lloyd George, *Memoirs of the Peace Conference*, Vol. II, p. 722.)

plan that might result in Jewish emigration from Russia to Palestine or anywhere else.

The Central Powers had early appreciated the usefulness of offering the Jews a homeland in Palestine, but Palestine was in the hands of the Turkish ally, who could not be expected to look with favor on any German Balfour Declaration. German and Austrian Jews had fought patriotically in the ranks of the German and Austrian armies, but Britain permitted the formation of a Jewish Mule Corps, the only country that had a specific Jewish contingent formed with one eye on Palestine.

Zionism had had its devoted, zealous advocates long before the Balfour Declaration (as well as those like Lord Palmerston, who sixty-five years before that document was drawn up said he favored a Jewish homeland in Palestine), and they might have gone to work, again buttonholing legislators, writing books and editorials and letters to the press, convening congresses, but accomplishing little of solid political substance, had it not been for the crisis of conscience that overcame the Western world when it discovered how pervasive and deadly its own anti-Semitism had been.

It was a simple truth that the Jews in the course of World War II had had no place in all the world to escape to. Pogroms there had been before in Russia, in Poland, and in Rumania. Anti-Semitism was an accepted fact of life in many societies, but planned wholesale extermination, genocide, as it came to be called, was something new. Between the years 385 and 1918, one author has calculated that 1,380,000 people had been slain in religious wars. Jews had been slaughtered, but so had Protestants by Catholics, 30,000 of them on St. Bartholomew's night, and Protestants under Cromwell in their turn had killed 3000 Catholics in one town in Ireland. Muslims had slain heretics and nonbelievers by the thousands. Christians had killed Muslims as well as one another for centuries on end.[1] So killing for religious or quasi-religious reasons was not new in the twentieth century; what was new was the scale of the massacre and the planned extermination of an entire trapped people as a state policy. Hitler was the state, commander-in-chief of its armed forces, its chief justice, and its lawmaker, and he had summoned the Wannsee Conference of 1942 to arrange for the destruction of all the Jews in Europe. How many were executed can probably never be known, but the number of European Jews who were killed during World War II is certainly not less than 5 million and may approach 6 million.[2]

Not only the killings lay on the conscience of the West. There was also the indifference and the imperfectly concealed antipathy of the relatively friendly nations. Franklin D. Roosevelt, for one, had done very little to ease the lot of the desperate Jews in the years before and after the start of World War II. On a memorandum submitted to him by one of his aides in 1939 asking for his views on a bill that would have permitted the entry of 20,000 Jewish children from the Third Reich, Mr. Roosevelt wrote: "File no action." And when in 1943 Sweden proposed that the Reich permit 20,000 Jewish children to leave Germany to be cared for in Sweden until after the war, the costs to be shared by the United States and Britain, who would permit food and medical supplies to be shipped through the blockade, the plan was approved by the British Foreign Office, but the American State Department delayed five months before it decided against the proposal, suggesting another, watered-down solution that was never adopted.

Nor did Mr. Roosevelt give support to other rescue plans despite the evidence pouring in to him beginning in 1942 that the "cleansing" measures undertaken against the Jews were becoming large-scale exterminations. Not until 1944, when only a small percentage of the European Jews could be saved, did the President take serious action, and its success on a minor scale was evidence of how much more might have been accomplished had he moved earlier. It is true that the American public, according to polls, was overwhelmingly opposed to raising immigration quotas, but even so more than 400,000 places on the permissible quotas went unused between 1933 and 1943 by countries under the control of the Third Reich. The State Department found all kinds of obstacles to prevent visas from being issued. Proof in the form of bank balances and affidavits was demanded that the applicant would never be likely to become a public charge, and he was required to produce a police certificate testifying to his good behavior*—this, in the case of German Jews, from a country where all Jews were considered criminals.

The United States up to May 1939 admitted 63,000 refugees. Some other countries did better in relation to their population, and many of them did worse. Sweden before and during the war admitted all the refugees who could reach her shores, Holland took in some 25,000 Jews, but only as temporary visitors, and Denmark, limited by its population density, admitted as many as it could. England

---

* A provision that remained in force after World War II.

took in 40,000 refugees including some 9000 children. France, with 30,000 refugee Jews and many other refugees and aliens in addition, had reached a saturation point, its representatives said, by 1938. The Dominican Republic offered to accept a sizable number of immigrants—100,000—but they would have to work in agriculture. A spokesman for the British Commonwealth declared that no territory in the Empire was suitable for large-scale immigration. Australia refused to admit Jews, saying it had no real racial problem and wanted none. Canada had room, it said, only for farmers. Peru, Nicaragua, Honduras, Costa Rica, the Argentine, and Mexico wanted no Jewish immigrants. Cuba, which in 1939 had issued landing permits (sold in Germany by the Hamburg-America line at $150 each) to 930 Jews, changed its mind in the person of President Bru when the liner *St. Louis* entered the harbor of Havana and Sr. Bru failed to receive further monetary inducements (they turned out to amount to $1 million) to permit the passengers to land. The ship had to leave, disembarking only twenty-six of its passengers, those who had farsightedly hired lawyers in Europe to arrange for credentials more solid than their landing permits. For an extra $500 they had obtained authorization from the Cuban State, Treasury, and Labor departments to enter Cuba, but the other passengers were not so fortunate, save for one man who cut his wrists and jumped overboard. He was rescued and brought to a Havana hospital to be shipped out later. All the passengers had been given quota numbers by the United States and would have been admitted there in intervals ranging from three months to three years.

The sympathetic German Captain of the *St. Louis*, Gustav Schroeder, did manage eventually to distribute his passengers among England, France, Holland, and Belgium, although for a time he had considered beaching his ship, as a last resort, on the British coast to prevent the return of his cargo to the Third Reich.[3]

Thus National Socialists could and did point out to their Western critics that their own countries seemed no more anxious than Germany to accept Jews, although they disguised their antipathies with more humane rhetoric. Poland in 1938 announced that it would rescind the citizenship of Polish Jews who had remained out of the country for more than five years, and when the Reich promptly attempted to deport its Polish Jews back to their native land, Polish border officials refused to let them in. These wandering Jews, like the passengers on the *St. Louis*, moved back and forth for two days in a no-man's-land between the countries that wanted no part of them, and it was a member of a family from among these refugees who killed the German Legation's councillor of embassy in Paris, Ernst vom Rath, in November 1938.* The murder of vom Rath became the excuse for the Kristallnacht and the savage destruction of Jewish property, an event that led Hermann Goering to say he would rather have seen 200 Jews dead than so much valuable property destroyed.⁴

The St. Louis was only the first of a fleet of vessels to be chartered by Jews that would never reach their destination because no one wanted their passengers. Another ship that sailed in December 1941 from the Black Sea port of Constanza, the Rumanian vessel Struma, a battered, leaky hulk with defective engines, had set sail for Palestine. It broke down off Istanbul and Turkish authorities would not permit the passengers ashore without landing permits for Palestine issued by the British authorities. The British refused to grant the permits, the Struma was towed out to sea by the Turks, and six miles from shore she sank with all but two of her passengers; 70 children, 269 women, and 428 men were drowned. The Jews would have been illegal immigrants violating the conditions of the latest British White Paper and, as the British Undersecretary for the Colonies, Harold Macmillan, said: "It is not in our power to give guarantees nor to take measure of a nature that may compromise the present policy regarding illegal immigration."⁵

Palestine, promised as a homeland for the Jewish people in 1917, had been closed to any sizable immigration since May 1939 when a British White Paper reversed the Balfour policy. The paper was drawn up at a time when Britain again had to find allies wherever she could, above all in the Arab world where the Axis was poised to mount an attack against her not only with tanks and planes and troops but also with an intoxicating message of anti-Jewish purposes that found a mighty resonance in Egypt and all the other Arab countries. Nasser for one said plainly he had hoped for a German victory and so did the Mufti of Jerusalem and other leaders of the Arab independence movement. Iraq waged a "war" lasting for thirty days against Britain in 1941, and the bedouin in Transjordan cut British oil pipe lines. Britain, as had not been the case in World War I, could count on the support of the Jews no matter what her policies.

* Herschell Gruenspann, who mistakenly shot vom Rath, intended to kill the German ambassador, Count Welczek. (Helmut Heiber, Der Fall Gruenspann, pp. 134–172.)

The Jews had nowhere else to turn but to the Western powers, while the support of the Arabs had to be won, and so the Balfour Declaration of 1917 was controverted in the White Paper of May 9, 1939. Although this was a document the Zionists were far from accepting, they had no choice but to live with it because they had no way of efficaciously rejecting it. Ben-Gurion summed up the matter by saying the Jews would fight the White Paper as if there were no war and the war as if there were no White Paper. Their enemy was Hitler, their allies the Western powers. The rest could wait.[6]

But the White Paper was bad news for the Zionists and a bad augury. They were striving to found a state Jews could freely migrate to, and the White Paper announced that in the mandated territory of Palestine, Britain would permit no more than 75,000 Jews to enter in the course of the next five years, and after that the number of Jews to be admitted would be determined only with the consent of the Arabs. From the British point of view this was no doubt a sensible and even necessary measure under the circumstances, when for Britain far more than the lives of foreign Jews was at stake, but it was another heavy blow on top of all the others to a people living under the increasingly brutal anti-Jewish laws and regulations of the Third Reich.

Although many British leaders, including Winston Churchill, had long been pro-Zionist and undoubtedly would have preferred to see issued a confirmation, in concrete terms, of the Balfour Declaration in place of the White Paper, Britain was being pressed in Europe, Africa, and Asia and her own security demanded that she obtain the help or at least neutrality of the Arabs. After the war a compromise might be reached where, as both the White Paper and the Balfour Declaration foresaw, an Arab-Jewish state would arise in which both peoples could live together in some condition of peace and where account would be taken of the aspirations of both Jews and Arabs, the one for a homeland, the other for independence.

But there was no way whatever of accomplishing this end. From the Arabs' point of view, Palestine was their country, a country from which they had driven the Crusaders centuries before and in which the Jews, if they came in large numbers, would be threatening interlopers. As the Zionists saw it, Palestine was their immemorial home from which they had been driven 2000 years ago, sung of in a Bible which was read in every country of their persecutors, including Germany.

The Jewish claim to Palestine, always a powerful one, would ac-

quire an enormously increased emotional charge following the holocaust. From the Zionist point of view, not only was the claim established in the sacred scriptures of the Old Testament* and confirmed,
if ambiguously, in secular documents including the mandate granted
by the League of Nations in 1922, not only had the lands the Jews
acquired up to the founding of the Israeli state in 1948 been bought
and paid for at prices far exceeding the $24 worth of beads ex-
changed with the Indians for Manhattan Island, but it was also a
state that two thirds of the nations of the world (Britain abstaining)
had voted to create because it was a psychological as well as a historical necessity. For the Arabs this was all hypocrisy and verbiage.
What it meant was that part of an Arab country would be ruled by
Jews, and Palestinian Arabs would live on sufferance on their an-
cestral lands.

The Rise of Zionism

A few Jews had remained in the Holy Land after the Babylonian
Captivity and after the destruction of the Temple in A.D. 70, but only
some 8000 lived there in the beginning of the nineteenth century.†
Although the French Revolution had liberated Jews in feudal Europe, it had not given rise to any back-to-Palestine movement. That
movement started in the nineteenth century in widely separated
parts of Europe as a direct result of pogroms or milder anti-Semitic
outbreaks. Colonists from Russia began to appear in Palestine in
the eighteenth century. In 1878 a colony was founded by Russian-
Jewish emigrés near Jaffa. In 1882 a total of 167 major anti-Jewish
incidents took place in Russia alone and a manifesto was issued by
a group of Jews calling themselves "Lovers of Zion," condemning the
"false dream" of assimilation, and asserting the necessity for a homeland of their own. Theodor Herzl had been a member of a predomi-

---

* Psalm 137: "By the rivers of Babylon, there we sat down, yea, we wept, when
we remembered Zion. We hanged our harps upon the willows in the midst thereof.
For there they that carried us away captive required of us a song; and they that wasted
us required of us mirth, saying, Sing us one of the Songs of Zion. How shall we sing
the Lord's Song in a strange land? If I forget thee let my hand forget her cunning. If
I do not remember thee, let my tongue cleave to the roof of my mouth; if I prefer not
Jerusalem above my chief joy. Remember, O Lord, the children of Edom in the day
of Jerusalem; who said, Rase it, rase it, even to the foundation thereof. O daughter of
Babylon, who art to be destroyed; happy shall he be, that rewardeth thee as thou hast
served us. Happy shall he be, that taketh and dasheth thy little ones against the stones."

† After the Diaspora centers of Jewish life had shifted with political and social
changes from the Mideast to Spain, France, Central Europe, Poland, and Russia.

nantly Christian duelling fraternity in the University of Vienna, and although the anti-Semitism he had encountered in Austria and Germany was unpleasant, it was in France at the time of the Dreyfus affair that he came to see anti-Semitism as a growth that would never be uprooted but only left behind for a Jewish homeland where it could not exist. Other early Zionists came to the same conclusions from similar experiences. While at times it seemed possible that land might be acquired elsewhere than in Palestine, it was always eventually to the country of the historic past that Zionist aspirations would return. Empty lands in South America, Cyprus, Madagascar, and Africa were theoretical possibilities, but for a people that had been held together mainly by a common religion and religious tradition for 2000 years, nothing could adequately replace the country of their scriptures and their origins, the country they had prayed for in their synagogues: "Next year in Jerusalem" and of which the Talmud had taught "Better to live in the deserts of Palestine than elsewhere in palaces."

There is some truth in the legend that up to the twentieth century it had been Arabs, not Europeans, who had shown the Jews the most generous hospitality and imposed the fewest restrictions on them. Jews welcomed the Islamic invaders of Spain, who treated them far better than had the Christians. Maimonides wrote freely in Arabic in a Muslim country, and other Jews played leading roles in Muslim states. In England, in the Germanic and Slavic states, in Spain and Portugal, on the other hand, Jews were placed under heavy disabilities, tortured under the Inquisition, or forced to become Christian converts to escape such penalties. These Marranos (the Spanish word meant swine), who while professing Christianity secretly remained Jews, had no counterpart in the Islamic world. Arab medicine and learning were world-renowned and part of the reason for their preeminence was the presence of learned Jews who were permitted to make their contributions to Islamic culture without becoming Muslims. This state of affairs, however, was precarious. As was the case in Algeria, Jews were often as penalized in Muslim countries as they were in the Christian ones, although in the view of Islam Abraham, common ancestor of Muslim and Jew, is one of the prophets as are Moses and Jesus, and the Jews, like the Christians, are people of the Book and have a tolerated place among them. Nevertheless, their Semitic kinship never prevented the Muslims from conducting pogroms of their own. All the Jews of Damascus were

thrown into prison in 1840 and many of them were tortured after
a priest had disappeared whose blood the Jews had allegedly drunk
in one of their cannibal orgies. This was a Muslim version of the
medieval Christian notion of how the Jews conducted secret religious
rites and a precursor of the Protocols of Zion invented in later nineteenth-century Russia.[7]

When the Zionists toward the end of the nineteenth century began to acquire sizable sections of land in Palestine, they were more
often than not welcomed by the native Palestinian population and
by the commonly absentee landlords who were glad to sell at prices
far beyond the going ones. It was desolate farmland they bought,
for the most part desert and swamp and all of it disease-ridden. The
German Emperor William II, to whom Herzl had appealed for aid
in obtaining the approval of the Sultan for a Jewish settlement in
Palestine, said what everyone else had observed—what the land
needed was water. Without irrigation Palestine was a wasteland
from which only the meanest of livings could be had, a country in
which no improvements of any kind had been made for centuries.

In the late nineteenth century there were few signs of Arab or
Palestinian nationalism. Palestine had never, except under the Crusaders, been an independent territory. It had been ruled by Romans,
Turks, Jews, Arabs, and Christians, but never in modern times had
it been a state or even a political entity. The Turk ruled it as part of
Syria and, as he did Algeria and other Arab lands, with an eye to the
taxes that could be collected from the subjugated peoples. When
Herzl inquired of the Sultan Abdul Hamid whether Jews might be
admitted in large numbers, the answer was they could be if they
adopted the Muslim religion, accepted him as their suzerain, and settled anywhere in his domain except Palestine. The Turks had an
eclectic tradition; in general, people of all creeds and races were admitted to the Turkish realm as long as they accepted the status quo
and its rulers.

But the Jews who migrated to Palestine in the course of the nineteenth century and the beginning of the twentieth did not leave the
land as it was. They instituted irrigation and modern farming, and
what had been a well-nigh worthless plot when they arrived became
in their hands an oasis often in bright contrast to the dusty plantings
of the Arabs. It soon became evident to those who had sold the land
that it was far more valuable than they had believed and the sellers
came to have second thoughts. Also, the Jewish settlers competed

in the local labor market and offered alternatives to the fellahin when they hired Arabs as laborers, sometimes in preference to their own people. The Arabs were good workers and cheap, whereas the Jews, who more often than not had come for political or spiritual reasons, had European standards in mind when they hired out for work in the Promised Land. When Arab workers were later replaced by Jews, one of the chief reasons for the Zionists being tolerated by the local populations disappeared. Arabs who had been watchmen on the farms sometimes joined in raids on them after they lost their jobs.

The period just before World War I was a time when Asian and African nationalisms began to stir and Arab nationalism made its appearance along with similar movements in China and India. Land in Palestine that had seemed worthless and merely to be gotten rid of when a buyer could be found became in the minds of many Arabs a native soil to be defended at almost all costs. Such sentiments, however, were limited to an Arab elite. Arab nationalism was still as remote to the simple farmer who knew and cared nothing about the world beyond his native village as it had been to his ancestors.

In addition, the Jews brought to the region ideas that went beyond agriculture: the ethos of a dynamic Western culture that was not only clearly superior in its adaptation to desert farming than the ancient symbiosis of a camel and a farmer with a stick, but that included social change as well, a democratic community that the Arab fellahin might compare favorably with his own ancient feudal structures. So the Effendi were soon not so ready to sell their lands as they had been, and as Arab nationalism grew, it became easier to obtain popular support by declaring the land to be indefeasibly Arab.

In support of this view they were given considerable hope by the British promises and statements of policy in two wars. During World War I, when the British were fighting the Turks and, through T. E. Lawrence and General Allenby, mustering all the allies they could find among the Arab sheikdoms, the British High Commissioner in Cairo, Sir Henry Macmahon, had written a letter on October 24, 1915, to Hussein, then Sharif of Mecca and later King of Hedjaz. In this letter Macmahon promised on behalf of his government Arab independence in the Palestine region, except for the two districts of Mersine and Alexandrette and portions of Syria to the west of the district of Damascus that, as the letter stated, "cannot be said to be purely Arab." The British would later maintain that these exceptions included Palestine and also the territory Britain promised to France on May 16, 1916, in the secret Sykes-Picot Agreement (disclosed when the Bolshevik government of Russia in 1917 published the texts of secret treaties made among the Allies carving up other nations' territories). The Arabs, however, understood the British promises differently. One writer has pointed out that despite all the later British clarifications and disclaimers, if indeed Macmahon had meant to include Palestine in the exceptions, why did he not write "west of Amman" or of a point farther south?

At any rate the Macmahon letter, like the Balfour Declaration two years later, was ambiguous and was undoubtedly designed to be so because some of the same territory was being promised to three peoples, the Arabs, Jews, and French. Promises of independence linked with high moral purpose are made freely in times of stress, and France in 1917 joined in making them. The French Foreign Minister, Jules Cambon, also wrote a letter, which became known as the Cambon Declaration, on June 4, 1917, four months before the Balfour Declaration but similar to it. Cambon wrote to the representative of the Zionists, Nahum Sokolov: "You have wished to explain to me the project to which you are devoting your efforts and which has as a goal the development of an Israeli colonization of Palestine. You believe that if circumstances permit and the independence of the Holy Places is assured, it would be a work of justice and of reparation to help in the rebirth, under the protection of the allied powers, of a Jewish nationality on this territory from which the People of Israel were banished so many centuries ago.

"The French government, which entered the present war to defend a people unjustly attacked and which pursues the battle to assure the triumph of right over might, can only feel sympathy for your cause whose triumph is bound to that of the Allies."[8]

Hussein's vision of a united Arab kingdom under his rule was no more than a dream. Like all Arab leaders, he had many rivals, and when the British and French allies did business together to divide their influence in the Arab world, neither the Jews nor the Arabs, nor, for that matter, the Italian ally, who also had claims to make in the Middle East, were invited to be present.

But there was perhaps a moment at the end of World War I when some kind of Arab-Jewish compromise might have been reached. Following the issuing of the Balfour Declaration on November 2,

1917, Chaim Weizmann headed a Zionist delegation to Palestine to meet Prince Faisal, the son of King Hussein, near Aqaba. They agreed that Jews and Arabs must support each other at the coming peace conference if they were to have any chance to secure the aims of both parties. And at Versailles an agreement was duly drawn up and signed by Weizmann on behalf of the Zionist organization and by Faisal for the kingdom of Hedjaz on January 3, 1919, that might have led to the solution so many Jews and Arabs and Christians had been searching for. The document spoke plainly of the need for creating two states, one to be in Palestine, the other in the adjoining Arab territories; for mass immigration of the Jews into Palestine; for the protection of the Arab peasants and farmers there; and for technical and economic assistance to be supplied by the Jews for the benefit of the Arab population.*

This agreement, made with the necessity in mind of a common front at a peace conference run by and for the great powers, was con-

---

* The agreement declared: "His Royal Highness the Emir Faisal, representing and acting in the name of the Arab kingdom of the Hedjáz and Dr. Chaim Weizmann representing the Zionist organization and acting in its name, Taking into consideration the kinship and the ancient bonds existing between the Arabs and the Jewish people . . . [and wishing] to establish the closest collaboration possible in the development of the Arab state and of Palestine, and . . . to consolidate the good understanding that reigns between them have agreed on the following articles:

"Article 1. In everything that concerns their mutual relations and on the occasion of the negotiations to take place, the Arab state and Palestine will be inspired by a desire for understanding and reciprocal good will, and to this end Jewish and Arab representatives duly accredited will be appointed and maintained in the territory of the other state.

"Article 2. Immediately after the end of the deliberations of the peace conference the definitive frontiers of the Arab state and of Palestine will be fixed by a commission named following an accord between the two parties.

"Article 3. In the establishment of the . . . administration of Palestine all measures will be taken to guarantee the practical execution of the declaration of the British government of 2 November 1917 [The Balfour Declaration].

"Article 4. All necessary measures will be taken to encourage and stimulate the immigration of Jews into Palestine on a large scale. . . . It is agreed that in the execution of these measures, the protection of the rights of the peasants and Arab farmers will be assured and that these latter will be aided in the future in their economic development."

Article 5 provided for the free exercise of the various religions in the territory and for the free exercise of civil and political rights; Article 6 provided that sacred Muslim places would be under Muslim control; Article 7 for an economic commission of experts for the development of the region with the Zionists agreeing to furnish the Arabs with recommendations for such development and to help the Arab state obtain the means to exploit their natural resources and economic possibilities. Article 8 declared that both parties saw the need to act in complete accord and perfect harmony in all the above questions to be brought before the Peace Conference. And finally, Article 9 provided that any disagreements between the two parties should be submitted for arbitration to the British government.

firmed in a letter of March 6, 1919, from the Emir Faisal to Felix Frankfurter, then a prominent American Zionist and a member of the American delegation to the Paris Peace Conference. Faisal wrote: "We are convinced that the Arabs and Jews are closely related [sont des parents de race très proches], both of whom have been persecuted at the hands of forces stronger than they. But by a happy coincidence they have been permitted to take together the first step toward the realization of their national ideals. We Arabs, especially the intellectuals, regard the Zionist movement with the greatest sympathy. Our delegation at Paris knows exactly what proposals the Zionist delegation submitted yesterday at the Conference of Paris and they consider them moderate and well founded. We will do everything in our power to help in the success of your proposals. We wish to address to the Jews our cordial wishes of welcome on the occasion of their return to their country. . . . We will work together to reconstruct and revivify the Near East and our two movements complement one another. . . ."[9]

Faisal made it clear to the British that his premises of cooperation with the Zionists were based on the precondition of Arab independence. These were moments of reason and truth that were never to reappear. The Peace Conference disappointed both Arabs and Jews, as it did so many other peoples including the victorious Italians, for while it created Arab states, it also conferred authority over Arab territories on Britain and France, and in place of the harmoniously cooperating states foreseen by Hussein, Faisal, and the Zionists, came, following the Conference of San Remo and the unratified Treaty of Sèvres, the British and French mandates over Palestine and Syria along with an independent kingdom of Hedjaz under Hussein.* The mandate for Palestine repeated the provisions of the Balfour Declaration and the aim to establish a Jewish homeland in Palestine and then proceeded to give all administrative power to the British. The Jewish political organization in the country was advisory; effective control over Palestine's internal and external relations was placed entirely in the hands of the mandatory power. English, Ara-

* The British during World War I had conquered Damascus from the Turks, and according to promises made Faisal, it was there that an independent Arab government was to be established. Both Britain and France had declared their intention during the war to support Arab governments in Syria and Mesopotamia. Faisal was duly chosen as king, but after the French mandate was approved at San Remo, a French army drove him from Damascus and his throne. He was later elected King of Iraq, which he ruled for twelve years.

bic, and Hebrew were the three official languages and disputes were to be settled by the League of Nations, an organization that gradually withered away in the course of the treaty violations before World War II.

Both England and France had made enormous sacrifices to win the war. While they were far from seeking to make the world safe for democracy, they were intensely concerned with making it as secure and tolerable as possible for themselves. Faisal might address the Peace Conference in eloquent phrases on the subject of Arab aspirations, but the French asked dryly why the desert kingdom of Hedjaz should rule the sophisticated Syrians. What they meant by this was that Syria should be placed under French authority, and so it was. Palestine went to the British, who in their private deliberations at the Peace Conference agreed that no other power could do as well there as mandatory. It would not be long before the French would drive Faisal from Damascus and take over all of Syria.

What was meant by a Jewish homeland was never clearly defined and never intended to be. Balfour said he had not used the phrase to mean the establishment of a Jewish state because a state would have to be developed by natural evolutionary means and could not be delivered in any agreement.* Chaim Weizmann, when asked by the American Secretary of State, Robert Lansing, if he had a state of Israel in mind, said he did not, only the free immigration of Jews and a protectorate under either Britain or the United States with an administration that might or might not be Jewish. Premier Orlando of Italy, too, professed himself as favoring a Jewish national center, as did Woodrow Wilson, but everyone was treading cautiously. Too precise a definition of homeland, if it meant a sovereign Jewish state, would lose all Arab, as well as British and French, support. Immigration was the crucial issue, and if the Jews could immigrate freely, it would not be long before the demand for such a state might be made with some likelihood of its being accepted by the great powers. The British had discovered in the course of World War I, as an official memorandum from the Foreign Office to the Cabinet pointed out, that Palestine was the strategic buffer of Egypt,

---

* In an official interpretation of British policy with regard to the mandate the then Colonial Secretary, Winston Churchill, while denying that the Arabs or their culture would be placed at a disadvantage, nevertheless affirmed that the Jews were in Palestine "as of right and not on sufferance," and that Palestine was a place that could "become a center in which the Jewish people as a whole may take . . . an interest and a pride." (Ronald Sanders, *Israel: The View from Massada*, p. 133.)

a part of the world Britain was convinced was vital to her strategic position.[10] To buttress the security of the passage to India and the Far East, she needed a peaceful and friendly population of both Jews and Arabs, especially Arabs.

Arab chieftains other than Prince Faisal and King Hussein immediately showed signs of resistance to the plans for admitting large-scale Jewish immigration, as observers like Lord Curzon noted during the British discussions at the Peace Conference. These warnings were borne out when the first of what would be a long series of Arab riots against the Jews occurred in 1921. Despite the statesman-like documents about a shared living space, Jews were an easy target for any Arab leader disposed to rouse a following against them and the mandatory power. Nor were Arab fears imaginary. It was true that what the Zionists were demanding, which always included the right to large-scale immigration, would inevitably lead, over a period of time, to Jewish domination of a land where Arabs would no longer be a majority. And this was so not only because of the numbers of Jews who might come in but also by reason of the manifest superiority of their scientific methods of farming, and what was wholly new in the land, a dedicated, self-sacrificing, communal way of life that was to make the kibbutzim unique. Collectivist settlements of a similar kind had been tried before, especially in Canada and in the United States, but they had almost always died out as the early enthusiasm faded. But in Israel this communal experiment had an extraordinary success. People worked not only for themselves but for one another on behalf of a classless community, owning no private property except a few personal belongings. They turned desolate, unhealthy, often dangerous settlements into flourishing garden spots, and they demonstrated year after year that the stereotype of the money-loving, self-seeking Jew did not apply to immigrants to the Holy Land.

Although only 3.3 percent of the population of Israel in 1967 was in kibbutzim, a considerable proportion of the leaders of Israel had spent years in a kibbutz. It was a spiritual as well as an economic and social experience, and it had a great role in the morale of the society and the army. In this respect, too, the Jewish settlements were in marked contrast to the farms and way of life of the Arabs. On the one side were luxuriant crops, an efficient, literate people bringing with them modern medicine, housing, higher learning, and modern techniques in all their forms; on the other side, a people of another century, fallen from their time of greatness, undernourished, often diseased, illiterate, impoverished, with the widest cleavages in their class structure. In order to achieve the Zionists' purposes, however, the Jews would need more and more land, and that could only be had from the Arab proprietors glad enough to be rid of it until the refusal to sell became a protest against the alienation of a sacred soil, of a *patrie* that had never existed in reality but that the Arabs came to feel more and more must one day come into independent being. As Faisal had said, both peoples had known persecution at the hands of stronger powers, but soon, in the eyes of each, it became the other that had caused all the suffering.

In the 1939 White Paper it seemed as though the Arabs had won a decisive battle in the struggle, but the White Paper was written before the death camps began their operations. After World War II the British, holding on to their key strategic positions as best they could, strove to carry out the provisions limiting Jewish immigration, and in the course of that effort many new variations of the *St. Louis* and *Struma* voyages occurred. Fifty-seven transports with the Jewish survivors of Hitler's Europe on board were intercepted by the British navy, rammed, boarded, and captured in an effort to keep Jews in excess of the quotas from reaching Palestine. One ship was blown up by the Jewish underground to prevent the refugees from being returned. Only 1500 Jews a month were permitted to enter by the Labour government that had come to power in 1945 at a time when almost all the hundreds of thousands of Jews who had survived the death camps were trying to reach Palestine. But morally, how could the war fought to end a system of savage violence be followed by herding the survivors of its horrors into new concentration camps, under the aegis of the power professing to be motivated by the transcendent principles that had brought it into combat? How could a war fought against National Socialist barbarism lead to the arrests and manhandling of the tattered survivors of Hitler's gas chambers? The concentration camps that Britain erected in Cyprus were far more humane, no doubt, than the Nazi camps, but they were used to imprison the survivors among the same harried people who had died in the extermination camps. When Jews were killed, as some of them were in the police actions Britain undertook against them, their deaths were a bizarre replay of measures everyone in Britain and the West thought they had been fighting against.

The Jews were convinced the British were at bottom pro-Arab not only in their quota system but in their administration of Palestine. They thought Arab excesses were treated differently from Jewish reprisals against them. In one case they accused the British of turning over four Jewish prisoners to an Arab mob that killed and mutilated them. Jews complained that the British sold arms at the end of the mandate to Arabs but refused to sell to them. They also claimed that the British obviously held them collectively responsible for Jewish terrorist activities. In one incident British soldiers rioted in the streets of Natanya and Be'er, smashing windows and beating up any Jews they encountered. Almost all the Jewish leaders in Tel Aviv and Jerusalem, 2600 of them, were arrested shortly before the bombing of the King David Hotel, and Ben-Gurion escaped only because he was not there. One British general ordered that the troops take action against the terrorists that would demonstrate their disgust, adding: "I understand that these measures will create difficulty for the troops, but I am certain that if my reasons are explained to them they will understand their duty and will punish the Jews in the maner that race dislikes the most—by hitting them in the pocketbook."[11]

The British attempt at continuing the mandate was countered on every front: by public outcry against their tactics; by an intergovernmental commission formed under American pressure urging partition; by armed force and terrorism. The resistance ranged from that of the fanatical Stern gang, many of whose members were oriental Jews, the Irgun, with a good many Polish migrants, to the Haganah, formed as a self-protection body in 1920 with an elite corps, the Palmach. The Stern gang specialized in killings; the Irgun in destructions. A mixed group of terrorists was responsible for the murders at Deir Yassin and of the Swedish emissary from the UN, Count Bernadotte, who had proposed a compromise solution for Palestine rejected by both Jews and Arabs and who was shot down in the streets of Jerusalem. It was the Irgun that blew up the King David Hotel, the center of the British army administration. By 1947, however, even the Haganah was engaged in sabotage and blew up two ships in the harbor of Haifa. Zionists of almost all persuasions were singlemindedly determined to get the British out and to found a Jewish state in Palestine. A total of 84,000 Jews had illegally been brought out of Europe to Palestine in a kind of underground railway run by Jewish groups. For the Zionists, extremists and moderates both, the bottleneck of British limitations on immigration had to be broken, and to this end every weapon had to be used. The Zionist paramilitary formations were mainly formed of men trained in the

British army, to which they had flocked in the course of World War II (26,000 had fought for the British compared with 8000 Arabs), and they wanted to hear nothing more of compromises that would keep Jews out of the only country they could go to. The Arabs, too, had their terrorist organizations, formed mainly of Palestinian and Syrian forces, which blew up and killed Jews and British impartially as the Irgun and Stern groups killed Arabs and British.

After World War II the plan for a divided Palestine had become widely accepted as the best solution for both Arab and Jew in the councils of Europe and the United States. This was a compromise, and compromises are always highly thought of in reasonable circles. A divided Palestinian region was implicit in the Faisal-Weizmann agreement, and it had a respectable advocate in the Peel Report of 1937, a British document that recommended the creation of a small Jewish state and an Arab state consisting of Transjordan and the hill country of Palestine with a British mandate over Jerusalem and Galilee. After the issuing of the White Paper, however, no one again had spoken plainly in formal documents of the establishment of a Jewish state until the Zionist Biltmore Conference held in New York in 1942 as the exterminations were beginning in the Eastern camps. What the Zionist sought, said Ben-Gurion at the Biltmore Conference, was the establishment of a Jewish commonwealth after the war. He did not say "state," although that is what he meant.

The idea both of partition and of a sovereign Jewish state had long been popular in the United States, although Franklin Roosevelt was not one of its supporters. During the war he would permit no criticism of Britain by the Jews despite the White Paper that shocked many of his close advisors. The World Conference on Zionism held in 1945, however, called on the British to announce without delay the creation of a Jewish state, a step Mr. Roosevelt's successor, President Truman, came to accept, and the Anglo-American Commission, which made its report in 1946, recommended much the same solution of the Palestinian problem that was eventually adopted by the UN in 1947. Other theoretically reasonable solutions such as a divided state bridged by an economic union, or autonomy within an Arab-Jewish state, were bound to founder on the hard rock of irreconcilable Arab and Jewish goals. The Arabs were increasingly determined to keep their numerical predominance in Palestine, which meant keeping down Jewish immigration. The whole purpose of the Zionist movement was the opposite—to have one part of the world where Jews might enter freely, where as one writer has put it, they would be free to have hooked noses and bandy legs. But that observation was made before the holocaust, and what the Jews needed after a catastrophe of such dimensions was a place where they were not a minority, where they could recover a collective persona and their membership in the human race, where they might be accepted and admired or hated or rejected as other peoples who had a state and a nationality were. They had built up their numbers in Palestine slowly and unsteadily, but the number of Jews there had risen despite Turkish and British prohibitions of immigration. Turkish edicts had not been difficult to circumvent; migrants could always get to Palestine by way of Egypt and bribery. After World War I and until 1924 a total of some 30,000 Jews had migrated to Palestine. By 1925, when an additional 34,386 Jews had moved there to escape anti-Semitic measures in Poland, Tel Aviv alone had a Jewish population of 30,000. But then the Arabs reacted. Jews were slaughtered at the Wailing Wall, and after that incident far fewer entered the country. Nevertheless, because the pressures on their leaving some part of the world never ceased, by 1928 they numbered 151,000. Although in 1932 only 4075 Jews migrated to Palestine, in 1933, when Hitler came to power, 30,327 emigrated from Germany alone. In 1934 the figure rose to 42,359, and the year the Nuremburg racial laws were promulgated (1935) the number went up to 61,854. The total number of Jews in Palestine was some 200,000 in 1933, a figure that doubled in the next few years as Jews rushed to get out of Europe.[12]

At the end of World War II hundreds of thousands of Jews would be knocking at the gates, if only they could reach the gates. A total of 100,000 Jews were in DP camps alone, and how many of them, and of Jews in the rest of Europe, were trying to emigrate may be estimated from the number—750,000—who did go to Israel between 1945 and 1954 when the barriers were lowered.

The British decision to leave Palestine was only partly of their own making, although it was in line with their other withdrawals from the outposts of empire. When they departed from Palestine, however, they did so with less grace than they displayed elsewhere. On the day they left, May 14, 1948, no preparation had been made for the transfer of power, and the Arabs were free to march into the state the UN had approved and Britain had ruled. Now 600,000 Jews were in Israeli Palestine, and in and around their new country 30 million Arabs were intent on driving them out.

Wars Won and Battles Lost

Britain had long had considerable interests in the area, interests that if not permanent were certainly long-lived, and they did not disappear with the British troops. Like the French in Algeria, the British had brought amenities to Palestine—roads, the first telephone and automobile in 1917, political advice, and a police force—and they left only under duress. They had sought to meet the terror of the Irgun with harsh reprisals, and some of the manifestos they issued in the course of the running battle they had with the Jewish terrorists were not very different from those of the National Socialists. After Jewish terrorists had blown up a street in Jerusalem, the British League is said to have issued the following statement: "On the 22 of February 1948, we attacked the center of the Jewish quarter of Jerusalem with high explosive, inflicting heavy losses on the vermin; more than 200 dead and 200 wounded, all Jews. We are proud to announce that no distinction has been made between the cowardly gangsters of the Haganah and the Sternist assassins. Jewish women and children, young and old, will be destroyed. We will finish the work that Hitler began."*

But the memories of nations when it is expedient can be short, and after the Israeli repulse of the Arab attacks in 1948 came a period of cool but not unfriendly relations with Britain that culminated in the quasi-alliance at the time of Suez. And by then other major changes had occurred in the policies of the major powers with regard to Israel. Russia and the Communist bloc, including China, were now pro-Arab, as they sought to move into the Muslim and Mediterranean world where Britain had once ruled. The United States, preoccupied as it had to be with increasing Soviet penetration into the Arab world, continued to try to hold the balance of power between Israel and the Arabs as even as possible. France under de Gaulle slowly shifted her markedly pro-Israel policy toward the Arab side, as de Gaulle tried to upgrade his country's minor position as a world power and to play a role as the leader of a third force mediating between East and West.† Only three years after the attack on Port Said, France's vote was cast in the UN for a resolution favoring the return of Arab refugees to Palestine, although Israel had asked her to abstain.

* Translated from Paul Giniewski: *Le Sionisme d'Abraham à Dayan*, p. 499.
† In addition, de Gaulle was not unaware that the oil resources of the Middle East were of increasing importance to France and all Western Europe.

As time went on, the Israelis lost almost everything they had won in the 1956 war. Eisenhower joined the Soviet bloc and that of their friends in the United Nations to insist on Israel's withdrawal from Sinai, the Gaza Strip (which had never been part of Egypt until 1948, when its army succeeded in occupying it), the Straits of Tiran, and Sharm el Sheik. The President, pursuing his hope of collective security, favored the imposition of sanctions including the prohibition of sending aid even from private persons in the United States if Israeli troops did not withdraw. Senator William Knowland, a Republican, asked why, then, sanctions could not be demanded against the Soviet Union after its occupation of Hungary? The answer came from Henry Cabot Lodge, American ambassador to the United Nations, who said the United States must take account of the facts of life—which was true but not quite in line with the administration's lofty policy of applying the law equally to friend and foe.

Ben-Gurion resisted withdrawing the troops as long as he could, and before they left he succeeded in wringing some concessions from both the Arabs and the "peaceloving" powers, as they were represented in the United Nations. Sinai, the Gaza Strip, and Sharm el Sheik were to be occupied by an international force, the United Nations Emergency Force (UNEF), which Israel refused to permit on her territory, and Israel also received international guarantees that the Straits of Tiran would remain open to her shipping.* In an unpublished agreement between Dag Hammarskjöld and Nasser made in November 1956, Israel also was assured that the United Nations would not withdraw the UNEF from Egyptian territory on the sole demand of Egypt. The agreement declared that if either side were to act unilaterally, an exchange of views would be called for to harmonize their differences.[13]

Thus the boundaries were restored as they were before the Suez crisis, and the forces of international law and order could rejoice that aggression had borne no fruits for the victors, but only for Nasser.

Other factors, too, returned to the status quo. The raids began again, not from the Gaza Strip now policed by the UNEF but from Jordan and Syria. Egypt's credit skyrocketed after Suez in much of the Arab world. Her borders, patrolled by the UNEF, were also safe from Israeli retaliations so Nasser could aid any infiltration from

---

* See Chapter 3, p. 57.

Jordan and Syria and Lebanon without incurring the reprisal raids the Israelis again adopted to stop the forays.

Jewish settlements near the Jordanian and Syrian borders were bombed and shelled, kibbutzim continued to be raided by the guerrillas, bombs exploded in the streets of Israeli cities, buses were blown up by hand grenades and mines, and Israeli protests to the United Nations were in vain. No government acknowledged responsibility for the raids or admitted to arming the guerrillas, and the only form of protest that worked against the fedayeen was direct action exerted either on the spot or against their bases.

Israeli policy was to let incidents accumulate and then to retaliate with a large-scale raid often involving tanks and planes against Syria or Jordan. Syria, which had a much shorter border with Israel and had its artillery dug in on the Golan Heights, was not as easy a target for these raids as was Jordan; it could shell kibbutzim with relative impunity against reprisals on the ground. When the Israelis counterattacked, they had to do so with relatively massive actions, and their reprisals there and in Jordan gave rise to impassioned protests on the part of the Arabs and to stern condemnations in the Security Council, where Israel could count on few friends after the cooling of her relations with France and the British reversion to a kind of negative neutrality. Israel's main support was in the United States, but the Americans, too, joined in the resolutions condemning the Israeli raids which they and many other speakers in the United Nations called out of proportion to the incidents that had provoked them.

The division between Right and Left sharpened in 1958 in the Arab countries, but it was blurred by local feuds. In Syria a nationalist-socialist group, the temporarily pro-Nasser Ba'ath party, took power, and Syria joined with Egypt in establishing the United Arab Republic. In Iraq young King Faisal, just out of Harrow, was murdered along with almost his entire family and the pro-Western Prime Minister Nuri Pasha in an uprising that shattered the alliance with Jordan and the other countries of the Baghdad Pact. General Abdul Karim Kassem, head of the new regime, promptly made a defensive alliance with Nasser, although a few months later pro-Nasser elements in the country attempted a coup which Kassem had to put down with the help of local Communists. Lebanon, with its precarious balance of power between Christians and Muslims and other contending factions, feared a leftist, pro-Nasser coup, and the government asked for American help. President Eisenhower, on the alert to counter what might have been a Communist-dominated revolution, sent in 10,000 marines who remained in the country until a new coalition government was formed.

Nasser, increasingly dependent on the Soviet Union, became the symbol of the "progressive" antimonarchical Arab forces despite his anti-Communist measures within Egypt. The search for Arab unity could only take the practical form of small-scale alliance or federations: the United Arab Republic was joined by the Kingdom of Yemen at the same time the alliance and short-lived federation of monarchical Jordan and Iraq fell apart. Jordan and its King Hussein were anti-Nasser, but a powerful opposition group of Palestinian refugees in the country was pro-Nasser, anti-Hussein, and pro-Moscow.

Between the monarchies, too, there were feuds. Ibn Saud of Saudi Arabia had been a hereditary enemy of the Hashemite family of Jordan. He had been succeeded by his son, Saud IV, but the oil-rich land was also rich in corruption and when Saud's brother, Faisal, who was Prime Minister, attempted to introduce a measure of austerity to the country, he was replaced by the King himself. Relations with Egypt had become strained when the Egyptian monarchy was overthrown and Nasser was elected President. In 1962, when civil war broke out in Yemen, Egypt and Saudi Arabia took opposite sides and remained there after Saud IV was deposed and Faisal became King.

Some twelve guerrilla organizations grew out of and mirrored the contradictions in the Arab world. El Fatah, schooled to some degree in the doctrines of Mao and Ho Chi Minh on partisan warfare, had its base in Jordan. Its views, congenial to the Ba'ath party, were echoed by the Damascus radio which told how half the American air force had been destroyed by the North Vietnamese. The Palestine Liberation Army, which by a revealing mistranslation had been called the Salvation Army in the war of 1948, was under the control of Ahmed Shukeiry of the Palestine Liberation Organization, supported by and centered in Egypt with units in Jordan. Like El Fatah, it was a threat not only to the Israelis but also to the throne of King Hussein, who relied for the security of his regime on the "reactionary" orthodox bedouin, who had placed him in power and kept him there. In the view of many of these Palestinians, Jordan like Israel was part of Palestine and belonged in a separate state without Hussein and without the Jews.

Anti-Israeli-ism was the one issue the Arabs could agree on. The

Ba'ath movement in Syria came to include pro-Maoist and pro-Castro groups, who both professed a deep admiration for Che Guevara while their sentiments toward Nasser warmed or cooled depending on their estimates of his true revolutionary fervor.

In 1963 the Ba'ath party of Iraq overthrew the government of General Kassem, who was executed along with a number of Communist supporters. Kassem's successor, President Aref, soon replaced the Ba'ath socialists in the government with more nationalist, pro-Arab Federation officials, and Iraq again drew closer to Nasser. A month later the Syrian Ba'ath party drove out the pro-Nasser Damascus government, and the rickety alliance of Syria and Egypt collapsed. Iraq, in addition to its factional rivalries, had a tribal rebellion on its hands, as the Kurds continued a large-scale revolt. Thirty-six plots against one government or another were incubated in Iraq between 1958 and 1965. Two coups were successful, and both of them were accompanied by bloody massacres.

In the midst of all these changes the Russians proceeded stolidly to build up their military and political influence, ignoring local Communist parties and permitting them to be flushed down the drain as the Soviets pursued their major drive to replace United States and British influence in the Arab countries. Whether under Khrushchev or his successors, Brezhnev and Kosygin, Soviet Near Eastern policy never wavered. They dealt evenhandedly with Nasser (whom they made "Hero of the Soviet Union" and presented with the Order of Lenin), with a moderate Ba'athist like General Hafiz when he came to power in Syria in 1964, and with the left-wing officers who staged a coup in 1966 and succeeded him. In that year the Soviet Union made Syria a loan of $250 million and agreed to build a dam on the Euphrates while they continued to pump economic and military assistance into Egypt. They used in Egypt the same tactics they had followed in Algeria: they permitted the dissolution of the Egyptian Communist party and the individual members were ordered to support Nasser and join the Arab Socialist Union. This was part of the technique of wooing the Third World—to support national liberation movements against the West and suspend the local Communist movements, expedients for which the Chinese Communists professed scorn. It was their uncompromisingly pro-revolutionary advocacy that gained the Chinese converts in Ba'ath and other left-wing movements, and their intransigence in turn prodded the Russians to greater efforts in their economic and military aid.

The Arab divisions into oil-rich and poor-desert states, into monarchies and republics, into forces roughly representing Right and Left, and Nasser's dynamism on behalf of "progressive" policies brought a new war, an Arab war. In 1962 Nasser took the part of the republican government of Yemen, where Saudi Arabia sought to support a monarchy. Thousands of Egyptian troops with tanks and air support were sent to Yemen, but here again victory would elude them. The number of Egyptian troops rose, but despite reinforcements and superior equipment including the only air force in the region, Nasser could not bring the war to a victorious end. What he did succeed in doing was to bring his country close to bankruptcy; the costs of supporting a large army in Yemen plus the high price of his domestic policy of heavy rearmament and social reform were far above Egypt's capacity to support. Prices had risen 40 percent in a few years. In 1965 Nasser had to sell thirty-seven tons of gold in Switzerland to pay for the support of his 50,000 troops in Yemen, and the deeper he became involved in his costly ventures at home and abroad, the more dependent he became on the Soviet Union. In 1965, 13 percent of the Egyptian gross national production went into the army. Expenditures rose from 250 million pounds for the army in 1965 to 300 million a year in 1967. The population continued to grow at the rate of one million a year, and nine out of ten Egyptians continued to live at a subsistence level; anything bought other than food and clothing was a luxury.

Nasser was deeply in trouble. In 1965 the United States stopped supplying free wheat which had provided bread for a majority of the population. Within the Arab world, when he failed to match his words with action against Israel, he was pilloried for killing Arabs instead of Jews and promising far more than he showed signs of being able or willing to fulfill. Such criticisms played no small role in his decision in 1967 to bring Israel down and to restore his role as pan-Arab leader.

During these years only one Arab voice spoke on behalf of a compromise settlement with the Israelis. It belonged to President Bourguiba of Tunisia, who proposed in 1965 that the Arabs recognize Israel on condition that she return to the 1947 boundaries, a suggestion that was called treason in Syria and found no echo in Israel.

The Refugees and the Fedayeen

The fedayeen came from the countries bordering Israel, but their base was among the refugees driven from their land or who had fled during the 1948 war. How many of these refugees there were is not easy to determine. Glubb Pasha, who led the Arab Legion of Jordan up to the mid-1950s, said there were a million. Other sources put the figure at some 800,000, the United Nations at 1,300,000. The Israelis said the number was about 600,000. The difficulty with all the figures is that they must be guesses. Subterfuges were constantly invented by the refugee population in the camps to keep the figures high: when people died, their deaths were not recorded so the rations of the deceased could be used by the survivors; women produced babies but also borrowed them to obtain increased rations; and the refugees were joined by other Arabs with dubious claims to refugee status but who chose to live on the pitiful dole of less than 10 cents a day allowed for their upkeep. The rations—providing some 1500 calories daily—were under what was needed for a minimal subsistence, but nevertheless the refugee colonies grew and not many of their members were absorbed into the economies and societies of the host lands. Rich Arab states like Saudi Arabia, Iraq, and Kuwait contributed nothing to their support, which came largely from the United States, Britain, and Canada. It was widely believed in Israel that the refugees were deliberately kept in a state of hunger, apathy, and despair by their own leaders and by the Arab countries that might have absorbed them to provide irresistible motives for their return to the lands they had left or had been driven from, as well as to have a constant witness before the world to the tragic results of the creation of the Israeli state. At least half of these refugees were living in camps in Jordan where they mainly worked at nothing, although some had minor jobs and a few were integrated into Jordanian life and others into the guerrilla forces. To their numbers, some 243,000 were added after the 1967 war.[14]

The causes of their flight, like everything else in the Arab-Israeli quarrels, were in dispute. The Arabs said they had been driven out as a matter of Israeli policy as well as by fear of repetitions of the murders at Deir Yassin. The Jews said they had tried to persuade many of them to stay, assuring them of their personal safety, but that the Arabs had succumbed to the propaganda urging them to flee so a free-fire zone could be set up where the Arab armies could wage war only against Israelis, and that the refugees were told they would return in a few weeks with the victorious armies of the Arab coalition.

Scarcely any Arabs were left in what had once been predominantly Arab cities like Haifa and Jaffa, although towns like Nazareth and Acre remained Arab centers within Israel. Ben-Gurion had certainly urged the Arabs to stay after the massacre at Deir Yassin, and the Arab forces had just as certainly urged them to leave. In July 1948 Israel had announced its willingness to permit 100,000 Arab residents to return, giving them until the end of August to do so, but the International Red Cross reported that all but 30,000 were afraid to go back.* In any event, the refugee problem continued to fester whatever Israel protested were her good intentions. And there was no question of Israel's being disposed to tolerate too large an Arab population within her borders. The dangers to security seemed too evident to them, and Arabs have never been permitted to join the Israeli armed forces even when they would like to do so. There is also the problem of the birth rate. Arabs tend to have large families, the Israelis small ones, and over a period of time the Jews would again be a minority in their own country if all the Arabs who claim they lost their land were to return. Again, from the Israeli point of view, many of the Arabs who fled may have had good reason to leave, and to permit the return of people with doubtful loyalties would be another grave danger to a state surrounded by sworn enemies. Israel holds that it can bear no responsibility for people who left despite pleas that they remain and that what property was taken over was deliberately abandoned. Israelis point out, too, that Jews have been displaced from Algeria, Iraq, and Yemen, 200,000 or more of them, and there is no disposition on the part of these countries either to take them back or to pay restitution to them. They do not mention internal Israeli economic factors, but they, too, doubtless played a role. Israel was experiencing a slow economic growth rate and relatively high unemployment; an increased Arab population would only add to such difficulties.

* The Arab fears were not groundless. Even respectable Israeli formations could sometimes use terrorist tactics that would not convince the Arabs of their benevolent intentions. At the time of the Suez war, refugees stated that Israeli troops driving into the Gaza Strip at Khan Yunis killed some 275 civilians after all resistance had ceased during searches for Arabs who had concealed weapons. And at the beginning of the invasion of Sinai, the Israeli border police came into Kafr Kassim on the Jordanian border at 4:30 in the afternoon to announce a curfew to begin only a half hour later, at five o'clock. This did not allow time enough to warn Arabs working the fields, and as they returned on foot, bicycles, and carts, the police shot and killed forty-seven people, including children. The incident caused an uproar in Israel, as it did in the Arab countries. Eleven of the police were tried; eight were found guilty and three acquitted. Those found guilty were sentenced to prison terms, a major to seventeen years. Similar incidents occurred in Rafah in the Gaza Strip in a search for fedayeen in a refugee camp of 32,000 people when the Israelis ordered the people to gather at screening points. Again the time was short; some of the refugees ran and were fired on by Israeli soldiers. A neutral observer said 111 Arabs were killed. (Lieutenant General E. L. M. Burns, *Between Arab and Israel*, p. 304.)

The arguments on both sides are made with passion, but when emotions are discounted, a large number of people still remain without homes they once had. And however humble these dwellings may actually have been, with exile and one-room huts to live in in a foreign country the past takes on an aura it may never have had in reality. Huts become houses, houses palaces, small arid plots of land luxuriant fields. But still the facts remain—these places, whether or not of fantasied size and beauty, were once theirs and are theirs no longer. It may well be that if the refugees—half of them are under eighteen —had been absorbed into the economies of the Arab states with unused lands—Iraq, for example—where they could have been resettled, they would be more ready to accept their situation. This has happened in the case of German refugees driven out mainly from East Prussia and the Sudetenland of Czechoslovakia who have more or less accepted their exile in a West Germany where they live well, many of them far better than they did in their lost homeland. But the Arab refugees have not fared so well. They live miserably, without jobs, brooding over their lot, and their only way out, or so it seems to them and so they are told by one another and by their hosts, is to win back the land that is rightfully theirs. Unfortunately for them, each time they have tried to accomplish this end they have succeeded only in adding more refugees from the state of Israel and the territories it occupies.

These refugees were the core of the infiltrating guerrillas, although they were joined by contingents from the armies of Syria, Jordan, and Egypt. Organized under extraterritorial organizations like El Fatah, the partisans took a high toll of lives and property. The whole border could not be guarded by Israel, some infiltrators could always get across, and in Israel itself the guerrillas were not always among the enemy because many Arabs living there sympathized with their missions. The fedayeen were the advance guard of the war to come, the war against the invader the Arabs promised continually over the radio, in the press, and in the public announcements of their leaders.

"We Will Liquidate Israel"

The Arabs had reason to be confident. The Soviet Union was supplying them, above all Egypt, with the latest and some of the best Russian equipment—tanks with infrared devices that permitted them to spot the enemy at night, that were faster and more heavily gunned than anything the Israelis might be able to buy or having bought, improve. The Arabs, readily given to large-scale propaganda victories (T. E. Lawrence said of Arabs that they knew no shades but black and white, only extremes), boasted of their growing strength and became increasingly convinced that the old stereotype of the Jew was still the true one. Jews could not fight, they were cowards, they had been successful in 1948 only because of the failure of the then corrupt governments of Egypt and her allies, and they had won in 1956 because the Egyptians had had their forces deployed along the canal to meet the threat of the Anglo-French attack. Then, too, in that war Israel had had the assistance of two great powers to win victories that would have been impossible had she fought on her own. It was a plausible story, and millions of Arabs believed it. The lost territory would be regained. Soviet Russia was a powerful ally, the armaments she was supplying were very different from the cast-off planes and out-of-date tanks and guns furnished by the Western powers.

The use of words like "imperialist" and "fascist aggressors" out of the Soviet lexicon became part of Nasser's political vocabulary. In an address at Al-Mansoura in May 1960 he declared: "Our battle today is a great battle. . . . We must mobilize our forces to wipe out imperialism and Zionism."[15] Other speeches continued in this vein, and two years later, speaking before the National Congress of Popular Forces, he said: "Imperialist intrigue went to the extent of seizing a part of the Arab territory of Palestine . . . the aim being to establish a military fascist regime which cannot exist except by military threats. The insistence of our people on liquidating the Palestinian aggression on a part of the Palestine land is a determination to liquidate one of the most dangerous pockets of imperialist resistance against the struggle of the peoples."[16]

Kamel Rifat, a member of Nasser's Presidential Council, told the Palestinian Student Congress: "The Palestinian tragedy is an outcome of an imperialist Zionist conspiracy designed to wipe out Arabism and to prevent Arab unity. Palestine will not be recovered by words but by force of arms."[17]

The Israelis carefully recorded the Arab pronouncements. They knew that they were propaganda, designed for an audience unused to anything in the denunciation of an enemy but that which demanded an end to him. Nevertheless, the promises of death and destruction were part of the arsenal of war and terror, and Arab armies and the fedayeen had used weapons more lethal than slogans before in the never-ending struggle with Israel. Threats of extermination were not new; since the founding of the Israeli state they had been part of the arsenal unlimbered against it in Cairo, Amman, Damascus, Baghdad, wherever Arab spokesmen were heard. One Arab leader promised: "A momentous massacre which will be spoken of like the Mongolian massacres and the crusades."[18] It was a refrain echoed from country to country and repeated year after year.

Nasser might appeal to the leftist sentiments of the "progressive" Arab parties with his use of Soviet slogans and his obvious ability to obtain large quantities of weapons from the Eastern bloc, but he never lost sight of his mission to create Arab unity out of warring factions that could be united only for the common purpose of driving the Israelis into the sea, a goal the Soviet union very likely did not seek. Russia provided planes and tanks and rockets, military advisors and training in Eastern bloc centers, but she would not supply Syria or Jordan with SAM II missiles with which they might unleash a war on their own terms. Russia would build up Arab armaments to a considerable and dangerous point, but Israeli observers were doubtful that the Kremlin sought the destruction of Israel, even though that is what the Arab radio in Cairo and Damascus and other news sources repeatedly promised. Nasser had to provide leadership for this Arab world accustomed to high political camp, and he did so with flaming words but with few matching actions.

The Arab propaganda was beamed to people with a long tradition of veneration for rhetoric and political high notes. The broadcasts and news reports varied little from year to year and from country to country. Nasser said in 1961: "We will act to realize Arab solidarity and the closing of ranks that will eventually put an end to Israel. . . . We will liquidate her and imperialism in our land. . . ."[19] A year before, Radio Cairo declared on March 17: "Israel is a crime that must be gotten rid of to the last vestige. Only in this way will we solve the problem and eliminate the cancer in the Arab homeland."[20]

Radio Amman said on June 16, 1961: "We see in Israel a plague that must be rooted out," and Musa Nasir, Jordanian Foreign Minister, declared on January 19, 1961: "The liquidation of Israel is the joint task of all Arabs."

Prime Minister Kassem of Iraq had said in March 1960: "We have made two strides forward and are about to make a third. Our fourth step will be the destruction of the so-called Israel."[21]

Nasser, speaking in Alexandria on August 11, 1963, told soldiers returning from Yemen: "The armed forces are preparing to restore the rights of the Palestinian people because the battle of Palestine in 1948 is a shame to all the Arab nations . . . therefore we must prepare to face Israel, Zionism and imperialism which backs Israel."[22]

The Cairo home service, monitored by the BBC on February 14, 1964, reported an interview with Nasser wherein he was asked whether there was any hope of settling the dispute with Israel. Nasser answered: "It seems that a second war in Palestine is inevitable . . . our Arab people have been living in Palestine for thousands of years. One million have been forced out, how can we tolerate this crime?" Question: "Does this mean war with Israel, sir?" Nasser: "We have always been at war with Israel and Israel has always been the aggressor. All past aggression such as the Suez war which you yourself witnessed and covered for your paper were engineered by Israel."[23]

On New Year's Day in 1964 a Cairo paper, Al Gomhouriya, printed the following: "The fact that another year has been added to our lives is unimportant. What is important is that we can shorten by one year the lives of our enemies. . . . But shortening the life of Israel by one year will add to the pride and glory of every Arab. . . ."[24]

In July of the same year Nasser told the graduating class of cadets of the United Arab Air Force: "The war between ourselves and Israel cannot be avoided because Israel is the aggressor." Israel, he said, had won in 1948 because it could get weapons from the West while Egypt had had no opportunity to obtain them and Egyptian tanks were vulnerable to any shell fired by the superior weapons the Israelis had been able to buy. Then he went on to say: "The Liberation of Palestine can be realized by deeds not by words. We do not face Israel alone, we face Israel and those who stand behind her."[25]

This was the talk while the fedayeen raids continued, and Israel conducted its reprisals. El Fatah dynamited roads and houses, infiltrating mainly from the long border between Jordan and Israel but training their formations in Syria where the government approved of their activities far more than did Hussein, who had to bear the brunt of the retaliatory raids as well as the caustic criticisms of the Palestinian leaders of the fedayeen.

Israel by 1964 had completed its oft-delayed project to divert part of the waters of the Jordan for irrigation of the Negev, a plan that had long been opposed not only by the Arabs but also by the United States, which favored an international construction project for the benefit of Jordan and Syria as well as Israel. With the Arab countries regarding themselves as still at war with Israel and Israel's well-founded doubts of the feasibility of such well-intentioned but unrealistic proposals, Israeli engineers had gone forward with a system of dams and water courses on Israeli territory. In 1964, at a summit meeting, Arab leaders decided on their own ambitious counterplan to divert the headwaters of the Jordan by way of its affluents lying in Syria and Jordan. This project, if successful, would deprive Israel of water essential to it, and the Israeli Chief of Staff, General Rabin, and General Dayan declared she would not permit it to be carried out. The Arab plans, for a number of reasons, including the Israeli warning, did not proceed very rapidly, and Nasser, as his detractors in the Arab countries pointed out, did nothing whatever to counter the Israeli threat. Syrian papers began to taunt him again on the wide differences between his speeches and what he actually did, saying he could fight other Arabs in Yemen while he only made warlike pronouncements against Israel. When President Bourguiba of Tunisia proposed the recognition of Israel in 1965, Nasser joined in the chorus of condemnation of such a notion, declaring that the Arabs would never accept a political solution of the Palestine problem. Bourguiba contented himself with saying that those who rejected his proposal should come up with a better solution, but no other Arab chieftain had any solution but war as far as their public pronouncements went.

High-ranking Soviet and Egyptian officials, including Brezhnev, Kosygin, Gromyko, and Nasser and his delegations, exchanged visits and joined in denouncing Israel's reprisal raids. The Russians had many reasons for supporting the Arab states against Israel, but it is doubtful that they seriously overestimated Nasser's military prowess or, at any time, wanted the State of Israel to disappear from the map. As Ben-Gurion had pointed out, Israel is a valuable political entity to the Russians. Without her, they would have small leverage on the Islamic states that on many counts are refractory to the inverse-dogmatism of the communism of both China and Russia.

But Nasser, in response to the pressures on him from other Arab states, could only keep moving further and further out on a long limb. Syria, feeling itself impregnable behind its heights, continued to mount its verbal and guerrilla attacks. Nasser, to express his solidarity with Syria, in March 1960 had used Damascus as a platform to speak, this time not about imperialism but about Arab unity and what it meant: "The holy march that began in Syria and Egypt will not content itself with the establishment of the United Arab Republic. Having struggled and fought and triumphed, we must struggle and triumph again. The establishment of the United Arab Republic in this part of the world represents a threat to the ambitions of Israel as well as to the existence of Israel altogether."[26]

President Al Atassi of Syria said in May 1966: "We raise the slogan of the people's liberation war. We want a total war with no limits that will destroy the Zionist base."[27] Such statements became responsive readings as Arab leaders competed with one another in their anti-Israel speeches.

The hue and cry for the extermination of Israel was to be heard throughout the Arab countries, in Saudi Arabia, in Jordan, in Lebanon. In Syria a cover illustration for *Salem in the Army*, a reading and writing primer for the Syrian army, showed a host of Arab soldiers trampling an Israeli flag and standing crouched with fixed bayonets on the shore while three Israelis are drowning in the sea they have obviously been driven into. The cover of a Syrian army weekly showed a huge Arab soldier with a rifle raised in his right hand while a tiny half-human mannikin with the Star of David on its chest plunges into the abyss. The caption read: "To Hell O Zionists." The same wishful cartoons appeared in the papers and publications of other Arab countries where the Israelis were always drawn miniscule and grotesque against the colossal figures of the Arabs. The stigmata of the *Stuermer* were there, too—the hooked Jewish noses, the bowlegs, the frightened Jews cowering before the overwhelming might of Islam.[28]

This was the propaganda picture as the Arab forces grew to some 300,000 men, their tanks to 3000, and their planes to 1000. In 1964 the editor of *Al Ahram* and a close friend of Nasser, Muhammed Heikal, said: "Egypt is building the most powerful offensive force . . . which will be capable of carrying out any assignment involving total conflict with the enemy." By 1967 the shrill tone was an octave higher. On May 17 of that year the Saut Al Arab radio commentator said: "All Egypt is now prepared to plunge into total war which will put an end to Israel," while Damascus radio exhorted: "To the front! More battles! Kill them! Butcher them! Wash your weapons clean of their blood in the waters of Jaffa, Acre, Haifa!"[29]

In March 1963 an Israeli patrol boat had been fired on in the Sea of Galilee by Syrian forces and in a massive retaliation the Israelis raided the Syrian villages of Nugeib and Al Kursi. The United Nations condemned the Israeli attack, and Israel categorically rejected the condemnation. In August 1963 Israel protested to the UN Security Council the murder of two farmers by infiltrating fedayeen from Syria, and the Soviet Union vetoed a Security Council resolution that would have placed the responsibility for the deaths on Syria.

In 1964, between January and March, seven raids were carried out from Syria by guerrillas, and between February and August ninety-six shooting incidents occurred in which fifty-one Israelis were killed and ninety-four wounded.[30] In July 1966 Israeli jets attacked a construction site near Baniyas in Syria and shot down one of the four MIGs that attempted to drive them off. An Israeli boat was fired on in the Sea of Galilee. Israeli forces replied: roads were mined, buses and cars blown up, tractors destroyed by mines planted in the fields. And so it went. Israeli sources said the fedayeen infiltrated with explosives, guns, knives, and a sack. The sack was to hold their plunder, the knives were for cutting off heads. Between July and November 1966 forty raids were carried out by Jordan-based guerrillas, and on November 13 two Israeli armed columns with seventeen tanks and eighty halftracks attacked what Israel said was a fedayeen base in Samu. A number of buildings were destroyed, and seventeen Jordanians in a relief column sent to the ruins were killed.* One woman was killed when she remained in a house that was dynamited.

Six successive United Nations resolutions condemned the retaliations of the Israelis. The United States, the Soviet Union, Britain, and France joined in demanding a vote of censure but no official body outside of Israel condemned the fedayeen raids. One resolution to censure Syria for not preventing saboteurs from using her territory was vetoed by the Soviet Union in the Security Council in 1967. The exploits of the fedayeen, far from being repudiated, were celebrated in Syria and Jordan, and those who returned from the raids were greeted with rapture. On January 1967 Radio Damascus declared that Syria would not hinder the fedayeen incursions even if this meant war with Israel. In the first three months of 1967 Israel filed 790 formal protests against Syrian violations of the 1949 armistice lines.

The Soviet Union became the chief protector of Islam and Arab

---

* How many buildings were destroyed and how many people killed are in dispute too. King Hussein wrote there were 47 buildings dynamited, other observers put the figure as high as 127. (J. Bowyer Bell, *The Long War*; Hussein, *Ma Guerre avec Israël.*)

unity against all comers. Russian military supplies for Egypt included 250 tanks in 1955, a figure that rose to 360 for 1967; 50 fighter aircraft were delivered in 1955, 360 in 1967. In 1955 Russia had delivered no bombers to Egypt and 10 transport planes; in 1967 the figures were 70 bombers and 60 transports. Twenty missile-carrying torpedo boats and 7 destroyers were supplied in 1967, as against 4 destroyers in 1955 and no torpedo boats. Syria got help on a smaller scale; 500 tanks and 100 fighter planes were delivered in 1967 as against 100 tanks and 15 fighter aircraft in 1955. As was the case in Indochina and other parts of the Far East, as well as in black Africa, the Soviet Union was in competition with the Chinese Communists in the Arab world. But the Chinese were not in a position to send military equipment on the Soviet Scale.[31]

While the Kremlin showed no desire to risk a direct encounter with the United States, its propaganda policy in the Arab countries as everywhere else had as a continuing theme, as did China's, the world-wide aggression planned and conducted by the United States with Israel as an outpost. The chief difference between the Chinese propaganda line and the Soviet Union's lay in the Chinese accusation that the Russians, too, were imperialistic, and in their policies of revisionism and coexistence were becoming the running dogs of the capitalist imperiums.

Israel, according to the Russian line, as the advance guard in the Near East of American imperialism, had as its mission to prevent and destroy Arab unity, and the battle against Israel was also one against the nation that inspired and armed its aggressions. The Russian polemics in the 1960s were in marked contrast to what they had said a few years before. In 1948 the Soviet Union had repeatedly, in its support of Israel, upheld the moral and legal position of the new state in its conflict with the Arabs. On May 28, 1948, a Soviet representative had pointed out to the Security Council that Israel had never penetrated into foreign territory, and another speaker in June denounced the Arabs for seeking to destroy Israel. In July a Soviet spokesman said that world public opinion condemned the aggression of certain Arab groups against the Jewish state, and declared the Arab attack on Israel had occurred without the slightest provocation, adding that Soviet public opinion resolutely condemned the aggression.

By 1956, as we have seen, all this had changed and the same charges once leveled against the Arabs were made against Israel. In

1956 Russia had demanded in the UN that the committee charged with defining aggression include ideological aggression on the part of any state "that encouraged the propaganda of Nazi-Fascist ideas, racist and nationalist exclusivism as well as hatred and dislike of other nations." In 1964 Nasser, Hero of the Soviet Union, wrote in a letter quoted in the preface to *Palestine and the Human Conscience*, a book that repeated the charges of the notorious forgery, "The Protocols of the Elders of Zion," that the Protocols were "a gift of history." The author of the book was Mohammad Aly Allouba, commandant of what was then East Jerusalem in Jordan, and the author of still another book, *The Danger of World Jewry for Islam and Christianity* (Cairo, 1964), in which he wrote that "the god of the Jews is not content with the sacrifices of animals . . . the Jewish practice is to kill children to mix their blood with the unleavened passover bread. . . ."[32]

Allouba's books were but two of a number of blatantly anti-Semitic publications produced in Cairo, resurrecting the ancient charges against the Jews of ritual murder, and the Cairo daily, *Al Gomhouriya*, added the accusation that the murder of President Kennedy had been committed by Zionists, again citing the *Protocols of the Elders of Zion* as evidence "for the diabolical system of infiltration of the Zionists."[33]

The Soviet Union had often in the past declared itself against economic aggression, which, it said, could take the form of an economic blockade, and in favor of putting an end to warlike propaganda while economic ties were developed. But the Arab boycott of Israel, enforced since the armistice of 1949, under which a blacklist was kept of foreign firms trading with Israel, roused no criticism of any kind in the Soviet Union.

By 1967 Nasser was inexorably led by the Syrian guerrillas among others into taking action on his own account. Since he could not point to the exploits of fedayeen operating out of Egypt, he had to keep up his credit by extolling the military potential of his own well-equipped army and the fury of its coming onslaught against Israel. In February 1966, talking as much to his Arab critics as to Israel, Nasser said over the Cairo radio: "The perspectives for us are for a war with Israel. But it is we who will decide on the battlefield." On May 26, 1967, he went further: "The Arab people aim at combat. We await the propitious moment. Since a short time ago we have had the feeling that our forces have become sufficient and that if we confront Israel in combat we will be able, with God's help, to carry off the victory."

Syria was the most bellicose in its threats against Israel as well as against Hussein or anyone else failing to take as hard a line as its own. The Syrian press campaign against Hussein reached the point where Damascus accused Jordan of planning an attack on Syria in alliance with Israel and the United States. The Palestine Liberation Organization, under Ahmed Shukeiry, which was supported by Egypt, was as much anti-Hussein as it was anti-Israel. Hussein was target number two for the organization (and sometimes he even took precedence over the Israeli enemy), and Shukeiry declared that before capturing Tel Aviv the Palestinians had to win in Amman. When in 1966 an Israeli raid was made against Palestinian villages near Hebron and Jenin in Jordan, Shukeiry denounced Hussein, saying the King had done nothing to protect them. And in the course of the year Syria went as far as to offer arms openly to the anti-Hussein forces to help in his overthrow. Hussein, like his grandfather Abdullah,* may well have nourished the idea of coming to some kind of agreement with Israel, but any such attempt would certainly have cost him his throne and probably his life. Although he broke diplomatic relations with Syria when a Syrian truck loaded with explosives and destined for Amman blew up prematurely, he had little choice but to move toward Nasser and a reconciliation with the fedayeen. To save his throne he flew to Jordan, met with Nasser and Shukeiry, and made a military alliance that placed the Jordanian army under an Egyptian general.

Israel was determined by any means open to her to put an end to the attacks from Syria. On April 7 a tractor moved into the narrow strip of no-man's-land near the Israeli villages of Tel Katsir and Ein Gev, where the kibbutzim workers had never farmed before, and Syrian artillery opened fire as the Israelis doubtless knew it would. The Israelis thereupon ordered a large task force into action, including air and armor. In the course of the afternoon Israeli Mirages and Mystères engaged intercepting Syrian planes and shot down six. The Israelis lost no planes and the embittered Syrians again asked their ally Nasser where he had been with his air force of which he talked so much.

---

* In 1948 Abdullah had offered Israel autonomy in an undivided state with Jordan, with equal representation in Parliament, an offer declined by Golda Meir who had gone disguised as an Arab woman to Amman.

Early in May Soviet and Egyptian intelligence both agreed that an Israeli attack on Syria was imminent, even the date was reportedly given—May 17. Reports spread of Israeli troop concentrations on the Syrian border. Soviet sources said eleven brigades were deployed, although actually there was but one company stationed there against fedayeen attacks, as Israel could readily demonstrate to UN observers or to the Soviet ambassador at Tel Aviv had he cared to investigate.[34]

But Nasser had to act with some display of strength under the pressure from Damascus and from the Soviet Union with its warning of an impending Israeli attack on Syria. Nasser had declared at the Casablanca summit conference that he would not permit the presence of the UN emergency forces to inhibit his freedom of action, and at this point he set about to demonstrate his firm resolve.

On May 15, facing what it believed to be a major Israeli assault, Syria appealed to Nasser for help, and on May 16 the Egyptian chief of staff, Mohammad Fawzi, told the UN contingent of Indian units in Sinai to move into Gaza so that Egyptian forces could occupy the eastern frontier and be ready to attack Israel if she invaded Syria. U Thant, the Secretary-General of the United Nations, then made a decision that has been sharply criticized. Thant told Nasser he could not order the partial withdrawal of the UNEF; he had either to keep all or none of the UN troops on Egyptian territory. On May 17 Egyptian forces entered the frontier observation post of El Sabha, and the commander of the Indian troops, General Rikhye, was given twenty-four hours to evacuate all his UN troops. On May 18, the Egyptian commander in the Gulf of Aqaba area gave the UN forces, made up of Yugoslav troops, fifteen minutes to move out of Sharm el Sheik and this they did.*

Nasser had thus been put in a position by U Thant where he either had to back down or demand complete UN withdrawal from Egyptian soil. U Thant, in his own defense, pointed out that under the conditions of the UN occupation in which Egypt retained full sovereignty over Sinai and Gaza, Nasser had every right to ask the UNEF to withdraw and he had no choice but to agree. As for the Hammarskjöld-Nasser agreement, he first denied that it existed, and when it was published, said it was merely an unofficial private document and not binding on the UN.

---

* The UN troops had no serious armaments; they could not have resisted if ordered to.

Aside from that document, which certainly had played a role in Israel's agreement to evacuate Sharm el Sheik, it seems that U Thant was technically correct in acceding to Egypt's demand for the withdrawal of the UN contingents, half of which were composed of Yugoslav and Indian troops whose governments supported the Arab cause and might well have ordered them out in any event. But U Thant was open to criticism in the haste with which he acted when he might have delayed by calling for a meeting of the Security Council. Had he done this and referred to the Hammarskjöld-Nasser agreement, he conceivably might have gained another of the cooling-off periods that had prevented the eruption of major hostilities in the past. Abba Eban, the Israeli Foreign Minister, asked what good it was to have a fire department when the firemen left for home at the first sign of a blaze, and although U Thant could reply that Israel for its part had never agreed to permit UN troops to occupy any of her territory, it remained true that the peacekeeping forces had left at precisely the moment when they were most needed.

Why U Thant acted as he did was not because of any anti-Israeli sentiments. In 1958, when he had been Burmese ambassador to the UN, he had made a speech before a Jewish group, telling them that the state of Israel was welcomed by the Asian nations "as the return of their long lost relatives to their own hearths and homes."[35] It is unlikely that he had changed his mind; as one writer has said, he possibly thought Nasser was bluffing, that Egypt would not demand total withdrawal and the UN forces would stay. Nasser, despite his flamboyant oratory, was known to be a pragmatic politician and few close observers of the Middle East thought he wanted war.*

Israel conceivably might have tolerated the occupation of Sinai and Gaza by an Egyptian army whose fighting qualities she did not value highly despite its numbers and equipment. But the occupation of Sharm el Sheik and the closing of the Straits of Tiran was, her leaders had said many times in the past, an act of war that Israel could not accept in 1967 any more than she had in 1956.

Nasser accompanied the forward movement of his army with appropriate speeches. On May 23 he said: "Our armed forces yesterday

* Mohammad Heikal, Nasser's friend and advisor, writes in his biography of Nasser that the Egyptian President, when he sent his troops into Sinai, had wanted to draw off Israeli forces from Syria and had expected that UN forces would be withdrawn from only a few checkpoints. Heikal says that U Thant misunderstood Nasser and pulled out all the UN troops. (*Chicago Sun-Times*, December 6, 1971; Mohammad Heikal, *Das Kairo Dossier*, pp. 233–234.)

have occupied Sharm el Sheik. We will no longer authorize under any circumstances, whatever they may be, the passage of the Israeli flag through the Gulf of Aqaba." A week later Radio Cairo said: "With the closing of the Gulf of Aqaba, Israel has two choices: either to let herself be suffocated by strangulation by the economic and military blockade imposed by the Arabs, or to perish under the fire of the Arab forces which surround her from north, south and east."[36]

On May 26 Nasser said: "The meaning of Sharm el Sheik is a confrontation with Israel. Adopting this measure obligates us to be ready to embark on a general war with Israel." And he continued on May 28: "We plan to open a general assault on Israel. This will be total war. Our first aim is the destruction of Israel."[37]

On May 18 Nasser said over the Cairo radio: "The forces which were the guardians of the peace are gone. They are leaving and will not return.... Their duty is done."[38]

On May 29 Nasser spoke again over the Cairo radio: "We have succeeded in reversing the situation to what it was in 1956. The Lord will help us and will lead us in reversing the situation to what it was before 1948...."[39]

By May 30 military pacts had been signed by Jordan with Egypt, and the high command of the Jordanian army was taken over by the Egyptian General Riad. Troops from Iraq, which had joined the alliance, moved to the Jordan-Israeli border, and the Cairo radio announced that Israel was encircled in the full sense of the word.

Prime Minister Eshkol, although he had mobilized the Israeli army, to the surprise of many observers did not attack. Instead he sent his Foreign Minister Abba Eban to Washington, London, and Paris, all of which had guaranteed the right of free passage in the Gulf of Aqaba after the Suez War.* But Eban was received with varying degrees of coolness in all three capitals. De Gaulle warned him against firing the first shot, and when reminded of France's promises of assistance in the matter of the Gulf of Aqaba, merely said that the situation had changed. Harold Wilson in London was noncommittal, and Lyndon Johnson, who had long been a strong

---

* In 1957 the American State Department in a note sent to the Arab diplomats in Washington had reaffirmed its position, which was also that of France and Britain, that "the waters of the Gulf of Aqaba are international and no state has the right to prevent the free and peaceful passage through the Gulf and the straits that give access to it." (Ives Cuau, *Israël Attaqué*, p. 82.)

supporter of Israel as against the vacillating attitudes of both Eisenhower and Kennedy, kept Abba Eban waiting a day before he would see him and then told him to be patient, that the United States would try to gather together fifty or sixty nations who, as an international armada, would if necessary force the straits and open them to Israeli shipping. Of the international flotilla, however, not much remained when the volunteers were counted—two countries, Holland and Australia, agreed to join Johnson's naval force, not nearly enough for his purposes.

The first Egyptian battle orders were issued on May 18 to the air force, which was ordered on D-Day to support the offensive operation designed to cut off the southern Negev and to capture Eilat. Early on May 26, 1967, Battle Order No. 6 was issued to stand by for total readiness from the dawn of the same day.

On May 30 Nasser declared over Radio Cairo that all the Arab states were ready for the coming combat. He said: "The armies of Egypt, Jordan, Syria, and Lebanon are poised on the borders of Israel to face the challenge while standing behind us are the armies of Iraq, Algeria, Kuwait, Sudan, and the whole Arab nation. This act will astound the world. Today they will know that the Arabs are arraigned for battle, the critical hour has arrived. We have reached the stage of serious action and not of mere declarations."[40]

Two days later the President of Iraq confirmed that the hour had struck. He said to his pilots on their way to Syria: "My sons, this is the day of battle and of revenge for your brothers who fell in 1948. It is the day of the removal of the shame. With the help of God we will meet together in Tel Aviv and Haifa."[41]

Such were the tones of the Arab broadcasts beamed from Damascus, from Algiers, and even from Amman where a reluctant King Hussein had joined the war party and was striving to show how belligerently pan-Arab he was too. In fact, one Jordanian battle order captured by the Israelis ordered the troops that would raid the Motza colonies to destroy and kill all the people (800) in them when the code word launched the attack.*

If Ben-Gurion is correct in his estimate that the Soviet Union had no intention of permitting the state of Israel to disappear from the map, there is little evidence that the Kremlin had been able to con-

---

* Hussein, in his book *Ma Guerre avec Israël* (p. 68), says the order was given only in case a retaliatory raid was to take place after an Israeli attack like that in Samu. But even if that is true it does not adequately explain the "kill everybody" orders.

vince their Arab allies of the desirability of waging a limited war with limited objectives.

Soviet Positions

The Soviet Union praised the Egyptian takeover of Sharm el Sheik, although in 1933, when Russia was confronted with the rise of National Socialism, the Soviet delegation to the Disarmament Conference held in February of that year that the naval blockade of a coast or port was one definition of an aggressor. The same sentiment was repeated as late as 1956, when a resolution submitted by the Soviet Union to the Special Committee on Defining Aggression to the United Nations included among the evidence of aggressive war: "To submit another state to an economic blockade." However, when Egypt occupied Sharm el Sheik the Soviet Union made no objection; on the contrary, it hailed the act as another step forward against the imperialist powers. On May 22 the Straits of Tiran were closed. The next day Moscow announced that any state committing an act of aggression against Egypt would be answerable to the Soviet Union.[42]

On May 23, two hours after Nasser had announced the closing of the straits, the Palestine Liberation Organization radio station broadcast a note the Soviet Union had sent to Nasser, affirming its support for Nasser's stand "in defense of his country and territorial waters against the imperialists." On May 28 Marshal Gretchko, in a farewell address in Moscow to the Egyptian Minister of Defense, said: "The USSR, its army, its people and its government will stand behind the Arabs and will continue to encourage and support them. . . . In the name of the Ministry of Defense and of the Soviet People, we wish you success against Imperialism and Zionism. We are with you and ready to help at all times." Then Nasser declared on May 29 that he had been given a verbal message from Kosygin "in which he [Kosygin] announced that the USSR is taking a stand on our side in this conflict and will not permit any country to intervene. . . ."[43]

It is difficult to believe that the Kremlin, or those in the Kremlin who were making the decisions, did not foresee the inevitable war that must arise if Russia continued to increase its supplies of armaments to Egypt and the other Arab countries while the fedayeen raids continued and Moscow did nothing to stop them. If the Soviet

Union did not urge Nasser to occupy Sinai, Gaza, and Sharm el Sheik, she obviously did nothing to block him, but on the contrary approved what had been repeatedly characterized as an act of war—the closing of the Straits of Tiran—as a defensive measure taken against Zionism and imperialism. How could such steps lead to anything but war, and if war came, how could a peace be negotiated between the Arabs and even a truncated Israel to preserve a state the Arabs had sworn to destroy?

Of course the high key of Arab prose should not be mistaken for the substance of high policy. According to Hussein and others to whom Nasser talked, the Egyptian President did not think Egypt and Syria alone could defeat Israel, but no one has reliably reported his estimate of the situation after Jordan, Iraq, and Saudi Arabia promised they, too, would send troops. All Israel could judge by were the increasingly menacing words and armaments and her estimate of what they would lead to. Both, despite Nasser's reputation in some quarters for pragmatism and relative moderation, seemed lethal.

Russia became gradually committed to the Arab cause by her general design to weaken Western influence in Europe, Asia, and Africa and her readiness to take advantage of any opportunities to this end placed in her path. Soviet involvement in the Middle East had modest beginnings. Before 1954 it scarcely existed, and only through the blunderings of the West, which as the Suez crisis demonstrated had no concerted Mideastern policy, and the Arab-Israel hostility was the Soviet Union able to make use of the dazzling possibilities of military bases on land and sea in the Mediterranean. Russia had called the coup against King Farouk of Egypt by Nasser and his brother officers in 1952 the result of a "fascist uprising"; in Algeria, as well as in Egypt and Syria, the Soviet Union had demonstrated that it held few illusions about the revolutionary quality of Arab leadership. But the situation became too promising to pass up because of local disadvantages. Revolutions, in the Soviet view, need careful preparation. They require a proletariat and a Communist party to organize it, and these countries had neither. Furthermore, while the Soviet Union had been pro-Israel, it had never been pro-Zionist from an ideological point of view. All international movements, especially those affecting the behavior and attitudes of peoples within the Soviet Union, have always been held suspect and dangerous. The overriding consideration governing Russian policy in the Middle East was the possibility of improving the Soviet Union's strategic position. Russia did not need Mideast oil, but she could make good use of the warm-water ports a grateful Arab constituency would place at the disposal of her rapidly growing navy, she could build up her political influence in this part of the Third World, and any such strategy that would diminish the influence of the West, especially of the United States, was clearly promising. This last had been the motive in 1948 when Russia had supported Israel against the Arabs and against Britain, in 1956 when she had supported the Arabs against France and Britain, and from the 1950s on when she had supported the Korean and Vietnam revolutions against the United States and its allies.

If Russia continued to pursue an activist, dynamic, pro-Arab policy, a point of no return must be reached when the incessant guerrilla raids and the Arab demands on Nasser for deeds as well as words would leave her little choice but to go along with a brand of fanaticism of which she was basically suspicious. Arab leaders, following Moscow, triumphantly declared that the United States wished to intervene on the side of Israel but that Russia prevented such intervention by asserting she would not tolerate it.

The Israeli Position

Israel's strategic situation was extremely vulnerable. The distance between Kalkilja on the Jordanian border and the Mediterranean is less than twelve miles, the distances by air from the Arab hangars to Israeli cities may be covered in a matter of minutes, and Israel was surrounded by hostile armies on three sides. The sheer numbers of the Arabs, some 30 million in the neighboring countries against 2.5 million Israelis, may not have bothered the Israelis for they estimated realistically the fighting qualities of the Egyptians and their allies.

Nevertheless, the superior military equipment was there in the hands of the enemy, and it was not clear to the Israeli Cabinet how long they could afford to follow the warning of their late ally France not to fire the first shot or of their friend in the White House who said the same thing. President Johnson asked for patience to give him time to summon an armada that showed no signs of materializing, while at the same time he reportedly told the Israeli ambassador to Washington that Israel was now on its own. Keeping the peace, doing nothing, refraining from firing the first shot might meet the canons of conduct approved for others, especially for small states by their betters, but how could Israel survive if the tanks and planes at her gates suddenly attacked?

This was the question the Israeli military men kept asking and to which the Israeli doves had no clear answer. The Arabs could afford to lose battles and wars, but not Israel. One defeat of the kind Nasser and other Arab leaders promised to inflict, and the state would be gone. The Free World had lamented and wrung its hands when Russia occupied Hungary, and beyond the shadow of a doubt public opinion in the West supported Hungary, but Soviet tanks had decided Hungary's fate, not UN resolutions or public opinion. How could Israel do nothing and survive? And it is, after all, the main job of any head of state or chief of staff to make certain that his people and their state do survive.

So Premier Eshkol, who had been one of the Israeli doves when a peaceful solution seemed possible, had no choice but to call in one of the renowned hawks of Israel, Moshe Dayan, to take over the portfolio of Minister of Defense. Eshkol had offered him the post of Minister without Portfolio, but Dayan and his friends would take nothing short of the Defense Ministry, so he entered the government in the critical ministry that would determine where and when Israel would fight.

Dayan had his critics: he had been no great success as Minister of Agriculture, a post he had held from 1959 until 1964, and many people considered him hard to work with in any kind of group enterprise, which could be an important defect in his new position. But whatever his disabilities, Dayan knew what had to be done and he lacked neither self-confidence nor the ability to inspire confidence in others. His becoming Minister of Defense could only mean that the time of inaction was over.*

Before Dayan accepted the defense portfolio the Israeli general staff had given consideration to a limited offensive, one that would enable their troops to occupy Gaza as far as Al Arish and thus lend

* Dayan, two weeks before his appointment, had offered his services to the Israeli chief of staff, Major General Itzak Rabin, and at his request had visited units at the front to suggest improvements in the operations plans. Dayan was a professional soldier who had fought against the British in the Haganah, and had served with the Australian army in Syria during World War II where he lost one eye. In 1948 he had commanded an Israeli unit around Jerusalem and in 1956 he had led the Sinai campaign against Egypt.

leverage to any negotiations for reopening the Straits, as well as provide President Johnson time to assemble his blockade-breaking armada. The Israeli army had intermittently been partially mobilized and it could not long remain in a state of immediate preparation for battle. The call-up of troops brought the entire economy to a near standstill, with the large number of young men and women taken from their civil occupations and the requisitioning of motor transport, private and public. Israeli soldiers, aside from the small standing army, come out of the civilian population. They keep their uniforms and guns at home and it is the business of the individual soldier to get himself to his unit when he is summoned by radio and messenger, not as in the European armies by posters or letters or telegrams. A country the size of Israel has time for nothing but direct action when it mobilizes.

It is a young army; generals may be in their thirties, they are retired in their forties, and the chief of staff is rotated every nine years. Israeli men eighteen years old serve thirty months in the standing army (women twenty-four months) of between 60,000 and 70,000 men and women. Within three days this army can become a force of 250,000 men and women who are called up from the reserves, which they join following their thirty months of active service. As reservists they spend one month of the year plus one day a month in military training until they are thirty years old.

Before Dayan had been appointed Minister of Defense, the Israeli army had been partially mobilized, and then as D-Day seemed to recede, many soldiers were given one or two days' leave. Such measures presented difficulties: one regiment of paratroopers refused to jump on their fourth false alarm. On the Arab side, the preparations for war were unmistakable and were meant to be so. Large Egyptian armored units rumbled through Cairo in daylight, detouring to pass in front of the American Embassy although they had often during former maneuvers traveled unobtrusively and at night. The same tactics were used in Jordan, where tanks and trucks on their way to the front rolled through the streets of Amman for all the population to see.[44]

The War

By early June the peace moves had come to a standstill. Canada had suggested Four Power talks, always dear to the heart of de Gaulle, but Russia courteously declined to participate. On June 2 Dayan called a meeting of the Israeli high command, and on June 5 at 7:45 A.M. General Hod, commanding the air force, gave the code word— "Focus, attack"—that sent his planes against their Egyptian targets. Following the planes, the ground troops were sent into action with the code word "Red Flag" against Gaza and Sinai. The Israeli government and press announced that Egyptian forces had attacked first but the statement was subject to question: Israeli papers had their headlines printed before the war started.

The performance of most of the Egyptian officer corps matched that of 1956. One Israeli general said the Egyptian soldiers were too thin and their officers too fat; in any event, the social and psychological gulf between them had not been bridged. Egypt had never succeeded in building an efficient officer corps from its beginning in 1820, when 5000 officers were conscripted from among the Mameluke slaves of Mohammad Aly, the Ottoman Viceroy of Egypt. A number of officers' training schools were later founded, including a staff college, and all of them were attended mainly by sons of the upper classes, landowners, and members of the Wafd party. The Wafd officers had strong reformist purposes and it was through them that the recruiting of officers from outside the upper circles was made possible. The Free Officer movement, which included Nasser among its numbers, was made up largely of men from lower-middle-class groups, although some of the Egyptian aristocracy were to be found in their ranks. Thus a beginning had been made toward an officer corps based on other criteria besides birth and money. But the corps remained a self-indulgent, relatively elite subsociety which had little or no rapport with its ragged troops and a good deal of disdain for them.[45]

An Egyptian brigadier, Abdel Nabi, interviewed by a British general after he was captured in 1967, lamented not the defeat but the loss of his fine London luggage and his transistor radio. Everyone had wanted to save his own skin, he said; vehicles were simply abandoned and the men took off across the desert to reach, if they could, the far shore of Suez. Another Egyptian commander, General Sharon, told a British interviewer that the Egyptian soldier was all right, it was the officers who were worthless.[46]

The Israelis captured some 5000 Egyptian officers. The men, for the most part, they let go as they had in 1956, for they could not stop to round up such large numbers nor had they any means of taking care of them. And again as in 1956, the fate of many of the Egyptian soldiers was lamentable. Hundreds of them wandered dazed, sometimes in the opposite direction from the canal, exhausted, without water, and it was reported that when survivors did reach the canal they were fired on by Egyptian forces from the east bank. In some cases Israeli soldiers shared their water rations with the Egyptians but they often did not; the memory of the fedayeen raids was too recent.

While the Egyptian air force and army were being defeated in lightning actions, the Cairo radio announced victory on victory to crowds delirious with joy. Speakers called for the mass murder of Jews. A voice over the radio asked: "What do we do with Zionists?" A moment of silence followed, then the sound of machine guns and hysterical laughter. In Damascus some hundred Syrian Jews were stoned and killed, in Egypt many Jews were arrested, terribly mistreated, and sent to concentration camps from which some of them have never emerged.[47]

King Hussein was told that 70 percent of the Israeli air force had been destroyed, and when the Jordanian radar reported planes flying in from Egypt he believed them to be Egyptian and not what they were—Israeli bombers returning from their destruction of the Egyptian air force.

Premier Eshkol, still hoping to keep Jordan out of the war, had told Hussein through the UN commander in Jerusalem, Odd Bull, that the Israelis would not open hostilities if the Jordanians did not. The Israelis ignored a bombardment of West Jerusalem, but when Hussein ordered his troops into action in an attempt to capture Mount Scopus, Israel attacked with planes, tanks, and paratroopers. The fighting in Jordan was bitter for a time. The Arab Legion again fought well but their resistance was quickly broken, as were the Jordanian defenses north and south of Jerusalem. Hussein lost the eastern part of the city which Jordan had held since 1948 and a third of his country as well. Despite the firm resistance of the Arab Legion, it was no match for the Israeli troops moving forward to capture in hand-to-hand combat the strongholds and, greatest prize of all, the holy places. It was Hussein who sustained the heaviest losses as a result of the war, and they included the center of the Golden City. After 2000 years the whole of Jerusalem was again in Jewish hands, the sound of the chief rabbi's Shofar* was heard at the Wailing Wall, or the West Wall, as the faithful called it, together with the

* The chief rabbi, Shlomo Goren, had the rank of general, and jumped regularly with the paratroops whose uniform he wore.

prayers of the Orthodox and the un-Orthodox and the impassioned speeches of men like Moshe Dayan who swore they would never leave this city again.

The last of the Arab states to be attacked in force was Syria, which had been largely responsible for the war. Dayan delayed giving the code word for the attack ("Hammer") for three days to be certain he had sufficient forces at hand for a decisive action. Syria, without having engaged in any serious fighting, accepted a UN call for a cease-fire on Wednesday, two days after the war had started, although the Damascus radio continued to denounce the "stinking Zionists" who "had thought the war would be over in a few days." But, Radio Damascus said: "We will have you know it will not be finished for years."[48]

The Israeli ambassador to the UN could point to the discrepancy between the words of truce and the words of war and thus explain why Israel could not accept the cease-fire just then.

The Golan Heights, a stronghold of formidable strength, were stormed with troops and tanks in a frontal assault against well-dug-in infantry and artillery protected by minefields and Maginot-like fortifications. The Israeli soldiers had to advance with lightning speed, for the UN machinery, of conspicuously small use heretofore, had been hastily set in motion by the Soviet Union under a crash plan for such emergencies. The Russians had been slow to appreciate the extent of the Egyptian defeat, and when they did, and Israel paid no attention to the demand for a cease-fire, they broke off diplomatic relations with Israel. The Kremlin had first demanded a cease-fire coupled with the immediate withdrawal of Israeli troops from Egyptian territory. Then as the Russians learned how badly the war was going for the Arabs, they were ready to join in voting for the American proposal in the Security Council for a cease-fire without conditions. Only months later, on November 22, would the Security Council adopt the Arab and Soviet demands for the withdrawal of Israeli troops, which was to be accomplished within a framework of another international recognition of Israel's sovereignty and territorial integrity.

It was the familiar design of a no-lose war for the Arabs and a no-win war for the Israelis. The war had been building for a long time, fueled with Soviet armaments and Arab promises of extermination; the UNEF, troops of a fictive one world with a common intent of keeping the peace, had pulled out as soon as hostilities could conveniently begin. Then as it became clear that the Arabs had once again been defeated, the Soviet Union, and eventually the Security Council, demanded that the victors retire to their bases and vulnerable boundaries with the same kind of international guarantees that had provided no security at all in the past.

Again the Egyptians discovered that other nations had been responsible for their debacle. Nasser accused the United States and Britain of intervening with planes from Mediterranean bases against the Egyptian air force.* He had some justification for this because the Israeli planes had first flown west over the Mediterranean before coming in from an unexpected direction to bomb the Egyptian bases (they had been expected to fly in from the northeast). In addition, Israel had given the impression of having far more planes than she possessed, her air force having flown a record eight missions per plane a day—that is, a thousand missions or more on one day against the Egyptian troops and airfields. The Russians, however, knew that these Egyptian accusations against the United States and Britain were false, and so eventually did King Hussein, who in a telephone conversation intercepted by Israeli special services on June 6, was questioned by Nasser as to whether they should declare that only the Americans had intervened or that the British had joined them.

The conversation, after preliminaries, went as follows:

NASSER: Hello, shall we say the United States and England or just the United States?

HUSSEIN: The United States and England.

NASSER: Does Britain have aircraft carriers?

HUSSEIN: (Answer unintelligible.)

NASSER: Good. King Hussein will make an announcement and I will make an announcement. . . . We are fighting with all our strength and we have battles going on every front all night and if we had anything at the beginning—it does not matter, we will overcome despite this. God is with us. Will His Majesty make an announcement on the participation of Americans and the British?

HUSSEIN: (Answer not clear.)

NASSER: By God, I say that I will make an announcement and we will see to it that the Syrians make an announcement that American and British airplanes are taking part against us from aircraft carriers. . . . We will stress the matter and we will drive the point home.

HUSSEIN: Good. All right.

---

* Egypt and other Arab countries broke diplomatic relations with the United States.

NASSER: A thousand thanks, don't give up, we are with you with all our heart and we are flying our planes over Israel today, our planes are striking at Israel's air fields since morning.

HUSSEIN: A thousand thanks, be well![49]

The Non-Peace

On another field of battle and in another time this might have been the end of a long war that had gone on since the founding of Israel in 1948. Victors had brought reluctant enemies to a peace table before to make their demands and derive as much as they could in strategic and political advantage from their victory. But not in the Middle East. The Arab countries were in a position to hold without budging that they have always been at war with an illegal state since its founding, to deny that the war has ever ended or that it can end without the disappearance of this spurious state or its reduction to a shadow, and, after every defeat they suffer, to demand a cease-fire and a withdrawal to boundaries as they were at the time the renewal of hostilities began. Thus the proposal for an international guarantee of Israel's existence, in the opinion of Israeli leaders, was the same kind of specious promise as had persuaded them to surrender Sharm el Sheik to the UNEF.

All this might be a charade whose players would one day take off their costumes and settle down to a *de facto* peace settlement or a peace conference were it not for the Soviet Union. Russia has its sights trained on far more tangible objectives than any moral case for the existence and security of the state of Israel. This is true, of course, of France and to some degree of the United States, where popular pro-Israel sentiment, as in France, Britain and, for that matter, West Germany, is overwhelmingly in favor of Israel while government policy reflects this fact only to a prudent degree or, at times, not at all. While the UN was discussing a cease-fire on June 5, 1967, the spokesman for the American State Department, Robert McCloskey, told the press that the United States was neutral "in thought, word and deed," a statement that so shocked not only the American public and press but also so many members of Congress that Secretary of State Dean Rusk, a little later, had to "clarify" Mr. McCloskey's remarks by saying that the United States was in a state of "nonbelligerence." A few months after that, the United States joined the other members of the UN Security Council in demanding that Israel relinquish her territorial gains and the security she had won with them in the Six-Day War. The only concessions made to the causes of the war would be the recognition of Israel's right to exist within her former boundaries and the assurance of free passage through the Straits of Tiran, something Israel had had up to a fortnight before the start of hostilities and a privilege that could be withdrawn again. Thus the new principles of international comity were repeated: Nations may no longer legally acquire territory by force of arms without the consent of the defeated, even if no peace conference is convened, unless they are superpowers like the Soviet Union, where the writ of the UN runneth not, nor the will of the United States and its allies either. And as a corollary, developing states like India may annex territory like Goa, if its former ruler, in this case, Portugal, may be classified among the reactionary powers.

President Johnson would testify later, on May 11, 1971, that on June 5, the day the war started, Premier Kosygin had used the hotline telephone to urge that both the United States and the Soviet Union stay out of the conflict and use their best efforts to bring about a peace. Then, according to Mr. Johnson, Premier Kosygin telephoned again on June 10, when the Israeli troops threatened to capture Damascus, to warn him that unless the Israeli forces stopped their advance within the next few hours the Soviet Union foresaw the gravest consequences and would support the Arab countries if necessary with military force. Under this threat, similar to the tactic used by the Soviet Union in 1956, Mr. Johnson said he had ordered the Sixth Fleet, stationed in the Mediterranean 100 miles off the Syrian coast, to move to within 60 miles, and the crisis was resolved with the cease-fire of June 10, accepted by Israel that day.*

---

* The United States was, however, directly involved in the hostilities, when the USS *Liberty*, an intelligence ship equipped with sophisticated spotting devices which was sailing within fourteen miles of the Israeli coast, was attacked by Israeli planes and a torpedo boat and badly damaged. Thirty-four men were killed and seventy-five wounded. The Israelis said they had attacked in error, had taken the ship for an Egyptian vessel, and offered their apologies and an initial indemnity of $3,325,000, both of which the United States accepted. What really lay behind the incident was never entirely cleared up, but the vessel looked like no Egyptian ship in the Israeli spotting manuals. The Israeli high command had warned shipping out of the area because of the danger and it seems not impossible that they did know the vessel to be American and were determined to stop such snooping on their orders and signals. When American destroyers set out to render the *Liberty* help, the hot line was used again, to tell the Soviet leaders that the ships were being sent on a rescue mission and had no other purpose.

This time, for a while, Israel had gained all her objectives. The Straits of Tiran were open; an Israeli ship could and did pass through them to arrive at Eilat. The Israeli border with Jordan and Syria were no longer an open field of fire and infiltration. The Jordanian boundaries were pushed back to points along the River Jordan where land mines and patrols would inhibit crossings, and the Golan Heights were in the hands of the Israelis.

Most important was the city of Jerusalem, the fount, source, and symbol of the historical, the biblical Israel. "Next year in Jerusalem" became "Now in Jerusalem," and no UN resolutions or Soviet or Arab demands seemed important in comparison with this overwhelming fact.

Jerusalem was restored to normal within a very short time; the Arab shopkeepers in the old city returned to their booths, the Arab hotel owners to their hotels, the Arab police to their beats—those who had not fled. The refugee quarter near Jericho that had housed thousands of Palestinians was almost empty now, but those who had stayed could remain. The Israelis would permit only what they called bona fide residents, that is, people who had not lived in refugee camps, to return. Nevertheless, in the course of the war, more than 240,000 Arabs had fled, many of them from territory on which they had lived for centuries, and the refugee population in the camps in Jordan and Syria climbed by another quarter of a million.

The Soviet Union moved right away to restore what the Arabs had lost in the way of military equipment. For a whole day the Cairo airport was closed while Soviet planes flew in supplies and planes to replace part of those that had been lost. Within a matter of months the Egyptian air force and tanks were up to strength. The loss of the war had been a heavy blow to the Soviet Union in material and prestige, including its credit in the mercurial Arab countries, which wanted to know why the Russians had not done more than they had, and even called them traitors. More galling still was the loss of $2 billion worth of Soviet military equipment, which represented the work of thousands of Soviet citizens who had available far fewer consumer goods than they would have liked. Worst of all, from the point of view of the Soviet Union, the Israelis had captured SAM missiles, tanks, guns, and planes, some of which were among the best the Eastern bloc could produce, and the war had shown Russian military doctrine, at least in the hands of the Arabs, no more competent than it had been in the summer of 1941. The Russians are extremely sensitive about their military secrets and equipment and now both turned up in the hands of one of the imperialist powers they had been designed to defeat. Nor could the problem be solved merely by sending new supplies. The Soviet Union continued to provide specialists and material, but even as they did, an Israeli foray in 1970 not only attacked a radar installation sent to Egypt, it took it back to Israel hauled by helicopters. Nevertheless, the overall Soviet position in the Middle East was undoubtedly improved by the defeat of Egypt, which it seemed had to rely more than ever on the Soviet Union for military and essential economic support.

The fedayeen raids diminished but did not stop, and in 1968 the Israelis conducted two major reprisals against Jordanian villages, both of which the Jordanians said were beaten back with heavy losses. The Israelis shrugged off such claims of Arab victory and said they had destroyed fedayeen bases and then returned to Israel as they had in the past. An Egyptian rocket sank an Israeli destroyer, the *Elath*. As a reprisal Israeli fliers set Egyptian oil refineries near Suez on fire and destroyed them. Hussein, still endangered by the Palestinian resistance, undertook in 1970 major reprisals against the fedayeen and succeeded in establishing the rule of his own army in what had been the partisan strongholds.

Nothing has changed basically in the Arab demands or in those of their supporters. The Eastern bloc countries, the United States, and the Security Council of the UN continue to demand that the Israelis withdraw from the Arab territory they conquered. Any negotiations to this end are still conducted by third parties because the Arabs refuse to recognize the existence of the state of Israel.

The decision of Nasser's successor, Anwar Sadat, in July 1972, to dismiss thousands of Soviet advisers and technicians seems to have been brought about by domestic political pressures. Many Egyptian officers and civil leaders were disenchanted with Sadat's failure to open hostilities against Israel, and they had become convinced that the Soviet Union was pursuing solely its own, rather than common policies when it refused to provide offensive armaments Egypt had repeatedly demanded. This was a marked shift in the sands of Middle-East politics, but it provided Egypt neither with the weapons nor the additional support Sadat had demanded in Moscow. Despite the withdrawal of Russian forces, Egypt had been well armed by the Soviet Union (receiving $2.5 billion in weapons in 1970 alone) and Cairo might now be in a position to make unilateral decisions on how and when to use them.

Despite the events of 1972, the Soviet Union remained committed to the Arab cause, whether or not this might lead to the destruction of Israel. The treaty of friendship and cooperation initialed by Presidents Podgorny and Sadat in May 1971, if placed in some jeopardy in July 1972, still remained in force, still useful both to Russia and Egypt. It may well be true that Russia would prefer Israel's continued existence as an alleged threat to the Arab states, but the stakes were too high to permit overly fine calculations. Before the June war, the Soviet Union had sent technicians and advisers to Arab countries and a number of their own fliers to Egypt, some of whom were shot down over the Suez Canal before the period of the formal cease-fire ended there in 1971. More and more Soviet and Eastern-bloc technicians went to Egypt after 1967, some of them in combatant posts or posts that could readily become so. The withdrawal of most of them (they were said to number 15,000 in 1972) while no doubt gratifying to Egyptian sensibilities, did nothing whatever on behalf of the Egyptian military potential, although it might increase Egyptian belligerency. But with or without Soviet advisers in Egypt, the Russian presence would remain in the Middle-East and the Mediterranean for an indefinite future.

The United States remains committed to some kind of balance of power in the Mideast, along with the preservation of law and order against an aggressor. To this end it supplies weapons to Israel (the only country now that does so), for despite the increased production of Israeli arsenals, Israel must still rely on the United States for maintaining its strength in planes and heavy armament. Its major reliance, however, it properly places in its own mission, its people, and its army.

NOTES

1. Ethelbert Stauffer, "Mord in Gottes Namen," pp. 28–42.
2. Raul Hilberg, *The Destruction of the European Jews*, p. 767.
3. Arthur D. Morse, *While Six Million Died*.
4. *Trial of the Major War Criminals*, p. 518.
5. Morse, *op. cit.*, p. 309.
6. Ronald Sanders, *Israel: The View from Massada*, p. 136.
7. Barnet Litvinoff, *The Road to Jerusalem*.
8. Paul Giniewski, *Le Sionisme d'Abraham à Dayan*, p. 208–209.
9. *Ibid.*, p. 229–230.
10. David Lloyd George, *Memoirs*, Vol. II, p. 745.
11. J. Bowyer Bell, *The Long War*, pp. 27–28.
12. Christian Zentner, *Die Kriege der Nachkriegszeit*, pp. 367–368.
13. Walter Laqueur, *The Road to Jerusalem*, pp. 88–89.
    Clifford Irving, *The Battle of Jerusalem*.

14. Lieutenant-General Sir John Bagot Glubb, *A Soldier with the Arabs*.
    Walter Pinner, "The Problem of the Palestine Refugees."
15. Voice of the Arabs, Radio Cairo, May 7, 1960. Israeli Ministry for Foreign Affairs, 1961.
16. Embassy of Israel, Washington, D.C., July 1967.
    Files, Israeli Ministry for Foreign Affairs, Jerusalem.
17. Files, Israeli Ministry for Foreign Affairs, Jerusalem.
18. Laqueur, *op. cit.*, p. 20.
19. Speech at Alexandria, August 17, 1961, quoted by *Al Manar*, August 18, 1961. Israeli Ministry for Foreign Affairs, 1961.
20. Voice of the Arabs, Radio Cairo, March 17, 1960. Israeli Ministry for Foreign Affairs, 1961.
21. Radio Baghdad, March 7, 1960. Israeli Ministry for Foreign Affairs, 1961.
22. Ministry for Foreign Affairs Information Division, Jerusalem, 1961.
23. Ministry for Foreign Affairs Information Division, Jerusalem.
24. Israeli Ministry for Foreign Affairs, January 1, 1964.
25. Ministry for Foreign Affairs Information Division, Jerusalem.
26. *Ibid.*
27. *Ibid.*
28. From *Selections of Cartoons From the Arab Press*.
29. "*Israel Must Be Annihilated.*"
30. Bell, *op. cit.*
31. *The Arab War against Israel*, p. 52.
32. *Principes Soviétiques et Pratiques Arabes*, p. 19.
33. *Ibid.*, p. 19–20.
34. W. Byford Jones, *The Lightning War*.
    Yves Cuau, *Israël Attaqué*.
35. David Kimché and Dan Bawly, *The Sandstorm*, p. 94.
36. *The Record of Aggression*, p. 15–16.
37. *Ibid.*, p. 16.
    Bell, *op. cit.*, p. 411.
38. *The Arab War against Israel*, p. 7.
39. *Ibid.*, p. 7.
40. *The Record of Aggression*, p. 16.
41. *The Arab War Against Israel*, p. 10.
42. *Principes Soviétiques et Pratiques Arabes*, p. 35.
43. *The Arab War against Israel*, p. 51.
44. Ernst Trost, *David and Goliath*.
45. P. J. Vatikiotis, *The Egyptian Army in Politics*.
46. Brigadier Peter Young, *The Israeli Campaign*, p. 112.
47. Cuau, *op. cit.*
48. *Ibid.*, p. 294.
49. *The Arab War against Israel*, pp. 43–44.

6

The Wars in Indochina

AGGRESSION, WAR CRIMES, CRIMES AGAINST HUMANITY

CHANGES decisively affecting the domestic and foreign policies of two Western nations in the postwar period have come about through their interventions in a relatively small, mainly rural area in Southeast Asia, a part of the world almost totally lacking in economic, political, and conventional military power but nevertheless the battlefield where both France and the United States have been tried beyond their endurance, or, more accurately, their willingness to endure. When the French general, Jean le Clerc, landed at the airfield of Saigon on September 23, 1945, declaring: "We have come to reclaim our inheritance,"[1] he was as far off the mark as was an American general, William Westmoreland, some twenty years later when he announced that his search-and-destroy operations would defeat the enemy in the next year. Whether or not Vietnam, Laos, and Cambodia were France's "inheritance," she was never again to make good her claim to rule them, and the United States, for all its enormous resources of fire and economic power, was equally unable to impose its will on Vietnam, a country that, in conventional warfare, would have been overrun in one vast sweep of air and sea and ground forces. Indochina, and especially Vietnam, has proved to be the "jungle," in terms of both geographical and psychological terrain, whose undernourished inhabitants could not be conquered by the computer technology that had explored the interior of the atom, sent men to the moon, and could move them in war and peace faster than the speed of sound.

The French Rule

France's vital misjudgments of her situation in Indochina were evident before the end of World War II, a few years after she had been defeated in Europe and Indochina had been overrun by the Japanese. The Japanese invasion of 1940–1941 had been an easy one; the French troops under the authority of the Vichy regime had capitulated to successive Japanese demands and resisted in the field for only two days, losing 800 men, one third of whom were European. Only 35,000 Japanese soldiers had been stationed in Indochina and these were not occupation forces but support troops for the adjacent combat areas.[2] The French had been allowed to remain in nominal control of Indochina; the Japanese required little of their administration but to keep the peace while their own forces fought in the battle zones.*

But toward the end of the war the situation changed as French leaders began to seek their way back to great power status. As early as December 1943 General de Gaulle spoke in Algeria of the need to restore French rule in Indochina, and General Wedemeyer reported from China in November 1944 that British, French, and Dutch interests were making "an intensive effort to ensure recovery of their prewar political and economic positions in the Far East."[3] De Gaulle, in 1945, asked for American shipping and supplies to enable Free French troops to take part in the final action of the war against Japan. Neither the French forces in Indochina nor those in Europe were in a position to give significant aid to the final American assault, but what de Gaulle wanted was to make a sufficiently impressive showing to enable the French to reestablish their sorely shaken position in Indochina and in the Allied councils of war.[4]

His request was turned down by the United States, which had little need of French troops in Southeast Asia and could use all the shipping space available for its own armies. The Free French forces did, however, have a few paratroopers in India and a detachment of these was dropped on Indochina in 1945 only to be promptly captured by the Japanese and never heard from again.

---

* The Allies believed the Vichy French to be much too favorably disposed toward the Axis powers and the Japanese and not much better than the enemy.

President Roosevelt had long been opposed to French colonialism. He was convinced that France had mismanaged colonies like Algeria and Indochina for decades. In 1940 the American Under Secretary of State, Sumner Welles, had told the French ambassador that if the Japanese attacked Indochina, France could expect no help from the United States. On October 13, 1944, Mr. Roosevelt told Cordell Hull to do nothing to aid the French resistance in Indochina, and in 1945 General Wedemeyer, commander of American troops in China, and General Chennault, commanding general of the Fourteenth Air Force, were told under no circumstances to give military aid to the French units that had fled to the jungle after the Japanese had suddenly decided to take over the administration of the country.[5]

The Japanese decision to create an autonomous state of Indochina had been made in March 1945 as a result of the deteriorating war situation and the imminence of an American invasion during which they thought the French would be all too likely to collaborate with the advancing Americans. The Japanese acted with dispatch, placing the country under the Vietnamese Emperor Bao Dai, disarming the French troops, arresting 750 civilians, 400 of whom died while in Japanese custody, many of them in the same jails the French had built for the Vietnamese. Only a few scattered French forces managed to escape the Japanese coup and these were lacking in supplies of every kind with small chances of survival without the aid President Roosevelt categorically refused to give them. General Chennault was himself ready enough to help with equipment and air support but, as one French general said, Washington's veto condemned the French to annihilation. He was not far from wrong: 1700 of them died during the retreat to China.[6]

President Roosevelt had a number of solutions for the settlement of world problems after the end of World War II. For Indochina, he said at Yalta on February 8, 1945, he favored a trusteeship under the United Nations, a suggestion opposed by Britain because, Roosevelt thought, of the implications for a trusteeship of Burma. Mr. Roosevelt had also proposed to Chiang Kai-shek, when Nationalist Chinese fortunes were at a low ebb, that China resume authority over Indochina, whose territory she had left a thousand years before and had ruled for a thousand years before that. Later, Mr. Roosevelt came to favor a Chinese-Soviet-British occupation, a plan with which Stalin professed himself delighted. Stalin was always opposed to France's playing any role in Indochina. With President Roosevelt, he objected to the French trusteeship favored by Churchill, saying the Allies had not shed their blood to put the French back in Indochina.[7] After Mr. Roosevelt's death the Potsdam Conference provided for the occupation of Indochina by Nationalist Chinese and British forces, which also were to accept the surrender of the Japanese troops. Soviet Russia, not yet at war with Japan, was not included in the arrangement, nor were the French, who had not been invited to Potsdam. Only on October 25, 1945, did John Carter Vincent, on behalf of the American State Department, announce that the United States would support the restoration of French sovereignty in Indochina.

American opposition to the reestablishment of French rule by no means ended with the State Department's announcement. The Americans, mainly OSS men, who had come into contact with Ho Chi Minh in the latter months of the war had a high regard for him and his purpose—to create an independent Vietnam. Ho provided reliable information about the movements of Japanese soldiers and he spoke a language of anticolonialism, especially anti-French colonialism, that was not very different from the words of Mr. Roosevelt or the sentiments of the Americans he dealt with. One American officer visiting a prisoner of war camp where a French officer was held by the Vietnamese was asked for help. The American replied: "Those fellows must have had a reason for putting you there, why don't you just stay where you are?"[8]

The Truman administration in 1945–1947 steered a neutral course between the French and the Vietminh. Secretary of State George C. Marshall sent a cablegram to the American embassy in Paris saying that while the United States "fully recognized France's sovereign position . . . at the same time . . . there are two sides this problem . . . and our reports indicate both a lack of French understanding other side and continued existence dangerously outmoded colonial outlook and method. . . ." On the other hand, Marshall said, Ho Chi Minh had direct Communist connections and his cablegram ended helplessly: "Frankly we have no solution of problem to suggest."[9]

Ho Chi Minh

Ho Chi Minh was a man of many parts: a devoted Communist, a fanatical nationalist, a politician, a poet, a bearer of the party line, and at the same time, a flexible and adroit prestidigitator in his use of non-Communist and even anti-Communist factions in Indochina as long as they were on the side of the revolution that would drive France from the country. Like Lenin, Ho molded the revolution in his country, keeping it alive when it seemed dead, organizing its scattered cadres in the face of the overwhelming power of the enemy, steering his way between the hostile forces of Nationalist China, Vietnamese religious sects and their armies, Japan, and France, all of them bent on his destruction. He could be the benign Uncle Ho sending messages of love and gentle concern for the millions of his nieces and nephews, and he could also be the singleminded authoritarian leader who carried out his devastating land reform by slaying thousands of Vietnamese farmers whom he thought stood in its way. Ho betrayed an ally, the nationalist leader, Phan Boi Chau, to the French because, as Ho later explained, he thus disposed of a future nonparty rival, the money the French paid him could be well used in furthering the Communist cause, and if Phan were executed, this would increase anti-French sentiment in Vietnam.[10] Ho's own people, even his devoted followers, might regard him at times as too subtle, too ready to compromise his principles, almost a traitor to the cause when he seemed to be coming to terms with the enemy, but in fact, whatever his tactical twists, turns, and detours, he never lost sight of the one goal he lived for—an independent Vietnam as part of the Communist international world order.

Ho Chi Minh was one of a dozen of his adopted names. It was taken, in the Communist tradition, for its allegorical value (it meant "Enlightener of the People,"), and before he became Ho he had been Nguyen Ai Quoc ("The Patriot") and the bearer of other virtuous or merely clandestine names. He was born Nguyen Tha Than, the son of a minor Mandarin who had been a worker on the land of a well-to-do farmer whose daughter he had married. Ho attended a French lycée in Vinh until he was thirteen years old, when he left, according to his account, because his political views even at that age were incompatible with the teachings of the school, and according to the French, because of his low grades. His father then enrolled him in the lycée at Hué, from which he also failed to graduate.[11] In any event, he was one of the Vietnamese who could not tolerate the second-class estate of the native peoples ruled in their own country by the oppressive and arrogant white man. Without money, he could only hope to rid himself of a native's shackles by getting away from Vietnam, taking any kind of menial job he could find that would enable him to travel. In 1911 he shipped under the name of Ba as a mess boy on the French liner *La Touche Tréville* and saw much of the world, including New York and Boston and other cities of the West where white men, he noted, might be as poor as he. In London he was a kitchen helper, a pastry cook at the Carlton, and he joined a group of Asians in a secret organization called the Chinese Overseas Workers Association. When he moved to France in 1917 he was one of the 80,000 Annamites, as the French called them, imported either to serve in the French army or to work as coal miners. When French troops revolted in that year of catastrophic offensives that got nowhere, the Annamite troops were ordered to fire on some of the dissident units. Ho and the Annamite soldiers were seeing the French in a time of despair and brutality directed against Frenchmen, and what they saw was very different from the lofty ways of the white planters in their native land.

In 1919 Ho was one of the innumerable witnesses to appear at Versailles to voice the complaints and aspirations of the oppressed for the better world fashioned out of self-determination and democracy which, it had been promised, would emerge from the Peace Conference. At Versailles Ho made a modest appeal for Vietnam; not for independence but for equality, civil rights, and more schools. The next year he made another speech, this one before a Socialist congress held in Tours, where he told a sympathetic gathering that included Léon Blum and Clara Zetkin (the one a Socialist, the other a Communist intellectual), of the iniquities of French rule in Indochina, how the natives were being poisoned with French-owned opium and alcohol, how they were shamelessly exploited, imprisoned, forced to live in utter ignorance without civil liberties, tortured, and massacred—all, Ho said, for the benefit of French imperialism.[12]

It was a halting speech but its enumeration of grievances against the bourgeois order was well received by the left-wing gathering.* Ho was never a theoretician, but he was to become a superb organizer, using to every advantage the principles formulated by others, above all Lenin and later Mao Tse-tung, to fortify his countrymen to endure dangers and hardships in the revolutionary cadres. In France he supported himself as a photographer and retoucher of photographs at 45 francs each, writing occasional articles for *L'Humanité* and other newspapers on the Left, and in 1923 he departed for Russia.

* Soon after the Tours meeting the Socialists split and Ho became, on December 30, 1920, one of the founders of the French Communist party.

There he was enrolled for three weeks in the University for Eastern Workers, and although he never met Lenin, he came to know some of the foremost members of the founding Communist fathers, among them Zinoviev, Bukharin, Radek, Trotsky, and Stalin, all of whom, except for Stalin, would perish in the fires of the revolution they helped ignite.

From Russia Ho in late 1924 or early 1925 went to China to join the representative of the Comintern, Mikhail Borodin, who was organizing the revolution in Canton. There Ho founded the Association of Vietnamese Revolutionary Youth, the advance guard of what was to become the Communist party of Indochina and eventually of the Democratic Republic of Vietnam. The Communist attempt to control the Kuomintang ended in catastrophe when in 1927 Chiang Kai-shek, who had been one of Borodin's assistants at the Whampoa Military Academy in training the Chinese Revolutionary Army, turned his guns on the party adherents, killing many of them and sending Mao Tse-tung into the maquis and Ho back to Moscow.

Ho returned to his Asian mission by way of Siam where he started two front organizations: the League against Imperialism and the League for National Independence, forerunners of the Communist party of Vietnam, which was founded on February 3, 1930. The manifesto of the party, like Ho's demands at Versailles, proclaimed mild purposes: an eight-hour day, nationalization of banks, education for all, the abolishing of poll taxes, and also the overthrow of French imperialism and in its place a government of workers and peasants in an independent Vietnam.

Soon after, Ho was arrested and imprisoned in Hong Kong for his Communist activities. It was rumored that he had died and a funeral oration was actually delivered in his memory, but he managed to escape, apparently from the prison hospital where he had been sent suffering from tuberculosis. After hiding out in Amoy and then Shanghai, where he resumed his clandestine organizational activities, Ho again made his way back to Moscow, where he studied and taught for a time at the Lenin Institute, giving a course on the history of Vietnam.

Japan was on the march in China when Ho returned in 1938, after four years in the Soviet Union, untouched by the purges, to help organize a new coalition, a front of national unity of all parties against the Japanese invaders. Moscow belatedly had come to recognize the need for such an alliance following the bankruptcy of its doctrinaire policies that in Europe had branded the Social Democrats more dangerous than the National Socialists, and in the Far East had failed to organize an anti-Japanese coalition. The call in the mid-thirties was to unite against fascist aggressors in Europe and the Far East, and while the line changed abruptly in Europe when Stalin made his nonaggression pact with Hitler in August 1939, it held reasonably fast in Asia despite the treaty of neutrality Stalin would make with Japan in 1941. Russia and Japan remained wary of each other; the Kremlin had no illusions about the "coprosperity sphere" Japan was building in the Far East nor the threat of Japanese military power to the Soviet Union.

The Indochinese Communist party did not operate independently in the 1930s. It was under the control of the French Communist party, and the United Front, designed to stop Hitler in Europe, forced Ho to accept, temporarily at least, French colonialism in Indochina. Such a concession, tactical though it was, cost Ho and the Vietnamese party the backing of nationalist organizations like the Dai Viets and forced Ho after World War II started, and he could operate again on behalf of Vietnamese interests, to rebuild the Communist party from a smaller base of support than he would otherwise have had. Ho, like the leaders of the French Communist party, for the time being had accepted the Paris Establishment. He had announced, on behalf of the Vietnamese resistance, a new soft-line policy in 1939, saying this was not the time to call for national independence but instead to organize a Democratic National Front that would win French progressives as well as Vietnamese, the bourgeoisie as well as the workers. He proclaimed a policy of cooperation with the French Popular Front in which the Communist party would assert its leadership by demonstrating the greatest zeal and readiness to sacrifice in order to win the masses.

The enemy for the time being was Japan, and Ho, like Chiang and Borodin before him, helped school the Kuomintang in guerrilla warfare. In 1941, with France at war, Ho could return to the attack on French colonialism. He founded the League for Vietnam Independence, the Vietminh. It was another anti-Japanese coalition but it was also anti-French, made up of Vietnamese of every political complexion. Its well-organized nucleus was the Indochinese Communist party, which was, however, no more than 10 percent of the membership of the new party.[13]

In a letter written on June 6, 1941, Ho called on the Vietnamese to unite against the Japanese and the French. The Japanese, he said, were bogged down in China and confronted by formidable American and British forces, the French were defeated in Europe and no longer able to dominate Vietnam. It was a prescient letter written before the German attack on the Soviet Union and the Japanese attack on Pearl Harbor, and Ho proceeded to fight the war of national liberation by its light.

Vo Nguyen Giap

In Kunming, Ho had been joined by the ablest of the men who would be his collaborators in the years to come. He was Vo Nguyen Giap, called by Sainteny, head of the French military mission in southern China, "one of the most brilliant products of our culture."[14] In 1944 Ho and Giap met again to concert their guerrilla tactics. Giap, the warrior, wanted to call for the rising of the countryside; Ho, the more cautious Leninist, emphasized the need for intensive political organization first. Both men had attended the same lycée in Hué, but Giap, who had gone on to study law and teach history, was essentially a man of direct action. He had compelling reasons to fight. His wife had died in a French prison and her sister had been guillotined after both of them had been found guilty by a French military court of anti-French activities. Ho and Giap, combining their complementary talents, started the Armed Propaganda Teams for National Liberation, politically schooled guerrilla fighters mainly recruited from the Montagnard tribesmen.*

With the first unit of thirty-four men, Giap captured two French military outposts on December 22, 1944, and massacred the entire garrison. Giap used terror as an indispensable part of guerrilla warfare, routinely executing, along with the French, village chiefs who collaborated with them. He also followed Mao Tse-tung's doctrine of attacking when the enemy is weak and retreating when he is strong. Only once did Giap attack a Japanese force and that was when he was able to overwhelm a unit of 40 men with 500 Vietminh. But he was a skilled commander who learned his trade in the field as well as

---

* The Montagnards, aboriginal tribes numbering from 800,000 to 1 million people, were assiduously cultivated by the Vietminh and their successors in the National Liberation Front. They were promised autonomy in the new state-to-be, and freedom from their second-class status. Only much later, in the 1960s, were the Montagnards driven into open hostility against the NLF by the Vietcong demands, especially for food that was always in short supply.

from wide reading. Giap studied not only Mao and Lenin, but Clausewitz and Che Guevara and Mao's teacher of military strategy, Sun Tzu, who wrote *The Art of War* in 500 B.C.[15] Giap led small, well-schooled, and thoroughly indoctrinated units armed with odds and ends of rifles (Giap says they had sixteen kinds including Tzarist weapons the Japanese had captured forty years before) taken from the French along with a few supplied by the Americans and the rest from Japanese stocks. Only in 1949, after the victory of Mao's forces in China, when large Vietnamese forces could be trained on Chinese soil, could Giap's small detachments become an army. After the Chinese entered the Korean War, Giap was supplied with American weapons captured by the Chinese in Korea, which were more modern than those supplied by the United States to France.

The French Return

The French never learned how to deal successfully with Ho and Giap. General Le Clerc said he had come to Vietnam to claim the French inheritance, but it existed only as a memory. France had to rely on foreign help: it was a British major general who went so far as to arm former Japanese soldiers, no doubt to keep order, although it also had the effect of helping to reestablish French rule in Saigon. Anxious to assert their power, the French could readily become trigger-happy and this would lead to tragedies that would only harden the resistance. Even after the Japanese had departed and the returning French had succeeded in getting rid of Chiang's troops, who had been slow to leave with the pillage of North Vietnam still uncompleted, the French had had no peace with Ho and Giap on their flanks. In Vietnam, as in Algeria, there were times of respite and surface agreement. Ho was invited to France where, at Fontainebleau, on March 6, 1946, France formally recognized the independence of Vietnam in an agreement under which the French would be permitted to maintain troops in the country for five years while Vietnam would control its own army and finances within an Indochinese Federation and the French Union. Cochin China, the south of Vietnam, was to decide later by referendum whether it would be part of the Vietnamese state. The agreement lasted only a few months. It was effectively sabotaged by the *colons* of Indochina, with the strong support of Admiral d'Argenlieu, the French High Commissioner, against whom the wobbly Paris government could have taken no firm measures even had it wanted to. The agreement had contradictory meanings for each side. To the French it meant indirect rule, in which France would retain responsibility for the administration and defense of the country; to the Vietnamese it meant full independence. In June, as Ho Chi Minh was on his way to Paris to negotiate the details of the settlement, Admiral d'Argenlieu recognized Cochin China as an independent state, part of the Indochinese Federation and the French Union. No referendum had been needed.

The French did everything but carry out the agreement to make Vietnam independent. They installed Bao Dai, the ever-ready former emperor who had served both under them and under the Japanese, as senior advisor in Ho's Cabinet. Bao went to work this time as a commoner, under the name of Vinh Thuy, but he was no more successful as an advisor than he had been as an emperor. Bao had lived in France for most of his life, since he was twelve years old, and had been brought back to Vietnam to play the part of ruler first under the French and then under the Japanese. Now he stood ready to be of any further use the French had for him. Even the French negotiator, Jean Sainteny, however, preferred to deal with Ho, with whom he had a friendly relationship and regarded with respect. Nevertheless, the French in 1949, to counter the Vietminh, again installed Bao as Emperor, a post he retained, but only in the South, until 1955 when he was almost unanimously deposed in a referendum and again departed for Paris. Bao, an easy tool, was no match at all for Ho and the Vietminh, even with the French behind him.

Before World War II France had first tried to govern Vietnam (divided into three administrative regions: Cochin China in the South with Saigon as its capital; Annam in the center with Hué as capital; and Tonkin in the North, its capital Hanoi) by imposing French law and administrators on the country. The use of Chinese characters for the Vietnamese written language was forbidden and a system of romanization called Quoc Ngu was substituted. But the problem of communication had remained; few Vietnamese, even those given minor posts in the administration, spoke French well and even fewer French spoke Vietnamese. French citizenship, which was theoretically open to qualified Vietnamese, was always closed to an overwhelming majority by reason not only of barriers of language, but also of patriotism that prevented a Vietnamese official or villager from becoming a collaborator. The French had to rely for support mainly on the Catholic converts and the descendants of converts (only some 15 percent of Vietnam was Catholic), on whose behalf in 1850 France had come to Indochina—ostensibly to enable the Catholic missionaries to pursue their work of conversion without local interference. The French invasion army had even included some Spaniards who joined up to further the cause of these Catholic missionaries, who were far more important to government policy in Indochina than they were in France. Although the French with their superior weapons were able to suppress the uprisings that occurred from time to time, the resistance movement that arose with World War II was not the same as those that had gone before. The earlier revolts were much more romantic than the ones led by the Communists. One of them was called the "Go East Patriotic Movement"; it linked its cause with Japan and looked for liberation from the French to the Japanese army, not usually renowned for such enterprises. A peasant rising took place at the beginning of the twentieth century under a leader called Hoang Hoa Tham, who survived all the expeditions the French sent against him until he was murdered in 1913, and other revolts had erupted from time to time under the leadership of Vietnamese intellectuals striving to preserve Vietnamese culture. One of these was Tong Duy Tan, whom the French had put in a cage where he wrote poetry until he broke his bamboo pen to disembowel himself. Risings had also been led by intellectuals and Mandarins during the centuries of Chinese rule and there are many tales of guerrilla ruses used against the Chinese overlords not very different from the tactics of the Vietminh. Two national heroines were the Trung sisters. One was the widow of a local chief and she and her sister had fought Chinese rule in the first century A.D. and then drowned themselves rather than be captured.[16]

The Revolution Again

The main point of difference in the revolution under Ho from those of the past was psychological: a reaction to the French loss of face during the war, and the conviction that if France could fight for her freedom against the Nazi oppression, the Vietnamese had the same right and duty to fight for their freedom against French oppression. In addition, the Vietminh fought with the knowledge that their battle was being supported by powerful outside forces in the Soviet Union and China and in France itself.

It is hard to believe that the revolution could have been successful without the Communist cadres and men like Ho and Giap
who were sustained by a Marxist doctrine almost as comprehensive
as that of the Catholic priests who had brought the French to Vietnam in the first place. For Ho and Giap, France was the spearhead
in Indochina of decadent capitalist imperialism. The irresistible
forces of revolution were on the march, as Giap declared in 1945,
when he said that capitalism had been rocked to its foundations by
the war, the Soviet victory, the defeat of fascist Japan and Germany,
and of France, too, despite its technical presence on the side of the
victors. Nothing, Giap and Ho believed in 1945, could stop the
march of the Vietnamese revolution. The Communist party Ho
headed was very nearly the only one in the worldwide movement that
did not purge its leadership in the coming years. The men who
headed it in 1945 were still its leaders in 1969, a unique record in a
history of widespread, internal party violence.[17]

For a time the United States, as well as the Soviet Union, had been
the pattern for the Vietnamese revolutionaries. The Vietnamese
Declaration of Independence repeated word for word in its opening
paragraphs the American Declaration, a copy of which Ho had
been at some pains to obtain from his American friends in the OSS.
The Declaration suited him perfectly; it sustained his nationalist
sentiments and did nothing to damage his Marxism. Ho read the
Vietnamese Declaration on September 2, 1945, as the head of the
provisional government formed in May that had appointed him
President.[18]

In November 1946, eight months after signing the treaty creating
an independent Vietnam within the French Union, the French returned to their nineteenth-century tactics to assert their authority.
A Chinese junk was stopped in the harbor of Haiphong for its failure
to pay French customs duties and Vietnamese units fired on the
French to prevent their taking the ship, which in their eyes was under Vietnamese authority. As a result of intermittent fighting, the
French military commander, Colonel Debès, under orders from the
acting High Commissioner in Saigon, General Vallery, ordered
the armed forces of the Vietnamese to leave the city, and when the
Vietnamese soldiers concentrated in the Chinese quarter refused to
move, the French opened fire, killing, they said, 6000 (foreigners said
40,000), mainly civilians.[19] It was a massacre and with it any hope
of a peaceful settlement disappeared. Giap, with a sizable force in

Hanoi, retaliated, after a number of incidents in which civilians, both French and Vietnamese, were killed. Giap's troops attacked the French garrison, killing and destroying on a wide scale. The bloody events in Haiphong and Hanoi marked the end of the modus vivendi, as the treaty signed on March 6 was called.

The Dirty War in Indochina

The war that thus began was called a dirty war, a name that would be used long after the French were gone and the Americans had taken their place. Its fortunes varied. Giap fought with consummate skill and only once made the mistake of attacking French positions in the massive way the French commander, de Lattre de Tassigny, wanted him to. That was a serious setback but a salutary lesson for Giap and he never repeated the error. He operated mainly with small mobile units to which political commissars were assigned and they, as in the case of their Russian models, had the last word when decisions were made.[20] Forewarned of French moves by an excellent intelligence network, Giap fought in the cities, and when they became too hot he withdrew to the countryside, and after 1948 to bases in northern Tonkin backed up along the Chinese border (just as Mao had used the Chinese boundary with the Soviet Union to regroup his forces against Chiang). As General Navarre, who took over the command of the French forces in Vietnam in 1953, said, Giap imposed his pattern of war and his strategy on the French.[21]

The war was not fought according to any of the European conventions. Of 36,979 French prisoners of war, only 28.5 percent were repatriated; only one out of four came back alive from Vietminh prison camps.[22]

Guerrilla war as waged by Giap followed no rules taught at St. Cyr. The front was everywhere and every weapon available to them was used by the Vietminh to offset the French superiority in planes, tanks, and artillery. A thousand years before, against the Chinese, the Vietnamese had used broken pottery stuck in the ground to break the legs of the Chinese horses; against the French they used booby traps and punjii stakes—pointed bamboo or steel splinters, sometimes covered with excrement and buried under paths. These could pierce military boots and enter deep into the foot of the enemy, causing painful wounds and infections that could keep the soldier out of action for months. French civilians were murdered, as were

Vietnamese officials and villagers who collaborated with the French or refused to collaborate with the Vietminh. The French troops, composed of Europeans, Foreign Legionnaires, Senegalese, Moroccans, Algerians (Sainteny says that in the early stages of the war France had 38,000 men in the field of whom only 7500 were Europeans), used the rough-and-ready tactics they would later employ in Algeria. They tortured prisoners during interrogations and committed atrocities for the same reasons they would use to justify these tactics in Algeria: it was impossible to distinguish the Vietminh from the peaceful population and it was imperative to find out who among the villagers had perpetrated an attack and when the next one was planned. Interrogations were conducted with the electrical apparatus later to become notorious in Algeria. One soldier of the Foreign Legion has told how dogs were turned loose on prisoners when they refused to talk or gave unsatisfactory answers. As in Algeria, too, the heads of Frenchmen might be cut off by the partisans.[23]

The precepts of Mao Tse-tung on guerrilla warfare contained instructions on the treatment of prisoners of war and Giap made as flexible a use of them as did Mao. The Vietminh treated prisoners differently according to their rank and service. Members of the Foreign Legion were regarded as mercenaries seduced by the imperialists, the Senegalese, Moroccan, and Algerian troops as exploited native forces, potential brothers-in-arms of the Vietminh who could probably be reeducated. The French officers were considered as a separate group in a different category from their men, who were forbidden to do any work for them. The Vietminh did not go quite as far as Mao had recommended to his guerrillas in the treatment of prisoners of war: Mao had said that when a prisoner was captured, his mistaken choice of sides should be made clear to him by his captors and then he should be released. If he is recaptured, Mao said, the same treatment should be repeated. This was one of the many humanitarian views of Chairman Mao that was followed only laxly both in China and in Vietnam. Nevertheless, the Vietminh made every effort to point out the errors in the political education of the enemy soldiers who had come to Vietnam. Prisoners produced plays from Vietminh scripts in which they acted out roles of the French colonialist exploiter and his victims, and the Senegalese especially enjoyed taking the part of the white planter with a big cigar. The evils of colonialism were denounced every day in meetings of self-criticism where men were taught to speak candidly of their own misdeeds. "You are animals," said one Vietminh indoctrinator, "and I will make a man of you."[24] The aim, as the prisoners were told, was to speed up their evolution. If a man committed a breach of discipline, he was given to understand that he was not sufficiently evolved and that liberation would depend on his showing evidence that he had emerged from his primitive state. Committees of prisoners were formed and promising captives might be made members of the politburo of the camp where they were prisoners. The men were encouraged to become like Vietnamese and, in some cases, to marry Vietnamese women and then to fight in the ranks of the partisans. Such opportunities were rarely, if ever, open to the officers, who were regarded as class enemies who could never be capable of the inner reform and self-criticism open to the enlisted men and noncommissioned officers. Punishments could be severe. Many prisoners were shot trying to escape, and one man, who was recaptured, was roped to a tree for a month. Food was almost always scarce but extra rations might be bought or traded for with the scanty possessions of the captives—a belt, a watch, a pair of pants, a shirt. Sometimes such articles were confiscated, but for the most part they were bought or traded for. Medical care was primitive; few medicines or antiseptics were to be had. One French captive with a gangrenous arm was operated on by a relatively untrained Vietminh soldier acting as surgeon, and when the prisoner developed a secondary skin infection it was treated with tobacco juice. The Vietminh "doctors" were roughly the equivalents of American medics, and with the stiff pride of the formerly colonized, the Vietminh would not make use of the French doctors they captured nor did they want them to treat the sick French. All were to be treated by a Vietnamese doctor, whether they would survive or not. When French prisoners were freed after the fall of Dien Bien Phu, of 10,754, 6132 had to be hospitalized, although many of them had been captives only for a few months.[25]

Because food was always scarce, in one camp prisoners were given a day off if they provided their own rations from plants they might find in the fields around the camp, where they were free to wander as far as 1500 meters because escape through the jungle and across the mountains was almost impossible.[26]

The high death rate among French prisoners was doubtless caused mainly by disease, exhaustion, and lack of food and hygiene—a piece of soap was worth a fortune—rather than mistreatment. Prisoners were forced to march long distances, sometimes as much as 600 kilometers through the jungle, and many of them died on the way. French accounts tell of beatings but these occurred because of breaches of discipline, like refusal to work. Officers were often shot and killed attempting to escape, but no mass or wanton executions of Frenchmen or of soldiers serving in the French army seem to have occurred. Nevertheless, the death rate of prisoners was very high despite the task assigned Vietminh units to keep prisoners alive, to reeducate them if possible, and to get them to sign protests against the war. Such protests included the Stockholm petition, for which hundreds of thousands of signatures had been obtained in Europe, as well as more homemade denunciations of the role of the French army, and they might be accompanied by demands for the democratization of French society. Enlisted men and noncommissioned officers were forced to work, some of them for peasants in the neighborhood, and they were also encouraged to join propaganda organizations like the "Association of Repatriates of Indochina" or the "Committee for the Battle for Peace in Vietnam." If they took the oath of allegiance to such an organization (the Muslims swearing on the Koran), they were told they were considered free men; some of them were released and others were retained for reeducational duties with more slowly developing prisoners of war. Many of the prisoners taken from the Foreign Legion, made up, as it was, of many nationalities and often detested by its own soldiers, were among those who accepted the Vietminh conditions.

The treatment of prisoners of war was prescribed by the doctrines of Communist ideology—both the Moscow and Peking varieties. Workers and peasants in every country would be liberated once they were freed of the fetters fastened on them by the miseducation of the capitalists who had indoctrinated them with their false values. Every peasant or proletarian, every common soldier, was potentially capable of being reeducated. The officers, however, like those of the Polish army who were executed by the Russians at Katyn, were considered to be too stained with the doctrines of their own iniquitous class to be salvageable. Terror was also used coolly and calculatedly as a means of education for the recalcitrant or the reactionaries. It was practiced on both villagers and French troops when it was thought it would have a salutary effect on the survivors. Terrorist methods were not likely to be employed, as they were by the French, to elicit information from captives, but there was no hesitation in taking any measures if the means could be justified by the revolutionary ends achieved.

It was another war with which the French had little luck and not much belief in what they were doing. Even the most successful of French generals, de Lattre de Tassigny, believed victory impossible.[27] General Giap skillfully moved his highly mobile troops against the numerically superior enemy forces, giving the French no rest, turning their rear areas into front lines, striking and retreating and preparing the indispensable refuge and staging zone in the North against the Chinese border where the French could not dislodge him. His purpose was to disperse the numerically superior French forces so they could not bring their numbers and firepower to bear, and French general after general fell victim to his tactics. Only de Lattre de Tassigny scored significant successes against him and then only when Giap borrowed the Chinese human-wave tactics of massive assault and suffered high losses. Giap had always foreseen a protracted conflict, thought it inevitable and even an advantage for the Vietminh in the political and military context of a war of liberation waged thousands of miles from the home base of an enemy that had been too long and too inconclusively battling for ends unclear to much of the population of France.

The United States remained a spectator, despite President Truman's increasing uneasiness as to the degree and intensity of Ho's relationship with Moscow, until Mao succeeded in driving Chiang Kai-shek's troops from the mainland of China. The Truman Doctrine of containing the expansion of the Soviet Union had been successful in preventing Communist control in Greece, and it had been mainly the stiff resolve of the American President that had prevented the loss of West Berlin when the Soviet Union, in 1948, began the blockade of the city that could only be kept alive by round-the-clock flights of American military planes carrying coal and food. In the Far East, however, the Truman Doctrine had not been applied. The President had withdrawn virtually all American aid from the nationalist forces of Chiang Kai-shek, and Mao's armies, in 1949, had won victory after victory with the aid of weapons surrendered by the Japanese army in 1945 and delivered by the Soviet Union to the Chinese Communists, or surrendered by bought-out Chiang generals. With Mao's victory, the forces of international communism had taken a great leap forward, and with the defeat of Chiang, whom President Roosevelt had counted on as one of the four policemen to guard the peace and security of the world, Mr. Truman was widely accused of having let China fall to the enemy. He had failed to support Chiang mainly, it was charged, because of faulty and biased advice received from the State Department and academic sources, including the Institute of Pacific Relations, on the significance of Mao's movement. "Agrarian reformers," the phrase used by many such experts to describe Mao's Communists, became a term of derision characterizing a misconceived decision to withhold help from the Nationalist forces, and the Truman Asian policy fell under heavy criticism once it became apparent that Mao was both master of China and a Communist.

Korea, the United States, and Vietnam

Even before the Korean War started in June 1950, it had become clear to Mr. Truman and his military advisors that the United States would have to give considerable help to France if Vietnam was not to fall to the Communist-controlled Vietminh. American policy was generally to support Paris' decisions with regard to Indochina, for France was indispensable to the success of the Marshall Plan and to the reestablishing of political and economic equilibrium in Europe. The National Security Council had recommended in February 1950 that military aid be given the French; a $10 million grant was made and the United States recognized the Bao Dai government of Vietnam in May.

When on June 25 (June 24 Washington time) North Korea launched its full-scale attack on the South, President Truman ordered American planes and then troops into action. On June 27 he announced at a press conference that he was accelerating American aid to Vietnam and dispatching a military mission to aid the French.

The Truman Doctrine, designed to contain Communist expansion and "to assist free peoples to work out their own destinies in their own way," had to be stretched out of shape to make it apply to Vietnam. But the aid to the French came under its broad purpose to halt Communist expansion. Mr. Truman was searching for anti-Communist bulwarks at all the global danger points. NATO* had been created in March 1949 to unite the armies of the Western powers for their mutual defense. And the United States would soon, only a few years after the war against German National Socialism and mili-

* The Vandenberg Resolution adopted by the American Senate in 1948 called for "Progressive development of regional and other collective arrangements for individual and collective self-defense in accordance with the purposes, principles, and provisions of the [UN] Charter," and "Association of the United States, by constitutional process, with such regional and other collective arrangements. . . ."

tarism, demand the approval of its wartime allies for the rearmament of West Germany to help balance the huge Communist armies at the borders of Eastern Europe. The French, battling Communist forces in Indochina, were part of the common fighting front in Southeast Asia, a front that extended from Korea to Indochina and might well widen. The American government recognized the Bao Dai government of Vietnam, while Soviet Russia and the People's Republic of China recognized Ho Chi Minh. In each case, Ho or Bao was recognized as head of state for the entire country, not just for the North or South, respectively. It appeared that the battle lines had been plainly drawn and that the United States was finally committed to stop Communist expansion in Southeast Asia as it had in Europe.

In 1950 this seemed to be, on the whole, a sensible decision. France was doing the fighting in Indochina, and the United States was carrying the main burden of the war in Korea as well as providing the considerable economic support of the armed forces of the Free (that is, anti-Communist) World all over the globe. With the American military mission and planes and supplies in Vietnam, the Communist advance might be halted there as successfully as it would be in Korea, with the expenditure of far less money and no American troops.

But French military fortunes did not improve markedly despite American aid, the infusion of fresh troops, and a succession of generals. Any French military successes were few and short-lived and American aid had to be stepped up. In 1952 the United States was already bearing one third of the costs of the war in Vietnam and this was plainly not enough to turn the tide. By 1954 American aid amounted to $1.1 billion, 78 percent of the cost of the war.[28]

After the election of Dwight Eisenhower in November, but before he took office, the American Secretary of State, Dean Acheson, wrote to President Truman that the Vietnamese war was being waged by the French without enthusiasm either in the field or on the home front.[29] The newly-elected President and his Secretary of State, John Foster Dulles, soon had considerable evidence that no matter how much money and weaponry they provided the French, more of both would soon be needed. As the military situation deteriorated, French appeals for American intervention became more importunate. Military missions to the United States played hard on the anti-Communist theme and found sympathetic ears in Washington. In early 1954 Admiral Radford, chairman of the Joint Chiefs of Staff, was convinced that the United States had to commit pilots and planes to action, and on March 29 Secretary of State Dulles told the Overseas Press Club the United States could not passively accept a Communist takeover in Indochina.[*29a]

Vietnam and the Domino Theory

President Eisenhower and many of his advisors were certain, early in 1954, that without American airpower Vietnam would be lost, communism would have scored another great success, and not only France would have been defeated but the cause of the Free World as well. If Vietnam fell, then Burma and other countries in Southeast Asia would go. This was President Eisenhower's "domino theory," that his successors, Messrs. Kennedy and Johnson, would also adopt. Vice President Nixon was one of the hard-liners who believed it might be necessary for the United States to do more than stop communism in a succession of little wars around the world. In March 1954 he said: "Rather than let the Communists nibble us to death . . . we will rely in future on massive retaliatory powers."[30] Nevertheless, the decision for active intervention was a difficult one for Eisenhower to make and he proceeded with caution.

On the one side, it was evident that France had already lost much of its zeal for any mission whatever in Southeast Asia. In 1953 important French political leaders like former Premiers Edouard Daladier and Edgar Faure declared France would not stay in Indochina whether or not she won the war, French interests were no longer being defended there.[31]

On the other side, as both Truman and Eisenhower saw it, the Communists had to be prevented from overrunning any more non-Communist countries. Both American presidents spoke, too, of the need to uphold collective security, that still undimmed vision of the peace-loving nations of the world uniting against the peacebreaker. Only collective security, President Truman had told René Pleven in 1951, would save the peace of the world.[32] Without collective security the world would return to its former unhappy state of lawlessness where aggressors went unpunished.

In Korea, as we have seen, the United Nations had officially con-

---

* Not all the American High Command were convinced of this. General Ridgway, for one, opposed any American armed intervention.

demned the aggression of North Korea, and the war became, through the fortuitous absence of the Soviet delegate to the UN Council, Jacob Malik, an approved war, with armed contingents from a number of member nations, although they were very small in comparison with the American forces there. While not much hope existed for turning the Vietnamese war into an armed intervention by the United Nations against aggression, both Truman and Eisenhower were determined that the fruits of aggression would not be enjoyed by the guilty forces if they could prevent it.

When Dien Bien Phu was under siege early in 1954, the French chief of staff, General Ély, went to Washington to ask for the immediate dispatch of 60 B-29s and 150 pursuit planes, with American pilots. The planes could be painted with French markings, General Ély said, and with them Dien Bien Phu could be held. Eisenhower made the tentative decision to intervene on April 14, 1954, subject to congressional approval and, above all, the participation of Britain. Both Dulles and Eisenhower were in favor of sending the planes but did not want to act alone. The doctrines of collective security demanded the collaboration of other peace-loving states, and Eisenhower and Dulles sought the support of Britain, Australia, New Zealand, Thailand, and the Philippines, as well as that of the recognized governments of Laos, Cambodia, and of Bao Dai in Vietnam. While the siege was still in progress, Dulles summoned a group of congressional leaders and spoke pointedly to them, asking their approval for intervention. The leaders, mostly members of the Democratic party, demurred, and advised Dulles to consult America's allies. Dulles flew to London to ask for Britain's support in a joint enterprise of succor that could yet save the day. But Churchill, Eden, and the British Cabinet were unsympathetic; they had no desire to become involved in other people's wars through collective security or any other moral formula and they declined the invitation to contain communism in this fashion. In any event, Eden told Dulles, it was too late to save the French garrison at Dien Bien Phu.

American intervention at this point, April–May 1954, had been a near thing. With the approval of Congress, B-26s would have been flown in from Formosa, and other planes from carriers of the Seventh Fleet. France would have announced at the same time that it was accelerating its program for the independence of Vietnam, and the situation, it seemed to the American administration, would have been stabilized as it had been in Korea. The military plans, in fact, might even have involved more than the planes; suggestions had been made by responsible officers that tactical nuclear weapons be used against the Vietminh and President Eisenhower had more than once declared he would employ them if necessary to stop a mass attack against American forces.[33]

The decision reluctantly made, however, mainly because of the lack of support in London (given President Eisenhower's self-imposed restrictions on unilateral action), and secondarily because of the complete lack of enthusiasm (principally Democratic) in Congress, was to tell the French that American planes would not be sent to raise the siege.

But even after Dien Bien Phu, where 16,000 French troops were killed or surrendered to the Vietminh, the administration in Washington was not ready to accept the consequences of French defeat. The Geneva Conference began on April 26, 1954, and President Eisenhower on May 10 instructed Secretary Dulles to prepare a resolution he intended to bring before Congress authorizing the use of American troops in Indochina. This was never done, though, because the French were through with the war no matter who wanted to help them fight. They had suffered 370,000 casualties, 74,000 of them from Metropolitan France. The war, despite the huge American aid, had cost billions of francs and they wanted no more of it. The plans for American intervention were finally dropped when this became unmistakably clear to Washington and Dulles told the French ambassador, Henri Bonnet, that there would be no American troops.

The Geneva Conference

The Geneva Conference had been decided on the previous year when Molotov, at a meeting in Berlin, brought up the question of a five-power conference on Asia to settle the Korean conflict and to discuss related questions. As the French position in Vietnam deteriorated in the course of 1953–1954, Premier Laniel became more and more anxious to have the Geneva meeting held as soon as possible, and his successor, Mendès-France, openly favored a truce. Although the conference, attended by nine states—the People's Republic of China, France, the Soviet Union, Britain, and the United States, together with representatives from Korea, Laos, Cambodia, and North Vietnam—was nominally about Korea, almost the entire eighty-seven days were spent on Indochina. At Ho's insistence, Bao Dai was not invited to attend and his representatives were present only as advisors to the French. Dulles joined the meeting reluctantly; he was unhappy with the conference but said he hoped the aggressors would come to it "in a mood to purge themselves of their aggression."[34]

Matters, however, did not work out that way. The defeated French were enabled to withdraw from Indochina with a compromise they could not gain on the battlefield. The victorious Vietminh were prevailed upon, apparently by their Chinese and Russian allies, who were pursuing their own separate interests, to accept a military cease-fire before the political problems of the country had been dealt with. Only the military issue was settled and thus France was able to walk away from all the political responsibilities it had acquired in the course of seventy years in Indochina. The Vietminh, once they accepted a cease-fire, had no other cards to play; no means to put pressure either on their allies or on their enemies at the conference. Vietnam was rid of the French but not of its divisions or of the resolve of the Vietminh to complete their victory. The meetings resulted in "An Agreement on the Cessation of Hostilities in Vietnam" signed by the French and the Vietminh military commands, and a "Final Declaration" listing all the powers present at the conference but actually signed by no one. In the Final Declaration, agreed to by voice vote on July 21, the conferees took note of the cease-fire, the withdrawal of French troops, the recognition by France of the independence of all three countries (Vietnam, Laos, and Cambodia), and the agreement of both sides to withdraw their troops north and south of the 17th parallel in Vietnam. This was a temporary division of the country representing the *de facto* situation in which the French occupied much of the South including Saigon (roughly half the country still under the nominal rule of Bao Dai). In addition, the declaration noted the prohibition against introducing into Vietnam foreign troops and military personnel, as well as arms and munitions. Neither Cambodia nor Laos were to request foreign aid and no military base under the control of a foreign state was to be established in either of the two regrouping zones in Vietnam. The division of the country, it was foreseen, would last only two years until July 20, 1956, when nationwide elections would be held (what kind of elections, whether for a constitutional assembly or for a legislature or for a plebiscite was not specified) and the country then unified under one government. An international commission of representatives from Canada, Poland, and India, under an Indian chairman, was to supervise carrying out the cease-fire agreement, and to report to the British and Soviet co-chairmen of the expired conference on the execution of the Final Declaration. The United States, in a separate statement, affirmed its desire to see countries such as Vietnam that were divided against their will unified through free elections supervised by the United Nations. Peoples, the statement said, are entitled to determine their own future and the United States would not join in any arrangement that would hinder this.

Not many of the countries involved were pleased with the outcome of the Geneva Conference. The North Vietnamese had wanted, at the least, the demarcation line to be drawn at the 13th not the 17th parallel, control of the ancient capital of Hué and assurances of nationwide elections in the near future.[35] North Vietnam signed the agreement, but South Vietnam did not sign with the French for the other side, and in the years following the accords, observed July 21 as a day of mourning. North Vietnam came to believe it had been taken in: that it had thrown away the great victory of Dien Bien Phu at the urgings of its advisors from China and the Soviet Union and thus had lost the opportunity to unite the country under one government—that of Ho Chi Minh.

The American National Security Council regarded the accords as a "disaster." President Eisenhower said on July 21 that while the United States, in compliance with the UN Charter, would not use force to disturb the settlement, "any renewal of Communist aggression would be regarded as a matter of grave concern."[36] To bolster the anti-Communist forces in Southeast Asia, and give Dulles some luster to cover the tarnish of the Geneva Conference, the Southeast Asia Treaty Organization (SEATO) was formed on September 8, 1954. SEATO, the counterpart of NATO, was made up of the United States, Britain, France, Australia, New Zealand, Thailand, the Philippines, and Pakistan. Specifically aimed at Communist aggression, the pact stated that an armed attack against any one of the signatory nations would be deemed to endanger the security of all and each signatory would meet the danger in accordance with its constitutional practices. A protocol added that the treaty area to be defended included Vietnam, Laos, and Cambodia.

The United States and the Defense of the South

Only 342 American military advisors were present in South Vietnam when the Geneva Accords were signed, a number the Joint

Chiefs of Staff thought far too few to help prepare the defense of South Vietnam. A covert military mission, whose job was to sabotage Vietminh installations and directives, was dispatched under Colonel Edward Lansdale in August. It was a small group that did not add to the frozen numbers of the Military Assistance and Advisory Group (MAAG) personnel since its ten or so members were assembled in Saigon before the deadline of August 11. It did, however, reflect American skepticism of the possibility of the accords' being carried out as planned, by either side. It seemed, in fact, to Messrs. Eisenhower and Dulles that the cause of law, peace, and freedom had suffered a major defeat and they set about, by dispatching military and political advisors and direct economic aid to Vietnam, to prevent what they were certain would be a Communist attempt to bypass the agreements and to take over all Vietnam with or without the promised elections. This is what had happened, despite Stalin's solemn assurances at Yalta, in Poland and other Eastern European countries, and they had no reason to believe, in the light of the Soviet performance since the end of World War II, that Russian and party strategy had changed.

On October 23, 1954, President Eisenhower addressed the so-called Diem letter to Bao Dai's premier, Ngo Dinh Diem, telling him that he had asked the American ambassador "to examine with you . . . how an intelligent program of American aid, given directly to your government, can serve to assist Vietnam in its present hour of trial, provided that your government is prepared to give assurances as to the standards of performance it would be able to maintain in the event such aid is supplied."[37] The letter was far from a blank check and far from promising any American military contingents. It was a statement, characteristic of Eisenhower, Truman, and many other American leaders, of a desire to give foreign aid in a just cause and to foster the development of an entire people. It was, in short, a kind of Marshall Plan made subject to proper behavior. In the next paragraph of the letter Eisenhower, sounding more than ever like a schoolmaster, wrote: "The United States expects this aid will be met by performance on the part of the government of Vietnam in undertaking needed reforms," for only in this fashion, the President was convinced, could communism, which feeds on social ills and injustices, be fenced out. Meanwhile, as a result of the provision for repatriation in the Geneva Agreement, a massive trek south had begun in Vietnam, a movement that was to change the complexion of the South Vietnamese populace and was to have serious political results for the Saigon government. Some 860,000 people chose to leave the northern zone and move to South Vietnam. The United States navy and air force helped to transport 250,000 of them. Six hundred thousand of the migrants were Catholics, fearful of the Ho government's religious and political policies, and their fears were played upon by Colonel Lansdale's team, who had fake Vietminh leaflets printed telling of alleged plans of the new state against the lives and property of its citizens. Similar leaflets describing completely imaginary Chinese atrocities in the Tonkin region, including murder and rape, were also printed and distributed by the Lansdale "psywar" group. In addition, the Catholic devout were assured by their religious leaders that God had moved to the South and many wished to join Him. But of the 860,000 refugees who decided to go, the great majority undoubtedly did so because they had a chance to leave a Communist-run state whose manner of rule they had already experienced. Observers have estimated that another 400,000 would have liked to leave but were prevented by the Ho government from doing so.[38] A considerable migration of 60,000 to 90,000 people from the South to the North also took place, but these migrants included Communist troops who had been fighting the French in the South, some of whom would be retrained and sent back again.

Ngo Dinh Diem

The Vietminh left behind them in South Vietnam a skeleton organization of some 5000 to 10,000 men for political and propaganda activity on behalf of the Ho government during the preparations for the 1956 elections. It seemed likely to many foreigners, as it did to many Vietnamese in both North and South, that the promised elections would be won by the Ho forces. Bao Dai's Premier, Ngo Dinh Diem, succeeded him as President after elections were held in South Vietnam in 1955. These elections were like those in Algeria; in some parts of the country Diem got more votes than there were voters.*
Nevertheless, he was a good deal abler than the playboy ex-Emperor who, as President Eisenhower said, paid much more attention to the gay spots of Europe than to fighting Communists in Vietnam. Diem, himself the descendant of Vietnamese emperors, moved

* According to French reports 605,000 votes were recorded in Saigon which had 450,000 voters. (Dennis J. Duncanson, *Government and Revolution in Vietnam*, p. 223.)

quickly and efficiently to restore order but even with heavy infusions of American aid he had an overwhelming task to accomplish after the years of war and the influx of almost a million refugees.

An able but autocratic administrator, Diem, in the beginning, brought a measure of ordered life to South Vietnam. He disarmed the major religious sects that had their own armies, something that no strong ruler could tolerate: those of the Cao Dai, a sect originally concentrated on the practices of spiritualist phenomena including table-tapping, the Union of Binh Xuyen, founded by bandits and river pirates, and the Hoa Hao, founded by a faith-healer just before the start of World War II.[39] Diem also entered upon an erratic program of land reform that set the government up as landlord of formerly French-held property where it imposed even more onerous terms on its tenants than did many private landlords. Only a quarter of the 2.47 million acres taken from the French was given the peasants; about one million, or 10 percent, received land. Two percent of the landlords, many of them absentee, owned over 45 percent of the riceland, and land owned by the Catholic Church, some 370,000 acres, was not subject to transfer.[40] A Catholic, Diem seemed to many south Vietnamese to have appointed an undue proportion of his co-religionists to offices and he was even more generous to members of his own family in the apportionment of the perquisites of power. He replaced village headmen with Saigon-appointed officials, a resented violation of Vietnamese traditions, although it should be noted that with the enormous problems posed by the refugees, Diem needed trained personnel in large numbers and these could come only in large part from the North where many Catholics had worked in the French administration. A bachelor himself, it was said that Diem had, when young, intended to be a priest. He was related not only to royalty but to the rich and powerful family of his brother's wife, Mme. Nhu, and another of his brothers was an archbishop.

An introverted man given to long periods of meditation, Diem sought to rule according to his Catholic-cum-Confucian copybook principles. His critics, whether Communists or disaffected Southerners, accused him of corruption, blatant prejudice, and the use of terror against suspected rivals. The latter two charges had substance, but Diem was personally not corrupt as so many Vietnamese administrators were. His chief political vice was his rigidity: his sure knowledge that he was doing God's work in the narrow parochial courses he followed. When his brother's birthday or a Catholic holiday was celebrated, religious flags flew from buildings and rejoicing processions moved in the streets, but when the celebration in May 1963 honoring the birth of Buddha followed the birthday gala for Diem's brother, Buddhist flags were forbidden, as was the gathering of the Buddhist faithful in the streets. It was no doubt possible, even likely, that the Buddhists had been infiltrated by Communist cadres and that the celebrations might well have taken on an anti-Diem coloration, but the repressive measures still seemed obviously one-sided. Diem formally consecrated South Vietnam to the "Immaculate Heart of the Virgin Mary" in a ceremony held in front of the Saigon cathedral. Since the overwhelming majority of Vietnamese were either Buddhist, Confucist, members of the sects, animists, or belligerent nonsectarians of the left, a large segment of the population, as a result of Diem's religious and secular biases, came to distrust and then detest him and his family.[41]

Diem and his relatives responded in kind, and when Buddhist monks burned themselves to death in public in protest against Diem's rule, Madame Nhu referred to the self-immolations as "barbecues" and said that if she had her way "they should be beaten ten times more." Nhu, not to be outdone, said he would be glad to supply the gasoline and a match.[42]

Neither Eisenhower nor his successor, President John Kennedy, was able to get the moderately high level of performance they had hoped for, but each in his turn supported Diem mainly because he was solidly anti-Communist. One of Diem's brothers, Khoi, had been taken prisoner by the Vietminh and, according to one story, beaten to death, according to another, killed by being buried in an anthill.[43]

In the north, Ho, too, dealt harshly with the population he loved so well as he proceeded to free the peasants from their feudal bonds with the aid of land reform battalions, sometimes accompanied by Chinese advisors. Under the land laws of the Ho government, anyone possessing a half-acre of riceland was considered a rich farmer and anyone who owned two acres or more was a landowner. In the course of this doctrinaire and hastily contrived land reform, organized, as in China, by the party, it has been calculated that tens of thousands of peasants were liquidated and others made outcasts and driven from their village communities. People's Courts, seeking to eradicate not only landlords but any desire to own property, demanded quotas of denunciations from communities and anyone who owned even a tiny plot might be denounced. So harsh were the measures that a sizable uprising took place in Northern Annam in 1956 that led, after its suppression and a period of breast-beating and self-criticism, to a scaling down of the program. The government freely acknowledged the gravity of the mistakes that had been made but no judicial action was taken against the perpetrators of the killings nor was restitution ever made to the victims or their families.[44]

Neither the North nor the South was a model of the good society, and the Communist party no more than Diem permitted an opposition party, a concept broadly defined on both sides of the 17th parallel.

The North Vietnamese and the Southern cadres, according to Giap, welcomed the rule of Diem in the South because he was such an easy target. So many millions of Southerners were soon disaffected by Diem's regime that it was easy to propagandize among them, or would have been if Diem had not moved so violently against the cadres the North Vietnamese had left behind. The Communist organization was reduced to a remnant as Diem made wholesale arrests that caught many more than Communists in its nets but captured hundreds of party workers too.

In any case, it seemed unlikely to the Americans and to Diem that he could win the elections planned for 1956 against Ho and they were never held. Eisenhower is often quoted as having said that he believed Ho would win the elections, but the remark was made while Bao Dai was still head of state and Bao was replaced by Diem who, even discounting the fake election, no doubt defeated him with an overwhelming vote. Nevertheless, as Diem continued in office, his popularity, which at first was relatively high in the South, diminished rapidly and any countrywide election contest conducted with reasonable honesty would have been at the least chancey and possibly would have resulted in another great victory for the Communist forces. In any event, Diem refused to hold the elections and the Americans supported his decision.

It was evident to many of the Communist cadres in the South that they had to shift their tactics back from the political to the military. Up to 1957 they had obeyed directives not to resort to arms despite the devastating roundups that had greatly reduced their numbers and effectiveness, but by the end of 1957 they again turned to guerrilla tactics. In the last quarter of that year thirty incidents of terrorism took place in which at least seventy-five local officials were assassinated or kidnapped and thirteen Americans wounded in three bombings in Saigon. It was the beginning of a campaign designed to rock the Diem government, to demonstrate that it was death to work in its administration, that no one who collaborated was safe. It was not until the end of 1958 and the early part of 1959, however, that the Lao Dong's (the Communist party) Central Committee meeting in Hanoi decided on full-scale guerrilla war to be directed from the North and began infiltrating large bodies of fresh units into the South. Up to then the Vietcong had largely operated on its own with only minor aid from Hanoi.

Diem's attacks on the Vietcong had done more than break into the party organization. The raids had been directed against any organized resistance and some 45,000 prisoners had been taken, the vast majority of whom had nothing to do with the Communist apparatus. Diem cared little if he was disliked and vilified by individual critics; it was organized opposition that he feared, and it might take the form of any kind of gathering, whether political or religious. It was these tactics of suppression that drove a wedge between him and the population and as early as November 1960 resulted in an attempt of South Vietnamese civilians and paratroopers to overthrow the Diem regime.

President Eisenhower's support of Diem had been continued despite the overall dubious performance of his government, partly because Diem himself was considered to have done pretty well, even to have accomplished "miracles," as was said in the early months of his regime, and later because he seemed to be the most reliable man at hand in an explosive situation. The vulnerability of South Vietnam became increasingly evident with the mounting Vietcong attack aided by North Vietnamese infiltrations. When President Kennedy took office in 1960, South Vietnam was one of the exposed positions on the wide front of American-supported anti-Communist deployment. The American military mission had grown under President Eisenhower to 685 advisors legally there under the Geneva Agreements (small increases had been approved by the International Control Commission (ICC), which was still in the country to supervise the carrying out of the cease-fire and the preconditions for elections that were never to take place).

President Kennedy Moves In

The limited-risk policy of Eisenhower was extended and then transformed under President Kennedy, who in the spring of 1961 ordered 400 Special Forces troops and 100 additional military advisors to Vietnam, a decision made in secret and contrary to the Geneva cease-fire agreements. The pressures on Mr. Kennedy to take such a step were considerable. Diem was calling for American help to build up a South Vietnamese army of 100,000 men, reports were coming in of the crumbling of the South Vietnamese defense system, and, as Vice President Johnson said after a quick visit to Vietnam, the United States either had to increase its aid or throw in the towel.

Not many Americans at this point were in favor of throwing in the towel. It was believed that by sending in agents to North Vietnam on a mission to form networks of resistance, harassment, and sabotage against railroads, highways, bridges, trucks, and depots, and by financing not a 100,000 but a 30,000 increase in the South Vietnamese forces, a beginning would be made to stem the intervention of the North and the dissolution of the Diem regime. Almost immediately, however, it became apparent in the recommendations of the Joint Chiefs of Staff and of President Kennedy's personal military advisor, General Maxwell Taylor, that more than a few hundred Americans would be needed. The Chinese were always a potential threat, as they had demonstrated in Korea, and one report to President Kennedy said China was preparing to send a division of combat troops to Vietnam. Various calculations were made—the Joint Chiefs estimated that 40,000 American soldiers would be needed to clean up the Vietcong threat, General Taylor thought 6000 to 8000 troops should be sent to the Mekong Delta and that an American task force was essential. It would not be long before the Joint Chiefs calculated that 205,000 American troops would solve all the problems of the defense of South Vietnam, including a possible Chinese Communist intervention. The chairman of the Joint Chiefs, General Lyman Lemnitzer, when asked by Mr. Kennedy about the importance of Laos, Cambodia, and Vietnam, said that if they were lost, the United States would lose Asia all the way to Singapore. The situation seemed so critical that American demands for the still-to-be-made reforms in the Diem government were softened and the demand for a voice in Diem's decision-making was dropped.

Therefore, early in the Kennedy administration the decision, as Vice President Johnson pointed out, had to be made to either get out or plunge in. What had been a minor American commitment in Vietnam and the other Indochinese states was nevertheless a segment of a global, overall bipartisan policy that held if communism was not stopped at what seemed critical points in Europe and Asia, it would overrun both. With the history of Soviet expansion in Europe, their ruthless Russian suppression of the Berlin uprisings in 1953 and the Hungarian revolt in 1956, and above all, with the success of the Chinese Communists in winning the mainland and then intervening in Korea, the need to shore up a defense against Communist dynamism was obvious. Not only were the Communist countries a formidable military bloc, the party itself was enormously resourceful as an arm of Soviet policy with its varied political organizations. The National Liberation Front (NLF), established in South Vietnam in 1960 with an elaborate and effective program for recruiting the peasantry, had its cadres in every village.

A Democratic administration was especially sensitive to criticism of a weak-kneed foreign policy with regard to communism. Under Roosevelt and Truman, their critics charged, much of Europe and Asia had been surrendered to communism, and President Truman had had to reverse Mr. Roosevelt's policies that had been based on continued concessions to Stalin and the Soviet Union soon after he became President or more would have been lost. Every American President from Truman on had agreed on this principle: communism had to be stopped, and each step taken in its turn seemed reasonable, even inevitable.

Few casualties occurred among the 685 American military advisors in Vietnam during the Eisenhower years and the sums expended would have been considered well spent had they accomplished their purpose of invigorating a strong anti-Communist South Vietnam, leading it gently toward democratic ways, and demonstrating again, as similar tactics had done in West Germany, the inherent superiority of the free societies and economies of the West over their totalitarian challengers in the East. It was not an ignoble dream, although it could not be realized anywhere in Indochina.

In the year 1961 the thrust of Communist expansion was evident in many parts of the world. Khrushchev confronted the young and inexperienced American President with the threat that the Soviet Union would sign a separate peace treaty with East Germany, a move that presaged a new Berlin crisis. The American-backed invasion of Cuba by Cuban refugees failed when President Kennedy refused to order the naval air support into action, and Russian support of Castro, it became evident, was far more potent than the irresolute American attempt to overthrow him. In Laos, the Pathet Lao, the Communist resistance forces, were reinforced by North Vietnamese units and threatened the overturn of Souvanna Phouma, who was striving mightily to keep his country together. Souvanna Phouma's policy was cautiously pro-American; he had the friendliest sentiments toward communism elsewhere but was opposed to it in Laos. The Soviet Union called for an international conference where the Pathet Lao would have equal status with the government representatives. When the conference, attended by fourteen nations, was held in Geneva in 1961–1962, it ended, after many recriminations on both sides, in an agreement on the neutralization of Laos which had, however, little or no effect on the heavy fighting in that country which was to continue with intermittent pauses for years to come.

What the United States did in support of its policies in Vietnam was never enough. The computers of the Pentagon whirred expensively, military and academic advisors furrowed their brows and made precise calculations. Mr. McGeorge Bundy in 1961 urged early a "hard-hitting" American intervention, figuring that this would have a 70 percent chance of arresting things and only a thirty percent chance the Americans would end up like the French because "white men can't win this kind of fight."[45]

Everything was quantified. General Taylor thought North Vietnam was extremely vulnerable to air attack, the Joint Chiefs that 205,000 American soldiers (apparently precisely the number the computers had determined) were all that would be needed even if the Chinese Communists joined the North Vietnamese. But none of the calculations or calculators seemed to have taken into account the well-known fact that all the bombing of a highly industrialized nation like Germany during World War II had not broken civilian morale nor prevented German war production from rising month by month until nearly the very end of the war. Above all, no computations disclosed the resolve of thousands of Vietnamese, Communist and non-Communist, to win the war no matter what the odds. President Kennedy could increase the American personnel to 16,732 during his term of office and his successor to over half a million; with American bombers, warships, and the modern weapons, the Pentagon could order enough firepower into action to win a conventional victory a thousand times over—but not in the jungle, not against well-trained, often fanatically determined men. Ho Chi Minh had compared his war against the French with the battle of a tiger against an elephant. At the end, he had said, the elephant would sink to the ground drenched in its own blood. The odds against the North Vietnamese and the NLF, once the United States committed its ground and air forces, were far more formidable than they had ever been when the Vietminh fought the French, but in the end, although there was no Dien Bien Phu, it was the Americans who wearied of the endless jungle warfare as the French had wearied before them.

Diem was ousted in 1963 in a putsch of dissident generals who had the tacit support of the United States, which included the recommendation from Ambassador Lodge that American funds be placed at their disposal to buy off officers who otherwise might not support the coup.[46] No evidence links the CIA or any other American organization or individual to an active part in the plot to murder Diem and his brother, but the American Embassy in Saigon, the military advisors, and Washington knew of the planned coup and encouraged it. Obviously a better man than Diem was needed if the war was to be prosecuted and the oft-repeated goal of winning the hearts and minds of the Vietnamese people achieved.

Diem had become unsupportable in Vietnam and in the United States. Soldiers and police acting under his and Nhu's orders had continued to attack Buddhist demonstrators and raid pagodas, and in one incident Nhu's special forces, together with the police, fired into a crowd, killing nine people. Wholesale arrests were made and they included 1400 Buddhist monks. Mme. Nhu, a strict puritan, had laws passed against dancing and against divorce and complained when Americans danced at parties. Two attempts to unseat Diem had been made before the successful coup, both of them by South Vietnamese army officers, one in November 1960, the other in February 1962. American stick-and-carrot methods to encourage reform by threats and promises were completely unsuccessful. As one foreign observer said, Diem and the Nhus gladly accepted American aid but not advice. The successful coup of November 1963 that took place shortly before the assassination of President Kennedy seemed to nearly all the Americans who wrote reports back and forth from Saigon to Washington a bleak necessity.

The situation in South Vietnam, however, never improved. Diem's immediate successors, General Duong Van Minh and Major General Nguyen Khanh, were not the hoped-for strong and honest democrats who would unite the South Vietnamese in their peril, nor would their successors fit this description. Americans could not find the equivalent in Vietnam of their own eponymous heroes who slew the dragons of corruption and treason nor could they find a non-Communist Ho. South Vietnam was governed in large part by people from the North who had no roots in the country and often regarded the South Vietnamese as more alien than the North Vietnamese Communists. Although many South Vietnamese officers had been among the fighters in the Vietminh who had defeated the French, many others held their jobs because of their connections and because they were considered politically reliable.

President Johnson's Solutions

It never worked, none of it. The Vietnamese were unaccountably different, both the friends and the enemies. The friends were to be supported and admonished to behave in the American image of virtue, and the enemies defeated by complicated calculations of so much lead and defoliants, napalm and ingenious bombs. Ten times the number of bombs were dropped on North Vietnam, the Ho Chi Minh Trail, and Laos and Cambodia than were used in the entire war in the Pacific in World War II, and still the enemy fought on.* It made no sense, it was science fiction turned around. President Johnson upped the American commitment over and over again, and then, after the Tonkin Gulf incident in August 1964, he declared a war by land, sea, and air, with bombing of the North and in 1965 the use of American ground troops. It was about as far as Johnson could go without nuclear weapons and without a naval blockade in a war never declared by Congress, although the resolution adopted at the time of the Tonkin Gulf incident came close to such a formal declaration. None of those tactics worked. Undoubtedly a lot of the enemy were killed, soldiers as well as noncombatants (in January 1967 the CIA estimated air war casualties in 1965–1966 at 36,000, 80 percent of whom were civilians), but the tactics did not destroy the enemy or his capacity to mount more offensives of the kind he excelled in. What they did succeed in producing was a self-loathing in the American people that matched the loathing of America in the rest of the world as they witnessed a superpower, the most super in the world, burning and slaying an enemy armed and unarmed that could not reply in kind. The enemy could, however, reply in other ways as the Tet offensive of 1968 would demonstrate.

Aggression at Tonkin Gulf

The Tonkin Gulf incident is an enlightening example of the loose way in which the term and concept of aggression are used. According to President Johnson's account to Congress and the American pub-

---

* Cornell University researchers, in December 1971, reported that 6 million tons of bombs had been dropped in Indochina compared with 2 million in the course of World War II.

lic, the American destroyer *Maddox*, while on patrol in international waters twenty-three miles from shore, was attacked on August 2, 1964, by North Vietnamese torpedo boats that failed to hit her. The *Maddox*, however, scored a direct hit on one of the torpedo boats and two others were damaged by planes from the *USS Ticonderoga*, which joined the action. The *Maddox* was then joined by another destroyer, the *Turner Joy*, and on the night of August 4–5, while continuing what Secretary McNamara called their routine patrols in international waters, they were again attacked. The ships had been ordered not to approach the coast more closely than eight miles on the day of the first attack, after which the prohibited distance was increased to eleven miles. The destroyers, however, had been much farther from the mainland than that, so when the attacks occurred there was no question of the ships' being in territorial waters. In retaliation for this unprovoked aggression, the President had ordered, eleven hours after the second attack, the bombing of targets in North Vietnam (sixty-four sorties were made against torpedo boat bases and oil depots) and had asked for, and obtained, from Congress a resolution giving him the power to "take all necessary measures to repel any armed attack against the forces of the United States and to prevent further aggression." Because, the resolution said, the maintenance of peace and international security in Southeast Asia was vital to the American national interest and consonant with its obligations under the Charter of the UN and SEATO, "the United States is prepared as the President determines, to take all necessary steps, including the use of armed force, to assist any member or protocol state of the Southeast Asia Collective Defense Treaty requesting assistance in defense of its freedom."*

For critics of the war, especially in the Senate, evidence available later would throw considerable doubt on the administration's version of what had happened. Six months before the Tonkin Gulf incident a contingency plan to bomb North Vietnam had been worked out and a congressional resolution had been drafted giving President Johnson substantially the war powers granted after the attack took place. The two American destroyers had been doing much more than routinely patrolling the international waters of the Gulf of Tonkin.

* The SEATO treaty provides that in the case of an armed attack, each signatory power will "meet the common danger in accordance with its constitutional processes." In other cases of subversion or indirect aggression they are to consult immediately on measures for the "common defense." Neither SEATO nor the American Declaration at Geneva would seem to have been designed for the use which President Johnson made of them on this occasion.

The *Maddox* had electronic detection apparatus that it used to "stimulate" the North Vietnamese radar and so locate it. Two North Vietnamese villages near the Laotian border had apparently been bombed by American T-28 planes on August 1 and 2, either deliberately or through a navigational error.[47] The ships were operating 100 miles from where South Vietnamese vessels were making an amphibious raid on two islands in the gulf, Hon Me and Hon Ngu, as part of an action called 34-A, directed by the American High Command with ships furnished South Vietnam by the American navy. It was, in fact, first thought in Washington that the initial attack on the *Maddox* had been made because the North Vietnamese had mistaken it for one of the vessels supplied the South Vietnamese. However, the second attack on the night of August 4–5, together with the radio intercepts, confirmed to Mr. Johnson and the Pentagon that the North Vietnamese did know the nationality of the destroyers the torpedo boats were attacking, although American Senators later questioned whether there had been any second attack at all.*

The night of August 4–5 had been heavily overcast, "like a knob of hell" one sailor said. The information obtained from sonar and radar was confusing. Warm, tropical air, especially over land-locked water, can cause "ducting" in the radar apparatus which makes distant objects seem close by on the screen. The sonar devices are difficult to interpret against the noise of the propellers, and the commander of the task force, Captain Herrick, expressed doubts soon after the recordings of enemy presence as to what had really happened.[48] The *Maddox* sonarmen, at the time, reported that twenty two torpedoes were fired, but later evaluations made that figure impossible since the Swatow boats carried no torpedoes and only some four to eight North Vietnamese torpedo boats were thought to be on the scene. The commander of the *Turner Joy* was certain he had been attacked and topside personnel had sighted two torpedoes, but none had been seen by the *Maddox* whose sonar picked up twenty-two. Secretary McNamara came to the Senate hearings in 1968 with a bullet in his possession that was the only tangible evidence that the ships had been fired on, and the bullet had been found after the first attack on August 2. The *Pentagon Papers*, however, indicate that President Johnson and his staff were convinced that an attack had been made, that it had been confirmed by North Vietnamese

* The North Vietnamese torpedo boats carried one or two torpedoes. They were accompanied by small patrol boats called "Swatow" that have no torpedoes but only 37-mm. guns.

radio reports and their admission that two additional torpedo boats had been sunk.

During the 1968 hearings of the Senate Foreign Relations Committee chaired by Senator William Fulbright, a question arose as to what kind of routine patrol it was, with the one destroyer equipped with apparatus to rouse the enemy radar and with both destroyers operating at the same time as a South Vietnamese task force was attacking North Vietnamese territory. Antiwar Senators like Wayne Morse and Albert Gore charged later that the destroyers had been cooperating with the South Vietnamese 34-A action to draw off the defending North Vietnamese ships from the South Vietnamese task force, and very likely, too, they thought, to provoke an incident President Johnson could use to get his equivalent-to-war resolution through Congress.

To Senator Morse, especially, the later evidence removed the incident a long way from President Johnson's and Secretary McNamara's "routine patrol in international waters." This dark suspicion of the United States deliberately provoking the attack is not borne out in the *Pentagon Papers*, which indicate that American officials did not expect a second attack on the reinforced patrol following a firm warning by the State Department that another attack would have "grave consequences," and the captain of the *Maddox* had not been told of the South Vietnamese raids and was on an unrelated mission.[49] On the other hand, the Tonkin Gulf attack did follow the administration "scenario" of a development that would provide an excellent reason for stepping up American intervention with congressional approval.

President Johnson called the incident deliberate aggression,* although it is not easy to see how that could possibly occur when clandestine and open attacks on North Vietnamese territory were being made and the ships were not far from a South Vietnamese task force using American-furnished warships to shell North Vietnamese islands and the mainland.

The President, eleven hours after the second attack, ordered the retaliatory sixty-four sortie air raid on torpedo boat bases and oil depots in North Vietnam.† This was an election year and the war

---

* On August 5, 1964, Mr. Johnson told an audience at Syracuse University: "Aggression—deliberate, willful and systematic aggression—has unmasked its face to the entire world." (Department of State Bulletin, August 24, 1964, Vol. 5, pp. 260–261.)

† President Johnson, whether consciously or not, was imitating President Roosevelt's actions in September 1941. Mr. Roosevelt had ordered American warships to join

was relatively low-keyed, but in December 1964 the bombing was stepped up. Operation Barrel Roll was ordered against the Laotian infiltration trails. NLF guerrillas made hit-and-run attacks on American troops and in reprisal American jets bombed Donghoi in North Vietnam in February 1965.

The American Forces Move In, Mr. Johnson Moves Out

The year 1965 is often called a turning point in the war in Vietnam, when the war became an American war, for at the end of that year the decision was made to increase the relatively modest force of some 23,000 men to 184,000 and to shift their combat assignments from supporting, defensive missions to those of attack and then search and destroy. On March 8, 3500 marines were landed in Danang to defend the airfield there and in April the number of American troops was increased by 18,000 to 20,000 men. A month later the marines in Danang were ordered to take a more active role in the fighting beyond defense of the airfield and in July an overall increase of 100,000 men was ordered. The troop movements were accompanied by an air operation called Rolling Thunder. Set in motion on February 15, it was the beginning of a sustained air war. On March 9 the use of napalm was authorized by the President against a naval base and munition dumps in the North. Even after the targets were multiplied to include petroleum, oil, and lubricant storage plants (the so-called POL targets) in March 1966, American intelligence reports soon said the bombings had not stopped or even slowed the enemy assaults. Demands for American troops became more frequent because the precarious situation of the South Vietnamese government and its armed forces never seemed to improve.*

Whether a turning point or not, 1965 was a year when the United States lurched more deeply into a conflict into which it had previ-

---

British patrols in the North Atlantic, convoying shipping, locating German submarines, and radioing their positions to the British. The USS *Greer* was tracking a German submarine, the U-652, having called in British planes, and when two depth charges were dropped the submarine fired two torpedoes, discovering only a day later that the *Greer* was American. Mr. Roosevelt, however, announced that the attack on the *Greer* was unprovoked, and called it "piracy." (Eugene Davidson, *The Trial of the Germans*, pp. 400–401.)

  * In November 1965 General Westmoreland asked that American troop strength be increased to 375,000. In December he asked for 443,000 by the end of 1966. In January the number was scaled up to 459,000 and in August the general asked for 542,588 men for 1967. (*Pentagon Papers*, pp. 460–461.)

ously entered cautiously, step by step. If it was a turning point, it was one among many; President Truman's decision to aid the French in 1950, Eisenhower's decision to send 800 military advisors, Kennedy's decision to increase their number to 16,000, were all turning points. What seems to have been crucial in 1965 was the fatal decision to let the war become a generals' war, a war fought by army standards with military success as the goal, and this came about because the political goals were unattainable.

Not that the generals got all the troops they wanted when they wanted them, and a green light to go anywhere and bomb anything they wanted to. Washington imposed checks on their strategy but could assign no goals that armed forces could secure. The simplistic formula of establishing a functioning democracy by permitting the people to choose their own form of government could not work because no viable South Vietnamese state existed. What there was was a government imposed on the peasantry partly by the circumstances of the revolution, and partly by an alien people building on the widespread rejection by the peasants of the North's communism. But a viable state could not be created by pumping in huge sums of money and troops, not in the face of an enemy determined to unify the country under his rule, with a program of getting rid of the alien white man and of social reform far more dazzling than those offered by Diem or Khanh or later Thieu. Up to the time President Kennedy increased the American forces to 16,000 men it would no doubt have been easier to pull out, but that would have been to sound retreat in the face of a dangerous worldwide enemy, and no administration could do that if a few more installments of American troops might yet dam the Red tide.

The use of more bombing and larger American military forces would have been necessary from the point of view of the State Department, the administration, and the Pentagon whether or not the *Maddox* had ever been fired on. The United States was already in the field with its military advisors, helicopters, and covert forces. Tonkin Gulf and the decisions made in 1965 stepped up the war effort, but the war escalation in 1965 was inevitable because a political solution was not possible.

The High Command of the American armed forces had always been optimistic about the course of the war. It may be recalled that the Pentagon had said 205,000 soldiers would be enough to provide victory even if the Chinese came in. But they were not enough even without the Chinese. Generals kept seeing light at the end of the tunnel. General Westmoreland predicted in 1966 that the war would be won in 1967. That seemed plausible enough until the Tet offensive of the North Vietnamese and the NLF opened in 1968. In Saigon, in scores of towns and villages, in all the cities of South Vietnam, NLF infiltrators and regular troops from North Vietnam began bomb, mortar, and combat assaults that captured the city of Hué, established their control of much of the countryside, and took weeks of bloody fighting and masses of American troops to put down.

The Tet offensive was a turning point in the war. General Westmoreland asked for 206,000 more troops and the dammed-up antiwar sentiment in Congress and in large segments of the American public became a torrent no President could resist. Mr. Johnson ordered an immediate increase in American troops of 10,500 men (later he approved an additional 20,000 men) but he could not accept the increase the Pentagon said was needed without a major revolt of influential members of his own party, the threat of ever increasing demonstrations accompanied by violence, and almost unanimous condemnation in the media. The dam had broken and the alternatives Mr. Johnson had accurately presented to President Kennedy six years before had to be confronted again: either do more, much more, or get out. As had been the case with the French in Indochina and Algeria, the American public was fed up with a war that got nowhere. In the Democratic primary in New Hampshire, despite the support of the entrenched party apparatus and the expenditure of considerable funds, the President won the nomination only by a relatively narrow margin over antiwar Senator Eugene McCarthy. Mr. Johnson knew a good deal more about political returns and polls of public sentiment than he did about how to wage war and peace in Vietnam. He reduced the bombing of the North, and when that seemed too little and too late, he stopped it altogether, at the same time that he announced he would not be a candidate for a second full term.

President Nixon and the War

It was Mr. Nixon, long an advocate of Communist containment and American military intervention in Vietnam, who came into office promising to end a war he had wanted to join a decade before. He chose the second of the two courses of action in Vietnam of which

Mr. Johnson had spoken earlier. Mr. Nixon's decision to withdraw American troops, to "Vietnamize" the war, was too hedged with ambiguities to be pleasing to either hawks or doves but it was irreversible. The battlefield might be momentarily enlarged with South Vietnamese incursions into Laos and Cambodia, supplied by American planes and helicopters, but American soldiers, if not their air and naval forces, were on their way out.

The invasion of South Vietnam by the North in the spring of 1972 did not alter this basic decision. When it seemed to Mr. Nixon and his advisors that the South Vietnamese army and government might collapse and a humiliating defeat be imposed on the United States by an enemy that refused to negotiate any, even face-saving terms of settlement, the President ordered the mining of North Vietnamese harbors and a large-scale air and naval bombardment. The alternatives—the abject acknowledgment of defeat, the surrender of thousands of Vietnamese to slaughter on a far larger scale than that which occurred at Hué,* the considerable increment in Communist leverage in many parts of the world—these could not be accepted if any way out, other than again sending in American ground forces, could be found. That thousands of innocent people might be killed as a result of the bombing is part of the insane calculus of decision-making in war,† and while ordering the bombing, Mr. Nixon offered to withdraw all American troops from Vietnam within four months and to stop all acts of force in Indochina with only two conditions—a cease-fire under international supervision, and the freeing of American prisoners of war. One way or another the American adventure in Vietnam was coming to an end, and without aggression's having been conquered.

American Goals

Both Johnson and Nixon had assured the world that the United States wanted nothing in Vietnam, had no territorial or other selfish ambitions but merely the purpose of letting the South Vietnamese, and if possible all Vietnamese, choose their own form of government. But even as political rhetoric this was to millions of Americans an inadequate justification for the sacrifices imposed by an endless war.

---

* See p. 205.

† It also seems to be far more acceptable to American public opinion than was the ground combat.

Half a million American casualties, 50,000 American dead, hundreds of thousands of Vietnamese dead on whose behalf the United States had intervened, millions of refugees throughout Indochina, billions of dollars spent to result in the ruin of much of several countries and their peoples—this was part of the balance sheet. As for going to war to permit the Vietnamese to decide their own fate, that was a very large order. Many nations since World War II, in fact, from the beginning of time, have not succeeded in self-determination, and if the United States were to send troops to all of them it would be depopulated. The only SEATO country to join the United States in the war was Thailand, which was paid generously for every man sent. (Korea committed troops but Korea was not a member of SEATO.)

Other reasons for American intervention seemed more substantial: the fulfilling of the obligations imposed by the American addendum to the Geneva Agreements and by SEATO, and the containment of Communist expansion. And yet, did the SEATO treaty demand American intervention? It merely provided that in the event of an aggression against one of the signatories or against a protocol state, each signatory would act to meet the common danger in accordance with its constitutional processes. The American statement following the Geneva Final Declaration was violated when the United States sent covert forces into North Vietnam immediately after it affixed its signature to the document. The statement no more than SEATO required American intervention. It merely said that the United States would view any renewal of the aggression in Vietnam in violation of the Geneva Agreements "with grave concern," and these were the agreements the United States promptly breached.

The containment of communism remains, and it is undoubtedly a desirable goal. But communism has not been contained in Vietnam; much more than firepower and generous sentiments are needed to combat it. The United States had only its good intentions and firepower and neither could sustain its presence there. The intervention was based on formulae for a defense against Communist expansion, valid enough directly after World War II, and on a belief in the universal application of collective security that it is doubtful ever had much validity. Giap writes derisively of the United States as "world gendarme," and the phrase has long been used with the same irony by many Americans and foreigners who are far removed from Giap's political beliefs. It is a mission the United States has assumed before —for example, when Wilson spoke in 1917 of making "the world safe for democracy," when Roosevelt promised the world the Four Freedoms, and to install the four policemen as a peace posse—but such morality plays are not genuine goals. Wars, as Clausewitz and many others have pointed out, are political acts, fought for political ends. If they are not perceived as such, the gendarme is bound to be trapped one day in the jungles of Indochina or Biafra or in the quicksands of a desert, on a barren mission whose results will bear no relation to his purposes.

The supreme crime at Nuremberg in the eyes of the chief American prosecutor, Justice Jackson, and of his government, was aggression; the other crimes were derived from it and Jackson linked the killing of 6 million Jews to the conspiracy to wage war. It is not easy, however, to disentangle the accusations of aggression from the crime itself. For the Communists, the aggressor is, of course, the United States and its running dogs, the South Vietnamese regime.[50] Many impeccable non-Communists agree that with the American disregard of the Geneva Final Declaration and its own statement, it was the United States that precipitated the large-scale war in which it became engaged. For successive American Presidents from Truman on, it has obviously been the Communists who, as in Korea, invaded from the North, organized the subversive cadres of the Vietnamese NLF, and attempted to impose their rule on the entire country who are the aggressors. It is unlikely that any court will ever decide the question, and if it did its decision would be based a good deal more on political than on any legal principles.

War Crimes and Crimes Against Humanity

The commission of war crimes and of crimes against humanity are not in dispute. They have been perpetrated by all sides, and the evidence for them is irrefutable. In large part they have resulted from the nature of guerrilla war where the enemy may be anywhere and anyone. Race differences have undoubtedly played a role, and in Vietnam as in Algeria, as in the old wars with the American Indian, no holds, no forms of torture, have been barred. But what is most striking is that the return to barbarism seems not to have shocked the Americans of the 1970s as it did the generation of the First and even the Second World War. An American lieutenant convicted of the killing of unarmed Vietnamese civilians, including babies, is hotly defended not only by soldiers in the field but by thousands of people at home and a ballad commemorates his heroism. The North Vietnamese and the Vietcong murder and torture as part of a battle plan to shake the morale of the unpersuaded, to destroy confidence in the South Vietnamese government and its ability to protect the people under its rule, and to provoke reprisals against the civilian population. They slay collaborators or those who, for any reason, fail to meet their incessant demands for men, money, and supplies. The war prisoners of the North Vietnamese are held with no attention paid to a humanitarian tradition, international conventions, or the customs and usages of war. Singlemindedly concentrated on their political goals, the NLF and the North Vietnamese use any means whatever to achieve them. The South Vietnamese have used torture as standard operating procedure when any suspect, man or woman, is to be questioned, and the use of electrodes or near-drownings, beatings with bamboo rods that tear away the skin and may leave the victims, including women, scarred for life, and other ingenious forms of physical violence have been described in detail by American and foreign witnesses.*

The North Vietnamese and the NLF have not enjoyed such sophisticated, scientific weapons as the Americans, but they have done the best they could with what they have. At Hué, before the city fell to the American counterattack in 1968, nineteen ditches full of corpses were found; it is said that 5800 people were killed or disappeared while the North Vietnamese held the city.[51] Some of them had been decapitated, some buried alive, some shot. These were victims who had been killed for political reasons, because they or their families had collaborated, and here, too, some of the bodies found were those of children. And Hué was no exception. In the South grenades might be hurled into houses or restaurants by members of the NLF, and bombs exploded that had been planted where civilians lived. Village chiefs have been killed in the presence of the entire population. In one village a chief, his wife, and daughter were brought to the village square where the chief was disemboweled before the eyes of his family and the villagers who were forced to attend. Then the

* Lieutenant Colonel Anthony Herbert, one of the most decorated men in the United States army, reports that he has witnessed such atrocities committed by ARVN soldiers in American prisoner of war compounds, and when he repeatedly protested to superior officers, he was relieved of his command. (*Dick Cavett Show*, Broadcast WABC, September 30, 1971.)

daughter was decapitated and the pregnant wife treated in the same fashion as her husband.[52] The daughter of another chief who was beheaded in Binh Dinh province had her arm cut off because her father had been a collaborator. A rifle was fired across the back of her six-year-old brother, leaving a long scar that would help him remember the day.[53] In at least one case an entire "social unit" was wiped out when a community leader, his wife, their daughter, and her husband, together with an unmarried daughter, two servants—a man and woman and their baby—were all killed by a Communist murder squad. Not only the human beings were exterminated, the family cat was strangled, a dog clubbed to death, and the goldfish scooped from their bowl and thrown on the floor.[54] Unlike the South Vietnamese, the NLF has often explained why they are killing* by pinning a note on the corpse of their victims or using a loudspeaker to tell the villagers what crimes those executed have committed.

The South Vietnamese have plundered and raped and killed because apparently they think that is mainly what a war is fought for. The Americans who saw them in action in Hué after it was retaken from the North Vietnamese were disgusted by their habit of plunder that seemed to the Americans in inverse proportion to their battle prowess.[55]

Crimes against humanity and war crimes committed over a period of years and on a broad scale have been charged against the Americans, who have been excoriated for mass bombing of civilian targets including hospitals, schools, and people working in the fields. The Americans are accused of wanton destruction of life and property, using biological warfare and gasses, napalm, white phosphorus, and bombs that release hundreds of smaller bombs spraying steel pellets that cut a swath hundreds of feet wide like a huge lethal bulldozer. The American army and its High Command are charged with dozens of Mylais by members and former members of its various services. Foreign and American observers have witnessed atrocities in which Americans have played a passive role, as when they merely watched the Vietnamese they were advising torture their prisoners, and Americans have also undertaken wanton killing and torturing on their

---

* Fifteen categories of people to be assassinated have been found in captured documents. They include: enemy forces engaged in espionage, police work, psy-war; members of "reactionary" religious or political parties, puppet government officials, leaders of organizations, defectors, and so on. (Douglas Pike, *Viet Cong Strategy of Terror*. Cited p. 88 in *The Human Cost of Communism*. Committee on the Judiciary, United States Senate, U.S. Government Printing Office, Washington, 1972.

own. Every unit of brigade size, said one American officer, has been responsible for its own version of Mylai; killing civilians, he reported, was a well-known and accepted practice.[56]

Whether or not such accusations of deliberate, wholesale, and protracted atrocities are all true, they have helped persuade American opinion that the Vietnam war is uniquely dirty and senseless, which is more or less what the Communist press of the world has wanted it to believe from the beginning. Usually, the revisionist history of a war begins some years after it is safely won and the patriotic fevers have subsided, but in Vietnam the revision has accompanied the action. The length and indecisiveness of the war, the woolly goals that could not be reached, the one-sidedness of the war reporting, the authoritarian way in which the United States became involved, the disarray on the American domestic front, the anti-Establishmentarianism of many intellectuals who believe that a society based on their notions of an enriched environment can change the nature of man—these are some of the elements that have set this war off from others the United States has fought.

No one saw the burned women and children of Dresden or Berlin or Tokyo on film during World War II or how noncombatants in Korea looked after napalm was dropped on them; Americans heard about the details of such events later on. It was not widely known during World War II that the British air force had orders not to waste bombs on dockyards or aircraft factories, that they were told: "the aiming points are to be the built up areas."[57] North Vietnamese and Vietcong atrocities are readily glided over; what films and reports come from the North are those they want the world to see and hear and read. The war is viewed by the American public through the magnifying end of a telescope in the South and through the reverse end in the North. But the American aversion to the war has not come about through manipulation alone. It is the longest, most frustrating war the United States has ever fought. Despite the overwhelming American technical superiority, and the huge sacrifices of lives and resources, there has been no victory, and only imperceptible progress toward subduing an enemy armed with relatively primitive weapons, seeking, as he tells us, no more than the unification of his country.

This is an excellent culture for the spread of Communist propaganda attempting to persuade the world, including Americans, that violence and indeed any evil in Vietnam would be exorcised once the Americans departed. This is the Dich Van program of the North Vietnamese which, like the art of Judo, turns the strength of the enemy against himself, and it has been very successful. Nevertheless, while Americans have been offered a one-sided picture of the brutalities of the war, the fact that war crimes have been committed by their armed forces in Vietnam as well as by their enemies is undeniable. A complicated attempt has been made to minimize them, the large American staff called MACV (American Assistance Command Vietnam) has issued precise "rules of engagement" in an attempt to establish what military actions may or may not be taken; the criteria for calling in air strikes or artillery barrages, when sniper fire may be returned, the definition of a free-fire zone. The rules impose restrictions on the use of napalm, defoliants, and antipersonnel weapons, and explain what to do if the ARVN are seen mistreating prisoners. They add up to a comprehensive, if theoretical, attempt to keep the war within humane bounds. No rule book, however, could cover the innumerable contingencies of guerrilla warfare and the program has been more impressive in its printed form than in the actual performance. In practice, the free-fire zone was often a place where everything that moved was considered a Vietcong, and therefore a proper target. The corpse of one boy was found with the child still holding on to the halter of the cow he had been leading before the machine guns of a helicopter brought him and the cow down. Deliberate attacks on enemy hospitals and medical installations have been reported by American units, and the body count tally put a premium on corpses whether or not they were those of soldiers. An American officer brought to trial for the murder of a prisoner of war argued that his action was consistent with official policy and the army's emphasis on a "high body count." The court thereupon revoked its verdict of premeditated murder, convicted him instead of involuntary manslaughter, and sentenced him to six months in jail. One witness saw a lieutenant deliberately kill a defenseless prisoner, and when asked why he had done it was told he needed to keep up his body count which was low for the day.[58] Without the body count the success of the American strategy could not be calculated. No frontlines were broken through, and if an area was occupied it might be infiltrated again as soon as the troops left. Therefore killing, piling up corpses, was the measure of success by which the efficiency of officers and men was judged. Also, the turkey shoots and target practice on anything that moved helped kill both the enemy and the monotony of the war. "Gonna get me a dink," a helicopter pilot is quoted as saying when he shot at a peasant and his buffalo who were at work in the fields.

Before the accelerated bombing began in the spring of 1972, ten million tons of bombs had been dropped on Vietnam, more than were used against the Third Reich and its allies, including the Japanese. Many of these bombs have hit civilian targets and at least some of them were intended to, as they were in World War II.

The use of napalm, a jellied gasoline that burns at a temperature of 1500 degrees centigrade, was authorized by President Johnson in 1965. It had been used in World War II against both the armed forces of the enemy and civilian targets, in Hamburg by the British in 1943, where some 50,000 people were killed, and in Dresden in 1945, a city undefended by antiaircraft guns and with no war industry; 120,000 to 150,000 people are estimated to have been killed as the city was attacked by three waves of British and American planes, dropping high explosives and napalm.[59] The improved napalm used in Vietnam burns at 2000 degrees centigrade, the magnesium bombs at 3500. During the bombing of North Vietnam children have worn hats of tightly woven textures against the cluster bombs that scatter 300 baseball-sized bombs, each with thousands of pellets, one of which can and has ripped out the eyes of a victim.

Civilian casualties have been high in Vietnam. As we have seen, the CIA is said to have estimated them as 80 percent of the total number killed or wounded by the bombing.[60] The war has created refugees in the millions; in Laos some 750,000 people, 2 million in Cambodia, 6 million in South Vietnam,[61] people who have been bombed out of their homes, or have left them for safer territory, or for refuges from the Vietcong tax collectors.

Entire villages had been destroyed for what has seemed to many observers, and no doubt to the people who had lived in them, little or no reason. Some of these were the so-called Zippo actions, where hutches were set on fire by GIs who held their lighters to the thatched roofs until they blazed. Such burnings might be conducted for relatively small provocations—a single shot fired from a place vaguely identified as Village A—or the destruction of a village might be called for by a South Vietnamese official because it was "VC infested." It has been reported that in some cases where an official asked for a bombing run on a village he might not even have seen it for years; all he had to go on was a rumor. Or it might be decided that a village was supplying food to the Vietcong and so it was ordered burned. It was hit and miss, except for the village and the people made homeless.

Other ways of depriving the NLF, and also a good many civilians, of food have been found. Rice crops have been destroyed by means of chemicals like Agent Blue, in use since 1961 for what the army euphemistically calls "a resource denial program." In addition, some food has been destroyed in the course of using defoliants on forest areas, and how much permanent damage has been done the land is disputed, as are the statistics.* In the attack on the crops it has been calculated that 560,000 acres were sprayed up to 1970, along with 5,200,000 acres of forest land, the total amounting to one-seventh of South Vietnam's land area.[62] One of the defoliants used— Agent Orange—was found to be teratogenic, that is, fetus-deforming, and its use was suspended, although in 1971 a million and a half gallons of it were still stored.[63] Vietnamese villagers might also be forcibly removed from their sometimes rich fields to a barren part of the country where they would allegedly be safer, as well as hungrier. The Strategic Hamlets Program, under which the South Vietnamese were removed to more secure areas in the neighborhood or kept from supplying the NLF with food, has been called a form of genocide by the Russell International War Crimes Tribunal.†

* A critic of the statistical methods used in some surveys points out that only certain areas are militarily worth defoliating, and since the jungle growth is stubborn these have had to be sprayed repeatedly. For example, an area of some 50 square miles along the Saigon-Vung-Tau highway was defoliated twice a year for five years, which in some interpretations appears as the defoliation of not 50 but 500 square miles. (Personal communication to author from Douglas Pike.)

† The Bertrand Russell International Tribunal met in Stockholm, Sweden, from April 30 to May 10, 1967. Set up on the initiative of Lord Russell, it was presided over by Jean-Paul Sartre, with two vice presidents, Laurent Schwartz, professor of mathematics at the University of Paris, and Vladimir Dedijer, a well-known Yugoslav historian and political figure. Other members of the tribunal included Simone de Beauvoir, Peter Weiss, the Swedish playwright Isaac Deutscher, historian and biographer of Stalin, a number of Americans, a Japanese jurist, and an Austrian writer. What the members of the tribunal had in common aside from their learning was a double standard of international law and morality, one for communist nations and another for the United States. They condemned American aggression and war crimes, found that not only had the United States been guilty of aggression as defined at Nuremberg, but had added a new and vicious turn by committing it against an entire people, aggression engaged in, not to settle a political dispute, but to prevent a people from defending their fundamental rights. Thus the American aggression was linked to genocide, of which the United States was also guilty. The United States has conducted, the tribunal said, a characteristically neo-colonialist war with the use of gas, chemical warfare, napalm, and phosphorous, as well as with fragmentation and other bombs designed for use against human beings and not against fortifications. The tribunal, while it in part confirmed testimony of other witnesses, had nothing to say

Almost none of the mitigations, whether of Hague or Geneva or the Genocide Convention, adopted by the United Nations in 1946 have been adhered to in Vietnam. It is illegal under American military law to bomb civilian targets unless they are fortified or harbor troops. But when refugee camps became too overcrowded, it is reported that army units in Guang Ngai province were told not to "generate" more refugees and no longer to issue warnings when search-and-destroy operations were under way.[64] Night bombing operations were conducted against obscurely identified enemy activity at specific map coordinates and a former intelligence officer reports that hospitals were second only to fixed installations as the targets of such bombings. In another kind of action ordered by the American High Command, Operation Thor, air strikes, some as wide as three kilometers, were made by B-52s in South Vietnam regardless of the villages that lay in their path.[65]

One of the principles of the legal use of military power cited in the *American Manual on Field Warfare* is that no more force will be used or more damage caused than is necessary to attain a military end. Such principles, too, have been disregarded in the Vietnamese war, although they were cited against the Germans in the trials after World War II. German generals who came before the Nuremberg courts were charged with causing the needless destruction of civilian dwellings, but General Jodl's counsel, Franz Exner, pleaded that the destructions in Norway, for example, had been made because of military necessity and had been kept to a minimum. Both the Nuremberg and Norwegian courts seem to have agreed with Professor Exner, for the charges were not upheld.[66] It is interesting to note however, that aside from the rule book issued by MACV no similar attempt by the American High Command to minimize the destruction of dwellings and villages seems to have been made in Vietnam.

My Lai

Almost every charge leveled against the German generals at Nuremberg has been made against the Americans in Vietnam: barbarous treatment of prisoners of war, wholesale and indiscriminate

---

about the atrocities committed by the North Vietnamese or by the NLF. In this respect, it bore some resemblance to the Nuremberg Tribunal, which was composed of members of the victorious powers, with the mandate to judge and punish only the crimes committed by the Axis powers.

bombing of civilian targets, involuntary mass transfer of civil populations, inhuman methods of warfare. How far these last may go is to be seen in one relatively small incident that has been carefully scrutinized at Mylai. In the slaughter at Son My, usually referred to as the Mylai massacre, more than 400 people, all of them civilians, were killed by American troops sent on a mission to clear the hamlet and subhamlets of Vietcong. The troops were members of C Company, First Battalion, 20th Infantry of the Amercal Division. They killed everyone they could find. A few refused to obey orders and did not shoot; the rest obeyed. Some of them raped women and then killed them; children and babies were shot and even animals. According to surveys in the United States after disclosure of the incident in the press, Americans questioned about the event mainly approved or condoned it.*

One writer explains that Charlie Company included an unusual number of men with subnormal intelligences. They had been inducted as an experiment by Secretary of Defense McNamara, who believed it a good idea to take men who would otherwise have been rejected because of their low IQs and, by educating them, bring them up to the level of the rest of the army. IQs cannot be very much improved in this fashion, but in any event, the men received no special education or training and like many other American soldiers many of them used drugs. One third to one half of them, the author points out, were either black or Puerto Rican, the commander of the company was a Mexican-American whose chief ambition was to be recognized as a true American, and his second in command, Lieutenant Calley, was a drop-out from a junior college who had held only odd jobs before he joined the army and was sent to Officers Training School.[67]

For weeks these men had been fighting an enemy they never saw, but who planted booby traps that maimed or killed the unlucky man who tripped into them. Charlie Company had also been caught in a lethal mine field, probably laid by South Koreans, that had blinded, made deaf, and blown off the foot of one man and killed and wounded others. The company lived in a nightmare of frustration, fighting in a war whose purpose was incomprehensible, against an enemy they could not see but that could and did kill and mutilate

---

* *Time* magazine reported that of 1,608 people questioned, 65 percent denied being upset by the Mylai disclosures. (Erwin Knoll and Judith Nies McFadden, eds., *War Crimes and the American Conscience*, p. 119.)

them. So their enemy was the Vietnamese, any Vietnamese, for they were all Vietcong, all the people who had set the booby traps or who knew where they were and did not tell.

That, if not the defense, is one explanation given for the events at Mylai. And what of the other Mylais? Were the perpetrators of these also ethnics trying to prove their 100 percent Americanism, drop-outs from the eighth grade, officered by drop-outs from junior colleges? And why did General Westmoreland give Charlie Company a letter of commendation for its victory over the Vietcong, when, as Martin Gershen has observed, a four-star general must know that something is wrong when it is reported to him that 128 people have been killed but only three rifles captured?[68] And why, when rumors of other Mylais have been widespread, has the army been so slow, even after charges have been made, to investigate and act on them?

The American rules of war, as amended in 1944 so the old ones could not be cited by the Germans in the coming trials as a defense, inform the soldier that he will be held responsible for obeying an illegal order, although superior orders may be regarded by a court as mitigating the crime. No one at Mylai inquired whether what they were doing was legal or not, although a few soldiers refused to participate in the slaughter. Killing women and children and rape were not unknown in the war fought in Vietnam, and up to the time Mylai became a public scandal it would have been absurd, some witnesses said, to ask if orders to kill civilians were legal.

American advisors had watched their Vietnamese troops torture and drag prisoners of war across fields tied to a tank or truck.* They themselves had collected fingers and ears of the dead Vietcong, but they had also taken part in a thousand acts of kindness. For example, the wife of a Vietcong guerrilla had been flushed out of hiding, carrying her nursing child who had been shot through the belly, and the Americans had sent her with the child to the rear where the child's life was saved by American doctors and the woman supported by the contributions of the soldiers who had captured her. A marine captain had reorganized the economic life of a village occupied by his command and made it possible for the people to set up small hand

---

* Such bizarre practices may have had their origins in the strategems of the Vietcong, who often made booby traps of the corpses of their dead enemies that exploded when anyone tried to remove the bodies. These measures were countered by dragging the bodies, attached to a tank or truck, before attempting to retrieve them for burial.

industries so they would not be dependent on the thin local market for tenant farmers. American volunteers had carpentered and built houses, adopted orphans, taught school, provided medical aid and supplies, and paid for the relief of the native population out of their own pockets. They had done all these things as well as laying waste and destroying the country and hundreds of thousands of its people. The official attempt to win the hearts and minds of the people did not have much success; as one marine officer summed up the matter: "If you get them by the balls, the hearts and minds will follow."

Racial War?

It seems evident that Vietnam was, like Algeria, in some degree a racial war. The use of terms like "slopes," "dinks," and "gooks" is not conclusive evidence of racism, and it has been noted that American Negro soldiers use them as readily as do white troops. "Kraut" in its day served as well as "gook" to describe friend or foe, but no doubt race marks the enemy off in more convenient fashion than does nationality. The notion cultivated by the National Socialists of the *Untermenschen*, the race of subhumans, is especially useful if you wish to destroy a people. Lieutenant Calley was charged in the indictment against him with killing "Asian Human Beings," a curious locution that would scarcely have been used had it read "Negro" or "Caucasian Human Beings."

But atrocities have been committed by white against whites, by Asians against Asians, blacks against blacks; the racial component is certainly not essential for hatred and inhuman practices. Guerrilla warfare, whether in Algeria or Vietnam, is always ruthless, and if all wars, if they last long enough, tend to deteriorate beyond the provisions of the Hague and Geneva conventions, guerrilla war begins with deteriorated standards. If anyone may be the enemy, if he is mostly unseen, striking out of and disappearing again into the darkness, if he wears no uniform, masquerades as a peaceful peasant, a harmless child or woman, and one's comrades are blown up, the reprisals tend to resemble the methods of the perpetrators. No guerrilla war has ever been fought according to accepted military conventions. Although in the course of such wars prisoners have been captured and treated decently, these conflicts are invariably marked by torture and casual executions contrary to military law and the customs and usages of war. Air war, with or without guerrilla warfare, destroys whole populations, as it did during World War II even before the atomic bomb was used.

Who Was Responsible?

We are speaking, however, of modern times. In the sixteenth and seventeenth centuries, it will be recalled, both Francisco de Vitoria and Francisco Suarez denounced the treatment of the Indians by the *conquistadores*, maintaining that the same law, the *jus gentium*, applied to all mankind. The American advisors did not have to condone the tortures they witnessed being administered by the South Vietnamese troops even if the same measures were being used by the other side. The American High Command was not compelled to order chemical and gas warfare, and the use of bombs with the most ingenious killing devices against civilian targets. The war ran down morally very quickly, and for this, if Nuremberg and Tokyo are any precedents, the highest echelons of the military and political leadership of the United States bear the responsibility. Atrocities were either condoned or, as in the case of the free-fire zones and the bombing without warning of civilian areas, ordered. The causes of such crimes of commission and omission are complex and obscure. Nevertheless, it may be tentatively suggested that while wholesale bombings of civilians as well as other atrocities occurred during World War II, as they did on a smaller scale in World War I and in Korea, a war fought with illusory political goals must be left mainly to military tactics and the military's job is to carry out assignments with the most economical means at its disposal. The difference between the damage done the population of a Dresden or a Tokyo, whether caused by fire bombs, high explosives, or napalm, seems neither impressive nor important to the generals. Such attacks, with the approval of London and Washington, were made to break civilian morale and thus end the war more quickly. High-ranking American officers have maintained that gas should have been used as a more humane and efficient weapon against the Japanese in island warfare and they can doubtless make a reasonable case for their contention. What before World War II mitigated the barbarities of war was a Judeo-Christian ethic which, however submerged, was nevertheless part of the military tradition of Europe, and a similar ethic appeared in non-European countries as well—in Algeria, for example, as Abd-el-Kader taught the French.

That such chivalric traditions were often observed more in the breach than in the fighting does not change the fact that thousands of human beings survived as prisoners of war and as noncombatants who would have been killed had the ethic and the conventions not existed. These were elitist traditions, held by a relatively small group, often against the resistance of a corrupt court, and those who held them might come from any stratum of society, although only through the acceptance of the powerful could they be put into force. An individual ruler or general might be guilty of the most horrendous crimes, including war crimes and crimes against humanity, but the chivalric ideals remained and in updated form were codified in the conventions of the democratic societies. Abraham Lincoln, in a time of bitter civil war, maintained this humane tradition, as did the German generals who refused to carry out Hitler's orders to kill Russian commissars, whether in or out of uniform. Thousands of American officers and men maintained them, too, but other hundreds did not and for this the American High Command, civil and military, seems just as responsible as was the High Command of the Third Reich and the Japanese monarchy.*

Armies are hierarchies and the directives come from the top. Their enforcement, too, moves down through the chain of command through the commissioned and noncommissioned officers to the GIs. Many, probably most, of the members of each of these categories have behaved well in Vietnam, but never enough of them to prevent the torture and illegal slaughter. The plan of campaign was distorted from the time of the first directives that sent American troops into battle. The army was assigned a job it could not possibly carry out without a functioning South Vietnamese state and national consensus, with the civilian arm approving or instigating any military measures that promised to bring the North Vietnamese to the conference table. Because it was not a war in the constitutional sense, the Pentagon could not use the relatively humane means of blockade that would have been open to it in a declared war. The impossible goals made the available military means all-important, and the means, like the body count, became the ends. How

* Members of the Hitler government, as well as party officials and army officers, were tried at Nuremberg and in 1948 the Tokyo War Crimes Tribunal held that a Cabinet member was guilty of war crimes even if he could not prevent them. The tribunal pointed out that if a cabinet member had knowledge of such crimes he could have resigned. (Na., "Judgment of International Military Tribunal for the Far East," typescript photo-offset [no publisher, 1948], pp. 1178–1179.)

could a man fight a war for the right of a people to govern itself when he saw all around him the corruption of a state that had never governed itself? When a "friendly" might become an enemy in a split second, a peaceful peasant turn into an assassin, and the GI was an enemy to both sides?

The malaise goes deeper than such symptoms. Sixty-five percent of Americans questioned said they were unmoved by what went on at Mylai and the ballad in praise of the man who ordered defenseless people "wasted" was a considerable popular success. Are Americans simply hardened to crime and violence, or do they believe that the really guilty ones in high places have not been tried and that the minor people who are found guilty are merely scapegoats? Has the elitist tradition of another century all but disappeared in a universal rage for egalitarianism that is not much more than a return to barbarism armed with lethal, mass-produced gadgets? Are the evidences of brutality and corruption in the American society and its army symptoms of a decomposing ethos in one country or of a worldwide return to the jungle accompanied by some modern hygiene?

Some of these questions have a partial answer in the atrocities committed by other armies as well as by Americans in the recent past: in the behavior of the SS during World War II, of the British commandos and the orders given them to act like gangsters, in the mass bombing of civilians, in the methods of warfare of the partisans in Europe, Africa, and Asia, in the behavior of the French High Command and paratroopers in Algeria and Indochina, of the Nigerians against the Biafrans, of the Congolese against the Europeans, of the Pakistani against the people of their eastern provinces. These are widespread phenomena, and it is not that laws have been lacking to discourage their occurrence but that no serious effort has been made in the highest quarters to prevent them.

An army, especially a conscript army, is a projection of a society, and the American society endures one of the highest crime rates among the "civilized" countries of the world. How could its army not reflect its origins? The United States has a rickety educational system in which semi-literates may have college degrees; what kind of officers do such men make?

On the political side, the President may make wars that are not wars because Congress has not declared them; he may make them on valid or spurious grounds, and if they do not go well, the disillusion of a people accustomed to victory but beset by deep trouble in their own society surfaces in civilian life as well as in the army. Atrocities are seemingly built into the weapons of mass destruction of modern war, but many of the crimes that occurred in Vietnam were also endemic to American society, blown up and multiplied in the free-fire climate of a military campaign with no credible purpose. A cease fire can cover the final American withdrawal, but the political problems remain as unresolved as they were in 1954 or 1945.

NOTES

1. Douglas Pike, Viet Cong, p. 28.
2. Edgar O'Ballance, The Indochinese War.
3. Foreign Relations of the United States, Conference of Berlin, p. 915.
4. Jean Lacouture, Ho Chi Minh.
5. Bernard B. Fall, The Two Vietnams.
6. Joseph Buttinger, Vietnam: A Dragon Embattled.
7. Chester L. Cooper, The Lost Crusade.
8. Fall, op. cit., p. 69.
9. Neil Sheehan et al., The Pentagon Papers, pp. 7–8.
10. P. J. Honey, ed., North Vietnam Today, pp. 3, 4.
11. David Halberstam, Ho.
12. Lacouture, Ho Chi Minh.
13. David Schoenbrun, Vietnam.
14. Jean Sainteny, Histoire d'une Paix Manquée, p. 83.
15. Vo Nguyen Giap, People's War, People's Army, Praeger, 1962.
16. Pamphlets on Vietnam, President Ho Chi Minh, pp. 77–79.
    Edgar O'Ballance, op. cit.
17. Halberstam, op. cit.
18. Truong Chinh, op. cit.
19. Lacouture, Ho Chi Minh, pp. 162–163.
    Schoenbrun, op. cit.
20. O'Ballance, op. cit.
21. Henri Navarre, L'Agonie de l'Indochine.
22. Bernard Fall, Le Viet-Minh.
23. Henry Ainley, Mourir pour Rien.
24. Pierre Richard, Cinq Ans Prisonnier des Viets.
25. Fall, Le Viet-Minh.
26. Claude Goëldhieux, Quinze Mois Prisonnier chez les Viets.
27. Jean Lacouture and Philippe Devillers, La Fin d'une Guerre, p. 34.
28. Sheehan et al., op. cit., p. 10.
29. Harry S Truman, Memoirs, Vol. I, p. 519.
29a. Jean Lacouture and Philippe Devillers, La Fin d'une Guerre.
30. Robert H. Ferrell, American Diplomacy, p. 519.
31. Navarre, op. cit.
32. Truman, op. cit., p. 438.
33. Dwight D. Eisenhower, Mandate for Change.
34. Donald Lancaster in Wesley R. Fishel, ed., Vietnam: Anatomy of a Conflict, p. 41.
35. Cooper, op. cit.
36. Eisenhower, Mandate for Change, p. 371.
37. Department of State, American Foreign Policy 1950–1955, Vol. 2, pp. 2401–2402.
38. Fishel, op. cit., p. 56.
39. Pike, op. cit.

40. Fall, *Le Viet-Minh.*
Buttinger, *op. cit.*
41. George A. Carver, Jr., in Fishel, *op. cit.*
42. John Mecklin, *Mission in Torment*, pp. 170–178.
Buttinger, *op. cit.*, Vol. II, p. 995.
43. Christian Zentner, *Die Kriege der Nachkriegszeit.*
44. Dennis J. Duncanson, *Government and Revolution in Vietnam.*
45. Sheehan et al., *op. cit.*, p. 80.
46. *Ibid.*, p. 229.
47. *Ibid.*, p. 261
John Galloway, *The Gulf of Tonkin Resolution.*
48. Galloway, *op. cit.*
Eugene G. Windchy, *Tonkin Gulf.*
49. Cooper, *op. cit.*, p. 239.
50. *U.S. Crimes in Vietnam.*
51. Douglas Pike, *The Vietcong Strategy of Terror*, cited in "The Human Cost of Communism in Vietnam," Committee on the Judiciary, 92nd Congress, 2nd Session, U.S. Government Printing Office, Washington, D.C., 1972, p. 89.
52. Malcolm W. Browne, *The New Face of War.*
53. Jay Mallin, *Terror in Vietnam.*
54. Pike, *op. cit.*, p. 93.
55. *Vietnam: L'Heure Décisive.*
56. *The New York Times*, May 25, 1971: "Colonel Says Every Large Combat Unit in Vietnam Has a Mylai."
57. Noble Frankland, *Bomber Offensive: The Devastation of Europe*, p. 24 ff, quoted by Michael Walzer, "World War II: Why This War Was Different," p. 12.
58. Edward S. Herman, *Atrocities in Vietnam.*
International Herald Tribune, June 22, 1970: "Que Son Valley Massacre. Marine Gets Life for Helping Kill 16 Women and Children."
The New York Times, December 18, 1970: Book Review by John Leonard, "Who Is a War Criminal?"
Chicago Sun-Times, December 7, 1970: "Veterans Call Atrocities Usual."
59. David Irving, *The Destruction of Dresden*, p. 7.
60. "Bombs Killed 80% Civilians Vietnam," *Chicago Today*, June 27, 1971.
61. Raphael Littauer and Norman Uphoff, eds., *The Air War in Indochina*, pp. 63–89.
Cornell University Study, reported NBC December 24, 1971.
62. Raphael Littauer and Norman Uphoff, eds., *op. cit.*, pp. 93, 243.
Arthur H. Westing, "Agent Blue in Vietnam," *The New York Times*, July 12, 1971.
63. Thomas Whiteside, "Department of Amplification," *The New Yorker*, August 14, 1971, pp. 54–59.
64. *War Crimes and the American Conscience*, Knoll and Judith Nies, eds.
65. James B. Reston, Jr., *Saturday Review of Literature*, July 18, 1970, pp. 16–17.
66. Eugene Davidson, *The Trial of the Germans.*
67. Martin Gershen, *Destroy or Die.*
68. *Ibid.*

7

The New Colonialism: Russia in Eastern Europe

ON the night of August 20, 1968, the Presidium of the Central Committee of the Communist party of Czechoslovakia held a meeting at the party headquarters in Prague to discuss the preparations for a momentous occasion—the convocation of the XIVth Party Congress to be held in a little more than two weeks. Something extraordinary had happened, not only in the history of Czechoslovakia but also in the world Communist movement. An orthodox Communist party, an invariably dependable supporter of the policies of the Soviet Union, had set out to create a humane communism, "socialism with a human face," as they called it, to permit freedom of speech and of the press, a widened democracy within the party, the liberalization of the economy with a combination of market and planning techniques. They would complete the liquidation of the reign of terror and of the secret police that had marked the 1950s and continue the work of rehabilitating the surviving victims of Stalinist injustice. They would restore civil rights, resolve the nationality problem, give substance to the yearnings for freedom and independence of which so many Czechs and Slovaks had spoken but which had eluded them. These reforms had actually been set in motion in the course of the Prague spring of 1968, and they had electrified the world on both sides of the Iron Curtain. The Communist parties of eighteen countries including those of Italy and France,

Yugoslavia and Rumania, had greeted them with enthusiasm, and the XIVth Party Congress, scheduled for September 9, with its progressive-minded delegates, would approve everything that had been done since First Secretary Alexander Dubček and a new Presidium of the Czechoslovak party had replaced the oppressive regime of the Stalinists and their successors under Antonín Novotný.

Just after 11 P.M. Prime Minister Oldrich Černik was called from the meeting and returned a few moments later with the crushing news that the armies of the five "brother" Communist states of Soviet Russia, Bulgaria, Poland, East Germany, and Hungary were invading Czechoslovakia and already had crossed the borders. It was incredible news. Communists will not attack Communists, Alexander Dubček had maintained confidently, and now he wept openly. His life, he said, had been bound up with the Soviet Union and what had happened was a tragedy for the country, the whole Communist movement, and the greatest tragedy of his own life.[1]

Not only were most of the members of the Central Committee of the party shocked, few people in Czechoslovakia or in the West had expected an armed invasion. Not since the Hungarian revolution of 1956 had such an event of pure *Machtpolitik* taken place in the Communist world. Experts as well as the instant commentators of the media had declared it would not happen, could not happen; the Soviet Union would not dare affront not only world opinion and international communism, but the views expressed on many ceremonial occasions of Communist parties East and West. Nevertheless, the planes, tanks, and troops of the five "brother nations," some 200,000 men in the first wave, soon half a million, occupied Czechoslovakia. The chief members of the government and the Central Committee were arrested and taken to an unknown destination, and the freeze that settled over the Prague spring was felt far beyond the boundaries of a small state in East Central Europe.

The Revolts of the 1950s

The Czechoslovak revolution was the fourth of the risings against the Soviet Union that had taken place since the end of World War II. It was different, however, from those in East Germany, Poland, and Hungary. It lasted much longer, for months instead of days. Until the very end it was fought with polemics instead of tanks, and by a people many of whom were convinced and enthusiastic Communists. It was a revolution staged by the Czechoslovak Communist party, by dyed-in-the-wool party members, against co-believers in the fraternal countries and those they had welcomed as friends and saviors when Czechoslovakia was liberated. In the other countries of East Central Europe the Russians were regarded with mixed feelings dominated by contempt and hostility, emotions that could be readily extended to the secular army of Moscow, the Communist parties of East Germany, Poland, and Hungary. In Czechoslovakia, the opposite was true. The Russian was the traditional big brother, the shield against Teutonic oppression, and Marxist parties had the loyalty of a majority of the country.

In East Germany, in 1953, the workers themselves had risen, spontaneously. First the men on the showcase construction project on the *Stalinallee* had left their jobs to march on the government offices, and they had promptly been joined by thousands of their fellow workers in Berlin and then in the countryside. The incessant demands of the government for more work at the same pay that bought less and less food, the dreary harshness of life in a police state, had become unbearable. When the construction workers had been told the norms, the daily output of work expected of them, would be raised again—at the demand, party officials explained, of the construction workers themselves—it was too much. The men, relatively well paid, were experienced in the legends of Communist workers gladly volunteering to take on overtime jobs, and they were well aware that none of their number had asked to have their wages cut. "Show them to us," they yelled at the party bosses who had told them about workers asking for new norms at the *Stalinallee*, and then they simply marched off shouting their slogans against Ulbricht and the regime they detested. They had fought the police in the streets, and when the Russian tanks had come in, they had fought against them with homemade weapons and bare hands. Without the tanks the Ulbricht government would have crumbled, and as it was Ulbricht had barely survived. Moscow had little use for a party leader, however docile, who could not carry out his assignments. The party had played no role in the East German revolt except to bring it on with one of the most oppressive of the postwar Communist regimes that even after its ritual of self-criticism as a result of the revolt had, eight years later, to build a wall to keep the population from leaving. The uprising occurred on June 17, 1953. Between July 1952 and July 1953 almost 340,000 people had fled across the zonal boundaries to the West. By the time the Berlin

Wall was built in 1961, some two and a quarter million people, most of them young, in the most productive years of their lives, had left. In East Germany the revolt had been against the party, against the government, and the Soviet Union. It was made by the workers themselves with no help either from outside the country or from the party bureaucracy.[2]

In Hungary, too, in 1956, the situation at the time of the revolution was different from what it was in Czechoslovakia. After Stalin's death in March 1953, the thaw in Communist dogmas had been more evident in Hungary than in any other country. Czechoslovakia and East Germany remained Stalinist. They would be among the last of the satellites to be affected in their party structures by such events as the 30,000-word Khrushchev speech of February 1956 that had taken five hours to deliver at the XXth Party Congress in Moscow in which some of the crimes of the late Soviet dictator had been enumerated to the party faithful, many of whom had already known a good deal about them. Khrushchev's speech, nevertheless, exploded in the Communist world like a hydrogen bomb. The demigod, the infallible leader, the victorious generalissimo, the successor to Marx and Lenin had brutalized country and party, made colossal blunders during the war, and slaughtered the faithful as he had his enemies, by whim. These were not the deeds of a millenarian revolutionary leader demanding the terrible sacrifices needed to build a new world, they were the work of a paranoid monster.* Khrushchev's revelations were devastating news to thousands of party comrades who had believed they were waging a different kind of struggle for different ends, and while the speech was made to a select audience, rumors of what Khrushchev had said were soon heard far beyond party circles.

In Hungary, as early as 1953, after Georgi M. Malenkov had succeeded Stalin, peasants and workers were showing signs of discontent as threatening as those in East Germany, and in June, three months after Stalin's death, the Hungarian party leaders had been summoned to Moscow and ordered to form a new government. Imre Nagy, who favored milder courses than the Stalinist Mátyás Rákosi,

---

* The Soviet historian Roy A. Medvedev, who has had access to secret government materials, calculates that between 1937 and 1938 the Russian secret police killed more Communists than were lost in all the years of underground struggle, three revolutions, and the Russian Civil War. Between 4 and 5 million people were sent to prison or forced labor camps between 1936 and 1939 and "at least 500,000 most of them higher ranking individuals were shot." Harrison E. Salisbury, *The New York Times Book Review*, December 26, 1971.

was chosen as Prime Minister, although Rákosi remained First Secretary. Nagy had undertaken a program of reform, a new course that was to open the gates of the concentration camps, allow peasants to leave the collective farms, provide more consumer goods, and establish a People's Patriotic Front that would include non-Communists. Neither Nagy nor his regime had lasted long. The battle between the Stalinists and anti-Stalinists continued in Hungary as it did in all the Communist countries, and in 1955 Nagy was not only forced to resign his post as Prime Minister but was expelled from the party as well. Hungary, again under the heavy hand of Rákosi, steered away from the new freedoms and consumer goods back to the old policies favoring heavy industry and forced collectivization of farms that had alienated workers and peasants including thousands of Communists.[3] But there was no complete reversal of Nagy's reforms.

Nevertheless, the currents of anti-Stalinism ran deep throughout the Communist world and in the satellite countries they merged with anti-Soviet nationalism. The East Germans had denounced their Communist leaders Ulbricht and Pieck, but they also made their hopeless fight against the tanks of Soviet Russia. In Poland a secretary of the Communist party, Jerzy Morawski, accompanied the anti-Stalinist themes with a demand for closer contacts with the West and Latin America. The economic situation in Poland was no happier than it had been in East Germany; wages were low, living bleak. In Poznan, in June 1956, on the occasion of an international fair, workers in a locomotive and heavy machine factory rioted; 53 of them were killed and over 300 wounded. Again the party promised reform and shuffled the leadership. The rioters who had been arrested were treated leniently and given light sentences. Juliusz Tokarski, the Economic Minister, and Eugene Szyr, chairman of the State Economic Commission, lost their posts and in October a former party leader, Wladyslaw Gomulka, who had been imprisoned in 1951, was elected First Secretary of the Central Committee of the party.[4] This was but another turn in a new course that soon found its way back to the old channels as Gomulka, who had had time to meditate on his role in prison, tried to keep reforms within cautious limits and to make himself as pleasing as possible to his Moscow betters.

In Hungary, the former Minister of Interior and later Foreign Minister, Laszló Rajk, as well as other leading Communists who had been executed as Tito's agents in the Stalinist purges, were officially rehabilitated in 1956 and 200,000 people marched in a procession when they were ceremoniously reburied in a state funeral. Among the living, Nagy was reinstated in the party, and on October 22 students in Budapest took part in a mass demonstration demanding that he be made head of a new government, that free elections and a multiparty system be restored, and that the Soviet troops go home immediately. The next day the students demonstrated again to express their sympathy with the Polish freedom movement. Again a crowd of between 200,000 and 300,000 people gathered, calling for Nagy, who finally came to address them in careful, circumspect words. But Nagy was followed by an old party-liner, First Secretary Ernö Gerö, a former Comintern agent and colonel in the Soviet secret police, the M.V.D., who had just returned from a visit to Tito, now resanitized by the post-Stalin regime in Soviet Russia. Gerö spoke to the crowd in the fire and damnation texts of the Stalinist scriptures, referred to the demonstrators as "a rabble," and the crowd became infuriated. Police fired on them and the fighting was on. The Soviet Union, permitted by treaty to station troops in Hungary, immediately intervened, but the fighting intensified with some Hungarian soldiers joining the insurgents. On October 24, the day the Russian tanks appeared in Budapest, Nagy was again elected Prime Minister by the Central Committee of the Communist party and he was joined by other reformists in the Politburo and Central Committee, although the Stalinists in both remained a majority.

Throughout Hungary, however, the Communist party of 900,000 members very nearly disintegrated in the revolts in Budapest and the countryside. The masses of peasants and workers swelled the tide of a revolution against both the orthodox party and the government. The Kremlin, seemingly convinced that it could not cope with the revolution by force alone, on October 30 ordered its tanks out of Budapest and declared its willingness to negotiate with Nagy's government, which now included representatives of parties that had overwhelmingly defeated the Communists in the elections of 1945.* Non-Communist parties were quickly resuscitated as the country prepared for free elections; Nagy brought three of them into his government, the Social Democrats, the Smallholders, and the National Peasant Party, to share power with the Communists. He preached the crusade of reform communism, the dissolution of the Hungarian secret police, the reintroduction of the multiparty system, and renunciation of the Communist monopoly of power in

* The Communists had received only 17 percent of the vote despite massive Soviet support.

the state. But later he added, as we shall see, other nationalist goals —Hungary's withdrawal from the Warsaw Pact and a policy of neutralism for Hungary as between East and West. It was the rebirth of the dream of freedom from tyranny and a foreign yoke, but it was a dream. Soviet troops poured into Hungary from Russia and the tank divisions invaded Budapest again on November 4. This time the revolt was crushed. Tens of thousands of Hungarians died in the fighting and some 200,000 people escaped over the Austrian border to begin a new life somewhere else, anywhere else but in a country ruled by foreign tyrants and their puppets. Imre Nagy took refuge in the Yugoslav Embassy in Budapest and surrendered only when promised a safe conduct by the Soviet-installed Kádár government. However, they immediately arrested him and, as Moscow and Budapest announced more than a year and a half later, tried and executed him.[5]

Central and Eastern Europe

Communism had been imposed on the peoples of East Germany, Poland, and Hungary at the end of World War II by the bayonets of the Red Army. In no country of Central or Eastern Europe where the voters had had an opportunity in free elections to express their sentiments had the Communists received anything but a derisory small vote. Moscow's strategy to counter this lack of popular support was to establish a United Front party, an alliance of Communists with Social Democrats who had many more followers among the electorate than the Communists but who, in the new party, were permitted to play only the role of fellow travelers. In East Germany it was called the Socialist Unity party. In Hungary it was the National Independence Front, a coalition of the Smallholders party, the Peasant party, the Social Democrats, and the Communists, but as was the case in East Germany, the so-called coalition was completely controlled by the Communists.* In Poland, at the end of the war, it had been difficult to man the party and government apparatus with politically reliable personnel, there were so few Communists. The Soviet authorities in Warsaw, after having given a safe conduct in 1945 to sixteen of the most prominent members of the underground, all of them non-Communists, to enable them to par-

---

* The Social Democrats, the Peasant party, and the Smallholders party in Hungary, like the Social Democrats, the Free Democratic party, and the CDU in East Germany, were permitted to exist only as junior partners, with Communists holding the key positions in the government. The opposition parties had to accept Communist dominance or they would cease to exist. Nagy wanted to revive a functioning, multiparty system.

ticipate in forming a new government, had arrested them. The Communist party in East Central Europe ruled solely because of the presence of Soviet troops.

While in Czechoslovakia

In Czechoslovakia the case was different. There the Red Army had been welcomed in 1945 as liberators. Russia had had no part in the Munich agreement and the Czech government in exile, under Edward Beneš and Jan Masaryk, had been convinced that they must place their chief reliance for the country's future independence in the Soviet Union, not in the West that had delivered the Sudetenland to Hitler.

Beneš visited Stalin in 1944 and the Communists, after the war, formed the largest party in Czechoslovakia. In the election of May 1946 they had polled 37.56 percent of the votes as against 18.31 percent for Beneš' National Socialist party, 12.81 percent for the Social Democrats, and a scattering of votes for the other parties. The Marxists had succeeded in obtaining a majority in the National Assembly when the Social Democratic leader, Zdeněk Fierlinger brought his party into a coalition with the Communists, giving them 51 percent of the votes in the Assembly.

The coup that took place in 1948 had the formal appearance of legality. On February 20 the twelve ministers of the bourgeois parties had left the government in a protest against the strong-arm methods of the Communists who, through the Ministry of the Interior, were packing the police force with party members, and this action had precipitated the seizure of power. The new elections that were to take place in May had threatened a reduction in the Communist vote and the coup prevented any such development. After the bourgeois ministers had quit, President Beneš had done precisely what the Communists had expected of him; he accepted the resignations and approved a new Communist government, perfectly legal since they were the largest party in the National Assembly and with their allies, the Social Democrats, had a majority. When the May elections took place, the voters had only one list to approve, that of the National Front, which received 89.28 percent of the votes cast. The National Assembly, purged of its opposition parties, voted its approval of the new government. An opposition minister who fled the country, Hubert Ripka, later wrote that from 250,000 to 300,000 citizens were not permitted to vote because the

Communists claimed they were suspected of having collaborated with the Germans.

While the means employed by the Communists—the sending of time bombs to Czech leaders of the opposition, the purging of voting lists, the calling out of 15,000 Communist militia to patrol the streets of Prague, wholesale arrests, the closing down of opposition newspapers and radio stations—were extraconstitutional, the forms of parliamentary procedure and democratic voting had been maintained. Ripka charged that the Soviet Union in 1948 had committed indirect aggression. For although its troops had not invaded Czechoslovakia, the Soviet Union had sent Deputy Foreign Minister Valerian Zorin to Prague to direct the revolt and threaten direct Russian intervention if the Communist cadres and militia were not enough.[6]

Some violence had occurred, a good many people had been beaten up and jailed, the son of the first President and the then Foreign Minister, Jan Masaryk, who like President Edward Beneš had been persuaded to keep his post, had been killed in a fall from the window of his apartment in the Czernin Palace. The official verdict was suicide but from the beginning there were rumors that the secret police on orders from Moscow had murdered him.[7] When the reform movement twenty years later began its investigations into the brutalities of the Stalinist past, the Masaryk case was to be reopened, but with the Soviet invasion and subsequent suppressions the matter was dropped.

The Czechoslovak Communist party after 1948 controlled the National Front as the East German Communists did the SED. The Communist government had been voted into power by a unanimous vote of the National Assembly made up of their own members and Social Democrats, some of whom had long been crypto-Communists, and some of whom grudgingly went along with the change of regime as an alternative to civil war. But from its beginnings in 1945, the postwar Czechoslovak government had leaned heavily on its great ally and liberator, the Soviet Union, and the Communist party had been the dominant political organization.

The other countries that came out of World War II with large Communist parties, France and Italy, for example, were in a geographical and psychological position where opposition parties could function far more freely than in Czechoslovakia and in both countries, although Communists remained in the government until 1947, the Communist parties could not prevent the acceptance of such measures, frowned upon by Moscow, as the Marshall Plan. The Czech government, too, had first voted unanimously in 1947 to accept the aid the Marshall Plan offered, but after the Kremlin had irately summoned the Czechoslovak leaders to Moscow to lecture them on their duties, the same government, a couple of days later, unanimously reversed itself.

The Czechs had a special relationship to the Soviet Union. It might well have been possible for the Czechoslovak Communist party to seize power with the approval of a majority of the country in 1945, so overwhelming had been the sentiment of rejoicing over the deliverance from the National Socialist yoke by Russian troops. The Americans, too, had been given a tumultuous welcome when they appeared in Pilsen but they had gone no farther. Czechoslovakia lay within the Soviet sphere of influence and the American troops under the command of General Patton had been ordered to move no farther east than the line Pilsen-Karlsbad, close to the western border. The Americans could have liberated Prague and much of the countryside, but they were held back by the original directive given Patton and firmly repeated by General Eisenhower when Patton urged that he be allowed to relieve Prague, which was only 60 miles from Pilsen but 120 miles from the Russians, who had reached the district of Teschen.*

The delay in occupation had cost a good many Czech lives, but this did not dampen the ardor of the Czech reception of the Russian troops, nor had the Soviet acquisition of the easternmost region of Czechoslovakia, sub-Carpathian Ruthenia, in February 1945, which was ratified by treaty in June 1945.

Czechs and Slovaks

The Russians were the anti-Munichers as well as the deliverers of the country and it was the Communist party that had been the core of the resistance fighting the invaders in Bohemia and Moravia. In

---

* When Eisenhower had suggested that Patton's Third Army be allowed to move forward to Prague, the Russian chief of staff, General Alexei Antonov, would not agree. Antonov asked Eisenhower "not to move the allied forces in Czechoslovakia east of the originally intended line." (Ladislas Farago, *Patton*, p. 787.)

Britain and the United States, a year before, had indicated their acceptance of future Russian predominance in Czechoslovakia when they had refused to negotiate an occupation treaty the Czechoslovak government had suggested while the Soviet Union proceeded to make one. The Western powers did, however, make similar treaties with the governments in exile of Belgium, Holland, and Norway. (Ivo Duchacek in Stephen D. Kertesz, ed., *The Fate of East Central Europe*, p. 199.)

Slovakia the case was different. The nominally independent state set up by Adolf Hitler and Monsignor Tiso in 1938, the clerico-fascist state, as the Communists called it, was a Slovakia independent of the Czechs, and as such it was welcomed by many among the Slovaks who had little love for the clerico-Fascists but even less for the Czechs. Slovak troops had fought against the Soviet Union just as the Hungarians and East Germans had, but their ardor had cooled after experiences with SS formations that regarded them as subhuman and with German military defeats. In 1944 it had been the Communist party of Slovakia that had engineered the rising against the Germans in a revolt that had required the diversion of many more German military units than did the Prague rising of 1945.

The Czecho-Slovak state had been thought of by the Slovaks from its beginnings not as a unitary Czechoslovakia but as a hyphenated federal republic with an autonomous Slovakia linked to Bohemia and Moravia. Such a federation was what Thomas Masaryk had promised the Slovak delegation at Pittsburgh in 1918 when he was seeking support in the United States for the new state to be created from the ashes of the Austro-Hungarian empire. Masaryk had been eminently successful in obtaining American support for that state, so successful that he did not feel himself bound by an agreement made on foreign soil with Slovaks who had no official mandate. Nevertheless, the Pittsburgh Agreement bore his signature and it had been his assurances of a federal state that had drawn the Slovaks to join with him to convince President Wilson and the Allied powers at the Paris Peace Conference that he should have the state of mixed nationalities he desired, including 3.3 million German-speaking Sudetenlaender. The Czechs had been a minority in the country they ran effectively from Prague with only the minor participation of Slovaks, Ruthenians, Hungarians, and Germans, and they had never succeeded in winning the allegiance of these other minorities. It seemed to these people that the Czechs ruled the country with a heavy hand, portioning out jobs in the administration of the country, including the non-Czech territories, mainly among Czechs. After World War II only the Slovaks were left in any large number among the minorities. The Sudeten Germans had been expelled, often in the most brutal fashion. The Hungarian minority had been reduced by some 93,000 as they were exchanged or forced out of Slovakia.[8] In 1966 only 124,000 Germans were left in the country. Emigration to West Germany since 1961 had decreased their numbers slightly from 140,000, but they had gone down from over 3 million before the war.[9] The Hungarians numbered 559,000 in 1966, an increase over 534,000 in 1961, since few of them had cared to emigrate to their own socialist motherland. The Slovaks, although they participated in the postwar government, still demanded the long-promised autonomy; they wanted a federation resembling the Swiss model that had been foreseen in the agreement with Masaryk in Pittsburgh. But they were not in a very good bargaining position. They had welcomed the partitioning of Czechoslovakia in 1938 and many of them had fought against the Soviet Union. The Slovaks, to be sure, had risen under the leadership of the Communist party against the German occupants in 1944, but the Russians were very nearly as suspicious of foreign partisans as they were of those who collaborated with the German National Socialists. Just as Communist party members who had fought for the Loyalists in Spain had been among the first to be purged when Stalin was seeking out his enemies in the forties and fifties, most of the Slovak officers who had fought in the 1944 uprising were in prison when the anniversary of the revolt was celebrated in Bratislava in 1950. In the early 1950s a Slovak journalist recounts that when he brought together former officers of the Slovak national rising for consultation, only fourteen of them were left after the purges. Seven of eight generals who had participated in the rising had been reduced to the ranks, as had four of the colonels. Of twenty-one lieutenant colonels, one had been degraded to the rank of captain and one to the rank of a common soldier.[10] Stalin's orders for the wholesale arrests of wreckers, Titoists, Trotskyists, and deviationists had thrown thousands of men into Soviet prisons—Spanish patriots, liberals, socialists, and Communists who had fought gallantly in what the Western press of the thirties had overportrayed as a united battle against fascism. One of the reasons given by Soviet sources for the inclusion of the Spanish Loyalists in the purges was that many of them had been in the hands of the Gestapo and of the French Sureté and so were politically unreliable. But the Slovak Communists who had fought in the spring of 1944 were as suspect as the Spaniards had been. It was not, for the most part, the leaders of the Prague or Slovak risings who came into power when the Communist coup of 1948 took place. The new leaders were men like Klement Gottwald, who had spent the war in Moscow, and Antonín Novotný, who had been in the Mauthausen concentration camp. With the exception of a few leaders like Josef Smrkovský, who had fought in the Czech underground, the new leaders were far from romantic, legendary, dashing, partisan fighters who had daily risked their lives against the oppressors. The leading members of the Czechoslovak party hierarchy were dependable apparatchiki who knew the ways of Moscow and what was expected of them.

The popular sentiment in favor of the Soviet Union was very different from this. The people, workers and peasants, still remembered how their Western friends and allies had delivered them to the mercies of Hitler. They also knew that the creation of an independent Slovak state by edict of Adolf Hitler had been accepted by the Western powers, as well as the Soviet Union. All these countries had diplomatic missions in Bratislava; Soviet Russia had recognized the independence of Slovakia two days after it was proclaimed. The Soviet Union, while scoring the Munich agreement in 1938, nevertheless in August 1939, when it made its own nonaggression pact with Hitler, had accepted the dissolution of Czechoslovakia when it sent home the Czech ambassador to Moscow and later established a diplomatic mission in Slovakia.

So, although it was the Russians who finally had broken the chains forged by Hitler, neither they nor the West had lifted a finger against him until the start of World War II. And as for the fraternal Communist nations that invaded in 1968, three of them had come as invaders in 1938 too—the Poles, the Hungarians, and the East Germans. Only the Bulgarians, among the five, had taken no part in the partition of the country.

The Economy

The Czechoslovaks after 1948 had done moderately well for a time under their Communist government. Up to the early 1960s, they had very nearly the highest standard of living of the countries in the Soviet bloc, higher than that of the Soviet Union and just under that of the East Germans. It is true that they suffered, as did all the countries of the Eastern bloc, from the lopsided demands of the Soviet Union and later Comecon that forced them to produce for the needs, not of Czechoslovakia, but of the bloc. They had to concentrate on heavy industry, buy Russian goods, oil, for example, at twice their price in the world market, while they sold their own produce at figures that were far from inflated. Nevertheless, they had a sure market for their products and the functionaries who were responsible for production had no trouble at all in disposing of their wares because the brother Communist states, which included, in the late forties and fifties, Communist China, were short of everything. Czech shoes were often the only ones obtainable in Moscow, and only later, when Italian and Yugoslav shoes were also on sale in the Soviet capital, did Russians come to complain that the Czech styles were stodgy and inferior. Before that they gladly wore Czech shoes or went barefoot. Attempts to make the rigid Czechoslovak economy more flexible had been begun as early as 1957, when factories had been permitted to retain cash balances over the assigned norms for their own development. But such reforms had not compensated for the inefficient, overage machines, two thirds of which were obsolete, the stifling party bureaucracy, and the isolation of the country's technicians, cut off as they were from the West and receiving little help from Moscow. In 1963 industrial production was down and fixed capital had declined by 11.4 percent from 1962. A Czech economist, Robert Smelc, produced figures showing that Holland, with 12.5 million people, had earned two and a half times as much for each exported item as had Czechoslovakia, with a population of 14 million.[11] Costs of Czechoslovak production were very high, huge stockpiles of rejected goods rusted in warehouses, the efficiency of the industrial plants and machinery had fallen 30 percent from pre-Communist levels.[12] Long lines of people waited in front of food stores, for agricultural production had gone down 6 percent in 1962 and almost all commodities were in short supply.[13]

The plans for economic reform of Ota Šik, director of the Economic Institute of the Czechoslovak Academy of Science and member of the Central Committee of the Communist party, were given mainly lip service by the hard-line Novotný government. Šik, who was not a professional economist, had bold ideas; he favored a decentralized management system with more authority given the people directly responsible for a factory's production, a market economy that would be subject to supply and demand, incentives for both management and labor, and international convertibility of Czech currency. As matters stood, Czechoslovakia had large credit balances in the Comecon countries—$350 million in Soviet Russia alone—but Czechoslovakia could be paid only in goods its debtors were prepared to export, and in the case of the Soviet Union, at prices fixed by Moscow.

Absenteeism among workers was high, as was job hopping. Morale was low among the formerly self-respecting craftsmen who had turned out some of the best products of Europe; they had lost their pride in their work and their traditional standards of excellence. Pilferage was widespread. People said, "If you don't rob the state you are robbing your own family" and "If you hesitate you will go hungry."[14] Among the workers the chief crime was not theft but working too hard. Whether under the Austrians or the Germans, the Czechs had long thought of themselves as formed in the mold of the good soldier Schweik, that is, a man resists by elaborately dragging his feet. The job, in the Schweikian philosophy, is to stay alive, and what is not earned legitimately can be stolen. A man's life is not to be risked in foolhardy, open competition with the muscle of power. He should seem to go along cheerfully with the party and the government and then proceed to do as little as possible, or better still, nothing at all. His mission is to ignore or circumvent the endless exhortations to die gallantly for the Emperor, or to work better and faster with the broken-down machinery the state gives him. The Czechs had a long history of dealing in the Schweikian fashion with their oppressors, whether Hapsburg or National Socialist, and they used the same devices against communism. Schweikism, related to what the Germans call *Bauerschlauheit*, peasant shrewdness, although fully developed among the Czechs, is evident too in other societies where farmers and workers have to deal with grasping tax gatherers, officials, or estate owners, especially where these are of another ethnic origin.

Dubček

Alexander Dubček, who rose suddenly to prominence, was a Slovak, a devoted Communist who had spent a third of his life in the Soviet Union. His career until 1967 seemed to be that of the orthodox apparatchik, a party liner no better and no worse than thousands of others who believed what their readings in the party scriptures had told them. He was almost American. He had been conceived in Chicago, where his nineteen-year-old father, Stefan Dubček, had worked in a piano factory and as a carpenter. His elder brother was born in Chicago. Stefan Dubček was one of these idealistic international socialists more conspicuous in his time than in ours, who believed devoutly in the brotherhood of man and of all races and peoples, a follower in the United States of Eugene Debs and later a devoted supporter of the Soviet Union. Alexander Dubček's mother was a Communist. The family put down no roots in the United States, and after four years in the Middle West, they returned in 1921 to Slovakia where Alexander was born. In 1925 the Dubčeks moved to Kirghiz, north of the Caspian Sea in the Soviet Union, to work in one of the cooperatives then being established by Inter-helpo, an organization of fervent internationalists, socialists, and Communists who joined in a common effort to help build the new society where man would no longer exploit or be exploited. Their common language was to be the artificial *Ido*, from whence the name *Interhelpo* came. The cooperatives were not given much help nor were they highly regarded by the Soviet leadership, which had far more demanding tasks at hand than smoothing the way for these kibbutz types of common enterprise, but the Dubčeks labored on in the collectivist community, receiving no pay until 1926, with few material rewards and decreasing enthusiasm. They had eventually moved to Gorkiy, 200 miles east of Moscow, but after thirteen years in the Soviet Union, they returned to Slovakia shortly before the German occupation of the Sudetenland.

Alexander Dubček had acquired in these years fluent Russian and a profound admiration for the Soviet Union that, despite his family's spartan life in the remote Kirghiz and Gorkiy, would be proof against serious doubts of the greatness and high purposes of Soviet communism. He and his family had lived in Gorkiy during the Stalinist terror, apparently untouched by the arrests and disappearances of so many people both in and outside the party.

On their return to Slovakia, Alexander went to a school taught by Czech teachers. Only 7 percent of the employees in the civil service in Slovakia were Slovaks, and most of the teachers were Czechs, as were most of the officials of the Slovak Communist party. Dubček served an apprenticeship as a mechanic and in 1939, when he was eighteen years old, joined the Communist party. At the time of the Slovak rising in 1944 he became a partisan fighter and after the war took small jobs, one in a factory, another in a gasoline station, another as a chauffeur, and studied law at night. In 1949, following the Communist coup, he was given a full-time job working for the party. By 1953 he was a Regional Secretary, and in 1955 he was sent to the Soviet Union to study at the training center for party officials at the Party Higher School in Moscow. The Stalinist terror apparently had never troubled Dubček. During the purges of alleged Titoists, the fake trials that resulted in the execution of the former Czechoslovak party Secretary General, Rudolf Slánský, and of thirteen other high members of the party and government including former volunteers in the International Brigade, Dubček remained at his post, offending no one, plodding along the paths that twisted dangerously and were sown with booby traps for those who moved too quickly or not quickly enough.

No one took Stalin's place in the Soviet Union; he had ruled alone with a Politburo, an army, and a government that did what he told them to do. Malenkov and then Khrushchev occupied offices Stalin had once held but they were far from holding his absolute power. In Czechoslovakia, under Gottwald and Novotný, the party and government continued to follow the rigid pattern they had become accustomed to under Stalin. When the trials of the Jewish doctors were being prepared in the Soviet Union in 1953 before Stalin died, the Czechs had their similar trials: all but two of the fourteen defendants in the Slánský case accused of Trotskyism, Titoism, Zionism, and espionage for the West were identified in the indictment as being of "Hebrew origin," although the defendants were either Czech or Slovak by nationality and Communist doctrine in theory has no place for such religious or ethnic attributions. But since Stalin was trying Jews, the Czech and Slovak Communist parties followed suit, as they did when 100,000 Czechoslovak party members were jailed and 100,000 more fired from their jobs.

None of this touched Dubček. He had never been conspicuous, he was a dependable wheelhorse, and at the age of thirty he had been elected to membership in the Central Committee of the Slovak party at the same time as another Slovak Communist, Gustav Husák, was arrested, accused of Slovak nationalism and Titoism. Dubček was sufficiently circumspect and did well enough to be chosen to be sent to Moscow where the cadres destined for higher posts were trained. When the Prague Spring broke out with its heady flowering of freedoms, Dubček's contribution to it was mainly passive. The reform movement in Czechoslovakia was rooted in the party. Communists controlled the Writers Union, one of the chief sources of the demand for reform. The Czechoslovak television and radio, run by party members, aired the stories of the fake trials of the fifties and demanded the rehabilitation of their victims, a liberal, decentralized economic system, and a political program based on the consent and participation of the masses that resembled that of the West far more than that of Moscow or East Berlin. It may be that the choice of Dubček to replace Novotný as First Secretary of the Central Committee in January 1968, made by a party still divided between Stalinists and their opponents, came about precisely because he was not one of the men marked by any kind of extremism. The party progressives, intent on getting rid of the old regime, could accept him, and Moscow approved because nothing in his career showed him to be anything but a dutiful middle-roader, discreetly critical, a modest, hard-working man who loved football and moved up the party ladder without involving himself in the factional struggles that could deposit an ambitious man in high office, or in prison, or underground.

Dubček as First Secretary suddenly found himself at the head of the reform movement, holding the office because he was a mild opponent of the old Stalinist and anti-Slovak, Novotný. Dubček was placed in a key position when the call for reform was becoming a deafening roar. He was willing to be a reformer because he was a Slovak and therefore a partisan of one of the principal doctrines of the reform movement—the restoration of the original idea of two states, or two autonomous regions, within the federation of Czecho-Slovakia. It was the anti-Stalinist forces that had given him his post, and there is no doubt that his own convictions comported on the whole with theirs. He was convinced that the reform ideas were so sensible, so truly socialist, that they could be put into practice with the approval of Moscow once it could be made clear to the Kremlin how beneficent, far-seeing, and essentially pro-Soviet they were. All during the crisis that became steadily more acute in the course of the eight months before the armies of the five fraternal states marched into Czechoslovakia, Dubček kept assuring his critics in Moscow, Berlin, and Warsaw that the Czech reform could only strengthen their alliance. All the plans, he kept repeating, for trade agreements with the West, for democratic freedoms and a more independent course in foreign policy within the framework of international socialism, would only strengthen their common purpose. It would lead the Czechoslovak peoples to a marvelous flourishing of the spirit and to a hitherto unknown level of political well-being. Socialism, invigorated with some Western practices, could make of Czechoslovakia the promised land the pioneers of Interhelpo had been seeking, and this could only strengthen the common socialist cause.

Whether such views were those of a simple, idealistic Communist resolutely convinced that this was the true way to socialist salvation and that the vision must be shared by any reasonable party leadership as soon as its purposes were made clear, or whether they were elaborate Schweikian explications uttered by a friend to all parties concerned to explain why he had to loosen the ties to Moscow, they led Dubček, for the first time in his life, to take an uncompromising position.

The Czechoslovak revolution was a revolution led by Communists, its leaders were good and true party members. They were devoted to the principle of the leadership of the Soviet Union and of the party. They shared a common revulsion at the disclosures of what had gone on in the Soviet Union and in Czechoslovakia under Stalin and his lackeys, and their own experience of the failure of the party program in Czechoslovakia was corroborated by the writers and intellectuals who raged against the terror of the past and described how a decent society could now emerge where such things could not occur again. Writers and intellectuals are much more powerful in a small Communist country like Czechoslovakia once they are permitted to speak their minds than they are in those parts of the world where dissent is a commonplace and the views of reformers often tend to cancel out one another.

The intellectuals and party leaders were saying what the overwhelming majority of the country wanted to say and hear. Everyone knew how backward and inefficient the economy had become, everyone knew that the terror had claimed thousands of innocent victims, that the old party leaders had permitted the barbarities to occur, and that many of the leaders had played a part in the arrests, trials, and executions. Dubček had become the spearhead of those who demanded a fundamental change in the system that had dominated the country since 1948. He had ranged against him the old guard who had lived with and even prospered under the Stalinist rule, but behind him were not only the new men but the masses of the country, both Czech and Slovak.

The Styles of Soviet Imperialism

In Communist countries, where no political opposition is tolerated, the people, as Milovan Djilas has said,[15] are always in a latent war with the regime. What form their protests will take depends on the local opportunities, but their demands, once they can be voiced, tend to rise rapidly until such time as they are smothered in a torrent of overwhelming force. In the satellite countries, where historic differences lie just below the surface, the demands for change may readily be transformed into a nationalist revolt and then, if all goes well, into revolution.

The Hungarian revolution, begun with the demands for reform within the Communist system, had quickly become both antiparty and anti-Soviet. Nagy himself had been a Communist since 1919, and he had spent the war years in Moscow, but he had become more Hungarian than Communist when he renounced the Warsaw Pact, proclaimed Hungary's neutrality, restored opposition parties, and then called out the Hungarian army as the Russians invaded Budapest a second time. In the early stages of the uprising, from October 23 to October 28, peaceable demonstrators demanding economic and political reforms, free elections, and secret voting had become enraged combatants when the symbol of the Soviet system, the Hungarian secret police (AVO), had fired on them. The citizenry of Budapest, mainly workers and students, young people who had been educated and theoretically indoctrinated by the Communist regime, joined by some members of the Hungarian army who had been mobilized to reinforce the AVO, had stormed the radio station and captured weapons from the police and munitions depots. Russian troops had moved into the city at the request, the Russians said, in a formula they would repeat later in Czechoslovakia, of the Hungarian government. On October 25 the AVO and the Russian troops had again fired on the demonstrators, killing hundreds of them, most of them unarmed, young, and including many women and children. When Hungarian soldiers joined the revolt, the Russians understood that violence alone would not subdue these people. The Kremlin announced on October 30 that it would order the withdrawal of Soviet military units from Budapest and declared its willingness to negotiate with the Hungarian Democratic Republic and the other members of the Warsaw Pact regarding the presence of Soviet troops on their soil. The Soviets also promised complete equality of the Communist states of East Central Europe, respect for their territorial integrity, and no interference in their internal affairs.[16] Nagy, who had been expelled from the Communist party in 1955, was appointed Prime Minister on October 24, 1956, by the Central Committee, and set out on October 27 to reconstitute his government to include non-Communists in the Cabinet and to prepare for free elections. A few days after the Russians had departed from Budapest (they remained near the outskirts of the city), new Soviet armored divisions were again reported moving into Hungary. Nagy, determined not to be coerced, on November 1 went on the Budapest radio to announce that unless the Russians stopped their troop movements, Hungary would withdraw from the Warsaw Pact and adopt a policy of neutrality; a neutrality, it was even fatally suggested, that might be guaranteed by the United States, Britain, and France, as well as by the Soviet Union. By November 3, 2500 Russian tanks were back in Hungary, taking up strategic positions around Budapest as the negotiations for the agreed-upon withdrawal of the Russian armed forces were being conducted in Toekoel near Budapest. The Russian generals and the Hungarians were, in fact, discussing only the technical details of the agreed-on withdrawal, details that had to do with the honors to be paid the Russian troops as they departed and the restoration of monuments to the Soviet army that had been destroyed or damaged during the fighting. It was in the course of the banquet given in honor of the Hungarian delegation by the Russian military commander that the Hungarians were arrested by the Soviet secret police. Russian tanks and troops attacked on November 4 in force,[17] and when Nagy ordered the Hungarian army to resist, he had, in effect, declared war on the Soviet Union. The Russians had their satellite government under János Kádár, a member of Nagy's Cabinet who had spent years in jail under Rákosi, ready to take over, and after three days of fighting he and the Russians could announce that the counterrevolution under Nagy had been overthrown.*[18]

The Prague Spring

In Czechoslovakia a dozen years later it was the new leaders of the Communist party who were the folk heroes. The demand for change had come slowly, mainly from within the party. In Czechoslovakia, as in Poland, increasing pressure for reform remained under party control even when the popular demonstrations became mass risings.

---

* While the tanks and guns of the Soviet Union were crushing the revolution in Hungary, both Russia and the United States, along with a majority of countries in the United Nations, were denouncing the aggression of Britain, France, and Israel against Egypt. Washington and Moscow were demanding the withdrawal of the aggressors from Egyptian territory, and Marshal Bulganin was threatening to use atomic weapons against them. (CF. Chapter III, pp. 56–57.)

In Poland it was the dissident Communist Gomulka, seemingly reform-minded and once imprisoned for his apostasy, who could siphon the demand for liberalization into party channels, and Khrushchev did much the same thing in the Soviet Union. Khrushchev uttered in 1956 the words millions of Russians had been waiting to hear. They had all been living, he told the XXth Party Congress, whose members well knew the truth of what he was saying, under the tyrannical whims of a dictator; innocent people by the thousands had been imprisoned and executed. Khrushchev announced the thaw, the long-awaited freedom from the fake trials, the executions that had destroyed not the enemies of the state but a multitude of innocent victims within and outside the party. The terror of the Stalinist dictatorship with its mirror images in the satellite countries was everywhere admitted; the problem for the party leadership now was to remain within the compass of the Marxist-Leninist doctrines that they all cherished and at the same time make impossible a recurrence of the Neanderthal past. What Dubček, Černik, Smrkovský, and the others were trying to do was literally to re-form the party, to bring not only the slogans but the substance of democracy to it and the government it led. They repeated that the party would remain the leading force in the state but its leadership, they said, must be earned, not imposed.

In contrast to Imre Nagy's attitude in 1956, the Czechoslovak leaders maintained the supremacy of the Communist party within the state and ritually repeated their allegiance to the Warsaw Pact and their adherence to international communism. What they demanded was the right to adapt the Marxist-Leninist program to the specific needs of Czechoslovakia, to win a degree of independence within the Warsaw Pact resembling that of the Western allies within NATO, and to forward a program of inner reform that would lead the population to a willing acceptance of their socialist order. In short, the purpose of their socialism with a human face was to combine what they regarded as the scientific insights and humane purposes of Marx and Lenin with some of the genuine freedoms of the West. Dubček did not propose, as had Nagy, that a wide-ranging, multiparty system be reestablished. The Czechoslovak leaders said they had no wish to surrender the leading position of the Communist party. The parties that would be permitted to function, the Socialists and the People's party, would accept the guiding principles of the socialist state as did the non-Communist parties in the

East German coalition of the SED. The economy would continue to be socialist but with provisions made for private enterprise and trade with the West; joint companies would be established to combine with private, Western capital. The new Communist leadership proclaimed freedoms young people had been dreaming of: the right to travel abroad, to read what the critics of the government had to say, to listen to Western high-decibel music, and wear blue jeans and long hair. If Western youths felt themselves hemmed in by their calcified elders, they seemed like the free birds of the air to Czechoslovak youths who worked and scraped and then could only press their noses against the glass that separated them from the delectations they glimpsed in the West.* The Czechoslovak party leaders, like Communist leaders everywhere when the time for reform seemed to have come, told themselves and their countrymen they were truly striving to attain the aims of Marx and Lenin and of people like the Dubčeks when they had journeyed to Kirghiz, that they wanted to free the creative energies of the masses in a socialist and international community in a way that could not be accomplished under the monstrous, authoritarian rule of the Stalins or under the inequities of capitalism.

It never worked out that way in Czechoslovakia or anywhere else. Any thaws that took place in the Soviet Union or elsewhere in the Communist bloc could go only so far before freezing up again; the climate of one-party rule simply did not permit an eternal, or even a very long, spring. Nevertheless, it always seemed to the Dubčeks that it was possible to fashion a new way of life, better, freer, and more adventurous than any they had known before. It could be more humane and freer, they said, precisely because it was socialist, and Dubček and his friends spoke honestly when they said they had no idea of permitting anti-Communist, antisocialist groups to compete with the party. The supremacy of the party remained for all of them a principle that could not be compromised.

The Action Program

As early as February 1, 1968, Dubček had announced the need for an Action Program to be drafted by the Central Committee of

---

* Young people in Poland, Hungary, and Czechoslovakia were demanding rights considered elementary in the West—freedom of speech, of inquiry, of criticism, national freedom.

the party in collaboration with lower-ranking party organizations. The draft, in accord with the reform tenets, would be debated throughout the country before being adopted. The 24,000-word Action Program that was published on April 19 was written mainly by Ota Šik, Radovan Rychta, a member of the Philosophical Institute who had headed a group that made a broad survey of the need for adapting Czechoslovak policies to a technological age, and a historian, Pavel Auerspery, who had written speeches for Novotný. It was a wide-ranging, profoundly humane program that spoke of the need to guarantee the rights of all minorities in the country—of the Slovaks, Hungarians, Poles, Ukrainians, and Germans—to be separate nationalities within the state without being subjected to penalties. It prudently paid tribute to the heroic Soviet army that had liberated Czechoslovakia, but it pointed out, too, that 357,000 Czechoslovaks had died in the struggle against Hitler. It said that antagonistic classes had disappeared from the country and therefore no need existed for the harsh measures of the fifties that had deformed the socialist society. Power must henceforth be removed from the hands of the few; the imperative now was for more democracy, for the unimpeded flow of ideas in place of a monopoly of dogma and power. The parties of the National Front were to be partners with the Communists. They would, of course, be bound by the Constitution and would accept the irrevocably socialist character of the state, but within the socialist framework they would have guaranteed freedom of opinion. Censorship of news would be prohibited and citizens would be protected by a Bill of Rights. All political victims of the purges, Communist and non-Communist, would be rehabilitated. With far more energy and conviction than bourgeois countries, the socialist state could further the development of the individual personality in a cultural, economic, and political climate altogether propitious for human beings. The old plan of federalization was revived together with guarantees of equal rights for the minorities. The state security agency protecting the country against foreign spies and saboteurs would be separated from those responsible for public security, and political views were not to be subject to any kind of repressive measures. The National Assembly would really make laws and decide political questions instead of merely rubber-stamping drafts submitted to it. The Action Program pointed out that no economy could function efficiently without the entrepreneurial spirit, so independent enterprises not under state controls were essential. Industries were to meet the demands of consumers and to enlist workers as full partners in the common enterprise with the workers' movement linked to the scientific revolution. The market was necessary for the development of a socialist economy; it provided the evaluation of production goals and the country's goods needed to become competitive on the world market. Cultural development demanded more support and Czechoslovakian arts should become part of world culture. The alliance with the Soviet Union and the fraternal socialist countries would continue to be the cornerstone of foreign policy, but the program stolidly added a fateful phrase: it said Czechoslovakia "will formulate its own point of view on fundamental questions of world politics." Two German states existed, the Program noted, and while East Germany was the German state of peace, Czechoslovakia would like to have good relations with every country, and in West Germany, too, there were peaceful forces that should be encouraged. The desire of Czechoslovakia, in sum, was to live in peace with both East and West.

It was a beautiful program written with passion, exposing the errors of the past and promising what the entire country wanted. But it had fatal flaws. It took too little account of Czechoslovakia's critical geographic position, bordering West Germany, the neuralgic point for the Soviet Union of its European boundaries, and it gravely misconstrued the nature of the Czechoslovak alliance with Moscow, for example in the passages about improving relations with the Bundesrepublik, of living in peace with all nations, of formulating a specifically Czech foreign policy. The Kremlin was accustomed to reading between the lines, it had perfected the practice in the course of fifty years of double talk, and what the Czechoslovaks were saying was what Moscow most feared: that they were looking fondly to the West, borrowing capitalist notions for their economic program, relaxing the censorship without which no Communist country had ever been able to function, and worst of all, talking grandly about a national foreign policy. The Kremlin's reply was not long in coming. The Czechs were told by *Pravda* that what they were proposing was counterrevolutionary, they were coquetting with the common enemy —the imperialism of the United States and the revanchism of West Germany.

The polemics were harsh on the Russian side, stubborn and Schweikian on the Czechoslovak side. The reforms were necessary, they told the Russians and their other critics in the five brother states, to cement the allegiance of the Czechoslovak people to communism. They repeated their fidelity to the Warsaw Pact and the great Soviet Union, but they would also make their own way in foreign policy decisions. They could do this, they said, because Moscow itself had long agreed that all Communist parties were brother parties, that the socialist states were co-equal, each one sovereign and without the right to interfere in the internal affairs of the others. In Belgrade, in 1963, Khrushchev, who had charged Stalin with needlessly alienating Yugoslavia, repudiated Stalin's highhanded practices and announced a policy of nonintervention in the internal affairs of other Communist countries and affirmed the right of each to an equal voice in the common decisions. Khrushchev had been forced to adopt this egalitarian view because neither Peking nor Belgrade were now willing to accept a tutelage that amounted to Moscow's dictating important foreign and domestic decisions. They refused to accept the supremacy of the Russian party, and both the People's Republic of China and Yugoslavia declined to attend the world conference of Communist nations that the Soviet Union was anxious to convene to repair the breaches in its wall of Communist solidarity. Moscow had to content itself with regional conferences, it had to express its readiness to share the leadership in matters of doctrine, and while the satellite countries remained respectful of its achievements, the centrifugal pull of the away-from-Moscow-movement already evident in China, Yugoslavia, and Rumania, became evident in nearly all the satellite countries as well. Even in the Soviet Union the demand for decentralization was to be heard, and for a time during the brief post-Stalin thaw it seemed that a measure of local autonomy might, in fact, be achieved. People in Communist countries must live under code words more than those in other societies, and what the call for decentralization and polycentrism meant was increased independence in as many spheres as possible.

The Soviet Politburo itself in 1968 was widely reported to be divided in its opinions of what should be done in the case of Czechoslovakia. It was said that half of its members were opposed to using strong measures and commentators compared its divisions to those between the hawks and the doves in the struggle in the United States Congress over the war in Vietnam. Similar stories had gone the rounds in Stalin's day. The highest American officials had regularly been convinced, after the wartime Big Three conferences where Stalin had exhibited so much bonhommie (at Yalta Harry Hopkins told Mr. Roosevelt he thought Stalin had made extraordinary concessions), that he, too, wanted the kind of peace they sought, and when matters became difficult, as they always did after the banquets and toasts, it was believed that Molotov or some other person in the Politburo was sabotaging what generous Uncle Joe wanted done. The case in 1968 was very different. Neither Brezhnev nor Kosygin had Stalin's authority, the Kremlin was solemnly intent on pursuing the policies of collective leadership, and a division of opinion was far more likely to be operational than had been the case under Stalin.

But the Czechs gave the Kremlin peace party, imaginary or real, little to go on. The reform wave was cresting and good Communists outside the Central Committee were demanding much more than had the Action Program in the way of change.

The Two Thousand Words

Among the many revolutionary writings and speeches made during the Prague Spring, one of the most striking was the 2000-word Manifesto of Ludvík Vaculík, written at the suggestion of a group of scientists and writers. Vaculík was a novelist, one of the moving spirits of the Writers Union, and on June 27, 1968, when he published the Manifesto, it immediately became one of the most vital documents of the revolution. It called for a break with the old leaders of the Communist party who had failed to live up to their responsibilities, referring to them as egotists, calculating cowards, and unprincipled men. The troubles of the country, Vaculík wrote, had risen out of their failures, it was because of them that the Parliament had not governed, the government had forgotten how to rule, elections had no significance. People had lost their trust in such party leadership and in one another. The apparatus controlled by these evil and incompetent men made the decisions, said the Manifesto, and no organization, not even the party, belonged to its members but only to the manipulators of this inhuman machine. These men presented their arbitrary decisions as the will of the workers, but it was not the workers who had engineered the purges. A number of these discredited leaders had realized their errors and tried to return decision-making to the party and to the people, and thus the party in its formulation of reforms to be undertaken deserved no credit, it had merely paid a small installment on the debt it owed the society.

The revival in the country had only come about through the weakness of the old leadership, so the significance of the criticisms leveled by writers and students should not be overestimated. The truth had not been victorious, Vaculík said, but rather the truth was all that remained when everything else went to waste. He saw no cause in the reforms for national celebration but only for renewed hope. No democratic revival, he said, could be accomplished without the Communists (he himself was a member of the Central Committee), they had the organization, they were the experienced administrators, and the progressive wing they represented had to be supported. The Action Program the government had proposed was but a beginning. The men taking part in the forthcoming Party Congress had to be of a higher caliber than their predecessors and it was the job of each individual to see that such men were chosen. Workers should elect honest and capable leaders to represent them, the National Front should be revived, and the security agencies should be supported only when they prosecuted genuine criminals. Federation, Vaculík said, would solve the nationality problem, but it would not ensure better living conditions for the Slovaks. The task was for the reformers to hold their own. The people would back the government, they would defend it even with weapons if need be, if the government acted under the mandate the people gave it. The socialist allies were to be assured that Czechoslovakia would observe its alliances. Equal relationships would be secured, however, only if the domestic house was put in order. Again, Vaculík said, the Czechs and the Slovaks had the opportunity to take into their own hands their common cause which, for practical purposes, they called socialism, and "giving it a shape, that will better correspond with our own good reputation and with the relatively good opinion that we once had of ourselves."

The Manifesto was published in *Literární Listy*, in *Práce*, the trade union paper, and in two others, a youth paper, *Mladá Fronta*, and an agricultural paper, *Zemědělské Noviny*. It bore seventy signatures, mainly of Communists, including members of the theatrical world—film producers, doctors, a professor of philosophy, a biologist, poets, Olympic champions, stage managers, and composers—along with factory workers, farmers, engineers, lawyers, teachers, and economists. That was only the beginning, however. After the Manifesto was printed, tens of thousands of signatures were added.

To Moscow, the *Two Thousand Words* sounded a clear call to revolt; the most ominous phrases were those that spoke of backing the government with weapons if necessary. What could that mean but that the author and the signers of the Manifesto were ready to fight against the Soviet Union and its allies if they interfered with the Czechoslovak program for reform?

In Czechoslovakia the reception of the Manifesto throughout the country was overwhelmingly favorable. But in the National Assembly warning voices were immediately heard: one deputy, Major General Samuel Kodaj, wanted charges brought against what he called the inciters of "an open call to counterrevolution."[19]

The party leadership had no practical alternative but to disassociate itself from the *Two Thousand Words* it in general approved of, and it did so as circumspectly as possible. Josef Smrkovský, chairman of the National Assembly, fearful that Moscow would react sharply, telephoned Dubček to say that the government had to undertake some kind of action against the Manifesto. But a few days later he expressed his own views in a moderate reply entitled *One Thousand Words*, printed on July 5, declaring that socialism, democracy, and humanism were one and the same and that the chief present danger came from forces that wished to restore the regime that had ruled before January. He said that although he recognized that the author and signers of the Manifesto had the most honorable intentions, it was written with insufficient information; its proponents demanded in abstract terms the rejection of the unlawful, indiscriminate, and gross methods of the past, but its advocates were men removed from the practical considerations of government and it had been written with undue haste. It was time, Smrkovský said, to remove such discussions from the newspapers to closed rooms.

The reform leadership in the government cautiously distanced itself from Vaculík without rejecting the Manifesto. Minister President Černik said the leaders did not dissent from the criticisms, but the Manifesto could produce, in this phase of the negotiations, an atmosphere of nervousness, unrest, and legal uncertainty. The Presidium of the Central Committee called a special meeting and condemned "the politically irresponsible appeal." It added that the party would see to it that the state institutions were protected by all available means. Dubček cautiously said the party leaders would continue the renewal process, and he saw no reason to doubt the genuine motives of the author and signers of the Manifesto.[20]

But it was not in Czechoslovakia that the *Two Thousand Words* provoked answers foreshadowing the future. First, from the Soviet

Union, in classical Communist style, came an article by a man who obviously was one of the chief party ideologists. Written under the pseudonym of I. Alexandrov, the article, published in *Pravda*, denounced the Manifesto, calling it "an attack on the socialist foundations of Czechoslovakia." Then, on July 15, the attack was broadened and made international. A letter came from Warsaw, from the five fraternal parties, addressed to the Central Committee of the Czechoslovak Communist party. It was also published in *Pravda*. It called the Central Committee "Dear Comrades," and then went on to say that the developments in Czechoslovakia had aroused profound anxiety among the five brother parties. It spoke of the reactionaries' offensive, supported by imperialism, "against the Czechoslovak party and social system." The signers said they had no intention of interfering with Czechoslovakia's internal affairs, but they could not assent to hostile forces threatening to tear the country away from the socialist commonwealth. And then came a sentence that could not be misread: "This is no longer your affair alone. It is the common affair of all Communist and Workers' parties." The *Two Thousand Words* was an open appeal for struggle against the Communist party, a call for strikes and disorders. Antisocialist and revisionist forces were defaming the party, its foreign policy, and its alliances. Counterrevolution supported by imperialist centers had launched a broad offensive and this threat to socialism in Czechoslovakia jeopardized the common interests. American imperialism had not renounced a policy of force and intervention, it continued to fight a criminal war in Vietnam and supported the Israeli aggressors in the Middle East. The Federal Republic of Germany, where neo-Fascism had alarmingly reappeared, was demanding a revision of its borders and access to nuclear weapons. The signers of the letter closed saying they knew that sound elements in Czechoslovakia were capable of upholding the socialist state and called on them to rally against the counterrevolution, to block the path of reaction, and added that they could count on the solidarity and assistance of the five fraternal socialist countries.[21]

The letter was even more ominous when read in the context of the military and political pressures being exerted from Moscow, Warsaw, and East Berlin. It preceded by four days the announcement by *Pravda* of the discovery of a cache of American arms, together with instructions on how to wage guerrilla warfare, allegedly found at Karlsbad, near the West German frontier. The weapons—20 machine pistols, 30 pistols, and 1500 rounds of ammunition—were not very numerous or imposing, but they served to document the danger coming from West Germany and the United States.[22] Since the end of May Warsaw Pact forces under their commander-in-chief, the Soviet Marshal Yakubovsky, had been engaged in military maneuvers on Czechoslovak soil.

The Maneuvers

First planned as routine staff maneuvers that would involve only a small number of troops, it soon was apparent that they would be much more, that considerable numbers of infantry and tanks would be involved in field exercises. The operations, it had been announced, would end in June, but the troops stayed on under one shallow pretext or another. Marshal Yakubovsky reported that the troops could march only at night as they withdrew in order to avoid disturbing traffic during the tourist season. Then it turned out that some of the Soviet units had to take part in still another exercise extending from Riga to the Black Sea, requiring them to march across Czechoslovakia. Thousands of Russian troops were still in the country in July when the Warsaw letter was dispatched. The Rumanian Premier Ceausescu had already complained of what the Czechs and all the other members of the Warsaw Pact knew very well: that the top jobs in the high command of the Warsaw Pact forces were all in the hands of Russians. Major General Josef Čepičky and his chief Lieutenant General Václav Prchlík, head of the military department in the Central Committee, could only repeat over radio and television that they expected the withdrawal in the near future of the brotherly armies, and then as the troops continued to stay on, General Prchlík admitted that apparently a new situation had arisen. He had boldly denied that the Warsaw Pact permitted troops to be stationed on the territory of a signatory state without its consent, but they came and stayed without such consent despite his interpretation of the pact's provisions.[23] The military pressure was coordinated with political moves and stern articles, especially in *Pravda* and in the East German press, that spoke openly of the alarming evidence that reaction and antisocialist forces were abroad. They named names and cited instances. *Neues Deutschland* reported that American forces were already in Czechoslovakia (what had happened was that a film was being made depicting the American crossing of the Rhine at Remagen, and the actors had worn American army uniforms). Other articles warned that neo-Fascism was raising its head in West Germany. They were referring to the rise of the National Democratic party that, after some minor local successes, never was to succeed in electing a single member to the Bundestag because it could not get the 5 percent vote required by the Basic Law.

High Noon in the Prague Spring

The warning signs seemed unmistakable to any trained eye. The Czechs were reminded of the fate of Hungary in 1956 and the chief of the Russian armed forces was reported to have said that the Russian army would do its duty if called on by Czechoslovak comrades to intervene to prevent the overthrow of the socialist regime. The thunder and lightning on the horizon should not have been misinterpreted by the sensitized Kremlinologists of the party, but they were. Tito, for one, told foreign journalists that the Russians would not invade, that an intervention would too greatly damage their already shaken position in the international Communist movement. Apparently the Czechoslovak leadership felt the same way because they continued euphorically on their course of reform and made it increasingly plain they were no longer willing to bow and click their heels when Moscow gave an order. They had refused to attend the Warsaw conference in mid-July and it had been held without them. They refused, in fact, to leave Czechoslovakian soil for any more conferences; they would not allow themselves to be summoned again to Dresden, or Warsaw, or Moscow to plead for their right to pursue purely Czechoslovak policies before a hostile tribunal of the fraternal workers' states. In the future, Dubček said, if these countries wished to discuss what was going on, they could come to Czechoslovakia for bilateral talks in place of the meetings where the Czechoslovaks were defendants and the five fraternal countries judges and prosecutors.

The reforms became more and more dazzling in what had been, for almost twenty years, a captive nation. After half a century the country was finally determined to end the nationalities question in a generous spirit, to do away with the Czech pretensions, so galling to the other ethnic groups, that they were the ones who were most competent to run the affairs of Bohemia and Moravia and of Slovakia and the Sudetenland as well. The sins of the past were openly confessed. One article in a German-language paper published in Prague, *Volkszeitung*, declared the Czechs owed a great deal to their German compatriots,[24] for the Germans, when they had first come to the Sudetenland in the thirteenth century, had brought with them a code of law with protections for the individual the Slav states had known nothing of before. As injustices of all kinds were being righted, the sufferings of the Sudetenlaender were recalled by Czechs, who now remembered that a large section of the German population had not been National Socialists, but Social Democrats, and that although many of them had supported the Beneš government against Hitler, they had nevertheless been driven from the country. For the first time since 1945 the German minority was to be given the same rights of citizenship as the Czechs, and a brave new day was dawning that resembled what Masaryk had promised the Slovaks at Pittsburgh. The Social Democratic party, which in 1949 had been absorbed by the Communist party, was now invited to reconstitute itself as an independent party, and the People's party, a Catholic organization, was also asked to start up anew.

The five fraternal states were enthusiastic about none of this. Janos Kádár in Hungary tried repeatedly to persuade Dubček to shift his course and then adopted the hard Kremlin line himself. Ulbricht was adamantly opposed to everything the Czechoslovaks were trying to do. He was appalled by the notion that Czechoslovakia might seek to "normalize," as they said, relations with West Germany, the center, as Ulbricht's press never ceased reminding its readers, of revanchism, neo-Nazism, and the staging area in Europe for the attack of the forces of American imperialism. *Pravda*, too, on July 19, warned that once the Americans had made their ideological preparations in Czechoslovakia, they would be ready for direct aggression.

They had swallowed much, the orthodox Communists of the five fraternal powers, along with the Czechoslovak conservatives who a few months before had supported Novotný as First Secretary and as President and dutifully carried out the Moscow line. A good many of these conservatives remained in the Dubček government—Drahomir Kolder, Jan Piller, Alois Indra in the Presidium, and some half-dozen others in other party and government positions.[25] Novotný had resigned as President, mainly as a result of the scandal that erupted when General Šejna defected to the United States in February 1968. Šejna had been closely allied to Novotný, he had urged the arrest and imprisonment of the liberal journalists who had caused Novotný so much trouble, so his choice of the United States instead of one of the hard-line Communist countries as refuge was widely attributed to material rather than ideological motives. Once Šejna had defected, not even the conservatives could readily support Novotný. Financial scandals came to light,* and worse still, a plot that had been blocked by General Prchlík for a military putsch under Šejna, which if successful, would have kept Novotný in power.

In the eyes of Dubček and his followers, so much of the past was tarnished with corruption, terror, and violence, and socialism with a human face by contrast was so beautiful, that it seemed impossible that the brother states would not, in time, understand how enormously useful it would be for all of them if Czechoslovakia were permitted to continue its experiments in socialist virtue. What the reformers were looking for resembled what Dubček and his parents had been seeking when the revolution was young. They wanted to return to the ideals of a selfless community without private profit or governmental terror, to the principles of cooperation and brotherhood that had somehow kept eluding them in Soviet Russia and everywhere else.

Final Negotiations

It cannot be said that Moscow showed itself unduly impatient. On May 4, when a Czech delegation of Dubček, Smrkovský, and Bil'ak flew to Moscow to try to obtain credits, grain, and raw materials, Brezhnev assured them the Soviet Union was ready to share its last piece of bread with them, only first they must deal firmly with the antisocialist manifestations in their country. On May 8 Soviet Marshal Konev, former commander of the Warsaw Pact forces, flew to Prague to celebrate the anniversary of Czechoslovakian liberation. Premier Kosygin flew to Prague on May 17, the same day the Soviet Secretary of War, Grechko, led a delegation there, and while the military discussions were going on, Kosygin took a week's cure at Karlsbad and talked with party leaders. On June 14 Brezhnev, First Secretary of the Soviet Communist party, received a delegation of

---

* Šejna was accused of having sold grain and other commodities belonging to the army for his personal gain.

Czechoslovakian members of Parliament in Moscow, talked with them for two hours, and according to an eyewitness, admitted with tears in his eyes that the Soviet Union had made mistakes in dealing with their country. In July Moscow made the final concession, in matters of protocol at least. The Russians had proposed a high-level conference in Moscow for July 19, to be followed a few days later by a meeting of the presidiums of both countries in Moscow, Kiev, or Lvov. The Czechs refused to go to the Soviet Union, and the Soviet Politburo made an unprecedented agreement to travel to foreign soil to meet with the Czechs.

The top leadership of the Soviet Communist party came on July 29—the full Politburo, Brezhnev and Podgorny among them—to meet for three days in the railroad workers' building in Čierná nad Tisou, formerly Schwarzau an der Theisse. At night the green train of the Soviet delegation would return to the security of Russian territory a few yards away in Chop, a frontier station that changed its nationality from Czech to Russian in 1945, but by day they sat with the Presidium of the Central Committee of the Czechoslovak Communist party. Included in the Czech delegation was the doughty President, Svoboda, who had fought with the Russian army in World War II and had been awarded the order of Supreme Hero of the Soviet Union, as well as Kolder, Piller, and Indra, Dubček's most relentless critics in the Presidium.[26]

At the first meeting Dubček painstakingly, all morning long, described what his government was trying to do and why he could not retreat from the course of reform. He admitted that antisocialist forces had appeared in the country but said they presented no possible danger of counterrevolution. Communists are accustomed to long speeches and Brezhnev heard him out, but neither he nor any others among the Soviet delegation appeared to have been listening. Brezhnev, when his turn came in the afternoon, spoke of the dangers of rising imperialism. He told the Czechoslovaks they did not know what was going on in their country and that they must reinstate press censorship and rid the country of liberals in leading positions. Kosygin, who was believed by some observers to be among the Kremlin doves, was one of the harshest critics of the Czechoslovaks. The conference lasted three days. The Czechoslovak delegates were treated with little formality. One of the members of the Presidium, František Kriegel, Kosygin called a "Galician Jew." Brezhnev made a personal attack on Dubček, who reacted stoically.

"I just try to smile at Brezhnev when he shouts at me," Dubček had said, "say yes, yes, and then I continue."[27]

Svoboda, who had succeeded Novotný as President, and for whom the Russians presumably had a high regard, made a speech and the Soviet representatives appeared to listen respectfully. But the tension continued, despite separate meetings between Brezhnev and Dubček and the long harangues. The Russians had brought a document with them containing, they said, ninety-nine signatures from the workers in a Prague factory, asking that the Russian troops (some 3000 Soviet soldiers were still in Czechoslovakia) not be withdrawn from the country. Later, it turned out that only forty signatures had been obtained from among 4000 workers asked to sign the petition.[28]

A bland, final communiqué was issued on August 1, reporting that the conferees had met in an atmosphere of mutual understanding and friendship and that the five fraternal powers would meet on August 3 in Bratislava. Thus, the Russians, although they were willing to meet again in Czechoslovakia, had succeeded in bringing the Dubček government again before a tribunal that would speak for international communism and not merely for the Soviet Union.

The press of the Free World was, on the whole, pleased with the results of the Čierná conference, as it would be with the Bratislava meeting, and spoke of the victory of the stubborn Czechoslovaks who had refused to budge from their principles, had forced the Russians to come to visit them, and apparently had kept their Action Program intact. This interpretation was given some support as the Soviet press stopped its attacks on the Czechoslovak leadership, and President Svoboda and other delegates to the two conferences went on radio and television to assure the country that no secret pacts had been signed, nothing had been surrendered.

The Bratislava conference lasted only one day and the Czechoslovaks heard the same old record. They again, apparently, were reminded that the basic policy of the Warsaw Pact was to fight revisionism and imperialism in the German Federal Republic and not to make accommodations with it, that the party must play the leading role in Czechoslovakia, that press controls must be reestablished, and so on. The conference ended with another noncommittal communiqué, this one signed by the six powers on August 3, the day the last of the Soviet troops left Czechoslovakian soil. The communiqué spoke of the brotherly solidarity of the socialist countries vis-à-vis the imperialists, of their desire to continue their common policies and to reaffirm the unity of the socialist countries against those who wanted to revise the results of World War II. It spoke of the unbreakable friendship of the peoples of the six countries, and their purpose to serve the interests of peace, democracy, national independence, and socialism.* Dubček, in his Czechoslovakian television appearance, called the Bratislava conference a success and promised that the government would continue the policies adopted in January. He again assured his nationwide audience that the only decisions that had been made appeared in the communiqué, but he also announced that press attacks on the Soviet Union must cease and told viewers that the government was unanimously behind the Warsaw Pact and Comecon.

Again the press of the world rejoiced, complimented the Czechoslovaks on their courageous stand, and some commentators spoke of the defeat the Soviet Union had suffered. On the television screens of the West this was another happy ending like those of the soap operas that had preceded and would follow the news broadcasts.

The United States and the United Nations

In the United States, 1968 was an election year and the President, in deep trouble in Vietnam, was eager to obtain any possible political gains in other parts of the world, especially in Soviet Russia, which was, among other unfriendly activities, supplying all North Vietnam's sophisticated weapons and 90 percent of its other war material. Mr. Johnson had long wanted to arrange for a summit conference with Soviet leaders, and Premier Kosygin, with the Czechoslovak military operation fully prepared, was ready to oblige him. On August 19 Kosygin informed Mr. Johnson he would be pleased to meet with him in Moscow. When a day later the troops of the five fraternal countries invaded Czechoslovakia, Mr. Johnson was indignant but not bellicose, deplored the invasion, and called for an emergency meeting of the Security Council, a move that one of the

---

* One or two phrases, if read hypercritically, might be seen to cast the shadow of coming events. The communiqué spoke of the common international duty of all socialist countries to support the gains they had made, of the need to intensify cooperation among them based on "principles of equality, respect for sovereignty and national independence, territorial integrity," and then it added "and fraternal mutual aid and solidarity." (Isaac Don LeVine, *Intervention*, p. 46; Robert Alison Remington, ed., *Winter in Prague*, p. 257.)

chief critics of his war program in Vietnam, Senator Eugene Mc-
Carthy, declared out of proportion to its cause. No emergency session
of the Security Council of the United Nations had been needed,
said Mr. McCarthy, because what had happened was not a major
crisis that endangered the peace of the world. And indeed nothing
happened outside Czechoslovakia that would have the slightest adverse effect on what the five brother nations sought to achieve. Mr.
Johnson would eventually have to forego his summit meeting, although a White House spokesman said, on August 21, that the
conference would proceed according to plan. The former ambassador
to the Soviet Union, George Kennan, urged that 100,000 American
troops be sent to West Germany and brought back only when the
Russian troops left Czechoslovakia, but Mr. Johnson declined to
take his advice.[29] It was hard to see what such a gesture would accomplish other than the exercise of marching the troops up the hill
and then down again. Mr. Johnson declared that the invasion violated the UN Charter but said at the same time that there was no
safe course open to the United States other than that of leading the
protests in the United Nations and mobilizing world opinion. This
is what was done, and country after country deplored the invasion,
as did Communist parties outside the Soviet Union. The People's
Republic of China compared the invasion to Hitler's occupation of
the Sudetenland in 1938; in France Charles de Gaulle and Jean-
Paul Sartre both had harsh words to say about it, as did Harold Wilson in Britain and Tito in Yugoslavia and the Communist parties of
France and Italy. Fidel Castro called the invasion illegal but an essential measure against the counterrevolution. Premier Ceausescu of
Rumania denounced the invasion on August 21, but on August 26
he softened his attack asserting that all Communist parties must make
common cause against imperialism. Albania condemned it, North
Vietnam wholly approved of it. In Soviet Russia small and isolated
demonstrations also took place against the invasion and arrests
were made in Red Square where Larissa Bogaraz Daniel, the wife
of the imprisoned poet Yuri Daniel, and the grandson of Maxim
Litvinov, the physicist, Paul Litvinov, with two others were taken
into custody. A scattering of Russian intellectuals praised the Czechoslovaks; Andrei D. Sakharov, a physicist and member of the Academy of Science; Piotr Yakir, the son of a general who had been executed in the 1937 purge; the poet Yevgeni Yevtushenko; the author
of an unpublished book on his experiences in a slave labor camp,

Anatoly T. Marchenko; and others. But the protests stopped with the intellectuals; no echoes were to be heard among the people.[30]

A United Nations spokesman declared on August 21 that another serious blow had been dealt international order and morality and ten members of the Security Council approved a draft resolution on August 23 which condemned the invasion, calling it a violation of the UN Charter, under which member states were to refrain from threatening and/or using force, and demanded the withdrawal of the occupying troops. But the Soviet Union held all the cards of peace and war; joined by Hungary, it vetoed the Security Council resolution. Moscow was also able to stifle any attempts of the Czechoslovak representatives in the UN to plead their case.

The acting head of the Czechoslovak delegation to the United Nations, Jan Muzik, had read a communication from Czech Foreign Minister Jiri Hájek on August 21, saying there was no justification for the invasion and demanding that the illegal occupation be halted and the troops withdrawn. A second message from the Czechoslovak Presidium called the invasion contrary to international law, the Warsaw Pact, and the principle of national sovereignty. Foreign Minister Hájek flew to New York on August 23, and when he appeared before the Security Council on the following day he said again there was no justification for the illegal occupation. But on August 25 the Czechoslovak delegation to the United Nations asked that debate on the question be halted, and on August 27 Foreign Minister Hájek declared his delegation would not participate in further discussions of the issue before the Security Council. In the United Nations Assembly references were made to the invasion but that was all; the subject was never formally put on the agenda because, as the Russian delegate, Mr. Malik, had argued in the Security Council, this was an internal matter concerning the Czechoslovakian government and they did not wish it discussed.

Moscow

President Svoboda had been flown to Moscow on August 23, where he was received with full Soviet ceremony at the airport and driven past cheering crowds in an open limousine with Brezhnev, Kosygin, and Podgorny to the Kremlin. He would not begin the talks, however, until the Czechoslovak leaders who were still under arrest, Dubček, Smrkovský, Černik, and the others, were allowed to attend the conference. Svoboda was the only man the Soviet officials had to deal with during the conference who could cause them any serious embarrassment; he threatened to shoot himself in the Kremlin if Dubček and the others were not released from custody and permitted to join the talks, and the Soviet Politburo evidently saw less harm in the presence of their prisoners than in the effect Svoboda's suicide might have on the outside world. Therefore the Russians agreed to free everyone, but would not permit František Kriegel, chairman of the National Council, whom they regarded as a Zionist and implacably hostile, to come to the meeting. They did, however, when Svoboda said he would not leave without him, permit him to fly back to Prague with his compatriots after he had been so roughed up he could scarcely speak.

The Czechoslovak leaders were now, at long last, fully aware of their situation. They had been unceremoniously handled. Černik said later his life had been threatened. Dubček had been telephoning when he was arrested in the offices of the Central Committee on the morning of August 21, the phone was ripped from his hands, and he and the other members of the Presidium were lined up with their faces to the wall. They had been, it was reported, handcuffed and taken off by Soviet paratroopers, and since many of them were old hands at being political prisoners, they had gone quietly. Smrkovský had taken two lumps of sugar from the table before he left, saying: "We will need these."[31]

But more than the safety and comfort of their persons was involved as they found themselves sitting again around a conference table with the representatives of the five fraternal powers. The Soviet leaders threatened to make a separate state of Slovakia and incorporate it into the Union of Soviet Socialist Republics, using a strategy similar to that of Hitler when he conferred independence on Slovakia in 1939. Bohemia and Moravia, the Russians pointed out, could be made into an autonomous state. The Czechoslovak delegation could only agree to what concessions were demanded of them and gain small points—a promise of troop withdrawals, the safe return of the entire delegation. For the time being, they were needed by the Russians because the Soviets had no one immediately prepared to take their places who would also be acceptable to the home population.

On August 26 the Czechoslovak leaders ended their talks, or more accurately, their being talked to, in the Kremlin. The Soviet Politburo members had been joined by Ulbricht, Kádár, Gomulka, and Shivkov, representing the four fraternal parties, but the final communiqué was issued in the names only of the Czechoslovak and Soviet participants.*

The Dubček government had to agree to abandon any notion of a neutralist position in international affairs. The decisions of the XIVth Party Congress, which had been held clandestinely after the invasion, were declared invalid. The Communist Party, it was agreed, would reassume its leading role in Czechoslovakia, censorship would be reimposed, and no one who had collaborated with the occupying powers would be prosecuted. Economic ties with the Soviet Union would be strengthened, no new political parties would be authorized, and the nonsocialist clubs† would be dissolved. Foreign policy would be conducted within the framework of the Soviet alliance. These were reported as the secret agreements made at the conference[32] and subsequent events indicate that they were, in fact, accepted by the Czechoslovak delegates in Moscow.

The official communiqué issued at the end of the Moscow conference was as unctuous as the statements following Čierná and Bratislava. It stated what might be expected to calm and admonish the Czechoslovak population: During the open-hearted comradely discussions the two sides had considered the present international situation and the imperialist machinations against the socialist countries. The Soviet government would support the leadership of the Czechoslovak Communist party and the decisions made by the Central Committee in January and May to improve the management of the society, socialist democracy, and the socialist system. The communiqué spoke of the "temporary" entry of the troops of the allied countries and said they would not interfere with the internal affairs of Czechoslovakia. They would be withdrawn from the territory of Czechoslovakia "depending on the normalization of the situation in the Republic." The Czechoslovaks had agreed that the government would do everything possible to prevent incidents and conflicts that might disturb public order. The communiqué affirmed that the representatives of the republic had not requested the submission of the Czechoslovak question for consideration by the Security Council of the UN and had demanded its removal from the agenda. The par-

* Walter Ulbricht was chairman of the State Council of the German Democratic People's Republic; Wadislaw Gomulka, First Secretary of the Central Committee of the Polish Workers party; János Kádár, First Secretary of the Hungarian People's party; and Todor Shivkov, First Secretary of the Bulgarian Communist party.

† A number of organizations had been formed by non-party people. One such organization was a discussion club, "The Club of Committed Non-Party Members, with the acronym of "Kan." Kan had also drawn up a political program.

ticipants in the meeting, who were all representatives of the Communist parties of both states, confirmed their determination to strengthen the solidarity of the socialist movement "and the cause of peace and international security. As heretofore the Soviet Union and Czechoslovakia will resist with determination the militaristic, revanchist and neo-Nazi forces that strive to reverse the results of World War II. . . ." Both sides were determined to do everything they could to strengthen the defensive forces of the socialist community and to increase the effectiveness of the Warsaw Pact treaty. The talks, the communiqué said, were held in an atmosphere of frankness, comradeship, and friendship.[33]

Svoboda and Dubček, on their return to Prague, revealed more of what had gone on and they made the dose as palatable as possible. President Svoboda, in a broadcast made at 2:50 P.M. on August 27, after expressing his sorrow at the deaths caused by the invasion, thanked his fellow citizens for their support and told them he had done all he could to avoid bloodshed. The situation, he said, must be "normalized" as quickly as possible and to this end an agreement in principle had been arrived at for the gradual withdrawal of the occupation armies. Meanwhile, however, their presence was a political reality. The President admitted that painful wounds had been inflicted in the last days, but he said confidence had to be restored and sincere cooperation between countries linked by destiny. "The place of our country in today's world," he said, "is and cannot be anywhere but in the socialist community."

The government, he declared bravely, wished to continue to strengthen the humanist, democratic character of the socialist system as expressed in the Action Program and would not retreat one step from this goal. It would not, however, allow its aims to be misused by interests alien to socialism, and Svoboda urged on his listeners wisdom and circumspection.[34]

The exhausted Dubček broadcast a few hours later, at 5:30 P.M. He, too, thanked his listeners for their enormous demonstration of confidence, and said they must now prevent further suffering and losses. But, he added, the fact that "we are determined to prevent bloodshed does not mean that we want to submit passively to the situation. . . ." The government, together with the people, would find a way to "normalize" conditions. ("Normalize" was another code word meaning getting rid of the occupation troops, which would not happen if there were mass protests.) From time to time Dubček's emotions overcame him, but he did the best he could to reassure his listeners. The Warsaw Pact troops, he promised, would leave Czechoslovakia in a phased withdrawal, and would depart immediately from towns and villages to special areas.* Order was needed, conscientious discipline, no one should act in passion. Temporary measures would restrict the "degree of democracy and freedom of expression." Some broadcasts, following President Svoboda's speech, had already spread doubts about the Moscow negotiations and Dubček warned against such tactics. The people, he said, would never retreat from the ideas of socialism, humanism, national independence, and Czechoslovak sovereignty. The party must have the confidence of the citizenry under today's "incredibly difficult conditions," bear its responsibilities, and guard "decisively . . . our socialist policy in Czechoslovakia for the future." (At this point Dubček paused, nearly fainted, some said, and then asked his listeners to forgive him if every now and then he had to stop. He added: "I think you know why this is.") The future course would not be easy and the fulfillment of the Action Program would be more complicated and take longer than they had thought. Czechoslovakia and its people belonged in the community of socialist nations, and its relations, despite what had happened, would be resolved in harmony with this reality. Dubček begged that there be no provocations, that the country remain united, calm, and above all, prudent.[35]

It was a difficult speech to make. Dubček had to prevent a hopeless uprising, make promises that were as vague as possible, and above all, play for time to keep the peace and eventually get rid of the armies of the five fraternal powers, while saving whatever he could of the Action Program. Soviet pronouncements had explained the presence of the Warsaw Pact armies in Czechoslovakia by saying they had been called in by high authorities of the Czechoslovak government and party to prevent the dissolution of the socialist regime by counterrevolutionary forces. The story had been prepared in advance and was an old one, always at hand. It had been used, on among other occasions, against the Finns in 1939, when Moscow announced it was invading Finland at the request of the Finnish People's Government under Otto Kuusinen in Terijoki.†

---

* Dubček spoke on August 27. The occupation troops began to evacuate key buildings in Prague on September 3. The evacuation of villages came later.

† The Kuusinen government, composed of Finnish Communists in Moscow, never functioned and may never have been in Terijoki. (David J. Dallin, *Soviet Russian Foreign Policy*, p. 141.)

In the Leninist-Marxist scriptures, Soviet Russia could not commit an aggression as could capitalistic countries, whose motives were unfailingly imperialistic. All war in this view was class war, and since Soviet Russia's mission was to defend the workers and peasants of the world, it had always been able to call on devoted friends in time of need to invite the Soviet armies to invade foreign territory, whether in Tannu Tuva or Hungary, if such was Moscow's purpose. But this time, no Czech or Slovak could be found who would admit to having invited the Soviet troops and their allies to come into the country. Those who might have been so used, like Indra, Kolder, and Bil'ak (Dubček had been arrested in the name of the "Indra Revolutionary Workers and Peasants Government"), must have realized how little popular support they could count on and did not play out the roles expected of them. The reasons, therefore, that Moscow gave for the invasion would vary with some disregard for what had been said a few days before. First the announcements from Moscow said the fraternal troops had been invited by unnamed high officials, and when the Kremlin could not produce these officials, it said the invasion had occurred to rescue the country from a counterrevolution. Finally the explanation was given that would need no further elaboration—it was the enunciation of the Brezhnev Doctrine, the view that the Soviet Union would always have the right and duty to intervene if socialism was threatened in any country within the socialist commonwealth.

The Brezhnev Doctrine

The Brezhnev Doctrine, as it came to be called, although its author has denied that such a doctrine exists, was first formulated in *Pravda* on September 26, 1968, in an article signed by S. Kovalev. Mr. Kovalev moved like a talented ballet dancer among the conflicting pronouncements that had been made by Soviet leaders in the past. The article agreed with the position that the socialist countries and their Communist parties have the right to determine the paths of their separate development but, and this was the important point, they must damage neither socialism in their own country nor world communism. Every Communist party was responsible not only to its own people but to the socialist community as well. Marx, said Mr. Kovalev, had opposed one-sidedness; every phenomenon had to be examined from both sides, seen in its specific nature and in connection with other phenomena and processes. The sovereignty of an individual socialist state could not possibly be antagonistic to world socialism and the revolutionary movement. Each Communist party had the right to apply the principles of Marx and Lenin in its own country, but it could not depart from those principles and remain Communist. Therefore, the socialist states had to take account of the struggle against capitalism, a struggle led by the Soviet Union. No plea for self-determination could be used as a mask for neutrality that would enable NATO troops to approach the Russian border. The Bratislava agreement of the Communist and Workers parties had underscored the common duty to support the socialist gains of the past. Neutrality would lead straight to the jaws of West Germany's revanchism, and this kind of self-determination would be self-determination for the benefit of the enemy. In class societies no such thing as a nonclass war can exist; all laws are subordinated to the laws of the class struggle and of social development. These truths could not be disregarded for legalistic formulations. If they could be, there would be no stopping fascism and Nazism, the butchers of Franco and Salazar, and of the colonels in Greece. The United States and its Saigon puppets admit they cannot support the strivings of the progressive forces. The five powers had aimed at defending the fundamental interests of Czechoslovakia, the socialist commonwealth, and the sovereignty and independence of Czechoslovakia.[36]

The doctrine, while inconsistent with such pronouncements as those made at Belgrade and on other occasions, was nevertheless completely in line with what Lenin had said in 1920 when he declared that socialist international proletarianism in one country was the common interest of all. Lenin's position was adopted by Stalin, who held that the workers of the world had the duty to defend the Soviet Union, the base of the world revolution. Khrushchev had attempted to water down these principles when, on June 2, 1955, he had signed the Belgrade Declaration with Marshal Tito, that proclaimed the complete equality of all socialist states and recognized the need for national differences in the development of socialism. The XXth Party Congress had adopted the Khrushchev line in February 1956, and for a time it had seemed that the pluralistic, decentralized development of the Communist orthodoxy might well become the new course. But the revolts in Poland and Hungary in 1956 had led inexorably to the adoption of a harder line, and when

Mao, like Tito, attempted to assert China's right to independent judgment, Moscow and Peking found themselves at the same opposite poles that had formerly been occupied by Stalin and Tito. From 1961 on, the chief danger seemed to Moscow to be reform communism, and soon Mao, as well as Tito, was added to the list of perils. On July 3, 1968, Brezhnev had said the Soviet Union could never be indifferent to the fate of socialism in other countries, and on June 27 Gromyko said the strengthening of socialism was the most important task of the Soviet Union. Brezhnev denied that what the five powers were seeking was a limitation of sovereignty; rather, he said, the act of intervention was a display of proletarian internationalism. On November 28, speaking before the Polish United Workers party, Brezhnev again formulated the doctrine he would later deny existed. He said: "When enemy forces react against the development of a socialist country and attempt to restore capitalism, when a serious danger to the socialism of one country becomes a danger to the security of the socialist community, then this is not a concern of that country but is a common problem . . . for all socialist countries."[37] This, despite the subsequent tactical shifts, had become socialist international law, the law for the world revolution. Mutual help is the right of each and each has the duty to give it. Any counterrevolution justifies intervention if the counterrevolution would restore capitalism and help imperialism. The chief of the Rumanian Communist party, Ceausescu, rejects this doctrine, as do Tito and Mao and the Albanians. The Chinese called it a gangster theory, but it is a foundation stone of Soviet hegemony in the Eastern bloc, and when Brezhnev, in Belgrade in the autumn of 1971, again denied there is such a thing as the Brezhnev Doctrine, the words were designed for that occasion only; the doctrine would reappear when it was needed.[38]

The Logistics of the Brezhnev Doctrine

The invasion machinery had worked smoothly. Half a million men had marched, been driven, or flown into Czechoslovakia. The elaborate maneuvers of the preceding weeks had served as a reconnaissance for the invasion, the pinpointing of the disposition of Czechoslovak troops, and the strategic places to be occupied. The spring maneuvers of the Warsaw Pact countries had been held under the command of Russian Marshal Yakubovsky, but the commander of the invasion forces was not he but another Russian general, Ivan G. Pavlovsky, chosen apparently to avoid the Warsaw Pact channels of command where the Czechoslovaks might learn of the plans. The Czechoslovak Presidium, when it first heard of the invasion, had ordered that the Czechoslovak troops remain in their barracks and there they stayed. This was the third time the expensive Czechoslovak army had failed to fight when the hour of decision came. It is true that in none of the crises could resistance have been successful: the Czechoslovak army in 1938 was no match for Hitler's legions; in 1948 resistance would only have resulted in civil war against the pro-Communist militia and Communist elements in the army supported by Soviet troops; and in 1968 a call to fight would have resulted only in a hopeless battle against the overwhelming forces ranged against them.

Nevertheless, there were criticisms. The army had always cost the Czechoslovak people large sums out of a slim national product and yet it never fought. In 1938 it had surrendered fortifications of considerable strength without firing a shot. But Finland had taken up arms in 1939, as had the Hungarian workers, students, and some military contingents in 1956. Impossible struggles had been waged before in history that led, if not to victory, at least to glorious legends. In the case of Czechoslovakia, it was the civil population who resisted and demonstrated their contempt for the invaders. They painted swastikas on the Russian tanks, and defamatory slogans on the city walls; they massed in the streets, they demanded to know from the Soviet soldiers what they were doing in a brother socialist state; they all, men, women, and children, refused to fraternize or to give the invaders a piece of bread or a drink of water. They tore down the street signs so the Russian troops would wander in a Kafkaesque city where the streets led anywhere and nowhere. People were killed and wounded as they painted their demands that "Ivan go home" on walls, or when they disobeyed the curfew, or hurled Molotov cocktails at the tanks. Nothing, however, like the furious uprisings in Hungary or East Germany took place in Czechoslovakia. The people were bitter and outspoken. They reminded the Slav big brother how closely he resembled Hitler, and they lashed back at him with scurrilous slogans and drawings. The clandestine radios told the people what to do, they summoned the meeting of the XIVth Party Congress that elected a new progressive Central Committee (which the government later had to repudiate), they reported the news, they responded to calls for a general strike, Schweikian strikes that were completely successful (though one lasted only fifteen minutes, another an hour). They kept the resistance mobilized but within bounds to prevent a holocaust. Signs said: "1938—Hitler: 1968—Brezhnev" and "Lenin, wake up; Brezhnev is crazy." Fake advertisements appeared: "Would exchange Soviet-Czechoslovakian friendship against any kind of crap." One placard read: "Take a good look at this poster; in a few minutes it will be torn down." The picture of a coffin was drawn with the words, "With the Soviet Union forever."

The invasion of the friend-turned-enemy was in many ways harder to bear than that of the traditional enemy, the German, who had been the chief overlord in the Austro-Hungarian empire and whose cousins had marched in 1938. Curiously enough it was now the ancient Germanic foe who was the friend, in the guise mainly of the Austrians,* who offered asylum for those who could flee the country, and the West Germans, who staged pro-Czech demonstrations and whose media, Writers Union, and political leaders were all on the side of the reform and the new freedoms. As for the East Germans, they had marched into the Sudetenland in 1968 as some of them had marched in in 1938, into a territory where many of the inhabitants still spoke German. It may be that one of the reasons the East German contingents were pulled out after only a token participation in the invasion was that the troops could understand the complaints of the German-speaking Czechs and what they said matched what the German soldiers thought of the Communist regime they themselves lived under. Another, and perhaps more important, reason for their withdrawal was the fact that their presence on Czech soil might be interpreted as a violation of the Potsdam accords, and of Articles 53 and 107 of the United Nations Charter according the right of intervention against "the renewal of aggressive policies by a former enemy state," which the Russians were always ready to cite when protesting the rearmament or aggressive tactics of West Germany.†

The Czechoslovak resistance to the invasion was long-lived be-

---

* The Austrians, uncertain whether the Russian invasion would stop at the Czech border and what the West would do if it did not, were friendly, but more cautious than they had been in 1956 during the Hungarian revolution.

† Not that the Kremlin regarded the Ulbricht regime as a former enemy state, but the West might make use of the same argument against East Germany's invasion of Czechoslovakia as the Soviet Union had advanced against the Bundesrepublik.

cause the Soviet troops stayed on. In 1971 60,000 of them were still on Czechoslovak soil where they could remain legally under an agreement signed by Černik and Kosygin on October 16, and ratified by the National Assembly in Prague on October 18, 228 votes to 4, with 10 abstentions.[39] The National Assembly resolution included a face-saving provision that the troops would not interfere in Czechoslovakia's internal affairs.[40]

The people, as opposed to the government, were still restive, and in November 1968 a student strike took place protesting the erosion of the Action Program. In January 1969 a twenty-one-year-old philosophy student, Jan Palach, following the example of Buddhist monks in Vietnam, immolated himself in Wenceslas Square in Prague in a fiery protest against the press censorship, dying a few days later. Again students staged anti-Soviet demonstrations. In March the Czechoslovak ice hockey team twice defeated the Soviet team in Stockholm, and celebrating crowds in Prague demolished Soviet property including the offices of Aeroflot, shouting "Ussuri, Ussuri." (The hockey victory had followed a bloody clash on the Ussuri River, separating Chinese and Soviet territory in the Far East, in which thirty-one Russians were killed and which the Chinese celebrated as a defeat for the Russian troops.) President Svoboda called the outbreaks "vandalism," and banned an outspoken journal, *Politik*, and thus marked the end of the reforms. Only the plan for the federalization of Czechoslovakia remained of the Prague Spring; the Soviets had no objection to more autonomy for Slovakia. Prague television announced that the allies of the five brother nations would give the country one more chance to put its house in order and that President Svoboda would have full authority to accomplish this end, including the use of Soviet troops if need be.

The Soviet coils had tightened slowly. Ota Šik resigned his post as Deputy Minister on September 4, 1968, and others followed, including Foreign Minister Hájek who, despite his relatively quick change of front in August, was far from *persona grata* to the Soviet leaders. General Pavel, Minister of the Interior, quit on September 1, Smrkovský was ousted as chairman of the National Assembly on January 7, 1969, and from the Presidium on April 1. He was replaced by a strong Moscow supporter, Lubomir Strougal, who had been Deputy Prime Minister. Dubček was forced to quit his post as First Secretary on April 17, 1969, and replaced by Gustav Husák, a Slovak nationalist and, above all, a political pragmatist. Dubček was elected chairman of the National Assembly on April 28, but on August 27 he was denounced by his former ally, Prime Minister Oldrich Černik, for having allowed the situation to deteriorate before the invasion, and not having, for example, informed his colleagues in the Presidium of the date of the Warsaw meeting which they therefore had not been able to attend. On September 25 Dubček and Smrkovský were purged from the Central Committee, and in December Dubček was sent as ambassador to Turkey. In Ankara Dubček, to the distress of the Turks, called first on the Soviet ambassador before presenting his credentials to the Turkish President. Despite that gesture, six weeks after his arrival he could read in the newspapers that his membership in the Communist party had been suspended.

The post-Dubček government was composed mainly of apparatchiki who did what was pleasing to Moscow, and Dubček's old opponents, Alois Indra and Vasil Bil'ak, were prominent among them. In a Communist country there are few alternatives to power—either a leader is in the party and government or he is out, the high officials ride around in their black limousines and shop in the special stores where goods denied the ordinary citizens are to be had, or they lose these privileges and retire into obscurity as Malenkov or Khrushchev did in Russia, and Dubček and his friends in Czechoslovakia. If a man like Černik has been on the losing side of a dispute, he is lucky to be allowed to repent, attack his former friends and allies, and keep his job. Černik was adroit but no change of front could redeem his part in the 1968 reform movement and in January 1970 he was dropped as Prime Minister.

Dubček was not imprisoned or executed as were so many former leaders in the Stalinist purges of the thirties and fifties. He was merely cast aside, disowned, and the work of building socialism was continued by others. After a three months' stay in Ankara, Dubček was ordered to return to Czechoslovakia. He obtained a job in a Bratislava garage, where he was photographed in 1971 by a German newspaperman as he went to work in a bus, hanging on to a strap with the same wan smile on his lips he had worn when not only Czechoslovakia but much of the world hung on his words and praised his courage.

NOTES

1. Josef Maxa, *Die Kontrollierte Revolution*, p. 215.
   William Shawcross, *Dubcek*.
2. Eugene Davidson, *The Death and Life of Germany*.

3. Stephen D. Kertesz, "Hungary," in Stephen D. Kertesz, ed., *East Central Europe and the World.*
4. Oscar Halecki, "Poland," in Kertesz, *op. cit.*
5. Kertesz, *op. cit.*
6. Hubert Ripka, *Le Coup de Prague.*
7. Claire Sterling, *The Masaryk Case.*
8. Kertesz, *op. cit.*
9. Jacques Marcelle, *Le Deuxième Coup de Prague.*
10. Ladislav Mňacko, *The Seventh Night,* p. 80.
11. Quoted in Isaac Don Levine, *Intervention,* p. 30.
12. Radislov Selucky, *Czechoslovakia: The Plan That Failed.*
13. Tad Szulc, *Czechoslovakia since World War II.*
14. Mňacko, *op. cit.,* p. 182.
15. Milovan Djilas, *The New Class,* p. 87.
16. Ferenc A. Vali, *Rift and Revolt in Hungary,* p. 345.
17. Vilmos von Zsolnay, in Werner Frauendienst, ed., *Ungarn Zehn Jahre Danach.*
18. Vali, *op. cit.,* p. 384.
19. Fritz Beer, *Die Zukunft functioniert nicht,* p. 315.
20. Almar Reitzner, *Alexander Dubček.*
21. Robert Alison Remington, ed., *Winter in Prague,* pp. 225–231.
22. Heinz Brahm, *Der Kreml und die ČSSR,* p. 48.
23. Robert Rhodes James, ed., *The Czechoslovak Crisis.*
24. Reitzner, *op. cit.,* pp. 95–98.
25. Brahm, *op. cit.*
26. *Ibid.*
27. Shawcross, *op. cit.,* p. 175.
28. Reitzner, *op. cit.,* p. 115.
29. Brahm, *op. cit.,* p. 91.
30. Levine, *op. cit.*
31. Josef Maxa, *Die Kontrollierte Revolution,* pp. 220–221.
32. Facts on File Incorporated, *Facts on File,* August 26, 1968.
33. Klaus Kamberger, ed., *Der Fall ČSSR,* pp. 70–73.
34. Robert Littell, ed., *The Czech Black Book,* pp. 248–249.
35. *Ibid.,* pp. 249–256.
36. *Ibid.*
37. Remington, *op. cit.,* pp. 411–416.
38. Boris Meissner, *Die Breschnev Doktrin.*
39. Reitzner, *op. cit.,* pp. 194–196.
40. Szulc, *op. cit.,* p. 431.

8

The Legacy:
The Present and the Past

IN the existential world where decision-makers act as well as talk, not much is left of the Nuremberg judgments, or of the amenities that had reduced the horrors of war in times that accepted armed conflicts as part of international life. As a result of the divided world, the loss of an international consensus, and what has amounted to the eclipse of legality, less protection is afforded a citizen of the United States on a civilian or military mission in foreign parts now than he could have counted on in the uncertain early days of the Republic or in any other period up to World War II. American citizens may be imprisoned because they are members of a crew of an intelligence vessel sailing the high seas off Korea; American fishing boats may be captured 200 miles at sea off the coast of Ecuador, which claims its territorial waters extend that far,* and forced to pay ransom.† Prisoners of war may be held in North Vietnam under any conditions imposed by the capturing power. Americans abroad have been arrested for alleged espionage or accused of other major or minor

* The generally accepted limits of territorial waters of from 3 to 12 miles are extended by some eight Latin American states to 200 miles in order to control fishing rights. The Soviet Union regards 12 miles as the limit but the People's Republic of China with Taiwan in mind, supports claims up to 200 miles. Iceland claims 50 miles on behalf of its fishing interests.
† In 1971 fifty-one American tuna boats were seized by Ecuador and the United States government had to pay fines and licensing fees of $2.5 million to free them. (*The New York Times*, January 7, 1972.)

offenses against an Eastern bloc state, as they have been in Poland, East Germany, Czechoslovakia, and Hungary, and sentenced to long terms of imprisonment with a minimum of diplomatic protection or none at all in the case of states like the German Democratic Republic or North Korea. It is doubtful that any one of these acts against American lives and property could have occurred in the eighteenth, nineteenth, or early twentieth centuries without energetic diplomatic action and reprisals being undertaken by the American government. As for peace in our time, wars have occurred at the rate of some four a year since Nuremberg, and the peacekeeping efforts of the United Nations are limited to those rare occasions when they meet the combined approval of the superpowers which, however, in areas near their own borders, reserve the right to intervene in the affairs of any country they believe to be adopting, or threatening to adopt, the political system of the other side.

The search for ways of mitigating the ravages and horrors of war has been a long one and until World War II had had considerable success. The observance of a flag of truce, the prohibition against attacking an enemy who had surrendered, the regulations for the humane treatment of prisoners of war and of civilian populations, and the distinctions between combatants and noncombatants had been codified in the nineteenth century, but written and unwritten laws for conducting a war according to accepted civilized norms, including the flamboyant courtesies of "Tirez les premiers, Messieurs les Anglais," long antedated the Hague and Geneva conventions.* These codes, even under the exigencies of near-total war, were fairly well observed through World War I. But during World War II they were often ignored and they have become largely irrelevant in modern guerrilla wars that involve the mass use of terror against civilian populations.

The All-Encompassing Military Necessity

The doctrine of military necessity permitting a commander to take measures, ordinarily forbidden, because they are indispensable for securing the submission of the enemy as quickly as possible has

---

* In the twelfth century Richard I of England issued ordinances, tables of punishment, for specific violations of articles of military and common law, as did Richard II in the fourteenth century and Gustavus Adolphus of Sweden in the seventeenth. The Salic Law of the fifth century is considered to be the origin of such European codes. (George E. Erickson, Jr., "United States Navy War Crimes Trials: 1945–1949.")

always been in conflict with humanitarian principles, but since World War II few limits have been imposed on it. Military necessity could be invoked to violate the rights of an innocent third party, or to justify the deliberate destruction of civilian dwellings to prevent their use by the enemy, or, because of the vulnerability of the submarine to increasingly sophisticated weapons, to justify the sinking of merchant ships without visit and search. But military necessity was itself placed in a humane context; the force used, the measures taken, "must not be out of proportion to the military advantage to be gained." This directive appears as part of the American code in the army manual, *The Laws of Land Warfare*, as well as in international agreements. The Geneva Conventions of 1949 kept the humane principles intact but made their functioning more difficult with sweeping clauses that declare that military necessity applies only in cases of "urgent necessity," and that it should not be invoked unless rendered "absolutely necessary" by military operations.[1] Almost any military enterprise, no matter how destructive, could be justified under these clauses.

Moreover, eminent proponents of the new order hold that an insurgent faction in an undeveloped country at the beginning of its struggle for power has no alternative other than to use terror to operate effectively, and the strategy of terror has certainly been used effectively by Mau Maus in Kenya, by Israelis in British-mandated Palestine, Arabs in Algeria and Israel, the Irish republicans in Belfast.[2]

This pragmatic concession to all-out military necessity when it is invoked on behalf of fanatically determined bands places no limit whatever on any kind of savagery if used by any people, however primitive their methods, for their "national liberation." Stretched, perhaps to its breaking point, such a claim on behalf of military necessity would apparently condone cannibalism if the threat of eating their enemies would advance the cause of the forces of liberation of a developing state. It is a curious reactive racism or ethnicism, the obverse of the position of John Stuart Mill, who said that the same rules of international morality and customs could not hold between a civilized and a barbarous state because they implied reciprocity and barbarians did not reciprocate. Mill was addressing himself to an audience that took for granted distinctions that social scientists and historians came to discard, after a closer scrutiny of the behavior of some of the civilized nations during their period of colonization. Genuine differences, however, between the behavior of peoples continue to be observed despite the leveling tendencies of guerrilla warfare. As one writer on the conduct of undeveloped countries in their new roles points out, they often are "primeval entities with no real claim to international status or the capacity to meet international obligations, and whose primary congeries of contributions consist in replacing the norms securing the common interest of mankind by others, releasing them from inhibitions upon responsible conduct."*³ It is the practices of such "primeval entities" that civilized nations are bidden to accept.

Neither War Nor Laws of War

Some supporters of the new order have gone so far as to declare that there was no longer a need for a *jus in bello,* a law of the customs and usages of war, because the aggressor was committing an illegal act and those defending themselves had therefore unlimited rights.

Nuremberg was believed to be the forerunner of universal justice, representing all mankind, minus Germans and Japanese, resolved to punish the inveterate criminals. The moral development of man, along with his lethal technology, had made war unacceptable to his conscience, and in addition, so ruinous to victim and victor alike that the political leader who led his country to war was no more to be tolerated than any other murderer; he was, in fact, far worse since the head of state who was guilty of the crime of aggression was responsible not only for the deaths of thousands, perhaps millions, of people, but he was also guilty of the ancillary crimes that could occur only because his war was being waged.

The assimilation of a head of state, or of a general, guilty of such mass slaughter into an ordinary criminal was not new. Seneca, for one, had written: "We check manslaughter and isolated murders, but what of the much vaunted crime of slaughtering whole peoples? Deeds which would be punished with loss of life when committed in secret, are praised by us because uniformed generals have carried them out."⁴

---

* The liquidation of colonialism has not meant more freedom and security for the individual in many of the "developing" countries. Discrimination of colored peoples against other colored peoples, as for example against Indians in Kenya and Uganda, is widespread in Africa and Asia.

What was new was the universal rejection, in principle, of recourse to war as a legitimate way to settle differences between states (Kellogg-Briand Pact), the unwillingness to recognize territorial changes imposed by armed conflict (Stimson Doctrine), and the attempt to answer Seneca's question at long last by saying there are no significant moral or legal differences between wholesale international and retail domestic killing. Pronouncements in this vein were often reiterated by statesmen while a war of which they disapproved was coming out badly from their point of view. An illuminating example may be seen in Soviet Russia's denunciation of Israel's alleged aggression in 1967, her demand that Israel accept a cease-fire and withdraw from Egyptian territory she had occupied, and the opposite position Russia took in 1971 when India invaded East Pakistan. In December 1971 the Soviet Union vetoed a Security Council resolution calling for a cease-fire and withdrawal of Indian troops from East Pakistan until India, like Israel before her, had occupied the territory she had set out to conquer.* What was aggression for Israel was legitimate defense for India. Also new was the rejection of the laws of war by those who denied any need for them, and by those who would grant the partisan forces of a country struggling for independence the right to use any barbarous methods they consider useful against their enemies who are conducting what is, by definition, an illegal defense of their lives and property.

As the New Order Worked

But the position that the conquests resulting from a war of aggression were not to be recognized was very lightly held. The People's Republic of China invaded Tibet in 1950, and in 1959 it decreed the dissolution of the Tibetan government, an act that, in accord with the principle that such acts of violence are unacceptable, caused the UN Assembly to adopt a resolution 45 to 9 with 26 abstentions deploring the events in Tibet and demanding that the Chinese respect the rights of the Tibetan people. The People's Republic of China, however, continued to govern Tibet, and thousands of refugees from its forward leap of progress escaped to India and Nepal.

* India aimed at replacing a hostile East Pakistan with a relatively weak and dependent Bangladesh to where the millions of Bengali refugees who had fled to India because of the mass terrorism of the West Pakistani army could return. The Soviet Union for reasons of power politics supported India.

But this, no more than the UN's denunciation of China's aggression during the Korean War, would not prevent the United Nations in 1971 from enthusiastically welcoming Peking into its membership and ousting the government of Chiang Kai-shek, although Chiang's Republic of China had invaded no one and was the successor of the same government that had helped to found the United Nations in 1945.

Soviet Russia, too, had been reproved by a large majority of the United Nations for its invasion and occupation of Hungary. Soviet forces, however, remained in that country and Soviet authority there was accepted *de facto* and *de jure* by the members of the United Nations despite the bloodshed, the universal admiration for Hungary's Freedom Fighters, and the resolutions of the UN Assembly. It would be difficult to demonstrate that Seneca's questions, after all, have been persuasively answered by the new order of Nuremberg.

A good many governments have been accused of committing the crime of aggression since World War II, but no one of their leaders has been tried for it, nor could he be unless he lost a war and came before the courts of his enemies. And who was the aggressor in the wars covered in the preceding chapters? Anthony Eden? Nasser? Eshkol? President Ho? President Diem? President Kennedy? President Johnson? Any answer can only be based on political and ideological judgments. The Kremlin and its satellites knew who was guilty long before any "aggression" took place; other countries, like France, denounced one side or the other as its short-term interests indicated or was itself denounced as it pursued them. What is clearly observable, although far from criminal, is that some peoples at some times are more aggressive than others. The Greeks and Romans in antiquity, the Germans and Japanese in the nineteenth and twentieth centuries, the Swedes in the seventeenth and eighteenth centuries, the French for some 300 years, have been on the march, each in their time. Britain, too, had her centuries of expansion, often by violence, but such periods of national dynamism could not be justiciable and civilizations flourished in them.

The notion that a just war of defense is being fought against an aggressor helps make a moral case and stiffen the military posture, but what a Soviet representative at the London Conference in 1945, General Nikitchenko, said of aggression remains true: "Although when people speak of it they know what they mean, they cannot define it." It remains undefined and undefinable; what was flagrant

Israeli aggression to the Arabs, the Soviet Union, and much of the Eastern bloc, was to the Israelis and the public opinion that supported them in Europe and the United States (although not to their governments represented in the UN) a war of survival against Arab aggression.

A vote on the subject in the United Nations could only result in a political verdict and could be predicted in advance from ideologies and alignments no matter how the war started. It is a supreme irony that the only man in Nuremberg to be sentenced for committing aggression and no other crime, Rudolf Hess, who is now the sole remaining prisoner in Spandau, was diagnosed by his British psychiatrists during his wartime captivity as schizophrenic, and it may be remembered that he flew to England under the delusion that he could make peace with at least one country.

The analogy often made between the gunman who attacks a peaceful citizen and a war criminal is as plausible and as heartwarming as a good Sunday sermon used to be. Actually, it is a weak parallel. In many such domestic cases the moral and legal issues are perfectly clear, but this is rarely true in international disputes, and what judicial body or United Nations would be competent to judge the kind of conflicting claims we have been dealing with? An International Court of Justice exists, but although under the United Nations Charter all its members are parties to its statute, only 38 out of 117 nations by 1967 had accepted the optional clause of the court which establishes compulsory jurisdiction for certain categories of cases. Only two of them, Haiti and Nicaragua, refrained from attaching such reservations as to make the court's compulsory jurisdiction of small value. A study of the decisions of this court and its predecessor, the Permanent Court of International Justice, reveals that since 1922 it is an unusual event when a judge has voted against his own state in cases coming before the court, and on twelve occasions a judge of the nationality of one of the parties or an ad hoc appointed national judge has formed a minority of one on the side of his own country.*[5]

No state has placed itself under the jurisdiction of the International Court of Justice in a case involving a major issue—Britain's possession of Gibraltar, for example, which is challenged by Spain

---

* National judges voted in favor of their governments in 70 percent of the cases and ad hoc judges in 90 percent. (II Ro Suh, "Voting Behavior of National Judges in International Courts.")

—and it is not surprising that the court has been little used, by few states, and only on minor occasions. Both the Permanent Court of International Justice and its successor, the International Court of Justice, heard cases involving states not individuals, whereas at the Nuremberg Tribunal judgments were made against individuals. The only way such a tribunal is likely to be reconstituted would be through the total defeat of one of the superpowers, and again, political and ideological, rather than judicial, decisions would result.

The Israeli government in 1967 was convinced it was acting to enable the country it represented to exist; Nasser was acting on behalf of Egypt and other Arab states who considered Israel a foreign and menacing aggregate in their midst. Neither Eshkol, nor Dayan, nor Nasser, nor Fawzi were international gunmen; they were all, as they saw it, defending a collectivity, present and future. They were responsible for the lives of millions of their compatriots, and if any of these leaders had been clearly identified in his own country as placing it in jeopardy, he would have been thrown out of office and replaced by a stronger man, more nearly resembling Adolf Hitler than Mahatma Gandhi. A head of state, acting for the state, lacks what for most European law is one of the chief stigmata of the criminal, the *mens rea*, the criminal intent.[6]

Were any national leaders to be convincingly judged, their cases would have to be heard before a court farther above the battle than was the Nuremberg Tribunal, which took account only of crimes committed by the enemy, found many of them guilty of a crime that had not been one when it allegedly was committed, heard evidence against the Germans for mass murders committed by the Russians, and found Admiral Doenitz guilty of aggression because his submarines had been in a state of readiness when the war started. This was a definition of aggression that, if generally accepted, could bring before an international court every able submarine commander in the world if his country went to war.

As for the United Nations being competent to decide who is the guilty party, the theory again bears little relationship to the realities. The UN lost any major peacekeeping function before it was launched, when the dream of one world exploded before the end of World War II. It is an organization with many useful functions, it serves as meeting place and propaganda forum, it performs various international assignments and errands, but it has had no peacekeeping role whatever in Hungary, in Czechoslovakia, in Greece, in Vietnam, or in

Pakistan, and in the Middle East it withdrew its forces as soon as hostilities threatened. The United Nations was not effectively constituted to act as an international police force. For it to be one, the nations of the world would have had to renounce their sovereign right to decide where their vital interests lay and to command their own armed forces, and no country was seriously prepared to do that. Given the ideological and political schisms of its membership, the results would have been either stalemate or catastrophe had the United Nations possessed such powers. The veto system in the Security Council prevents any attempt to intervene if one of the great powers considers itself right and the others wrong, and the General Assembly, with its majority of developing nations, will tend to adopt resolutions that reflect such political convictions as that wars of national liberation are always justified, or the Cuban view that a poor nation may expropriate American-owned sugar plantations without compensation because, as Castro maintained, it is "the duty of the peoples of Latin America to strive for the recovery of native wealth by wresting it from the hands of foreign monopolists and interests which prevent their development."*[7]

It is enlightening to observe the shifts in UN voting caused by the influx of the new states. On September 14, 1957, the General Assembly endorsed the report of its Special Committee on Hungary with 60 votes in favor, 10 against, and 10 abstentions. In the 1960–1961 session it placed the Hungarian question on the agenda with 54 votes in favor, 12 against, and 31 abstentions, the latter mainly from the newly independent African states.[8]

Return to the Jungle

The atrocities committed in the wars since World War II have shrunken the laws and usages of war to not much more than a jungle code. Since the ways of the jungle are never far beneath the surface of any culture and the struggle against them lasts longer than any single war, it is easy to return to them. In 1901, during the Philippine insurrection, an American brigadier general, Jacob H. Smith, gave orders to a Marine Corps major, L. W. T. Waller, who was attacking the guerrillas of the island of Samar that were not very

---

* No way exists for peaceful change to be effected in international relations unless both parties agree to it. In any other circumstances only an international government could act to enforce a decision binding on both parties.

different from those of Mylai. A treacherous massacre of a detachment of American troops had occurred and the general told Waller: "I want no prisoners, I wish you to kill and burn; the more you kill and burn the better you will please me." General Smith said he wanted everyone capable of bearing arms killed, and when Major Waller asked what the age limit was to be, the general replied: "Ten years."[9]

Both General Smith and Major Waller were court-martialed. The general was found guilty of "conduct prejudicial to good order and military discipline" and sentenced to be admonished by the review authority. The sentence was a very light one and the court explained: "The court is thus lenient in view of the undisputed evidence that the accused did not mean everything that his unexplained language implied; that his subordinates did not gather such a meaning; and that the orders were never executed in such sense, notwithstanding that a desperate struggle was being conducted with a cruel and savage foe."[10]

President Theodore Roosevelt delivered the admonishment and ordered the general, who was sixty-two years old, retired from active service. Roosevelt wrote: "The findings and sentence of the court are approved, I am well aware of the danger and great difficulty of the task our army has had in the Philippine Islands and of the well nigh intolerable provocations it has received from the cruelty and treachery on the part of its foe. I also heartily approve of the sternest measures necessary to put a stop to such atrocities and to bring this war to a close."[11]

Secretary of War Elihu Root also confirmed the sentence of the court and justified its leniency on a number of grounds; one being that: "no women or children or helpless persons or non-combatants or prisoners of war had been put to death." Root observed that General Smith had hitherto been an exemplary officer and had been seriously wounded in the Civil and Spanish wars. But, said Root, it was no longer "in the interest of the service that General Smith should continue to exercise the command of his rank." Root conceded that the natives were cruel and treacherous, and completely disregarded the laws of war, and he quoted General Washington's orders, in similar circumstances, to General Sullivan to destroy Indian settlements. Washington had written: "But you will not by any means listen to overtures of peace before the total ruin of their settlements is effected. . . . Our future security will be in their inability to injure us, the distance which they are driven and in the terror with which the severity of the chastisement they receive will inspire them."[12]

A Gresham's Law operates in the military field as it does in economics: bad behavior drives out good; the barbarous methods of the primitive are adopted by the so-called civilized forces and the spiral tends to move inexorably downward. Guerrilla war in the eighteenth and nineteenth centuries presented the same bloody dilemmas as it does in its contemporary forms, and the impulse to meet savagery on its own terms was as powerful then as it is now.* The difference is that atrocious behavior in the American army was not always as readily tolerated by civilian and military administrations or by the public. In Vietnam neither the High Command nor public opinion has been gravely disturbed by abominable conduct. The public is disgusted with the war itself, with both the friends and the enemy. As for the High Command almost any form of warfare, if it promises success and will not result in insupportable retaliation from the victim or his friends, or rouse too loud public outcries from influential sources at home, has been either ordered, condoned, or ignored. The only test is whether what is done promises to bring victory or promotion, and comports with the strategic game plan or scenario, as the chief players have spoken of what was going on. Aside from such considerations, few holds have been barred. In Algeria and in Indochina terror and torture of prisoners of war and of women and children have been officially countenanced as a means of conducting the war. Bombing is used as a weapon against almost any target, and we have seen how greatly the civilian casualties outnumber the military. It should also be recalled that in Vietnam these bombings and the slaughters at the Mylais have claimed as victims some of the very people Presidents Kennedy, Johnson, and Nixon have assured the world they were defending.

While it may well be doubted that human nature, as such, changes, there is no question that some epochs have accepted forms of human suffering that were absolutely unacceptable to people in other periods. The public executions of the seventeenth and eighteenth

---

* The massacres of American Indians, including women and children during the "winning of the West," is another example of how easily any laws of war or of humanity may be abandoned. Such crimes were condoned because they were regarded as justified reprisals against a subhuman enemy, and also, no doubt, because settlers wanted the Indians' land (cf. John G. Neihardt, *Black Elk Speaks*, Pocket Books, 1972; Dee Brown, *Bury My Heart at Wounded Knee*, Bantam Books, 1971.)

centuries, when war itself was hedged round with elaborate forms of chivalry, were shudderingly avoided by Victorian ladies and gentlemen whose ancestors had regarded them as entertainments a few years before. The nineteenth century was more squeamish in these matters than had been the preceding periods, but in half of it slavery was almost universally approved, as was the anathema of later decades, child labor, even in conspicuously nonjuvenile environments like coal mines. The twentieth century has witnessed similar incongruities; an enormous concern for human welfare and the high moral principles enunciated at Nuremberg exist side by side, in the developed states, with a toleration of savage behavior the early part of the century would have found impermissible either in foreign wars or within national boundaries.

The violence in American cities is projected in the conduct of American soldiers abroad, and the apathy of the Pentagon, the civil administration, and the public may arise in part from the emotional attrition stemming from one of the highest crime rates in the world. The well-known case of a woman's being murdered in New York City while a sizable audience did nothing about it, not even telephone the police, may not be dissociated from the public indifference to the crimes committed in Vietnam.

One of the officers who did revolt against the "interrogations" he witnessed in Vietnam and the indifference, not to say hostility, of his superiors to what he told them believed that part of the syndrome of moral anesthesia lay in that old devil, the machine.[13] From the high perspectives of a commander in a helicopter, people become marionettes, dehumanized toy figures that can be moved from place to place as children move lead soldiers. The colonel, or such, in a helicopter has no firsthand knowledge of what he is demanding of his men, and from where he flies the figures that fall are not unlike the paste targets in a shooting gallery.

Whether World War II ground down the sensibilities of a people so that they no longer react with indignation to senseless violence and terror may be doubted. The same officer who described the atrocities in Vietnam told how, in Korea, an American sergeant was sentenced to twenty years in prison merely for roughly shaking a Korean prisoner of war. Whether or not this was the sole offense of the sergeant, Korea was not the scene of a guerrilla war comparable to that in Vietnam, and neither was the army fighting, as it was in Vietnam—an interminable war rejected by its homeland that it had no means of winning. In Algeria, too, the French army developed its strategy of terror out of anger, contempt, frustration, and the repudiation of the war by the country at large.

The Working of Rules of War

Whatever the causes for the cruelties and the wide acceptance of them, they do not lie in the absence of laws of war. The rules for preventing military crimes are clear enough in the army regulations and international agreements already adopted. Passing more laws, negotiating more conventions, will not prevent a Mylai or the bombing of civilians or their torture. Murder was illegal before the Genocide Convention was adopted. The laws were already there when the French conducted their counterguerrilla war in Algeria and Vietnam and when Soviet Russia took over its imperium in Eastern Europe, complete with its institution of slave labor.

Attempts to limit the use of weapons considered especially cruel have had some, if limited, success. In 1925 the Geneva Protocol prohibited the use of poison gasses and of bacteriological warfare, but although approved with reservations by some sixty countries it was not ratified by the United States. The *American Army Manual of Land Warfare* explicitly states that the Protocol is not binding on the United States, although the army has never used poison gas and, in 1966, the American delegation voted in favor of a United Nations resolution calling for strict observance of its provisions. The use by the American army in Indochina of tear and emetic gases has been called by the Soviet Union a violation of the Geneva Protocol, but the United States defends its use of these nonlethal gases as relatively humane. They were mainly employed against enemy units holed up in bunkers, or caves, and the alternatives of subduing them by means of flamethrowers, grenades, and napalm were far more destructive than any gases that are only temporarily incapacitating.

The Western belligerents in World War II respected the provisions of the 1925 Geneva Protocol largely because lethal gases would have been counterproductive. Both sides considered using them. Martin Bormann and Josef Goebbels urged Hitler toward the end of the war to use the new gases Tabun and Sarin, which were five times more powerful than the former ones, but Albert Speer and the generals argued against them and Hitler decided against resorting to them because the Allies, with their superiority in the air, could have retaliated overwhelmingly. Speer was even able subsequently to stop the manufacture of the gases. Franklin Roosevelt threatened to employ gas against Japan as a reprisal after Chiang Kai-shek charged it was being used against his troops, and a number of American officers urged that lethal gases be used in the course of the Pacific Island campaigns where they believed gas would be more effective and more humane than conventional weapons. Since the war it has been used by Egypt in Yemen, but without tipping the scales of victory.

The decision against using gas in World War II no doubt was influenced by the universal abhorrence its employment evokes, but Captain Mahan may have been right when he argued, during the Hague Conference of 1899, that gas is no more inhumane than high explosives—and he had not encountered napalm, flamethrowers, and other contemporary weapons.

At any rate, world opinion and the Geneva Protocol seem to have had a positive effect on the decision not to use poison gas in World War II. Public opinion had not been heard from when the atom bomb was used against Hiroshima and Nagasaki or when Hamburg and Dresden were firebombed, although in the course of the latter raids, people, almost all civilians, were asphyxiated as thoroughly as they would have been by gas bombs.

The difficulty with limiting the use of weapons of destruction to the more humane ones lies in the conflict between the desire to win a war as quickly as possible with that of looking as respectable as possible while doing it. And public opinion is rightly suspicious of new weapons, although it may come to accept them. The cross-bow, when it was introduced, was considered a terrible and indiscriminate weapon, "hateful to God and unfit for Christians," because it could penetrate the armor of knights. Pierre Terrail Bayard, "le chevalier sans peur et sans reproche," as he lay dying in 1524 after he had been shot by an arquebus, was solaced by the thought that he had never given quarter to a musketeer.[14]

The submarine was considered an indispensable weapon by a country like Wilhelminian Germany without the means of contesting the control of surface waters with Great Britain, but it was regarded as hateful to God and man by the Allies and the United States in World War I, and then used in precisely the same way by all of them, including Germany, in World War II.

The ability of scientists to produce ever more ingenious and deadly weapons is, however, incontestable and it will not be easy for international conventions or public opinion to keep up with them. In

1970 President Nixon submitted the 1925 Geneva Protocol for consent by the Senate (forty-six years after the United States delegates had signed it at Geneva), and stated that the United States renounced the use of lethal and incapacitating chemicals and any biological and toxin weapons. The United States has also stopped using defoliants but it has not renounced their possible future employment nor that of the rest of the arsenal we have observed in action in Indochina. The nuclear stockpiles grow around the world and their use has been threatened more than once: by the Soviet Union during the Suez crisis; by the United States under President Eisenhower, in the event that the Chinese entered the war in Indochina; and Premier Khrushchev and President Kennedy, at the time of the Cuban missile crisis in October 1962, found themselves within the range of atomic warfare. Khrushchev and Castro declared that the Soviet missiles were defensive and had been supplied to Cuba because Cuba was threatened by the United States, which was mounting another attack after the failure of the Bay of Pigs invasion. But for the United States, with its long-lived tradition of preventing non-American expansion in this hemisphere, joined now by the Organization of American States, which in January 1962 had excluded Cuba "from participation in the inter-American system," the missiles with ranges of 2000 miles were a clear and present danger. This reaction had small relationship to the fact that the United States had nuclear bases with missiles of similar range in countries like Turkey, adjacent to the Soviet Union. Khrushchev had said plainly that nuclear weapons would be used if they promised victory; and ninety miles away, they presented an intolerable threat to the security of a country accustomed to oceans between itself and its foes. Nuclear weapons might start small and clean but it would be the end that determined how large and dirty they would become.

What Nuremberg Left Out

The Nuremberg doctrines did not and do not reflect the actual practices of states and statesmen. The trials* were fatally flawed from the beginning, from before the beginning; they were trials of

---

* There were thirteen trials in all. The first was the Trial of the Major War Criminals, of the twenty-two chief members of the National Socialist party, state, and military apparatus; the subsequent twelve, the Trials of the Generals, I. G. Farben, the Einsatzgruppen, etc., were called military, but they were held before American civilian judges.

the vanquished brought before the courts of the victors. No one in the world, neither Messrs. Roosevelt, Stimson, Jackson, nor the whole Nuremberg bench, could have dreamed of Comrade Stalin's being brought to judgment before any imaginable court for his invasion of Finland in 1939, although the League of Nations had declared it an act of aggression and ousted the Soviet Union from its membership. The expulsion took place during the period of the Hitler-Stalin Pact, when the Soviet Union was regarded as an accomplice of National Socialist Germany. The German defendants had been accused of having waged, or conspired to wage, aggressive war against Poland, but no witness in the course of the great trial was permitted to point out that the Polish campaign had been waged with the complicity of the Soviet Union, which divided Poland with the Third Reich a few weeks after the Germans invaded. No Italian was tried by the Allies for invading France in 1940 or Greece in 1941. Italy was regarded as a co-belligerent by the Allies after she declared war on Germany on October 13, 1943, although she had gone to war as a member of the European Axis.* The Nuremberg Court dealt with crimes of enormous magnitude committed by National Socialist Germany: the killing of between 5 and 6 million Jews, the mistreatment of millions of Russian prisoners of war, deportation of civilian populations and their forced labor, often under inhuman conditions. But it dealt with the crimes of only the one country, and along with crimes that every legal code in the civilized world regarded as punishable, it stigmatized as the chief crime aggression—which should perhaps be a crime in a better world but had no legal basis as such in this one. It would be difficult to maintain, even before a Western court, that the Soviet leaders, when they ordered their tanks into action in Hungary in 1956 or in Czechoslovakia in 1968, had any criminal intent. They were doing what they considered essential to preserve Soviet hegemony in a vital area, after, as Brezhnev said, oceans of blood had been shed to win it, and harsh as the fate of the Hungarians and Czechoslovaks may have been in their morally justified struggle for independence, their revolts could readily have triggered a world conflict.

The postwar polarization has had one marked advantage over the

---

* No Finn was tried either, although Finland had joined in the German attack on the Soviet Union. To have attempted to try anyone in that country would have raised inconvenient questions about the Russian invasion of 1939, which was the chief cause of the Finnish-German alliance of 1941.

prewar period. More than one major war in the past has come about when a small power demanded either the right to acquire or to retain disputed territory it could not hold on its own, or rights and privileges it could only attain with the help of the more powerful. World War I started over a murder committed by Serb terrorists in Bosnia; World War II over the Polish corridor and Danzig. In both cases the great powers were involved because they believed their own vital interests to be at stake, but also because the lesser ones had aspirations they could not fulfill by themselves, which even their allies considered excessive, but in the circumstances had to accept. Such maneuvers were much more difficult to accomplish in the years following the division of the world between the two great power constellations.

Actions Louder Than Words: The Johnson and Brezhnev Doctrines

The Brezhnev Doctrine's bearing on the Eastern bloc was derided in the West, and it is certainly glaringly opposed to Soviet pretensions with regard to maintaining the Nuremberg principles—self-determination, the indivisibility of peace, anticolonialism, and so on. But it is not easily distinguishable from the Johnson Doctrine that preceded it and under which the United States may intervene in the western hemisphere to prevent the establishment of any regime suspected of being Communist. In Guatemala in 1954 American planes bombed a harbor and American-trained troops invaded from Honduras and Nicaragua to help overthrow the pro-Communist government of President Jacobo Arbenz Guzmán. Arbenz Guzmán had been receiving shipments of arms from Poland, which the United States declared threatened "hemispheric security." The United States-supported rebels were successful, Arbenz Guzmán was deposed and went to Czechoslovakia.[15]

The 10th Inter-American Congress meeting March 1–28, in 1954, agreed, with Mexico and Argentina abstaining, that the intervention of international communism in the western hemisphere was not to be tolerated; communism by its nature was aggressive and therefore the aid given the Guatemala rebels was in self-defense. This view was confirmed by a concurrent resolution of the United States Senate on June 25, 1954, which declared it saw "strong evidence of intervention by the international communist movement in the state of

Guatemala . . ." and that the "pattern of communist conquest had become manifest. . . ."[16]

In the Dominican Republic in 1965 President Johnson ordered first 21,500 troops, then 25,000, to land on the island to protect the lives of Americans threatened by a left-wing revolt. Mr. Johnson declared he acted at the request of unnamed Dominican police and military officers who said they could not otherwise guarantee the Americans' safety. The presence of Communist forces was not observed by representatives of a number of Latin American countries, including those of Chile, Mexico, Uruguay, Colombia, and Venezuela, or by The New York Times correspondent, but President Johnson declared: "there were signs that people trained outside the Dominican Republic are seeking to gain control," and in a broadcast on May 2, 1965, he said: "Our goal . . . is to help prevent another Communist state in this hemisphere." Johnson said many of the Communist leaders had been trained in Cuba and he spoke of "the international conspiracy from which American servicemen had rescued the people."[17] Under the Johnson Doctrine, which it accepted, the Organization of American States had therefore the obligation to take collective military action, although the leaders of the revolution, Juan Bosch and Colonel Francisco Caamaño Deñó, were not regarded as Communists even in Washington.

These two cases, as well as the Bay of Pigs invasion by rebel Cuban forces trained and supported, up to a point, by the United States, the American representatives to the UN prevented being discussed in the Security Council. When the OAS voted to undertake an economic blockade of Cuba in mid-1962 because of Cuba's "intervention and aggression" in Venezuela's troubled politics, this decision, too, was arrived at without benefit of the UN. The dissident American states would certainly have found support in the Security Council from the Soviet Union and its friends, but the United States succeeded in keeping the debate and the decisions, including the economic blockade, within the OAS. It was not the UN's business. As Ambassador Lodge said: "The UN should be a supplement to and not a substitute for or impairment of tried and trusted regional relationships,"[18] and warned that if the UN did act it would impair its effectiveness, as well as that of the OAS. Ambassador Lodge and the OAS took their stand, as would later the Soviet Union and the Warsaw Pact countries, despite the plain words of Article 53 of the UN Charter which declares: "No enforcement action shall be taken under regional arrangements without the authority of the Security Council."

These events illustrate the fatuity of approaching international crises when they occur in the front yards of the superpowers by way of the Nuremberg doctrines or those of the UN, both of which were simply ignored. They are similarly ignored in the scenarios and game plans of the experts in the "Think Tanks" who work out the possible permutations and combinations of international behavior in the megaton and kiloton age.[19] The Johnson and Brezhnev doctrines have no relation whatever to the global legal order proclaimed at Nuremberg or in the Charter of the United Nations. Both the Soviet Union and the United States claim and exercise the right to exclude the system and machinations of the other from their zones of vital interest, and what they decide may be far removed from what the people of the country involved would choose. The Castro revolution in Cuba was not immediately recognized in Washington as Communist, but in the cases of Guatemala and of the Dominican Republic, the diagnosis of Communist aggression was made promptly and unilaterally by the United States, just as the Soviet Union made its findings about imperialist, revanchist, Western aggression in Czechoslovakia. Both the OAS and Warsaw Pact nations went along as their respective treaties intended them to. It seems clear that despite the oratory and the sonorous pitches about the indivisibility of peace and such, the ancient copy legends retain their authority in the capitals of the superpowers and what is left of global collective security is the right of regional allies to agree to go along with determinations made in Washington and Moscow.

The antennae of the superpowers are sensitive; they may often detect the infiltration of the enemy by means inscrutable to the rest of the world or to their own people. The risings in Hungary and Czechoslovakia came about not through any hanky-panky of the West but out of the bleak contradictions of Communist rule in those countries. In South America, too, the military dictatorships that have long been the prevailing mode inevitably lead to revolts by those living outside the golden largesse of the ruling clique. Nevertheless, the Communist parties and their allies are able to penetrate and propagandize in the camps of the enemy in a one-sided arrangement by which the West is shut out from the bloc countries. Riots in the Eastern bloc are called the work of subversives, revanchists, imperialist agents; in the West they are ascribed to social unrest. And the Communist party organizations of China and the Soviet Union compete as to which one will first bring down the rotten edifice of the capitalist states and build on its ruins.

The Peace We Have

The superpowers, despite their overwhelming collection of nuclear weapons, do not have anything like complete freedom of action. The war the United States has been fighting in Indochina, and the Russian invasions of Hungary and Czechoslovakia, have been limited by considerations of prudent risk; each superpower attempts to avoid actions that are likely to lead to a major confrontation with the other. Therefore, the United States refrained from declaring a blockade of Haiphong and North Vietnam (it would need a declaration of war to do this legally, and it would mean stopping Soviet ships). Mining was a risk, but in the dire circumstances, the administration thought it an acceptable one. For not until 1972, despite its massive bombing of the lines of North Vietnamese supply routes to the South, had the United States ever bombed the port where the concentrated war material would have been much easier to destroy. When in May 1972 the decision to bomb the harbor installations was made, that risk, too, was limited by Mr. Nixon's impending visit to Moscow, and the desire of both countries to pursue their antagonistic cooperation, wherever it seemed advantageous to their larger goals.

The Soviet Union did not invade Yugoslavia or Albania to maintain a pre-Brezhnev Doctrine; it preferred to attain its ends by longer-range means of the kind it must use with recidivist states not on its borders. The United States has been able to exert only a fraction of its power in Indochina without achieving anything resembling what it set out to do, which was to build a strong, stable, and, if possible, democratic bulwark against Communist penetration.

But the continuing struggle for supremacy takes forms other than those of direct military intervention, and the wars that arise, as they have for centuries, because it would be to one country's (India's) advantage to have a small, independent state on its eastern borders instead of a powerful rival (Pakistan) become part of a still larger power struggle, involving, although with relative discretion, the United States, China, and the Soviet Union.

So again, aggression becomes difficult to identify and the dynamic Communist movements of Moscow and Peking pursue their missions with and without bullets. Civil wars like those in the Congo or Pakistan, or in Korea, Indochina, or Latin America, readily involve the power politics of the rival systems if they promise a strategic advantage. No portion of the globe remains a truly neutral area in the ongoing struggle, and the ebb and flow of the continuing battle takes place within the limits imposed by Washington and Moscow in their desire to advance their causes and avoid all-out war. Atrocities, subject to no international control whatever, have been acceptable to both the Soviet Union and the United States as part of the operational necessities of any kind of war being waged.

Thus it may be argued that the uneasy peace that has endured between the major powers since World War II has been kept not because of, but despite, Nuremberg. Had the Nuremberg principles of the illegality of aggressive war been maintained as rigorously as many of their proponents would have liked, a world war could have started in Hungary, in the Middle East, in the Far East—in fact, anywhere at all. Fortunately for the human race, statesmen tend to act with a weather eye on realities and it is by ignoring the doctrines of Nuremberg rather than by trying to enforce them that the postwar world has lived through the cold war and then peaceful coexistence, which is another stage of the same process.

Nations do not sit passively with their collective hands folded, awaiting doomsday. It is in the interest of the Soviet Union and of the United States to limit the arms race with its astronomical demands on their economies and to come to agreements like the nuclear arms and nonproliferation treaties that serve their own purposes and security as well as the general peace. But other countries, Israel, for example, believe they must survive, too, and the forbidden weapons, including the nuclear arsenal, are not likely to remain frozen indefinitely in the hands of those who have them, nor will the researches producing the new ones be confined to the superpowers.

The extension of the Geneva Agreements must always lag behind the development of new weapons which are far more likely to be wholesale rather than selective killers. The outlawing of weapons like the bacterial ones that add only another indecisive increment of destruction may be to the advantage of the superpowers, as well as to that of the rest of the world, but probably no weapon in existence or to be constructed would fail to be used, if its use meant victory.

What Nuremberg attempted was to reduce the immemorial problems to a formula without content. Its doctrines bore only the vaguest relationship to the actual behavior of states in the past, present, and, no doubt, future. Collective security in the form of a universal order cannot be attained in the contemporary world, although it may be workable regionally, as both the United States and the Soviet Union have demonstrated. This, however, is not much different from the old system of alliances and what it expresses is again a rough balance of power. Such regional alliances function collectively only when they are perceived to serve the defense of the individual state, as in NATO, or are forced upon them, as in the Warsaw Pact. They do not function when they are called upon, as was SEATO, to operate in a war its members believe to be the business of someone else.

No one outside the United States and South Korea (which was not a member of SEATO) had any interest in a mission to preserve non-Communist governments in Indochina; the Thais and Filipinos had to be paid and paid highly for their participation in the war, New Zealand and Australia sent token contingents, France and Pakistan were outspoken critics. It was Washington's war and Saigon's.

An alliance such as NATO, with the Soviet system established west of Berlin, is another matter. Almost every Western European country considers NATO essential to its own defense, and when France in its pursuit of an elusive grandeur and a more significant role between the superpowers, sought to strike out on a quasi-independent course, it prudently remained a member with one foot in the door of the Western alliance.

The status of neutrality, of the right to stay outside the conflict, with the duty to treat the warring sides evenhandedly, was to be another victim sacrificed to the higher purposes of global collective security. All the members of the United Nations, according to its Charter, were obliged to join in collective sanctions against an aggressor when called on to do so by the Security Council, and the warring sides were not to be treated impartially, since one was waging a legal war of defense, and the other an illegal war of aggression. In practice, this notion, too, has had little practical significance in the wars since the Second World War. In Algeria, in Czechoslovakia, in Hungary, great and small powers have remained aloof from the conflicts, in deeds if not in words, or in the case of Korea, Vietnam, and Czechoslovakia, sent token forces. Countries, aside from the superpowers, have either been neutral and taken no official position with regard to Vietnam or, like France, kept outside the battle while denouncing one side for courses little or no different from those she herself had pursued earlier.

Neutrality in a major nuclear war promises to be irrelevant not on legal but on strategic grounds. The system of alliances, the nature of nuclear warfare with its lethal dust clouds, and the need for actual or potential use of bases around the world make it unlikely that many states would escape involvement in an all-out conflict if it lasted any length of time.

Some Ways Open

Atrocious warfare may be built into two modern forms of armed conflict: a war between the superpowers, where the macro-nuclear weapons would be used, and guerrilla wars. But neither of these dismal prospects should be fatalistically accepted by the United States, and if it does not accept them, some little hope remains that its example may be followed. Neither the United States nor Soviet Russia actually assumes the risks of thermonuclear war for anything short of what it regards as the ultimate threat, which is how the United States regarded the Cuban missiles. Any ultimatum involving the use of thermonuclear weapons is likely to be reserved for such rare occasions, and a bilateral agreement for a cooling-off period in these contingencies might be agreed upon in advance and actually carried out in a critical situation. As for the back-to-the-jungle spiral, the United States could quite simply stop the kind of warfare it has waged in Vietnam. Such a bold step could be taken both on military and on moral grounds. Had the United States and the French refused to adopt the methods of the adversary in their wars in Algeria and Vietnam, they might have failed to get some important pieces of information* but they would also not have demoralized large numbers of their own troops and half-destroyed the repute of their armies at home. The knowledge that an army was expected to fight under the laws of war and would punish any violators of their provisions would distinguish it from the barbarians of whatever stage of socio-economic development and restore not only the esteem the army once was held in but its own self-respect. To this end, the American army might institute, as part of its continual training program, courses prepared by competent historians, political scientists, and publicists that would set out to educate both officers and men in

---

* They might not have failed, however, since drugs like sodium pentothal might have elicited information just as readily as torture did.

the major issues that brought the troops into the areas where they serve. For those able to comprehend them, these could be, not propaganda courses, but genuine efforts to present the historical and political background of an enormously successful democratic society and its evolving, often ambiguous, values. The difficult issues would have to be presented along with the obvious ones that hinge on naked self-defense, and probably a majority of the troops would be given an understanding of why they are in uniform and part of an army that exists for something more than killing and body counts. These are not easy assignments, as West German military authorities have discovered, but they are probably realizable.[20]

The war efforts of nations like the United States and France have very likely been more damaged in their guerrilla campaigns than benefited. The self-loathing, the tarnished image of the army and of the American ethos that was once called the last best hope of mankind and evoked the admiration even of Ho Chi Minh is a major disaster. This decay can be arrested at any point by the President or by the Joint Chiefs of Staff, if they want it stopped and will use the means at their disposal to enforce the laws of war, no matter who breaches them. Air war can be rigidly confined to military targets, and free-fire zones abolished along with the other actions ordered under euphemisms the army has used as a cover for its unacceptable procedures. Such acts at least can be prevented, or punished if they occur; the crime of war is something else again.

The practices of the enemy in guerrilla warfare, where terror is used as a major weapon, can only be controlled by capturing or killing the perpetrators, or by reprisals. Terror, whether it is used by the guerrillas in Kenya, the Middle East, or Belfast, provokes counter-terror, which then becomes one of the most effective weapons of the revolutionaries and their always-on-hand sympathizers in the home country. Wholesale reprisals, more often than not, backfire, driving fresh contingents of fighters to the partisans and demonstrating the truth of the enemy propaganda that has claimed all along they are fighting for their freedom against pretentious barbarians. Guerrilla wars have never been fought according to conventions, but the country fighting guerrillas may do far better by observing unilaterally the traditional laws of war, limiting reprisals as far as it can, and making them commensurate with the offense than by imitating or improving on the savagery of the enemy.

During World War II, and increasingly since then, the Soviet Union and Communist forces in the Far East have made efforts to restructure the political views of their captives. French and American soldiers, in some instances, have been converted by these techniques, highly developed in the Soviet Union, and counterattempts have also been made, with some success, by the Americans, South Vietnamese, and South Koreans to reeducate Communist prisoners of war. In contemporary warfare prisoners of war remain participants as hostages in the power struggle. What privileges are accorded them in North Vietnam are granted by Hanoi, which regards the captives as useful criminals, kept alive for purposes of propaganda or trading. Countermeasures for or against prisoners of war held by the United States army have little or no effect on Communist treatment of American captives. Nevertheless, abiding by traditional rules of war with regard to enemy prisoners cannot possibly damage the lot of the American prisoners and conceivably could improve it. Here, too, the morale of the American army can only benefit from civilized behavior.

War remains the final arbiter in deeply schismatic disputes, although in its thermonuclear phase it threatens to destroy the entire race. A major war is no longer a test of valor, or national endurance, or readiness to sacrifice, virtues that had a genuine survival value in other centuries, however imperfectly the results of a war may have reflected them. A major war of the future threatens to obliterate the species along with any rules of war. Such a war will not be prevented by the United Nations or exhortations to behave as though there were a body functioning as such, but only by the mutually shared knowledge that the weapons of one side can retaliate with at least equally as devastating an effect as those of the other side. Nations historically have survived by good luck, favorable geographical locations, martial virtues, inwit, and their leaders' ability to strike a reasonable balance between ensuring the security of their country and the similar aims of the adversary. Never have formal renunciations of war, which were fashionable in the seventeenth century for monarchs to make regularly with one another after each war they fought, had a long life. The situation is different today only because the weapons are incomparably more deadly, but the chief means of man's survival has always been his intelligence rather than his armament.

In Sum

Insofar as Nuremberg was dealing with genuine crimes, as it did in points three and four of the indictment—war crimes and crimes against humanity—it had little new to say. War crimes were crimes long before the Nuremberg trials, as were crimes against humanity— mass murder or barbarous treatment of a people on a major scale— which violate both domestic and international law. Aggressive war remains a crime in embryo or in theory; as a full-blown criminal act it rarely, if ever, is identifiable as such by both sides, as well as neutrals, and has been nowhere clearly detectable in the cases we have examined.

Pacta sunt servanda, treaties are to be observed, but they can be observed only as long as they fulfill a function useful to both sides. A treaty that becomes insupportable to one of the parties must end in its abrogation. No preachments on the sanctity of treaties can compel a statesman to continue a policy, often one plotted by a predecessor, that appears to be disastrous to the country he represents. If conditions have changed fundamentally for only one of the parties since the treaty was made, it will be ignored or denounced. *Rebus sic stantibus*, things, conditions, remaining the same, is a solid rule of international law attaching to all treaties.

War is indeed reprehensible, primitive, and threatens universal catastrophe. All true, but it cannot be conjured away by calling it the crime of an individual, to be suppressed by a world community of peace-loving nations, when to responsible leaders it always appears as a final recourse against intolerable injury or national disaster.* War is more reasonably to be dealt with as disease is, with all the devices of man's ingenuity, which include a statesman's resourcefulness in maintaining the peace and security of the country for which he bears the responsibility, and part of this imperative is the quality of the weapons in its arsenals.

No statesman can possibly act intelligently if he relies on the presumed validity of the findings of Nuremberg, on the concept of one world, on the promise of a universal collective security. These principles have little more than a faint propaganda value and no state can live by them or expect that any other state will live by them. War continues to exist; scores of them have erupted since 1945 and many more are still to come. If we try to avoid any armed conflict by prudent diplomacy with tangible and attainable goals, confining our risks to territories vital to us and to people capable of making sacrifices for their defense equal to those required of the United States,

---

* Most peace treaties are concluded under duress. But duress does not make a treaty void or voidable in international law.

if we seek to compromise where it is possible, digging in where we know we must, if we clear our own Augean stables of corruption and atrocities, no matter who commits them, we may survive for a long time to come.

New weapons will be developed, perhaps planes that move with the speed of the revolution of the earth, laser beams that move with the speed of light and operate with the accuracy of a computer, weather control apparatus, a whole glistening arsenal of lethal machines yet undreamed of, along with the old weapons made more efficient. No matter what doomsday weapons are invented, the need for self-defense, called "aggression" by the enemy, will continue. All wars are not equally pernicious. Even the Kellogg-Briand Pact considered wars of defense legitimate, and that view may embrace a preventive war such as the one successfully undertaken by Israel against Egypt in 1967 and unsuccessfully by Adolf Hitler against Russia in 1941.

Hitler's war was abominable, not because he believed the Soviet Union would strike when it pleased Moscow and he set out to forestall the attack, but because of the way he ordered the war to be fought, because of its consequences, and because it would have been unendurable for all humanity had he won it. Hitler seems to have been convinced that Soviet Russia would attack the Reich at a moment Stalin thought favorable, but the evidence for this is flimsy, although German generals like Rundstedt, Winter, Jodl, and Gehlen thought the same way, as did Jan Masaryk, who believed Hitler's intuition had divined Stalin's intention.[21]

The consequences of the victory of the Soviet Union have undoubtedly been more tolerable to the people brought under its dominion than would have been those of a successful National Socialist war, but the difference in the damage done their sovereignty, independence, and the Four Freedoms so often promised them is quantitative rather than qualitative.

Southeast Asia, where the Soviet Union, mainland China, the Republic of China on Taiwan, and the United States all discern a vital national interest, and the seismic regions of the Middle East and Latin America are some of the explosive areas of the globe and the battles in them have been contained up to now because not enough was at stake to justify the risk of using the big weapons in the interventions of the superpowers. The arts of negotiation are still called upon even when the shadow of the rockets falls, as it did at the time of the Cuban crisis. No formula for maintaining peace exists, but the ingredients of preserving it are no secret; for the United States, they are military parity (as a minimum) with the Soviet Union, firmness of resolve in maintaining strategic positions essential to defense, even at high risk, the willingness to compromise in less important matters, the setting of achievable goals. None of these can comprehend treating war as nonexistent or mistaking a desire for peace and the maintenance of collective security as sufficient aims of foreign policy. In this case, the analogy between the individual human being and the state may hold. What is needed for the good life of a country, too, is based on its ability to act in the light of experience, to act intelligently, decently, on behalf of its national security in relation to other states seeking the same ends. The scale is larger on the international scene, the time scheme longer, but a state no more than an individual can deal effectively with an imaginary congeries of other entities, but only with those they actually confront and must live with. The conduct of foreign affairs remains an art with scientific admixtures; the survival of a nation cannot be successfully entrusted to simplistic formulae or to principles that reflect unworkable doctrines. No computers have been programmed for the wisdom that remains essential for survival. People still have to provide that from their own inner and outer resources, no matter how far the weapons may seem to have outdistanced them.

NOTES

1. H. C. H. Dunbar, "The Significance of Military Necessity in the Laws of War," pp. 201–212.
2. Richard A. Falk, quoted in Telford Taylor, *Nuremberg and Vietnam*, p. 137.
3. A. V. Freeman, in Richard A. Falk, ed., *The Vietnam War and International Law*, p. 141.
4. Seneca, "Epistulae ad Lucilium," Epis. XCV 30, quoted in Tom J. Farer, *The Laws of War 25 Years after Nuremberg*, Carnegie Endowment for International Peace, May 1971, No. 583.
5. Eberhard P. Deutsch, "A Judicial Path to World Peace," pp. 1115–1120.
6. Manuel R. Garcia-Mora, "Crimes Against Peace in International Law: From Nuremberg to the Present," pp. 35–55.
7. J. G. Merrills, "The Justiciability of International Disputes," pp. 241–269.
8. Ferenc A. Vali, *Rift and Revolt in Hungary*.
9. John Bassett Moore, A *Digest of International Law*, p. 187.
10. *Ibid.*
11. *Ibid.*, p. 188.
12. *Ibid.*, pp. 188–189.
13. Lieutenant Colonel Anthony Herbert, Telecast WABC, *Dick Cavett Show*, September 30, 1971, and November 2, 1971.

14. W. T. Mallison, Jr., "The Laws of War and the Juridical Control of Weapons of Mass Destruction in General and Limited Wars," pp. 308–346.

15. Thomas M. Franck and Edward Weisband, "The Johnson and Brezhnev Doctrines: The Law You Make May Be Your Own," pp. 979–1014.

16. *Ibid.*, p. 992.
   The New York Times, May 18, May 20, June 26, 1954; April 28, 1966.

17. Franck and Weisband, *op. cit.*, p. 1010.

18. *Ibid.*, p. 994.

19. Cf. Herman Kahn, *On Escalation: Metaphors and Scenarios.*

20. Siegfried Grimm, *Der Bundesrepublik treu zu dienen.*

21. Reinhard Gehlen, *Der Dienst*, p. 112.
   Eugene Davidson, *Trial of the Germans*, pp. 352, 542.

Bibliography

Adams, Michael, *Suez and After*. Boston: Beacon Press, 1958.

Ainley, Henry, *Mourir pour Rien*. Translated by Antoine Gentien. Paris: Stock, 1966.

Alleg, Henri, *Die Folter (La Question)*. Wien-Muenchen-Basel: Verlag Kurt Detsch, 1958.

Alquier, Jean-Ives, *Nous Avons Pacifié Tazalt—Journal de Marche d'un Parachutiste*. Paris: Robert Laffont, 1957.

Arnaud, Georges, *Mon Procès*. Paris: Les Éditions de Minuit, 1961.

Aronéanu, Eugène, *La Définition de l'Agression*. Paris: Les Editions Internationales, 1958.

Ashe, Geoffrey, *The Land and the Book*. London: Collins, 1965.

Avram, Benno, *The Evolution of the Suez Canal Status: 1869–1957*. Paris: Librairie Minard, 1958.

Barer, Shlomo, *The Weekend War*. Tel Aviv: Karni Publishers Ltd., 1959.

Barker, A. J., *Suez: The Seven Day War*. London: Faber and Faber, 1964.

Baroli, Marc, *La Vie Quotidienne des Français en Algérie: 1830–1914*. Paris: Hachette, 1967.

Barrès, Claude, *Pierre Lyautey: Un Héros Révolté*. Paris: Julliard, 1959.

Bar-Zahar, Michel, *Suez Ultra-Secret*. Paris: Fayard, 1964.

Bassiouni, Cherif, "The Middle East in Transition: From War to War, A Proposed Solution," *International Lawyer*, 4 (1970): 379–390.

——, "The War Power and the Law of War: Theory and Realism." *De Paul Law Review* XVIII (Autumn 1968): 188–201.

Beaufre, Général, *L'Expédition de Suez*. Paris: Editions Bernard Grasset, 1967.

Bedjaoui, Mohammed, *La Révolution Algérienne et le Droit*. Bruxelles: Editions de l'Association Internationale des Juristes Démocratiques, 1961.

Beer, Fritz, *Die Zukunft functioniert nicht*. Frankfurt/Main: Fischer, 1969.

Bell, J. Bowyer, *The Long War*. Englewood Cliffs, N. J.: Prentice-Hall, 1969.

Benoist-Méchin, Jacques Gabriel, *Le Roi Saud*. Paris: Albin Michel, 1960.

Bigelow, John, *Breaches of Anglo-American Treaties*. New York: Sturgis & Walton Co., 1917.

Bishop, William W., Jr., *International Law: Cases and Materials*. Boston: Little, Brown and Co., 1962.

Bloch, Johann von, *Beschreibung des Kriegsmechanismus*. Berlin: Puttkammer und Mühlbrecht, 1899.

Blunt, Wilfred, *Desert Hawk*. London: Methuen, 1927.

Bodard, Lucien, *La Guerre d'Indochine*. Paris: Gallimard, 1967.

Bondy, François, "Communist Attitudes in France and Italy to the Six Day War." *Wiener Library Bulletin* XXIII (1969): pp. 2–14.

Bouchet, Jacques, *Contribution à l'étude des fléaux qui menacent la mère et l'enfant indigènes en Algérie*. Paris: Carbonet, 1942.

Boumaza, Bechir, Francis, Mustapha, et al., *La Gangrène*. Paris: Éditions de Minuit, 1959.

Boutang, Pierre, *La Terreur en Question: Lettre à Gabriel Marcel*. Paris: Farqueille, 1958.

Brace, Richard, and Brace, Joan, *Ordeal in Algeria*. Princeton, N.J.: D. Van Nostrand Co., 1960.

Brahm, Heinz, *Der Kreml und die ČSSR*. Stuttgart: Kohlhammer, 1970.

Bridge, John W., "The Case for an International Court of Criminal Justice and the Formulation of International Criminal Law." *International and Comparative Law Quarterly* 13 (1964): 1255–1281.

Bromberger, Merry, and Bromberger, Serge, *Secrets of Suez*. Translated by James Cameron. London: Sedgwick & Jackson Ltd., 1957.

Broms, Burgt, *The Legal Status of the Suez Canal*. Vammala: Kirjapaino Oy, 1961.

Browne, Malcolm W., *The New Face of War*. Indianapolis: Bobbs-Merrill Co., 1965.

Brune, Jean, *Viet-Nam: Bataille pour l'Asie*. Paris: Compagnie Française de Librairie, 1967.

Bunn, George, "Banning Poison Gas and Germ Warfare: Should the U.S. Agree?" *Wisconsin Law Review* II (1969): 375–420.

Burns, Lieutenant General E. L. M., *Between Arab and Israel*. London: Harrap, 1962.

Buttinger, Joseph, *Vietnam: A Dragon Embattled*. Vols. I and II. New York: Praeger, 1967.

Callwey, Georg D. W., ed. *Permanente Revolution von Marx bis Marcuse*. Muenchen: Leonhard Reinisch Verlag, 1969.

Camille, Paul, *Suez ou la Haute Farce du Vaincu Triomphant*. Paris: Nouvelles Editions De Brosse, 1957.

Camus, Albert, *Actuelles: Chroniques 1944–1948*. Paris: Gallimard, 1950.

——, *Chroniques Algériennes*. Paris: Gallimard, 1958.

——, *La Chute*. Paris: Gallimard, 1956.

——, *L'Homme Révolté*. Paris: Gallimard, 1951.

——, *Noces*. Paris: Gallimard, 1947.

——, *Resistance, Rebellion and Death*. Translated by Justin O'Brien. London: Hamish Hamilton, 1960.

Carson, William R., *Vietnam: The Betrayal*. New York: Norton, 1968.

Changarnier, Général, *Memoires du Général Changarnier*. Paris: Éditions Berger-Levrault, 1930.

Charnay, Jean-Paul, *La Vie Musulmane en Algérie*. Paris: Presses Universitaires de France, 1965.

Chicago Sun Times. December 6, 1971. December 7, 1970.

Chicago Today. June 27, 1971.

Childers, Erskine B., *The Road to Suez.* London: MacGibbon & Kee, 1962.

Chomsky, Noam, *At War with Asia.* New York: Pantheon, 1969.

Churchill, Charles Henry S., *The Life of Abdel Kader.* London: Chapman and Hall, 1867.

Cohen, Maxwell, "Basic Principles of International Law: A Revaluation." *Canadian Bar Review* 42 (1964): 449–462.

"Congress, the President, and the Power to Commit Forces to Combat." *Harvard Law Review* 81 (June 1968): 1771–1805. Notes.

Conley, Michael Charles, *The Communist Insurgent Infrastructure in South Vietnam: A Study of Organization and Strategy.* Washington, D.C.: U.S. Government Printing Office, 1967.

Connell, John, *The Most Important Country.* London: Cassell & Co., Ltd., 1957.

Cooper, Chester L., *The Lost Crusade.* New York: Dodd, Mead & Co., 1970.

Cornell University Study, reported NBC News, December 24, 1971.

Corson, William R., *The Betrayal.* New York: Norton, 1968.

Courrière, Yves, *L'Heure des Colonels.* Paris: Fayard, 1970.

Crane, Robert D., "Basic Principles in Soviet Space Law: Peaceful Coexistence, Peaceful Cooperation and Disarmament." *Law and Contemporary Problems* 29 (Autumn 1964): 943–955.

Cuau, Ives, *Israël Attaqué.* Paris: Robert Laffont, 1968.

Daix, Pierre, *Journal de Prague (Décembre 1967–Septembre 1968).* Paris: Julliard, 1968.

Dallin, David J., *Soviet Russian Foreign Policy.* New Haven, Conn.: Yale University Press, 1942.

Darboise, J. M., Heynaud, J., and Jartel, J., *Officiers en Algérie.* Paris: Maspero, 1960.

Darboy, Marcel (pseud.), *Jeunesse de France en Algérie.* Paris: Renée La Coste et Cie., 1959.

Darcourt, Pierre, *De Lattre au Viet-Nam.* Paris: La Table Ronde, 1965.

Daumas, Général E., *La Vie Arabe.* Paris: Michel Levy Frères, 1869.

Davidson, Eugene, *The Trial of the Germans.* New York: Macmillan, 1966.

——, *The Death and Life of Germany.* New York: Knopf, 1959.

Dayan, David, *Strike First! A Battle History of the Six Day War.* Translated by Dov Ben-Abba. New York: Pitman Publishing, 1967.

Dayan, Moshe, *Diary of the Sinai Campaign.* New York: Schocken Books, 1967.

De Bourbon, Prince Michel, *En Parachute.* Paris: Presses de la Cité, 1949.

De Conde, Alexander, *A History of American Foreign Policy.* New York: Scribners, 1963.

Delarue, R. P. Louis, *Avec Les Paras du 1ᵉʳ R.E.P. et du 2ᵉᵐᵉ R.P.I. Ma.* Paris: Nouvelles Editions Latines, 1961.

De Latour, Pierre Boyer, *Cette Année à Jerusalem.* Paris: La Table Ronde, 1968.

——, *La Vie Quotidienne à Alger à la Veille de l'Intervention Française.* Paris: Hachette, 1963.

——, *De L'Indochine à L'Algérie—Le Martyre de l'Armée Française*. Paris: Les Presses du Mail, 1962.

De Launay, Jacques, *Les Grandes Controverses du Temps Présent: 1945–1965*. Lausanne: Editions Rencontre, 1967.

Delpey, Roger, *Soldats de la Boue: La Bataille de Cochin Chine*. Paris: Le Livre Artistique, 1961.

Démeron, Pierre, *Contre Israël*. Paris: Pauvert, 1968.

Denoyer, François, *Quatre Ans de Guerre en Algérie*. Paris: Flammarian, 1962.

Department of State, *American Foreign Policy 1950–1955*, 2 Vols. Washington, D.C.: U.S. Government Printing Office, 1957.

Department of State Bulletin 5 (August 24, 1964): 260–261. Washington, D.C.: U.S. Government Printing Office.

Deutsch, Eberhard P., "A Judicial Path to World Peace." *American Bar Association Journal* 53 (1967): 1115–1120.

——, "Problems of Enforcement of Decrees of International Tribunals." *American Bar Association Journal* 50 (December 1964): 1134–1139.

Die Algerische Revolution. Von einem Mitglied des politischen Büros der obersten Heeresleitung der algerischen befreiungs Armee (ALN). Stuttgart: Deutsche Verlagsanstalt.

Dinfreville, Jacques, *L'Opération Indochine*. Paris: Les Éditions Internationales, 1953.

D'Istria, Pierre, *De Suez à Akaba*. Paris: Les Éditions Cujas, 1968.

Djilas, Milovan, *The New Class*. New York: Praeger, 1957.

Dona, H., quoted in Robert D. Crane, "Basic Principles in Soviet Space Law." *Law and Contemporary Problems* 29 (Autumn 1964): 944.

Dubček, Alexandre, *Du Printemps à l'Hiver de Prague*. Translated by Ilios Yannakakis. Paris: Fayard, 1970.

Duchemin, Jacques C., *Histoire du F.L.N.* Paris: La Table Ronde, 1962.

Dudman, Richard, *Forty Days with the Enemy*. New York: Liveright, 1971.

Du Lac, André, *Nos Guerres Perdues*. Paris: Fayard, 1969.

Dunbar, N. C. H., Act of State in Law of War." *Judicial Review* 8 (1963): 246–278.

——, "Some Aspects of the Problem of Superior Orders in the Law of War." *Juridical Review* 63 (1951): 234–261.

——, "The Maxim *Nullum Crimen sine Lege* in The Law of War." *Juridical Review* 71 (1959): 176–196.

——, "The Significance of Military Necessity in the Law of War." *Juridical Review* 67 (1955): 201–212.

Duncan, Donald, *The New Legions*. New York: Random House, 1967.

Duncanson, Dennis J., *Government and Revolution in Vietnam*. London-New York: Oxford University Press, 1968.

Eden, Anthony, *The Memoirs of Anthony Eden—Full Circle*. Boston: Houghton Mifflin, 1960.

Eisenhower, Dwight D., *Mandate for Change*. New York: Doubleday, 1963.

——, *Crusade in Europe*. New York: Doubleday, 1948.

——, *Waging Peace*. New York: Doubleday, 1965.

El Moudjahid. Yugoslavia, 1962.

Ély, Général Paul, *Memoires.* Paris: Plon, 1969.

Epstein, Leon D., *British Politics in the Suez Crisis.* Urbana, Ill.: University of Illinois Press, 1964.

Erickson, George E., Jr., "United States Navy War Crimes Trials: 1945–1949. *Washburn Law Review* 5 : 89–111.

Étienne, Bruno, *Statistique du CNRS.* Aix en Provence, n.d.

Facts on File Incorporated, *Facts on File.* New York. 1968, 1969.

Falacci, Oriana, *Niente e così sia.* Milan: Rizzoli, 1970.

Falk, Richard A., "International Regulation of Internal Violence in the Developing Countries." *American Society of International Law Proceedings,* 1966–1967, 58–67.

———, ed., *Legal Order in a Violent World.* Princeton, N.J.: Princeton University Press, 1968.

———, *The Vietnam War and International Law.* Princeton, N.J.: Princeton University Press, 1968.

Fall, Bernard, *Le Viet-Minh: La République Démocratique du Viet-Nam 1945–1960.* Paris: Librairie Armand Colin, 1960.

———, *Street without Joy.* New York: Schocken Books, 1972.

———, *The Two Vietnams.* New York: Praeger, 1963.

Fanon, Frantz, *Aspekte der Algerischen Revolution.* Frankfurt/Main: Suhrkamp Verlag, 1969.

———, *L'An V de la Révolution Algérienne.* Paris: Maspero, 1959.

———, *Sociologie d'une Révolution.* Paris: Maspero, 1966.

Farago, Ladislas, *Patton.* New York: Obolensky, 1964.

Farale, Dominique, *La Legion à la Peau Dure.* Paris: Éditions France-Empire, 1964.

Faulkner, Stanley, "The War in Vietnam: Is It Constitutional?" *Georgetown Law Journal* 54 (June 1968): 1132–1143.

Favrod, Charles-Henri, *Le FLN et l'Algérie.* Paris: Plon, 1962.

Feingold, Henry L., *The Politics of Rescue.* New Brunswick, N.J.: Rutgers University Press, 1970.

Feraoun, Mouloud, *Journal 1955–1962.* Paris: Éditions du Seuil, 1962.

Ferrell, Robert H., *Peace in Their Time.* New Haven, Conn.: Yale University Press, 1952.

———, *American Diplomacy.* New York: Norton, 1959, 1969.

Files, Israeli Ministry for Foreign Affairs, Jerusalem.

Finer, Herman, *Dulles over Suez.* Chicago: Quadrangle, 1964.

Fishel, Wesley R., ed., *Vietnam: Anatomy of a Conflict.* Itasca: E. A. Peacock, 1968.

Flood, Charles Bracelen, *The War of the Innocents.* New York: McGraw-Hill, 1970.

Fontaine, Pierre, *L'Aventure Algérienne Continue.* Paris: Les Sept Couleurs, 1967.

Foreign Relations of the United States, Conference of Berlin. I: 915. Washington, D.C.: U.S. Government Printing Office, 1960.

Foster, Arnold, "American Radicals and Israel." *Wiener Library Bulletin*

XXIII (1969): 26–28.

Franck, Thomas M., and Weisband, Edward, "The Johnson and Brezhnev Doctrines: The Law You Make May Be Your Own." *Stanford Law Review* 22 (May 1970): 979–1014.

Francos, Ania, *Les Palestiniens.* Paris: Julliard, 1968.

Frauendienst, Werner, *Ungarn zehn Jahre Danach.* Mainz-Wiesbaden: Hase und Koehler, 1966.

Freeman, Alwyn V., "Some Aspects of Soviet Influence on International Law." *American Journal of International Law* 62 (1968): 710–722.

——, *The Vietnam War and International Law.* Princeton, N.J.: Princeton University Press, 1968.

Frei, Bruno, " 'Progressive' Auschwitz?" *Wiener Library Bulletin* XXIV (1970): 7–12.

Galloway, John, *The Gulf of Tonkin Resolution.* Rutherford, N.J.: Fairleigh Dickinson University Press, 1970.

Garcia-Mora, Manuel, "Crimes against Peace in International Law: From Nuremberg to the Present." *Kentucky Law Journal* 53 (Fall 1964): 35–55.

Gardner, Brian, *German East: The Story of the First World War in East Africa.* London: Cassell, 1963.

Gardner, Richard N., "The Soviet Impact on International Law." *Law and Contemporary Problems* 29 (Autumn 1964): 843–1017.

Gehlen, Reinhard, *Der Dienst.* Mainz: Hase und Koehler, 1971.

Gerassi, John, *North Vietnam: A Documentary.* Indianapolis: Bobbs-Merrill Co., 1968.

Gershen, Martin, *Destroy or Die.* New York: Arlington House, 1971.

Vo Nguyen Giap, *Big Victory, Great Task.* New York: Praeger, 1968.

——, *The Military Art of People's War.* New York: Monthly Review Press, 1970.

Giniewski, Paul, *Le Sionisme d'Abraham à Dayan.* Bruxelles: Éditions de la Librairie Encyclopédique, 1969.

Ginsberg, George, " 'Wars of National Liberation' and the Modern Law of Nations—The Soviet Thesis." *Law and Contemporary Problems* 29 (Autumn 1964): 910–942.

Glahn, Gerhard von, *Law Among Nations.* New York: Macmillan, 1965.

Glubb, Lieutenant-General Sir John Bagot, *A Soldier with the Arabs.* London: Hodder and Stoughton, 1957.

Goëldhieux, Claude, *Quinze Mois Prisonnier chez les Viets.* Paris: Julliard, 1953.

Goichon, A. M., *La Vie Féminine au Mzab.* Paris: Librairie Orientaliste Paul Guenther, 1927.

Golt, Maynard B., "The Necessity of an International Court of Criminal Justice." *Washburn Law Journal* 6 (Fall 1966): 15–23.

Goodman, Richard M., "The Invasion of Czechoslovakia—1968." *International Lawyer* 4 (October 1969): 42–79.

Greenberg, Eldon Van Cleef, "Law and the Conduct of the Algerian Revolution." *Harvard International Law Journal* 11 (Winter 1970): 37–72.

Grimm, Siegfried, *Der Bundesrepublik treu zu dienen*. Duesseldorf: Droste, 1970.

Habart, Michel, *Histoire d'un Parjure*. Paris: Les Éditions de Minuit, 1960.

Hadsel, Winifred N., "Foreign Policy Report, American Policy towards Greece." New York: F P Associates, Inc. Vol. XXIII, September 1, 1947.

Halberstam, David, *Ho*. New York: Vintage Books, 1971.

Halderman, John W., special ed., "The Middle East Crisis: Test of International Law." *Law and Contemporary Problems* 33 (Winter 1968): 1–183.

Halle, Gunther, *Légion Étrangère*. Berlin: Volt und Welt, 1952.

Hammer, Richard, *One Morning in the War: The Tragedy at Son My*. New York: Coward-McCann, 1970.

Harkabi, Yehoshafat, "The Meaning of 'A Democratic Palestinian State.' " *The Wiener Library Bulletin* II (1970): 1–6.

Hazard, John N., "Why Try Again to Define Aggression?" *American Journal of International Law* 62 (1968): 701–710.

Heiber, Helmut, "Der Fall Gruenspann." Vierteljahreshefte fuer Zeitgeschichte, April 1957, pp. 134–172.

Heikal, Mohammed, *Das Kairo Dossier*. Munich: Fritz Molden, 1972.

Henissart, Paul, *OAS—L'ultimo Anno dell'Algeria Francese*. Translated from English by Marilena Rescaldani. Milan: Garzanti, 1970.

Henriques, Robert, *A Hundred Hours to Suez*. London: Collins, 1957.

Herman, Edward S., *Atrocities in Vietnam*. Boston: Pilgrim Press, 1970.

Hersh, Seymour M., "Cover Up: 1." *The New Yorker*, January 22, 1972, pp. 34–69.

——, "Cover Up: 2." *The New Yorker*, January 29, 1972, pp. 40–70.

——, "My Lai 4: A Report on the Massacre and Its Aftermath." *Harper's Magazine*. 240 (May 1970): 53–84.

Hesse, Erich, *Der Sowjetrussische Partisanenkrieg: 1941–1944*. Goettingen: Musterschmidt Verlag, 1969.

Heynowski and Scheumann, *Piloten im Pyjama*. Munich: Kindler, 1967.

Hilberg, Raul, *The Destruction of the European Jews*. Chicago: Quadrangle Books, 1961.

Hitti, Philip K., *The Arabs*. New York: St. Martin's Press, 1968.

Ho Chi Minh, *On Revolution*. New York: Praeger, 1967.

Honey, P. J., ed., *North Vietnam Today*. New York: Praeger, 1962.

Hughes, Larry, *My Year at War*. New York: Morrow, 1970.

"Human Rights Symposium." *Howard Law Journal* 11 (Spring 1965): 257–373.

Hurwitz, Ya'akov, "The Kibbutz: Its Socialist and National Roots." *The Wiener Library Bulletin* No. 4: 70–71.

Hussein, *Ma Guerre avec Israël*. [As told to] Vick Vance and Pierre Lauer. Paris: Albin Michel, 1968.

II Ro Suh, "Voting Behavior of National Judges in International Courts." *American Journal of International Law* 63 (April 1969): 224–236.

International Herald Tribune, June 22, 1970.

Irving, Clifford, *The Battle of Jerusalem*. New York: Macmillan, 1970.

Irving, David, *The Destruction of Dresden*. London: William Kimber, 1963.

Israel Must Be Annihilated. Tel Aviv: Zahal Information Office, 1967.

James, Robert Rhodes, ed., *The Czechoslovak Crisis*. London: Weidenfeld and Nicolson, 1969.

Jeanson, Francis, *La Révolution Algérienne*. Milan: Feltrinelli, 1962.

Jescheck, Dr. Hans-Heinrich, *Die Verantwortlichkeit der Staatsorgane nach Völkerrecht: Eine Studie zu den Nürnberger Prozessen*. Bonn. Ludwig Rohrscheid Verlag, 1952.

Johnson, Paul, *The Suez War*. London: MacGibbon & Kee, 1957.

Jones, W. Byford, *The Lightning War*. London: Robert Hale, 1967.

Kagan, Colonel B., *Combat Secret pour Israël*. Paris: Hachette, 1963.

Kahle, Wolfgang, "Jewish-Arab Coexistence." *Der Monat*, December 1969, pp. 9–12.

Kahn, Herman, *On Escalation: Metaphors and Scenarios*. New York: Praeger, 1965.

Kamberger, Klaus, ed., *Der Fall ČSSR*. Frankfurt/Main: Fischer, 1968.

Katz, Michael, "When a Nation Is at War—The Supreme Court in a Post-Utopian Era." *Rutgers Law Review* 23: pp. 1–32.

Kende, Istvan, "Twenty-five Years of Local War." *Journal of Peace Research*. Oslo: International Peace Research Institute, 1961, pp. 6–22.

Keramane, Hafid, *La Pacification*. Lausanne: La Cité, 1960.

Kern, Erich, *Algerien in Flammen*. Göttingen: Plesse Verlag, 1958.

Kertesz, Stephen D., ed., *East Central Europe and the World*. Notre Dame, Ind.: University of Notre Dame Press, 1962.

——, *The Fate of East Central Europe*, Notre Dame, Ind.: University of Notre Dame Press, 1956.

——, *The Quest for Peace through Diplomacy*. New York: Prentice-Hall, 1967.

Kimché, David, and Bawly, Dan, *Israël Face aux Arabes*. Paris: Cercle Européen du Livre, 1968.

——, *The Sandstorm*. London: Secker and Warburg, 1967.

Knoll, Erwin, and McFadden, Judith Nies, eds., *War Crimes and the American Conscience*. New York: Holt, Rinehart and Winston, 1970.

Kraslow, David, and Loory, Stuart, *The Secret Search for Peace in Vietnam*. New York: Random House, 1968.

Krieg. E. *La Tragédie Indochinoise*. Paris: Editions de Saint-Clair, 1966.

Kuehnrich, Hans, *Der Partisanenkrieg in Europa: 1939–1945*. Berlin: Dietz Verlag, 1965.

Kutner, Luis, "Due Process of War: An Ad Hoc War Crimes Tribunal: A Proposal." *Notre Dame Lawyer* 43 (April 1968): 481–502.

Lacheraf, Mostefa, *L'Algérie: Nation et Société*. Paris: Maspero, 1965.

Lacouture, Jean, *Ho Chi Minh*. Paris: Editions du Seuil, 1967.

——, *Vietnam: Between Two Truces*. Translated by Konrad Keller and Joel Carmichael. New York: Random House, 1966.

——, and Devillers, Philippe, *La Fin d'une Guerre*. Paris: Editions du Seuil, 1960.

Lafont, Pierre, *L'Expiation*. Paris: Plon, 1968.

Lancaster, Donald, *The Emancipation of French Indochina*. London: Oxford University Press, 1961.

Lanon, Henri, *Comment a débuté la guerre du Viet-Nam: Le Massacre de Haiphong (23 Novembre, 1946)*. Paris: Supplément des Cahiers Internationaux, 1952.

Laqueur, Walter, *The Road to Jerusalem: The Origins of the Arab-Israeli Conflict, 1967*. New York: Macmillan, 1968.

Lartéquy, Jean, *Les Centurions*. Paris: Presses de la Cité, 1960.

Lauterpacht, H. ed., *Oppenheim's International Law*. 7th ed. London, New York, Toronto: Longmans, Green & Co., Ltd., 1948.

——, *Oppenheim's International Law*. 8th ed. New York: David McKay, 1955.

Lavergne, Bernard, *Problèmes Africains*. Paris: Editions Larose, 1957.

Le Cornec, Michel, *Appelés en Algérie*. Paris: Editions de la Pensée Moderne, 1964.

N. a., *Les Enfants d'Algérie—Temoignage et dessins d'enfants réfugiés en Tunisie, en Libye, et au Maroc*. Paris: Maspero, 1962.

N. a., *L'Etat Algérien Avant 1830*. Paris: Editions Résistance Algérienne, n.d.

Levine, Isaac Don, *Intervention*. New York: David McKay, 1969.

Littauer, Raphael, and Uphoff, Norman, eds., Air War Study Group, Cornell University. *The Air War in Indochina*. Boston: Beacon Press, 1972.

Littell, Robert, ed., *The Czech Black Book*. New York: Praeger, 1969.

Litvinoff, Barnet, *The Road to Jerusalem*. London: Weidenfeld and Nicolson, 1965.

Lloyd George, David, *Memoirs of the Peace Conference*. New Haven, Conn.: Yale University Press, 1939.

Loebl, Eugen, and Pokorny, Dusan, *Die Revolution rehabilitiert ihre Kinder*. Wien/Frankfurt: Europa Verlag, 1969.

Loebl, Eugen, *Stalinism in Prague: The Loebl Story*. Translated by Maurice Michael. New York: Grove, 1969.

Love, Kenneth, *Suez: A History*. New York: McGraw-Hill, 1969.

Luce, Don, and Sommer, John, *Viet Nam—The Unheard Voices*. Ithaca, N.Y.: Cornell University Press, 1969.

Maas, Johannes, "Algeriens politische Geschichte bis zur Unabhängigkeit 1962." *Institut fuer Auslandsbeziehungen* 20 (1970): 116–129.

MacMahon, Maréchal de, *Memoires du Maréchal de MacMahon: Souvenirs de l'Algérie*. Paris: Librairie Plon, 1932.

Mallard, William D., Jr., "Nuremberg." *International Lawyer* 4 (July 1970): 673–680.

Mallin, Jay, *Terror in Vietnam*. Princeton, N.J.: Van Nostrand, 1966.

Mallison, W. T., Jr., "The Laws of War and the Juridical Control of Weapons of Mass Destruction in General and Limited Wars." *George Washington Law Review* 36: 308–346.

Mandouze, André, *La Révolution Algérienne par les Textes. Documents au F.L.N.* Paris: Maspero, 1961.

Mandrou, Robert, *Les Sept Jours de Prague: 21–27 Aout, 1968*. Paris: Editions Anthropos, 1969.

Manvell, Roger, and Fraenkel, Heinrich, *The Incomparable Crime*. London: Heinemann, 1967.

Mao Tse-tung, *Ausgewählte Werke*. Vols. I, II, and III. Peking: Verlag für Fremdsprachige Literatur, 1968.

——, *Quotations from Mao Tse-tung*. Peking: Foreign Languages Press, 1967.

——, *Vom Kriege*. Gutersloh:Bertelsmann, 1969.

Marcelle, Jacques, *Le Deuxième Coup de Prague*. Paris: Les Editions Vie Ouvrière, 1968.

Marchand, General Jean, *L'Indochine en Guerre*. Paris: Les Presses Modernes, 1954.

Marks, Richard E., *The Letters of Pfc. Richard E. Marks, U.S.M.C.* Philadelphia: J. B. Lippincott, 1967.

Martin, Claude, *Histoire de l'Algérie Française: 1830–62*. Paris: Editions des 4 Fils Aymon, 1963.

Marx, Werner, and Wagenlehner, Guenther, eds., *Das tschechische Schwarzbuch vom 20–27 August 1968*. Stuttgart: Seewald Verlag, 1969.

Maugham, Viscount, *UNO and War Crimes Trials*. London: John Murray, 1951. Quoting from *The Histories of Polybius*, Vol. 2, p. 549, Shuckburgh. London: Macmillan.

Maxa, Josef, *Die Kontrollierte Revolution*. Hamburg-Wien: Paul Zsolnay Verlag, 1969.

McAlister, John T., Jr., *Vietnam: The Origins of Revolution*. New York: Knopf, 1969.

McCarthy, Mary, *Hanoi*. New York: Harcourt, Brace, 1968.

McDougal, M. S., *Studies in World Public Order*. New Haven, Conn.: Yale University Press, 1960.

McNeill, William Hardy, *Greece: American Aid in Action—1947–1956*. New York: Twentieth Century Fund, 1957.

Mecklin, John, *Mission in Torment*. Garden City, N.Y.: Doubleday, 1965.

Meissner, Boris, *Die Breschnev Doktrin*. Koeln: Verlag Wissenschaft und Politik, 1969.

Merrills, J. G., "Morality and the International Legal Order." *Modern Law Review* 31 (1968): 520–534.

——, "The Justiciability of International Disputes." *Canadian Bar Review* 47 (1969): 241–269.

Michaux, P., *Criminalité et Terrorisme en Algérie*. Paris: Editions de l'Ordre Français, 1957.

Michel, Bernard, *Les Grandes Énigmes de Notre Temps*. 3 volumes. Paris: Amis de l'Histoire, 1967.

Mňacko, Ladislav, *Death Is Called Engelchen*. Translated by George Theiner. Prague: Artia, 1961.

——, *The Seventh Night*. Translated by Harry Schwartz. New York: Dutton, 1969.

Moore, John Bassett, *A Digest of International Law*. Vol. VII. Washington, D.C.: U.S. Government Printing Office, 1906.

Morganthau, Hans J., *Vietnam and the U.S.* Washington, D.C.: Public Affairs Press, 1965.

Morice, André, *Les Fellaha dans La Cité.* Nantes: Editions de Société d'Editions du PO., *N.d.*

Morse, Arthur D., *While Six Million Died.* New York: Random House, 1968.

Mudge, George Alfred, "Starvation as a Means of Warfare." *International Lawyer* 4 (January 1970): 228–268.

Murphy, Robert, *Diplomat among Warriors.* New York: Doubleday, 1964.

Murray, R., *Vietnam.* London: Eyre & Spottiswood, 1965.

Mus, Paul, Viet-Nam: Sociologie d'une Guerre. Paris: Editions du Seuil, 1952.

Nasinovsky, Eugene N., "The Impact of 50 Years of Soviet Theory and Practice on International Law." *American Society of International Law Proceedings*, 1968, 1969, pp. 189–196.

Nasser, Premier Gamal Abdal, *Egypt's Liberation: The Philosophy of the Revolution.* Washington, D.C.: Public Affairs Press, 1955.

National Liberation Front EAM, *White Book.* New York: Greek American Council, 1945.

Navarre, Henri, *Agonie de l'Indochine.* Paris: Plon, 1956.

Nerone, F. Regan, "The Legality of Nuremberg." *Duquesne University Law Review* 4: 146–162.

Neumann, Robert L., "The Arab-Israeli Dispute: Legal Issues and Possible Solutions." *International Lawyer* 4 (1970): 360–363.

Newman, Bernard, *Background to Viet-Nam.* London: Robert Hale, 1965.

Nourreddine, Méziane, *Un Algérien Raconte.* Paris: Editions du Seuil, 1960.

Nutting, Anthony, *No End of a Lesson—The Story of Suez.* New York: Potter, 1967.

——, *The Aftermath of Suez.* London: Hollis & Carter, 1958.

O'Ballance, Edgar, *The Algerian Insurrection.* London: Faber & Faber, 1967.

——, *The Indochinese War: A Study of Guerrilla Warfare.* London: Faber & Faber, 1964.

Oppermann, Thomas, *Le Problème Algérien.* Translated by J. Le Cerf. Paris: François Maspero, 1961.

Osborne, Milton E., *The French Presence in Cochinchina and Cambodia: 1859–1905.* Ithaca, N.Y.: Cornell University Press, 1969.

Paillat, Claude, *Dossier Secret de l'Algérie.* Paris: Le Livre Contemporain, 1961.

——, *Dossier Secret de l'Indochine.* Paris: Presses de la Cité, 1964.

Paine, Laurance, *Viet-Nam.* New York: Roy Publishers, 1965.

N.a., *Pamphlets on Vietnam.* Hanoi: Foreign Language Publishing House, 1966.

Patai, Raphael, ed., *The Complete Diaries of Theodor Herzl.* New York: Herzl Press and Thomas Yoselof, 1960.

Paulson, Stanley L., and Banta, John S., "The Killings at Mylai: 'Grave Breaches' Under the Geneva Conventions and the Question of Military Jurisdiction." *Harvard International Law Journal* 12 (Spring 1971): 345–355.

Péju, Marcel, *Le Procès du réseau Jeanson présenté par Marcel Péju.* Paris:

Maspero, 1961.

Perez, Gilbert, *Recueil des Journeaux d'Algérie: Sélection du 2 Novembre 1954–4 Juillet 1962*. Vols. I and II. 1967.

Peyrefitte, Roger, *Les Juifs*. Paris: Flammarion, 1965.

Pike, Douglas, *Basic Causes of the Vietnam War*. Taiwan: Regional Information Office, U.S. Information Service, September 1971.

——, *Viet Cong*. Cambridge, Mass.: The M.I.T. Press, 1966.

——, *Viet Cong Strategy of Terror*. Saigon: United States Mission Viet-Nam, February 1970.

Pinner, Walter, "The Problem of the Palestine Refugees." *The Wiener Library Bulletin* XXIII (1969): 29–35.

Principes Soviétiques et Pratiques Arabes. Jerusalem: Ministère des Affaires Étrangères, January 1970.

Redish, Martin, "Military Law." *Harvard International Law Journal* 9 (1968): 169–181.

Reibstein, Ernst, *Völkerrecht*. Freiburg/Muenchen: Verlag Karl Alber, 1957.

Reitzner, Almar, *Alexander Dubcek*. Munich: Die Bruecke, 1968.

Remington, Robert Alison, ed., *Winter in Prague*: New York: The M.I.T. Press, 1969.

Renald, Jean, *L'Enfer de Dien Bien Phu*. Paris: Flammarion, 1955.

Rentsch, Helmuth, *Partisanenkampf*. Frankfurt/Main: Bernard und Graefe Verlag fuer Wehrwesen, 1961.

Reston, James B., Jr., *Saturday Review of Literature*, July 18, 1970, pp. 16–17.

Richard, Pierre, *Cinq Ans Prisonnier des Viets*. Paris: Editions de la Serpe, 1964.

Riffaud, Madeleine, *Au Nord Viet-Nam*. Paris: Julliard, 1967.

Ripka, Hubert, *Le Coup de Prague*. Paris: Plon, 1949.

Rosenne, Shabtei, "Directions for a Middle East Settlement—Some Underlying Legal Problems." *Law and Contemporary Problems*. Durham: Duke University, Winter 1968.

Roskill, Captain S. W., *White Ensign*. Maryland: U.S. Naval Institute, 1960.

Roy, Jules, *Autour du Drame*. Paris: Julliard, 1961.

——, *La Bataille de Dien Bien Phu*. Paris: Julliard, 1963.

——, *La Guerre en Algérie*. Paris: Julliard, 1960.

Rudolf, Walter, *Voelkerrechtliche Aspekte des Vietnam—Konflikts*. Bad Homberg, Berlin, Zurich: Verlag Gehlen, 1967.

Russ, Martin, *Happy Hunting Ground*. New York: Atheneum, 1968.

Sabatier, Général G., *Le Destin de l'Indochine*. Paris: Plon, 1951.

Safran, Nadar, *U.S. and Israel*. Cambridge, Mass.: Harvard University Press, 1963.

Sager, Lawrence W., "Charter vs. Constitution: An International Criminal Tribunal in American Law." *Howard Law Journal* 11 (Spring 1965): 607–620.

Sager, Peter, and Bruegger, Christian, eds., *Prague 1968*. Benne: Verlag Soi, 1968.

Sainteny, Jean, *Histoire d'une Paix Manquée*. Paris: Amis de l'Histoire, 1967.

Salisbury, Harrison E., *Behind the Lines—Hanoi: December 23, 1966–Janu-*

ary 7, 1967. New York: Harper and Row, 1967.

——, *The New York Times Book Review*, December 26, 1971. Roy A. Medvedev, *Let History Judge*. Translated by Colleen Taylor. New York: Knopf, 1972.

Sanders, Ronald, *Israel: The View from Massada*. New York: Harper and Row, 1966.

Sartre, Jean-Paul, *Situations*. Vol. V. Paris: Gallimard, 1964.

Servan-Schreiber, Jean-Jacques, *Lieutenant en Algérie*. Paris: Julliard, 1957.

Scheer, Maximilian, *Algerien Jugend im Feuer*. Berlin: Verlag der Nation, 1959.

Schlesinger, Arthur M., Jr., *The Bitter Heritage*. Boston: Houghton Mifflin, 1967.

Schoenbrun, David, *Vietnam*. New York: Atheneum, 1968.

Schuetze, H. A., *Die Repressalie*. Bonn: Roehrscheid, 1950.

Schwarzenberger, Georg, "From the Laws of War to the Law of Armed Conflict." *Journal of Public Law* 17 (1968): 61–77.

Selections of Cartoons from the Arab Press. Tel Aviv: Zahal Information Office, July 1967.

Selucky, Radislov, *Czechoslovakia: The Plan That Failed*. London: Nelson and Sons, 1970.

Selver, Paul, *Masaryk*. London: Michael Joseph, 1940.

Seneca, "Epistulae ad Lucilium" Epis. XCV 30. Quoted in Tom J. Farer, *The Laws of War 25 Years after Nuremberg*. Carnegie Endowment for International Peace, No. 583, May 1971.

Shaw, *L'Algérie un Siècle avant l'occupation française (au 18ᵉ siècle)—Temoignage de Shaw, Religieux Anglais*. Paris: Carthage, 1968.

Shawcross, William, *Dubcek*. London: Weidenfeld and Nicolson, 1970.

Sheehan, Neil, Smith, Hedrich, Kenworthy, E. W., and Butterfield, Fox, *The Pentagon Papers*. New York: Bantam Books, 1971.

Shull, Brigadier General Lewis F., "Counter-insurgency and the Geneva Conventions: Some Practical Considerations." *International Lawyer* 3 (October 1968): 49–57.

Silverberg, Robert, *If I Forget Thee O Jerusalem: American Jews and the State of Israel*. New York: Morrow, 1970.

Simon, Pierre-Henri, *Contre la Torture*. Paris: Editions du Seuil, 1957.

Sinha, S. Prakash, *New Nations and the Law of Nations*. Leyden: A. W. Sijthoff, 1967.

Smith, H. A., *The Crises in the Law of Nations*. London: Stevens & Sons Ltd., 1947.

Smith, Ralph, *Vietnam and the West*. London: Heinemann, 1968.

Smothers, Frank, et al., *Report on the Greeks*. New York: 20th Century Fund, 1948.

Sohn, Louis B., *The UN in Action*. New York: The Foundation Press, 1968.

Spencer, Floyd A., *War and Post-War Greece*. Washington, D.C.: Library of Congress, 1952.

Stauffer, Ethelbert, "Mord in Gottes Namen." *Der Monat*, December 1969, pp. 28–42.

Sterling, Claire, *The Masaryk Case*. New York: Harper and Row, 1968.
Sviták, Ivan, *The Czechoslovak Experiment*. New York: Columbia University Press, 1968–1969.
Szasz, Paul C., "How to Develop World Peace through Law." *American Bar Association Journal* 52 (September 1966): 851–857.
Szulc, Tad, *Czechoslovakia since World War II*. New York: The Viking Press, 1971.
Tatu, Michel, *L'Hérésie Impossible*. Paris: Grasset, 1968.
Taylor, Telford, *Nuremberg and Vietnam: An American Tragedy*. Chicago: Quadrangle Books, 1970.
The Arab War against Israel. Jerusalem: Ministry for Foreign Affairs, 1967.
"The Legality of U.S. Participation in the Defense of Vietnam." Symposium. *Yale Law Journal* 75 (June 1966): 1085–1160.
The New York Times. May 18, May 20, June 26, 1954. April 28, 1966. October 4, 1968. December 18, 1970. May 25, July 12, 1971. January 7, 1972.
The Record of Aggression. Washington, D.C.: Embassy of Israel, 1967.
Thomas, Hugh, *The Suez Affair*. London: Weidenfeld and Nicolson, 1966.
———, *The Suez Affair*. Rev. ed. Harmondsworth, England: Pelican Books, 1970.
Thompson, Robert, *No Exit to Vietnam*. New York: David McKay Co., 1969.
"Time Limit for War Crimes." Notes. *International and Comparative Law Quarterly* 14 (April 1965): 627–632.
Trial of the Major War Criminals. 1816 PS, Vol. XXVIII, p. 518. Nuremberg, 1948.
Trost, Ernst, *David und Goliath*. Vienna: Verlag Fritz Molden, 1967.
Truman, Harry S, *Memoirs*. Vols. I and II. New York: Doubleday, 1955–1956.
———, *Reports to Congress on Assistance to Greece and Turkey*. Reports 1–8. Washington, D.C.: U.S. Government Printing Office, 1945–1949.
Ulam, Adam B., *Expansion and Coexistence*. New York: Praeger, 1968.
U.S. Crimes in Viet-Nam, Hanoi: Juridical Sciences Institute under the Viet Nam State Commission of Social Sciences, n.d.
Vagts, Alfred, *Jahrbuch für Amerikastudien*. Vol. XV. Heidelberg: Karl Winter Universitätsverlag, 1970.
Vali, Ferenc A., *Rift and Revolt in Hungary*. Cambridge, Mass.: Harvard University Press, 1961.
Vatikiotis, P. J., *The Egyptian Army in Politics*. Bloomington, Ind.: Indiana University Press, 1961.
Verdross, Alfred, *Völkerrecht*. Vienna: Springer Verlag, 1964.
Vietnam: L'Heure Décisive. N.A. Paris: Robert Laffont, 1968.
Von Clausewitz, Karl, *On War*. Translated by O. J. Matthijis Jolles. New York: Modern Library, 1943.
Wallach, Jehuda L., *Die Kriegslehre von Friedrich Engels*. Frankfurt am Main: Europaeische Verlagsanstalt, 1968.
Walzer, Michael, "World War II: Why This War Was Different." *Philosophy and Public Affairs* I (Fall 1971): 1–21. (Quoting Frankland's *Bomber*

Offensive: The Devastation of Europe) pp. 12, 24 ff.

Wasserstrom, Richard, "On the Morality of War: A Preliminary Inquiry." *Stanford Law Review* 21 (June 1969): 1627–1656.

Watt, D. C., ed., *Documents on the Suez Crisis: 26 July to 6 November 1956*. London: Royal Institute of International Affairs, 1957.

Weinstock, Nathan, *Le Sionisme contre Israël*. Paris: Maspero, 1969.

Weiss, Charles J., "Submarine Warfare." *Intramural Review of NYU* 22 (July 1967): 136–151.

Westing, Arthur H., "Agent Blue in Vietnam." *The New York Times*, July 12, 1971.

Thomas Whiteside, "Department of Amplification." *The New Yorker*, August 14, 1971, pp. 54–59.

Wilner, Alan M., "Superior Orders as a Defense to Violations of International Criminal Law." *Maryland Law Review* 26 (Spring 1968): 127–142.

Windchy, Eugene G., *Tonkin Gulf*. New York: Doubleday, 1971.

Wint, Guy, and Calvocoressi, Peter, *Middle East Crisis*. New York: Penguin Books, 1957.

"World Conference on World Peace through the Rule of Law." *Kentucky Law Journal* 53: 5–55.

Wright, Quincy, *A Study of War*. Chicago: The University of Chicago Press, 1965.

——, "The Middle East Problem." *International Lawyer* 4 (1970): 364–373.

Yacet, Saadi, *Souvenirs de la Bataille d'Alger*. Paris: Julliard, 1962.

Young, Brigadier Peter, *The Israeli Campaign*. London: William Kimber, 1967.

Ysquierdo, Antoine, *Une Guerre pour Rien*. Paris: La Table Ronde, 1966.

Zentner, Christian, *Die Kriege der Nachkriegszeit*. München: Südwest Verlag, 1969.

Zsolnay, Vilmos von, in *Ungarn zehn Jahre Danach*. Edited by Werner Frauendienst. Mainz: Hase und Koehler, 1966.

INDEX

Index

Abbas, Ferhat, 87, 96n
Abd-el-Kader, 62, 69n, 74–76, 78, 79, 86, 89, 101n, 215
Acheson, Dean, 179
Aggression: and capitalism 18–21; definitions, 15–17; in Polish criminal law draft, 17; as political tool, 274–75, 290–91
Aggressive War (*see also* Kellogg-Briand Pact): changing concepts of, since Nuremberg, 1, 4, 5–8; and Christianity, 10–11; and conquest, 11–12; declared illegal at Nuremberg, 1–2, 4; and humanitarianism, 12; and the League of Nations, 13–14; and military necessity, 272–274; and partisan warfare, 17–19; and post WWII balance of power, 4; and question of responsibility, 12–15, 276; and "Reason of State," 14; and sovereignty, 11; views on legality of, 2n, 4, 10 ff., 271
Al Atassi, President, 136

Algeria: and Abd-el-Kader, 62, 69n, 74–76, 78, 79, 86, 89, 101n; after independence, 100–101; attitude of, to Vichy Government, 86; Barbary pirates in, 65–67; beginning of independence movement in, 85, 86–89; Berber population of, 65, 67, 70, 73; Communist party in, 62, 87; state of, at time of French conquest, 65–66; economy of, under French rule, 81; French education rule, 83, 85, 94; French citizenship policies, 84–85, 86, 87, 94; French conquest and colonization of, 62–63, 64, 65, 67–70, 77–87; elective government under French rule, 83–84, 89; racial and tribal makeup of, 62–63; resistance to French rule, 64, 69–70, 74–81; Sétif massacre, 87–88, 95; Turkish rule in, 63, 65, 67, 70–74, 79, 80, 85; war for independence, 24, 62—casualties, 64, 95—ceasefire and independence granted at